CHANGING ORGANIZATIONAL BEHAVIOR

CHANGING ORGANIZATIONAL BEHAVIOR

Edited by

Alton C. Bartlett
University of South Florida

Thomas A. Kayser
University of South Florida

Prentice-Hall, Inc., Englewood Cliffs, New Jersey

658.4
B289

Library of Congress Cataloging in Publication Data

Bartlett, Alton C.
    Changing organizational behavior.

    Includes bibliographies.
    1. Organizational change—Addresses, essays,
lectures.   2. Organizational change—Case studies.
I. Kayser, Thomas A.   joint comp.
II. Title.
HD38.B27   658.4'06   73-7859
ISBN 0-13-127928-9

Printed in the United States of America

10 9 8 7 6 5 4 3 2 1

Prentice-Hall International, Inc., *London*
Prentice-Hall of Australia, Pty. Ltd., *Sydney*
Prentice-Hall of Canada, Ltd., *Toronto*
Prentice-Hall of India Private Limited, *New Delhi*
Prentice-Hall of Japan, Inc., *Tokyo*

To
SUE and CAROL

Contents

Preface

The manager of the future will certainly be called upon to operate within both a technical and a social system that becomes ever more complex, dynamic, interrelated, and synergistic. The probabilities seem high that the structure and governance of organizations will vary considerably from that of the present-day bureaucratic model as we know it.

This manager of the future will need, of course, to be fully cognizant of the total organization as a gestalt—that is, "an organized, meaningful whole," in which his subsystem is an integral part rather than a fragmented part.[1] He will need to assimilate, in a real-time framework, the mission and goals of the total organization. Of more importance, however, will be the need—and demand—of his organization that he function as the "complete manager" of his own component within the total system.

As a complete manager he will have to be much more adept in the planning function so as to elaborate clear, concise, operational goals that are not only attainable but also consistent with those of the total organization. He and his subordinates undoubtedly will be quite facile in utilizing a concept such as management by objectives.

Once these objectives are fixed, however, tomorrow's complete manager will shift to a framework similar to management by results. In this framework he will

[1] Muriel James and Dorothy Jongeward, *Born to Win* (Reading, Mass.: Addison-Wesley Publishing Co., 1971), p. 6.

need to develop and maintain a control system which will: (1) provide him with accurate feedback as to when a deviation occurs; (2) assist him in understanding why there was deviation; and, (3) lend itself to ascertaining how to correct the deviation as well as to ensure that the same deviation will not recur. The emphasis is on problem-solving not blame-fixing. Since normal performance is expected, he will not want to know when the goals are being accomplished; instead, the complete manager will concentrate on dealing with the exceptions.

He will, of course, review the deviations from expected. Of far more importance, though, he will need to be capable both of formulating plans for change which will normalize the system again and of implementing the changes.

In addition, some change programs are either so time consuming or so involved that they may require the assistance of one or more change agents from outside the system. This suggests that the complete manager will have to be sufficiently knowledgeable to know what change agents do as well as how and why they do it.

Although there are many excellent books exploring change, they tend to be one-sided. Some emphasize organization development and laboratory training; others concentrate on the structural or technological aspects of change. But there is no book which attempts to provide a balanced and integrated approach to the change process. Our book was written to provide just such an approach, for it is our belief that there will be an ever-increasing demand that the manager of tomorrow be capable of planning, implementing, supervising, coordinating, and understanding the change process as one of his major functions.

A project such as this is always a labor of love for the authors. Still they must do a considerable amount of tedious and meticulous work which can be accomplished only with the help of research assistants and secretaries. This particular effort commenced with an intensive research effort at the State University of New York at Buffalo, where it was aided greatly by Miss Julie Hastings, Miss Carol Krakomberger, and Miss Janet Gehl.

At the University of South Florida, the project was advanced by Walter Bogumil, graduate assistant, and Mrs. Pat Martin, secretary. Over time, Mrs. Nadina Tuttle and Miss Suzie Bracken assisted with the typing. As the venture began to focus on a concerted effort to develop a coherent package of readings for use in our graduate and undergraduate classes in Changing Organizations at USF, the brunt of the research, typing, and organizing fell to Mrs. Lynn Howard. In preparing the final material for the publisher, Mrs. Janis Colgate contributed generously of her time and energy.

We also wish to express our gratitude to Professors Edgar Schein of the Alfred P. Sloan School of Management, Massachusetts Institute of Technology; John W. Slocum, Jr., College of Business Administration, The Pennsylvania State University; and Professor George Strauss, Institute of Industrial Relations, University of California, Berkeley for reviewing the manuscript and providing useful, constructive criticism at a time when our efforts to ensure a comprehensive, all-inclusive review of the field left us with one thousand pages of material for a four hundred page book.

George Strauss also reviewed much of the manuscript at an earlier stage. As usual, we paid great attention to his suggestions and criticisms because we hold his opinions in high esteem. We wish both to thank him for his support and to hold him blameless for any shortcomings. Arlyn Melcher of Kent State University also helped in the formative stages, and he, too, receives our warm appreciation for his efforts. We also wish to thank Mrs. Ruth Walsh of the University of South Florida who read the manuscript at various stages. Her suggestions on style, grammar, and punctuation were invaluable. To all of those students at Buffalo and USF who worked with this material in their classes and who made many significant suggestions toward improving the final product, we say thank you.

Finally, our sincere thanks to our wives, Sue and Carol, for their patience and encouragement during this undertaking. We feel certain they wondered—even more than we—whether our work would ever be completed.

Alton C. Bartlett
Thomas A. Kayser
University of South Florida
Tampa, Florida

part I

ORGANIZATIONAL CHANGE: ELEMENTS, PROCESSES, AND PERSPECTIVES

Part I is intended to acquaint the reader with the field of organizational change. The broad strokes are painted here; the fine lines of detail will come in later sections. This unit is based on the assumption that interest, and thus learning, will be increased if the individual is provided an incisive overview of a complex topic before commencing a detailed study of it. This portion of the book serves two useful functions: (1) it permits a mapping of the field of organizational change so that the reader has some notion of the direction in which he is headed; and (2) it provides a substantial base of information upon which to develop the rest of the material. Thus, although the readings in this unit are quite diverse, they are locked together to form a fairly comprehensive introduction to changing organizations.

The keynote article for this part, and for the book as a whole, is a piece entitled, "Organizational Change: A Trial Synthesis" by Alton C. Bartlett and Thomas A. Kayser. Written especially for this collection of readings, it sets forth fundamental concepts and terms of organizational change and then integrates them into a conceptual model. The reader then has a reference device to aid him in comprehending the remaining articles in the book and relating them to each other and to the problem of change as a whole.

Next, Louis C. Gawthrop's speculative paper, "The Environment, Bureaucracy, and Social Change: A Political Prognosis," elaborates on the environmental variables outlined in the previous reading. He examines the way public and private bureaucracies adapt to changes in their external environments and demonstrates the critical role played by the environment as a determinant of internal organizational change.

Harold J. Leavitt's exposition, "Applied Organization Change in Industry: Structural, Technical, and Human Approaches," presents an in-depth discussion of a major portion of the organizational elements comprising the Bartlett/Kayser model developed in the first article. Leavitt examines the change process from a *what*-is-to-be-changed-perspective.

Then follows Larry E. Greiner's survey of a number of organizational change studies, "Patterns of Organization Change," which is a macro view of the change process. Greiner elaborates on the role of various forms of power distribution within the firm relative to successful change. He explores the change process from a *how*-can-change-be-introduced viewpoint.

The pair of readings which wind up this unit delineate the two basic philosophies—behavioral and structural—for effecting positive modifications in organizational functioning and direction. Warren G. Bennis, with "Theory and Method in Applying Behavioral Science to Planned Organizational Change," tenders background material regarding the behavioral approach to change; Leonard R. Sayles examines the matter from the structuralist viewpoint in "The Change Process in Organizations: An Applied Anthropology Approach."

Organizational Change: A Trial Synthesis

The purpose of this article is to offer an integrated conceptual overview of change. It will attempt briefly to establish the importance of change, and the management thereof, in the world of tomorrow's manager. The lack of an integrated theory will be noted and lamented.

It then will present a model—or way of thinking systematically—about change. After the presentation of this model schematically, a listing of each of the several parts of the total organizational model will be made as if they were, in fact, separate entities.

Finally, an attempt will be made to tie the components together into one whole, for clearly a change agent ultimately must deal with the organization as one dynamic system composed of interdependent, integrated, and indivisible elements.

ORGANIZATIONAL CHANGE: A TRIAL SYNTHESIS

Alton C. Bartlett
University of South Florida

Thomas A. Kayser
University of South Florida

Change is inevitable. Sometimes it is the result of planned action, sometimes of reaction, and sometimes of no action at all. Change can improve things or it can make them much worse. However it occurs, change takes place almost continuously in virtually all organizations—unless they are already moribund.

A Needed Skill

We believe that no organization should desire that change take place in a vacuum. Decisions should be consciously made after a review of all known evidence and careful deliberation, rather than coming about by default. Decision-making under conditions of uncertainty is a part of managing. To change or not to change is a decision that requires managing. Change can be managed.

The point is that management of change is one of the many integrated, indivisible skills that every successful manager needs along with those of planning, organizing, staffing, directing, controlling, and so on. As Sayles puts it:

Alton C. Bartlett, Professor and Chairman, Management Department, and Thomas A. Kayser, Instructor of Management, both faculty from the College of Business Administration, University of South Florida. This original article was written especially for this collection of readings.

4

> *This means viewing change as an intimate, integral part of the administrator's task of managing. . . . Change, then, is not a special, for holidays only, activity. It is part and parcel of the normal administrative process. . . . .*[1]

It is essential, therefore, that every manager be totally familiar with all aspects of the change process, including ascertaining when it is required, what it is that needs to be changed, and how it is to be undertaken. This article will concentrate primarily on the first two aspects of change.[2]

A Conceptual Model of an Organization

There are many valuable and tested theories about one or more aspects of the total change process, but as Bennis put it in 1969:

> *. . . there is no integrated theory of organizational change with a set of interrelated hypotheses and variables . . . . However, and far more serious, in my view, is that there is, as yet, no tradition of* adding knowledge cumulatively *to the general theory of practice.*[3]

Figure 1 shows our diagrammatic conception of an organization from the *change agent's* (CA) point of view. It depicts the total organization existing within a set of environmental conditions including: economic, social, cultural, political, and legal constraints, as well as the firm's customers and competitors. The total organization is composed of two subsystems: (1) the *personal* system(s), and (2) the *formal* system with three interacting components in the latter: technology, structure, and leadership.

The interaction of these three components of the formal system with the personal system(s) results in the *emergent behavior.* The aggregate of this emergent behavior manifests itself as *behavioral consequences* or, if you prefer, results. Although it may seem strange, the CA looks first at the behavioral consequences when entering the client system.

Behavioral Consequences

When the CA is first approached by the client system he may be informed implicitly that "things aren't going right for us," or he may inquire in an offhand

---

[1] Leonard R. Sayles, "The Change Process in Organizations: An Applied Anthropology Approach," *Human Organization,* XXI, No. 2 (1962), 62, and reprinted in this volume, pp. 84-95.

[2] For one approach to *how* change might be undertaken, see Alton C. Bartlett, "Changing Behavior through Simulation: An Alternate Design to T-Group Training," in this volume, pp. 118-34.

[3] Warren Bennis, "Unsolved Problems Facing Organizational Development," *The Business Quarterly,* XXXIV, No. 4 (Winter 1969), 82.

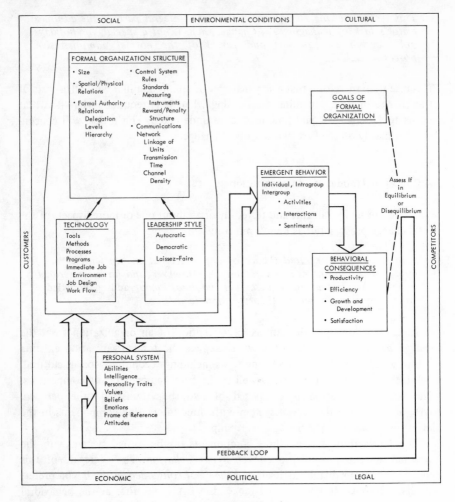

FIGURE 1.

manner, "How is the organization performing currently?" He will need much more than a casual response, however. Almost immediately he will need, among other things, hard data about production, costs, quality, sales, growth and development, and employee need satisfaction as manifested in absenteeism, turnover, and level of grievance activity.

The objective at this stage is to rapidly assimilate any and all data that might help to provide an answer to the following three questions: What results are being achieved by the organization now? What have the results been in several previous time periods? and, What might the results be like in the future?

Goals of the Formal Organization

The next step for the CA is to ascertain the goals of the formal organization through interviews with policy level managers. What goals and objectives do they identify for the short, intermediate, and long run? While it is undoubtedly useful to review policy statements and other written material presumably setting forth goals, at this point the CA can realistically do little more than accept what the policy makers say the goals are. Later these can be explored in depth and, if necessary, redefined. At the outset, however, we see them as *givens*. For this reason we show goals in our schema but they are not connected to the rest of the components in the model.

Assessment of Equilibrium or Disequilibrium

Once the CA has a solid grasp of both the goals and the results, it is time to compare and contrast them. Are they in harmony, or not? If the results being achieved are consistent with the goals desired, the finding of a state of equilibrium calls for no further action in most cases.[4] If, on the other hand, the results are not what the goals of the formal organization specify they should be, the diagnosis of disequilibrium calls for an analysis of the causes of this non-congruence.

Analysis

Further action, where called for by the state of disequilibrium, would take the form of an intensive in-depth analysis. Our own operating question at this point is simply, *What is going on here?* In more scientific terms we proceed from the premise that most human behavior within the workplace is caused by a myriad of identifiable—and some unidentifiable—variables. Although spread throughout several disciplines (including engineering, management, organization development, political science, psychology, sociology, and so on) the total literature provides, in the form of empirical research reports, considerable information as to what variables cause what types of work group behavior. We need to identify and isolate every variable which appears to be having an impact on the emergent behavior in the organization being analyzed.[5]

To accomplish this we may use questionnaires, interviews, observation, or any combination of them. Ultimately, we prefer to record the magnitude of each variable on a scale from one to nine. For example, the size and complexity of the organization could vary from three people in one small room to three million people in eighty cities in seventeen countries. In the first illustration we would score a one for both size and complexity (meaning very small and noncomplex)

[4]It might be possible, albeit rare, that a finding of equilibrium could still require a change if, for example, the goals were either dysfunctional or if they were 1920 goals in a 1980 society.

[5]The most exciting and extensive research effort we have seen in this area is that of Arlyn J. Melcher of Kent State University who is currently preparing a textbook, *Organizational Behavior: Towards a Systems Approach,* to be published in the near future by Prentice-Hall, Inc. We are using the "Melcher Model" in our organizational analysis course and have found it to be a most effective device for isolating the causal factors of organizational behavior.

and in the second we would score a nine for both (meaning very large and very complex). While this by itself tells you very little, similar rankings of fifty to one hundred variables provide a great deal of insight into the organization's formal and personal systems.

These rankings provide the information necessary to sketch a profile of the formal system (composed of technology, structure, and leadership styles) and the personal systems—including all of the constituent factors that go together to make up each of these categories. At this stage of the analysis we might find that *only three* causal variables *among the fifty* or more appear to *deviate significantly from what* the literature suggests as the *norm.* Such a finding would allow us to develop a working hypothesis that if we were able to move the variables in question toward the norm suggested in the literature, we would, in subsequent time periods, be able to alter considerably the emergent behavior. Further, this alteration presumably would result in the goals and results being far closer to equilibrium than before the change effort was undertaken.

In essence then, if action is called for because goals and results are in disequilibrium, analysis of the causal variables is required. Let us consider a few of these variables in more detail.

Formal System: Technology

The initial variable to consider is the technology of the organization. What is it like? How does it compare to the industry as a whole? How does it compare to other industries in the market area? Typical questions include: Is the technology modern or antiquated, labor or capital intensive? Is this a job shop or a continuous process operation? Is it dirty, hot, noisy, dark, or clean, cool, quiet, and well lighted? Is the technology designed to allow and encourage individual initiative, creativity, and control over one's destiny? Or is it designed to insure sameness via a rigid, inflexible, programmed flow? The questions that matter are almost endless when studying technology because they are the heart of the organization.

Technology includes such items as tools, machines, methods, processes, programs, job design, work flow, and immediate job environment; and some change agents approach their task by concentrating on these types of variables. Even though they usually pay lip service to other causal variables, these CAs end up attempting to alter the technology on the grounds that this is *really* how to change behavior of work groups in a significant, lasting manner.

There is no doubt that changing an organization's technology is of major importance in improving emergent behavior. Unfortunately, much of what we have defined as technology costs a lot of money to install and is acquired with the intention of using it for many years. No CA in his right mind could propose that General Motors tear down all of its plants and start over because, other things being equal, a different technology probably would modify emergent behavior, which in turn would see the goals and results become more congruent. Thus, if we are to rely on changing technology in any substantial manner we are going to have to wait until most of it wears out or some upheaval in the marketplace forces radical replacement. Short of that we will wind up with a piecemeal approach, which in many cases offers little in the way of improving behavior.

Formal System: Structure

Having become sufficiently acquainted with the technology, the CA would next want to find out all he could about the formal organization structure. Questions to be asked include: How large is the organization? How many layers of management are there? What is the degree of departmentalization? What are the spatial-physical relations like? What is the nature of the formal authority relations? In the control system: How are rules formulated and enforced? What type of bureaucratic pattern do most of the rules represent—*mock, representative,* or *punishment-centered?*[6] Are the standards characterized as sacred and inviolate, or, are they benchmarks to appraise you of where you are today relative to both yesterday and last year at this time as well as to tomorrow and next year at this time? In the reward-punishment structure, is the emphasis on reward or punishment? Do people know accurately what must be done to get ahead? Is the structure equitable? Does the present communications network move information accurately, in two directions, on both a vertical and lateral basis?

One implied assumption worth noting is that structure is to a large extent dictated by technology.[7] This makes the task of grasping the detail of delegation, rules, reward-punishment, and communications considerably easier than might be expected. Although every structure *is* different from any other, the similarities often outweigh the differences. So, although it would be technically incorrect to say, "once you have seen the structure in one automobile factory, you have seen them all," this is probably pretty close to the truth.[8] There is a fairly high probability that if you can describe a technology accurately to a good CA it is possible for him to predict the structure accurately without ever having seen the specific organization.[9]

Some CAs focus almost exclusively on this area in order to introduce change. Although they very probably do not deny that technology usually dictates structure, they are unwilling to live with present results until some future event

[6]Alvin W. Gouldner, *Patterns of Industrial Bureaucracy* (New York: The Free Press, 1954), Chs. IX-XII, pp. 157-228, has a superb, and perhaps the definitive, exposition on rules.

[7]Joan Woodward, *Industrial Organization: Theory and Practice* (London: Oxford University Press, 1965).

[8]We believe this is one of the strongest messages to come out of Leonard R. Sayles, *Behavior of Industrial Work Groups: Prediction and Control* (New York: John Wiley & Sons, Inc. 1958).

[9]As a matter of fact, we have found at this point that, given that technology and structure, we were able to go on and describe in great detail much of the emerging behavior going on.

mandates a major change in technology. Instead they note—and quite correctly—that one or more organizations in another industry approach, say, rule formulation and enforcement differently, and with seemingly better results than those in this industry.

They then concentrate on transplanting different forms of control systems, communication networks, formal authority relations, and so on, to their client system's structure. To illustrate this, consider an organization with fifty plants scattered around the country. If the industry utilized a centralized form of decision-making and other industries seem to get results more compatible with goals from decentralized forms, the CA may advocate a decentralization program.

This may improve things, but taken out of context from a total formal system in another technology it may very well not help. Joan Woodward underscores this point well:

> *The fact that organizational characteristics, technology, and success were linked together in this way suggested that not only was the system of production an important variable in the determination of organizational structure, but also that one particular form of organization was most appropriate to each system of production. In unit production, for example, not only did short and relatively broadly based pyramids predominate, but they also appeared to ensure success. Process production, on the other hand, would seem to require the taller and more narrowly based pyramid.[10]*

The fact that an ad hoc transplant from one system to another may make matters worse is the precise reason that we are attempting our first approximation of an integrated theoretical model. It is to be hoped that this systematic framework can keep the administrator or CA thinking of the organization as a total system and thus can help him see the ramifications of tampering with the parts.

Formal System: Leadership Style

The third part of this trio that composes the formal system is what we call styles of leadership. The CA may be asking whether, overall, the management follows an autocratic, democratic, or laissez-faire approach. We find it useful to use one of the many taxonomies that emanated from McGregor's Theory X/Theory Y,[11] such as those of Blake and Mouton[12] or Likert.[13]

Moreover, since it is possible to have a Theory Y oasis in the middle of a Theory X desert, the CA needs to explore the styles of leadership in several subparts of the organization at different levels. Failure to do this may result in a

---

[10]Joan Woodward, *op. cit.,* pp. 69-70.

[11]Douglas McGregor, *The Human Side of Enterprise* (New York: McGraw-Hill, 1960).

[12]R. R. Blake and Jane S. Mouton, *The Managerial Grid* (Houston: Gulf, 1964).

[13]Rensis Likert, *New Patterns of Management* (New York: McGraw-Hill, 1961).

totally erroneous conclusion about the styles of leadership employed. Our own approach, to insure the most accurate and thorough assessment possible, is first to nondirectively interview a reasonable sample of hourly employees as well as different levels of supervisors and then to design and administer a questionnaire based upon the interview data to a much larger random sample of employees and supervisors. We have been utilizing this approach, which we refer to conceptually as conducting the "behavioral audit," with considerable success since 1964.[14]

Some CAs also concentrate upon introducing system changes by altering styles of leadership. There seems to be little question about whether this can help. It can! Yet there are cases that give pause for reflection; introducing democracy in an army or autocratic centralized decision-making in a laboratory doing pure, basic research may result in a disaster.

Personal System(s)

The CA also needs to remember that every individual has his own unique personal system that he brings with him when he comes to work for the first time. Although these personal systems can be modified over time by the technology, structure, and leadership styles, each one is, in theory, different from all others.

Despite this apparent drawback many CAs devote their research and intervention activities to this facet exclusively. They capitalize on individual differences and attempt to create a climate where everyone is free to be himself and "do his own thing." In more academic terms, the objective is to create a climate where everyone seeks to satisfy his own unfulfilled needs on the grounds that in the process of attaining his own individual need fulfillment he will also fulfill the needs of the organization. *Interpersonal competence* is the password and the ingredients include: risk taking, willingness to own-up, and giving and receiving descriptive non-evaluative feedback.[15]

Clearly, improving interpersonal competence is worthwhile. It should lead to improved personal and organizational health and well being. By itself, however, we fail to see how it can lead to reaching equilibrium between goals and results in an organization with, say, a rigid, stifling technology, an oppressive structure, or the leadership style of a Genghis Khan.

Environmental Factors or Constraints

In addition to the internal elements of an organization discussed above, another element to be investigated by the CA is environmental factors or constraints, many of which fall in the category of a *given*. If, for example, we are

[14]For a detailed elaboration as well as the rationale of this approach see Alton C. Bartlett, "Human Asset Accounting and the Role of the *Behavioral Auditor*" (in press, 1972).

[15]Cf., Chris Argyris, *Interpersonal Competence and Organizational Effectiveness* (Homewood, Ill.: Irwin-Dorsey, 1962).

planning to *intervene* in a client system in the banking industry in Tampa, Florida, we undoubtedly already know much of the relevant data about the prevailing economic, political, legal, social, and cultural environment. We may or may not know enough about some of the constraints vis-à-vis customers, competitors, suppliers, transportation, and so on. If we went to Japan, however, we would be well advised to do a careful in-depth analysis of the environmental and other constraints.

Some CAs approach the environmental factors as the most important ingredient to concentrate upon in order to induce change. Stated in an overly simple manner the premise would be that if you pass a law requiring the company and union to engage in collective bargaining (in good faith) or if you elect leaders of a different political party to head the government, the mere fact of having done so would insure that the desired results were achieved.

It is impossible to deny that such an approach can result in change. We have all seen it happen, albeit not very often. Truthfully, we see it as just about as effective as trying to change the way a giant redwood tree faces by shining a fifty-watt lightbulb two hours every night in the direction you wish the tree to face.

It seems reasonable to assume that during the late 1960s some of the restiveness of the young and their disenchantment with *working for change within the system, through so-called normal channels by using time-tested procedures,* might have been the result of their realization of how long this takes, how imperfect the process is, and how difficult success really is to achieve.

Tools for Analysis

Having completed the data gathering step of the analysis, the CA is now ready to begin the actual analysis. We have found it useful to employ, initially, theoretical terms Whyte called "tools for analysis": *symbols; sentiments* and *norms; activities;* and *interactions.*[16] We will set forth the essence of his definition of these terms.

Symbols

These, in Whyte's terms, are principally *words* or *physical objects* that come to stand for relations of (1) man to man, (2) man to the physical world, and (3) relations between man and physical objects and other men. Examples include the flag, a chef's hat, a general's stars, love, peace, brotherhood.

[16]William F. Whyte, *Money and Motivation* (New York: Harper and Brothers, 1955), pp. 191-193. See also George C. Homans, *The Human Group* (New York: Harcourt, Brace, 1950).

Whyte made no distinction between *sentiments* and *attitudes*. These refer to the feelings people have toward each other and toward organizations, i.e., the department, management, government, union, or company. Sentiments are expressed in such statements as: "It is a *nice* place to work." "The management doesn't care about us." "Unionism is good for the working man." "Big government is bad government." "She is a catty gossip." "He is a braggart."

Whyte used norms as a subcategory of sentiments. They stand for the types of behavior required of its members of a particular group. For example: Output should not fall outside the range of 100-125 units per day. We do not share tools with other departments. Only department chairmen can drop in on the Dean without an appointment.

Activities

Activities are merely the physically observable things that people do: She walked. He typed. They talked.

Interactions

The term interactions is meant to cover *all* interpersonal contacts. He whispered in her ear. They glanced at each other knowingly. Sally spoke to Jane as they passed each other and Jane slapped her face. I telephoned Lou.

The purpose of the tools described above is to assist in answering such basic operating questions as: *Who goes where and does what with whom, when, and why?* and *how do they feel about it?* In other words, we are interested in knowing all we can about what we see and feel going on in the organization. By classifying activities and interactions, identifying the norms and symbols, and osmosing the subtle nuances of the sentiments of the social system, one can obtain a fairly accurate picture of an organization.

Furthermore, as discussed earlier in our section on assessment of equilibrium or disequilibrium, we have arrived by this time at a series of numerical rankings on our scale from one to nine for each of the so-called causal variables. We have also performed what we call a *behavioral audit*. These assist us in developing a profile of what we perceive the organization to look like.

Together these data become the basis for the synthesized statement we can call the consultant report.

Literature Review

When this description of the behavior manifested within the system is completed, there are still three steps left before we reach the stage where we think the Greiner model begins.[17] The first of these is to hypothesize why the behavior is occurring as described. To explain the why of it all requires a careful review of the literature in search of a consensus as to how certain variables affect behavior. Next, stipulate which direction on the scale (from one to nine) the relevant variables should be moved. Finally, some alternative change proposals should be formulated by the CA. These alternatives should have a statement of probability of success as well as of cost. Included in cost is far more than the dollar amount; for example, destroying people's dignity cannot be equated with money!

Presentation to Management

Our CA is now ready to present his report by means of one of the several viable methods to the policy makers in the client system. Our own preference is to do this orally in as informal a presentation as possible, for, although some of the data is "hard" and can be presented in a tabular or graphic format, much of it is impressionistic. Moreover, the real purpose of the presentation is to test the perceptions of the CA against the realities of the work-world in which the policy makers live. How do these two compare with each other? What is needed is a free and open interchange of ideas leading to a meeting of the minds between the principles, not a monologue!

The causal variables identified on the scale from one to nine can and should be reduced to charts including a brief explanation of why each one is scaled as it is, what it means, which way it is proposed to shift them on the scale, and why. Even these proposals, however, are tentative—until the meeting produces a consensus about both the findings and a plan of action.

At that point, if requested, the findings and recommendation can be finalized in writing as modified by the meeting and discussions with the policy level management.

The CA is now ready to proceed with the introduction of change.

---

[17]Larry E. Greiner, "Patterns of Organization Change," *Harvard Business Review*, 45, No. 3 (May-June 1967), 119-30, and reprinted in this volume, pp. 46-63.

The Environment, Bureaucracy, and Social Change: A Political Prognosis

Gawthrop's paper focuses on the interface between the organization and its relevant external environmental setting. Internal organizational change cannot be viewed in a vacuum inasmuch as the external environment is a critical variable—indeed, often the driving force causing the organization to make internal changes.

As Larry Greiner and Louis Barnes state:

> *Organizations are continually struggling to adapt themselves better to their external environment. Because the management of an organization cannot completely control its environment, they are continually having to introduce internal organizational changes which allow them to cope more effectively with new challenges presented from outside by increased competition, advances in technology, new government legislation, and pressing social demands. Most frequently organizational changes are introduced in "reaction" to these environmental pressures. In some cases, however, changes are made in "anticipation" of future pressures. This latter course, while more difficult to pursue because employees do not recognize its immediate importance, is a standard that can often be applied to organizations that lead rather than follow their industries. Such "proactive" organizations can be said to engage in attempting to change their environments as well as themselves.* [1]

[1] Larry E. Greiner and Louis B. Barnes, "Organizational Change and Development," in *Organizational Change and Development*, ed. Gene W. Dalton, Paul R. Lawrence, with Larry E. Greiner (Homewood, Ill.: Richard D. Irwin, Inc., 1970), p. 2.

In this reading Gawthrop follows the same logic and sets up organizational adaptations to the environment in two contrasting sets: responsive versus anticipatory and incremental versus comprehensive. The decision-strategies examined are the ones employed when firms attempt to deal with the problems generated by today's turbulent external environment. The environment is examined from the viewpoint of both public and private bureaucracies, and the author concludes that the public bureaucracies are not as adaptive to environmental changes as private ones, for the former can achieve only responsive or incremental change (adapting after the event occurs) whereas the latter are more flexible and thus are able to achieve anticipatory or comprehensive change. However, Gawthrop believes that multi-national corporations possess the greatest ability for comprehensive change.

In the author's words, this paper presents "that aspect of socio-political change which is critically related to, and directly affected by, bureaucratic response to the external forces of change."

The details of specific strategies that organizations utilize for altering their internal systems, at least partially in response to environmental changes, are chronicled in the remaining readings.

THE ENVIRONMENT, BUREAUCRACY, AND SOCIAL CHANGE:

A Political Prognosis

Louis C. Gawthrop
State University of New York

As broad and ambiguous as the concept of change may be, efforts by political scientists in the United States increasingly are being aimed at reducing the social and political friction which inevitably occurs when new and different ideas are set against existing, well-established behavioral patterns of the governmental process. Unfortunately, most of the recent contributions from political scientists on the subject of bureaucratic adaptation to broad socio-political change have been disappointing. An immutable faith in the persuasiveness of conventional political "wisdom" seems to prevail. Thus, if politics is the art of the possible then reasonable men can certainly iron out simple procedural breakdowns without questioning either the efficacy or the integrity of the structural foundations of their bureaucratic organizations, the prevailing decision-making strategy, or the public policy process itself. Viewed in this context, the future continues to be based on the present which is defined by the past, and the concept of a

"The Environment, Bureaucracy, and Social Change: A Political Prognosis," by Louis C. Gawthrop, as first published in *Environmental Settings in Organizational Functioning*, edited by Anant R. Negandhi (Kent, Ohio: Comparative Administration Research Institute of the Center for Business and Economic Research, 1970), pp. 19-33.

Professor Gawthrop's paper is published with the special permission of the Comparative Administration Research Institute (CARI), a research unit in the Center for Business and Economic Research at Kent State University. CARI has been organizing annual conferences in the area of organization theory since 1968. The reader interested in various theoretical developments in organization theory should refer to CARI's recent volume, *Functioning of Complex Organizations: Contextual, Environmental, and Socio-Cultural Explanations*, published by the Kent State University Press.

public bureaucracy's external environment still is narrowly defined in traditional terms of predictable, stable, constant, and limited relationships.

The relationship between environment, bureaucracy, and social change deserves much more attention (or, more precisely, much more of a different kind of attention) from political analysts than it has received to date. New organizational models, new bureaucratic alternatives, and new problem solutions are needed to meet the challenges of the post-industrial period. But political science will remain hopelessly landlocked as long as socio-political change is viewed solely in incremental terms, and as long as the relationships between bureaucratic organizations and their respective "relevant" environments are viewed as constants. Both of these points constitute the central focus of this paper, and each will be directly confronted by posing two basic propositions. The first is a basic notion intrinsic to the nature of change itself; one so elementary that, were it not for the fact it has been ignored frequently in the literature of politics and social change, I would be most reluctant even to raise the point at this time. I refer specifically to the fact that change—even radical change—is inevitable if certain other sets of conditions (socio-political, economic, organizational, etc.) are to prevail. The second is a more distinct notion which is fundamentally related to the concept of the environment—i.e., the extent and nature of change in any socio-political environment will be directly affected (either positively or negatively) by the bureaucratic complex which functions within the socio-political systems. Let me elaborate on the first of these points briefly before turning to the second which will constitute the main focus of this paper.

First, change is inevitable if any organism (biological or social) is to survive.[1] Due to the fact that no organism has complete control over its total (internal and external) environment, forces of change constantly are being exerted on the organism, changes which require adaptive responses if survival is to be achieved. Man must adapt to the forces of change imposed on him by the aging process if he wishes to extend his longevity. A family must adapt to changing social values affecting young adolescents if the familial bonds of love, affection, and respect are to be maintained. A political party must respond affirmatively to the forces of political change if it is to offer a meaningful and relevant appeal to the body politic. And finally, a national government must be prepared to adapt to a wide range of changing social, economic, political, and moral forces exerted both from inside and outside its formal jurisdiction if it is to maintain its sovereignty, its territorial integrity, and its *de facto* effectiveness.

Viewed within this context, the relationship between change and adaptation must be considered as different sides of the same coin. Change cannot be viewed in the abstract; it has no substantive content *per se;* it can only be analyzed in terms of forces of change and responses to such forces. While it is simply a truism to note that forces of change inevitably exert themselves on every

[1]For a more detailed discussion of most of the concepts presented in this section see, Gawthrop, *Bureaucratic Behavior in the Executive Branch* (New York: The Free Press, 1969).

organism, the manner in which the organism responds, or adapts, to such forces may vary substantially. In this connection it may be useful to distinguish between responsive change and anticipatory change. Both terms imply a state of mind or attitude that an organism assumes toward the forces of change. As such, neither is intended to provide an empirical determinant to be used as a measure of change, but merely to suggest conceptually useful attitudes which organisms may assume when confronted with demands for change.

Responsive change is defined as a reaction to clearly perceived forces of change. Thus, when it starts raining an individual puts on a raincoat; a college president creates a student policy committee after being confronted with a protest demonstration in his office; after a decade of transition, the character of a neighborhood finally becomes predominately black, and the local political party reacts by selecting a black candidate from that neighborhood to run for city council. In each instance the force or demand for change in the behavior of the subject is manifested overtly and is clearly perceived by the subject. In addition, the consequences of not responding to the demand for change also are clearly perceived. Thus, the response of the subject may vary according to his perception of the intensity of the forces of change. The extent to which the subject adapts successfully to these demands will depend on his perceptual accuracy of these intensities. However, in instances where the forces for change manifest themselves in a clearly perceived and overt fashion, the probability of error in the perception of intensity is low, assuming reliable data-gathering facilities are at the disposal of the decision-maker.

Anticipatory change connotes a fundamentally different means of adaptation to change. Essentially what is being suggested here is that the forces of change may be detected before they emerge in overt and dynamic form. As stated previously, all organisms must adapt to change if they are to survive. However, not all organisms are capable of anticipatory adaptation, and of those that are—human and social systems—it does not follow that this tactic will be applied. In the first place, to anticipate the forces of change effectively means that the subject (either an individual or an organization) must invest a high proportion of his resources in the routine scanning of the futuristic horizon. This means a high investment in data gathering and data interpreting facilities. In the second place, it means the subject is convinced that such an investment is worthwhile—i.e., the benefits received exceed the costs. These two factors obviously are related to the extent that a favorable attitude toward anticipatory change cannot be acted on by the subject in the absence of available resources. For example, the ability to read and write represents a rudimentary data gathering device. However, for the millions of peasant farmers and urban ghetto dwellers from all corners of the earth who are functionally illiterate, no matter how deeply they may desire to anticipate just a fraction of the total environmental forces which constantly bombard them, they do not have the basic skills or resources which are needed to act on this desire.

Of course, one may conclude that a routine scanning of the future for change simply is not worth the necessary investment, even if the required resources are available. Such an attitude is well-warranted when either individuals or organizations have complete confidence that they can respond effectively to any forces of change that may overtly manifest themselves in either their internal or external environment. A husband does not have to invest considerable amounts of time and energies in monitoring the behavior of his wife if he is confident of her fidelity. Minor adaptations to her changing moods may be required to maintain domestic tranquility, but these can be of a responsive rather than of an anticipatory nature. A political party need not make the high investment necessary to follow an anticipatory change strategy if it is confident that its candidates for public office inevitably will be elected. Nor need a nation concern itself with anticipating demands for internal democratic reform if it is confident that any such demands may be met successfully either by token cooptation or force. Of course, each example rests on a common assumption that the future is determined by the past, in which case concern for the present becomes the only relevant consideration, and responsive change or adaptation becomes the only sensible course to follow. This assumption appears especially persuasive in highly stable environments. The more stable the environment, the more the past controls the future, and, consequently, the more routinized responsive change can become. Then the feed-back loop completes the circuit in that the more systematically environmental forces of change can be routinized, the more static the system will become.

Probably the most necessary elements in achieving this condition of perpetual routine stabilization in any system are (1) a high sharing of values among the various members or sub-units of any system, and (2) a high degree of congruence between individual values and behavior. Both conditions are most likely to prevail in small group situations characterized by close, face-to-face interpersonal relationships. Within such social settings as the family, or within small work groups, these relationships work in a manner which tends to solidify a set of group norms and values. Such reinforcement may create a highly stable group environment in which routine responses to change are adopted on the assumption that the past is the most reliable guide to the future.

The critical point to be conveyed here is that small group situations tend to maximize the possibility of developing homogeneity of values and high congruence between values and behavior. Because of the close, face-to-face, interpersonal contact which prevails, group adjustment or adaptation to dynamic forces of change—be it either responsive or anticipatory adaptation—enjoys a potential unity, cohesiveness, and consistency which provides stability and agreement insofar as the internal decision-making process is concerned.

But what happens to the unity, the cohesiveness, the consistency, the stability, the agreement as the group expands into a large-scale organization? When close, interpersonal, face-to-face contact is no longer possible? As more and more individuals from diverse backgrounds are brought into the expanding group? As the functions and responsibilities of the group grow in both internal complexity and external diversity? In each instance unity, cohesiveness, agreement, and congruity are weakened, and internal decision-making consistency is lost.

It is at this point that the basic internal character of the organization has changed fundamentally, and the necessity to adapt to these forces of change becomes essential. In the case of the group which grows into a large scale, complex organization, a response is needed and the most effective response is the adoption of the bureaucratic model.

The Two Faces of Bureaucracy

In the current post-industrial, turbulent, computer age, the major topic of the day is bureaucracy. In fact, down through the centuries at most of the critical junctures of history where the forces of social change have had their most profound impact, a bureaucratic system usually has been involved. And, more often than not, at each of these moments of great social change, the bureaucracy—and its alter ego, the bureaucrat or administrator—has been cast in the role of the villain.

Of course, this is not surprising. The prime virtues of a bureaucratic system are stability, clarity, and simplicity. Within any bureaucratic structure maximum operating efficiency depends most critically on maintaining a highly stable, cohesive, and consistent internal environment. Furthermore, given the complex functions and responsibilities assumed by major bureaucratic systems—be they the Holy Roman Empire or General Motors—internal stability, cohesiveness, and consistency can be achieved only if the complex is made simple, if the abstract is made clear.

However, no bureaucratic structure exists in a vacuum. It is a system which must always interact with other systems, and which always exists within a larger system. For its internal operating system, stability is a general prerequisite for overall operating effectiveness. But for operating effectiveness to be truly maximized, stability must be maintained within its relevant external environment as well. The adjective "relevant" is appended to indicate that while logically everything that lies outside a particular bureaucratic structure comes within its external environment, only certain elements are perceived by the bureaucratic officials themselves as relevant. For example, the relevant external environment for many of America's early corporate structures consisted solely of their suppliers (including labor but most assuredly *not* labor unions), and their competitors. Likewise, for years the relevant external environment of numerous national governmental bureaucracies consisted solely of upper class social and economic elites, and/or their military elites.

For the purpose of clarification, it may be advisable to elaborate on several of the points presented in the previous paragraphs. In the first place, the elements included in any bureaucratic structure's relevant external environment are obviously subject to change over time, and the natural—i.e., "healthy"—progression is toward expansion. In the second place it is important to emphasize that the elements included in the relevant external environment are only those which are perceived by top level bureaucratic officials as being relevant. As will be discussed later, this places a high premium on the accuracy of their perceptions. And finally, while stability must be maintained both within the internal and external environments of any bureaucratic structure for maximum operating effectiveness, this is not to suggest that bureaucracies are able to control and manipulate the many other systems that are external to them. Bureaucratic systems undoubtedly are capable of influencing the behavior of other external systems or of the larger systems in which they are included, but the difference between influence and direct control must be underscored.

This point seems especially relevant if we now return to the main focus of this essay—the relationship between the environment, bureaucracy, and dynamic socio-political change. Forces of change are generated from the external environment of the bureaucratic structure. Broad scale demands for socio-political change inevitably disrupt the stability of that environment. Depending on the magnitude, scope, and duration of the forces of change, external environmental turbulence may cause severe damage to the internal stability of the bureaucratic system unless significant adaptations are effected. In view of the fact that a major portion of the world today—and, from all indications, for a long time to come—is engulfed in varying degrees and kinds of turbulence, the relationship between the traditional bureaucratic virtues and the modern forces of socio-political change suggests the image of two symbolic giants heading on a collision course. If this is so, the real question then becomes, how will the impact be absorbed? To what extent will, and can, bureaucratic structures adapt success-fully to the forces of dynamic change that are being manifested in their external environments?

Unfortunately, this implies the existence of a single, monolithic set of change forces, and this is obviously not true. One simply cannot discuss demands for socio-political change as if they were the same the world over. Nor can one assume that all bureaucratic systems will respond to demands for change in a similar fashion. Nevertheless, given the macro view this essay attempts to project, and given the basic assumption that all bureaucracies throughout the world today are forced to confront external environments which are growing increasingly unstable, then a conceptually useful dichotomy (albeit totally inadequate for analytical and empirical purposes) can be developed between advanced and transitional socio-political systems. For the purposes of this essay attention will be focused solely on the advanced socio-political systems of the world. A more extensive essay dealing with both advanced and transitional systems currently is being prepared.[2]

Advanced Socio-Political Systems

If bureaucracies are viewed simply in terms of large-scale, complex organiza-tions characterized by graded ranks of authority, superior-subordinate relation-

---

[2] This paper represents a shorter version of one being prepared for the Comparative Development Studies Center of the State University of New York at Albany in conjunction with the Center's sponsored seminar on Intercultural Negotiation and Change, November 3-7, 1969, Saratoga Springs, New York.

ships, a high degree of centralized decision-making power, and division of labor, then it should be apparent that the most advanced nations of the world contain numerous bureaucratic structures—public as well as private.[3]

For the public bureaucracies of most advanced societies, the decade of The Sixties has not been serene. In virtually every one of these nations a host of domestic crises, having been covered over by a blanket of tensions generated by the cold war during most of the 1950's, finally appeared like a mail train in the night as foreign policy tensions were relaxed during the 1960's. Moreover, domestic tensions have generated a turbulence in the external environments of these public bureaucratic structures which, on the basis of virtually every projected forecast, is likely to persist, if not increase, throughout the remainder of this century.[4]

The turbulence in the external environments of these public bureaucratic systems may be viewed from two perspectives, each integrally related. On the one hand, the environmental turbulence stems from forces demanding broad socio-political change of the role of the individual in these post-industrial, advanced societies. On the other hand, the turbulence stems from forces demanding even more extensive technological innovation. Thus, the turbulence which has developed emerges from an integrated set of socio-technological forces which seek meaningful solutions to the wide range of domestic problems existing in these advanced societies today.

The problems of human justice and human dignity, for example, necessitate the "invention" of meaningful socio-political solutions; the problems of garbage disposal and traffic flow in New York, London, Paris, and Tokyo require technical solutions. However, if a center city expressway is designed to cut a wide swath through low-income residential neighborhoods, an additional problem has been created which requires a socio-political-technological solution. One fundamental characteristic of the advanced societies in this post-industrial era is the growing social ramifications of every major technological change, and, conversely, the growing technological ramifications of any major social change.

If my characterization of the types of demands for change as being either socio-political or technical is correct, and if the two have become inseparably linked together, then it seems reasonable to ask if public bureaucracies have the necessary capability to respond effectively to these demands. In other words, demands for change are merely demands to solve problems; do the public bureaucracies in these advanced societies have the necessary problem-solving capability? In this connection, it might be helpful to separate the union just created between the socio-political and technical forces of change. Then a

---

[3]The communist nations, of course, do not have an extensive, highly developed system of private bureaucratic structures operating concurrently with the public system. The advanced socialist nations do reveal well-developed public and private bureaucracies even though private structures may be under the general policy direction of the government.

[4]Here one could cite numerous sources of projected aggregate data but the more relevant sources would be those which project the state of possible futures based on these data, e.g., "Toward the Year 2000," *Daedalus,* Vol. 96, No. 3 (Summer, 1967); "Tomorrow's Transportation," U. S. Department of Housing and Urban Development, 1968; P. Hall, *London 2000* (London: Farber and Farber, 1963).

two-step question unfolds which asks: (1) Are public bureaucracies capable of meeting the technical needs of their citizens; and (2) Are they capable of meeting the socio-political needs of their citizens?

Insofar as the technical capabilities of public bureaucratic systems are concerned, the best that may be said is that they are adequate when applied on a short range, limited, low-complexity basis. If the nature of the problem is limited, relatively non-complex, and amenable to relatively quick resolution, then public bureaucracies probably have the necessary capabilities. However, with the growing nationalization of political conflict in these advanced countries, incremental satisficing no longer appears as a viable alternative response to the forces of change. As national problems demand national solutions, the technical capacities of these public bureaucracies are revealed in their weakest light. The technical aspects of pollution control require long-range analysis, planning coordination, and implementation. The public bureaucracies in all but the smallest of nations are virtually incapable of responding to this kind of challenge. To an increasing extent more and more reliance is being placed on private bureaucracies to supply the rational comprehensiveness required to meet these technical challenges. The simple truth-of-the-matter is that in this computerized, systems analytical, post-industrial world, private bureaucracies have developed a comprehensive and analytical problem-solving capacity which makes public bueeaucratic systems appear anemic by comparison. The application of this capacity to the technical aspects of public policy problems has increased substantially in recent years and, in all probability, will increase even more dramatically in the immediate future.

But then the follow-up question becomes critical: Can the public bureaucracies satisfy the socio-political needs of their citizens? This, after all, gets to the traditional function of such public bodies—the one in which years, indeed centuries, of experience have been accumulated. Nonetheless, despite the presumed expertise in this area, the public bureaucratic structures in most of the world's advanced societies are infirm, and their respective prognoses are not bright. The cause of the infirmity is not difficult to locate.

In relation to the external forces of change there are really only two strategies any bureaucracy may adopt. Reference has already been made to the differences between responsive and anticipatory change. Another frequently cited distinction is between incremental and comprehensive change. Both sets of contrasting terms simply suggest two different decision-making strategies that may be applied in the search for problem solutions. The search may be aimed either at locating the optimal solution, or at locating a "less-than-optimal" solution but one which, nonetheless, would be satisfactory. Thus, the distinction is frequently made between "optimizing" and "satisficing" strategies. In seeking the optimal, or "best possible," solution, the decision-maker must be prepared to invest considerable time and effort in the search procedure. Thus, as Herbert Simon pointed out years ago, it is less costly, less-complicated, and just downright easier to come up with a solution which is satisfactory, or "good enough," than to search exhaustively for the "best" solution. In low-risk situations this is good advice to follow, and by low-risk I mean high stability, low anxiety environments. If not too many people feel too strongly about a particular social problem, then a "good enough" solution probably will satisfy the low murmurs of discontent until another "good enough" or incremental solution may be needed. In the United States particularly, as a result of the efforts of Charles Lindblom with excellent support from Robert Dahl,[5] this approach to change has become virtually sanctified by the public bureaucracies.

However, the breakdown of the incremental approach results when "good enough" no longer is enough to "satisfice." The utility of the incremental approach is lost when an individual or a group realizes that the losses which have been incurred over an extended period of time can never possibly be offset by any subsequent gains so long as the allocative strategy in which the losses were accumulated continues to operate. Under these circumstances, public bureaucracies become the prime targets for change.

But change comes hard to those for whom the bureaucratic system provides a state-of-mind, a frame of reference. Responsive change in public bureaucracies is deeply ingrained. To satisfy the socio-political needs of the present and of the future, the only alternative would seem to lie in the direction of anticipatory change. However, this approach and its innovative corollary require the invention of new solutions to new problems, and this implies a willingness to experiment, to discard, and most important of all, to adapt to turbulent situations. At this point in time it is not at all clear that these public bureaucracies can meet this challenge on their own accord.

What does seem clear, however (at least, insofar as the United States, Western Europe, and Japan are concerned), is that to an ever-increasing extent demands for solutions to pressing socio-political problems and needs are being directed at private bureaucracies. For example, part of the turbulence which has been generated within the external environment is a result of technological impersonality. An Orwellian image of dehumanized man in the face of a thoroughly impersonal technocratic machine is usually a characterization reserved for public bureaucracies. However, as the web of private corporate giants continues to expand and subdivide in these advanced societies, it becomes apparent that the everyday lives of average individuals are just as much affected by decisions made by General Motors, Unilever, or Renault as they are by the U.S. Defense Department, Britain's Ministry of Employment and Productivity, or France's Ministry of Finance. Public bureaucracies in advanced societies are capable of influencing the lives of millions of people; at the present time, no less is true of the large, complex private bureaucracies located in these same societies.

[5]Charles Lindblom and David Braybrooke, *The Strategy of Decision* (New York: The Free Press, 1963); Charles Lindblom, *The Intelligence of Democracy* (New York: The Free Press, 1965); Charles Lindblom and Robert Dahl, *Politics, Economics, and Welfare* (New York: Harper and Row, 1953); Robert Dahl, *A Preface to Democratic Theory* (Chicago: The University of Chicago Press, 1956). For a more detailed interpretative essay on incrementalism see Gawthrop, *The Administrative Process and Democratic Theory* (Boston: Houghton-Mifflin, 1970), Ch. 6.

Thus, insofar as the forces of change are concerned, public and private bureaucratic structures represent equally critical objects to which demands for socio-political change may be directed. In many respects, private bureaucracies—motivated by a composite mixture of altruism and competitive necessity—have reacted to these demands with much more imaginative innovation than public bureaucracies. Reflecting patterns established throughout Western Europe long ago, the private bureaucratic system in the United States is now becoming increasingly involved in a wide range of socially-related activities. Schools have been established to teach not only technical and clerical skills, but also basic literacy skills where the public systems have failed. Industry-related child day care centers are being developed. Corporate transportation systems have been established in instances where public systems have failed to provide low cost/high speed transportation for workers. Hiring practices have been drastically altered in recent years to expedite the hiring of hard core unemployed. Redevelopment programs for low income neighborhoods have proceeded in many instances on a private basis, especially in those areas which house a high percentage of a corporation's employees and/or potential customers. In a wide variety of other ways, the private sector has directly involved itself in providing solutions to pressing socio-political needs.

Private bureaucratic resources also have been combined with public resources to devise solutions to various socio-political and technical problems. For example, private management officials temporarily have been assigned to public units to provide technical expertise, especially in the area of systems analysis. Other specialists from the private sector have worked closely with public education officials to devise innovative changes in primary and secondary programs.

But probably most significant of all—at least in terms of long-range future change—has been the role assumed by many private bureaucracies on the transnational level. The literature on the multinational corporation is already substantial,[6] and as this phenomenon expands, so also will our understanding of its implications, both real and potential. At the present time, the future of the multinational private bureaucracy is being studied on an enthusiastic, albeit somewhat speculative, basis.

The rise of the multinational corporation has been rapid and is bound to accelerate even more. Therefore it is important to bear in mind that the ideal model of a multinational corporation is one whose decision-making system is totally unrestricted by purely national considerations. Thus, the pure model of this recent phenomenon reveals a global frame of reference which is clearly designed to transcend national political jurisdictions.

Needless to say, the pure model is, in actual fact, just that—a pure model. The

---

[6]Here one must be careful, however, to avoid traditional international business orientations being passed off under the guise of a new multinational approach. At the present time some of the most relevant and pertinent insights concerning the multinational corporation in a transnational world are being advanced—mainly in the form of articles—by Raymond Vernon, Howard Pearlmutter, George Steiner, and George Modelski.

closest approximation is the large (usually American) corporation that (1) draws more than 50% of its profits from outside the continental limits of the country which hosts its headquarters, (2) maintains subsidiaries in two or more countries outside of its headquarters country, and (3) maintains a decision-making system in which ultimate control is effectively monopolized by citizens of one particular nation—usually nationals of the headquarters country.

The incongruity between the actual and the ideal multinational corporation is apparent, but for the purposes of this essay the divergence is not important. What is important is the fact that the global expansion of private bureaucratic systems is, in part, a response to existing demands for socio-political change; but even in larger part, it represents a move in anticipation of future demands for such change.

Transnational communication and transportation systems have expanded the relevant external environment of those private bureaucracies which choose to recognize this development. The global transmission of information, technical as well as socio-political, public as well as private, has reached the near-instantaneous level. The globan transmission of people and material can now be gauged in hours. A free exchange zone accelerating these trends is evidenced among virtually all of the advanced societies, save the Soviet Union and the Soviet Bloc nations. And as private bureaucratic systems extend the scope of their networks on a transnational level, cultural barriers may very well diminish substantially.

This is not to suggest a direct, one-to-one correlation between transnational bureaucratic systems and cultural systems. It is to suggest, however, that the former may serve as effective devices in channeling the forces of change across national and cultural boundaries. Transportation and communication systems serve this function as well. Together, all three represent a potentially dynamic vehicle for the forces of socio-political change.

To a very real extent, socio-political conflict has already become "transnationalized." Among most of the advanced societies of the world, the causes and effects of urban congestion, ecological pollution, poverty, racial prejudice, mass education, and population expansion may be characterized in many ways, but certainly not in their cultural diversity. On a macro level these problems reveal a high degree of homogeneity, and demands for socio-political change become increasingly uniform.

Under these circumstances, environmental turbulence assumes global proportions. But as socio-political conflict escalates it transcends not only cultural barriers but also the capabilities of the national public bureaucracies to respond to these demands in an effective and meaningful manner. Nationally-bounded public bureaucracies will be forced to confront the transnational forces of change on an increasingly limited, consolidative, and incremental basis, while these dynamic forces of change will be seeking broad innovative, anticipatory, and comprehensive solutions.

The implications of such a situation are interesting and significant. Undoubtedly, the most important consequence which is suggested is the growing irrelevance of nationalism. With the development of a truly transnational communications system which links the advanced societies of the world together in an intimate network of free information exchange,[7] national efforts aimed at transnational socio-political turbulence assume band-aid proportions. By contrast, the only effective bureaucratic mechanism that would seem to be available to deal with transnational socio-political conflict in a relevant manner would be the transnational bureaucratic system of private organizations.

The implications of this suggestion insofar as the integrity of the nation state is concerned should need no elaboration. Transnational private bureaucracies represent a potential major threat to the viability of national public bureaucracies. Insofar as the future of socio-political change is concerned, a typical, and quite natural reaction to this threat would be to replace the diminished cultural barriers with imposing national political barriers. The transnational corporation is able to maintain its operational effectiveness only so long as the avenues of transnational intercourse remain open. And these avenues can be closed very easily by national political action.

Thus, the future of transnational private bureaucracies is bleak, indeed, to the extent that national public bureaucracies perceive its presence as a potential threat, or as a competitor for the allegiance of its citizens. If, on the other hand, this perception can be reversed—i.e., if a cooperative relationship can evolve between these two dissimilar units regarding problems involving broad socio-political change—then the future of transnational bureaucracies would seem much brighter.

The proposition is not inconceivable. Environmental turbulence threatens the international stability of *all* bureaucratic systems. At least within the United States, Western Europe, and Japan, the basis for a true symbiotic reciprocity appears to be present between the transnational private and national public bureaucratic systems. For each, effective adaptation to increasing environmental turbulence depends upon combining in a cooperative fashion with the other toward the solution of pressing socio-political problems. The success of one depends upon the extent to which it helps the other—which, of course, is simply another way of suggesting that the time-honored public-private dichotomy, especially in areas of vital socio-political importance, will continue to appear as an increasingly irrelevant consideration. As the forces of socio-political change in the external environments of public and private bureaucratic systems become more homogeneous and uniform in their attitudes and values, they also become less discriminating in their willingness to distinguish between public and private domains. In the minds of the young, the poor, the oppressed—and indeed, many of the affluent, well-educated groups, as well—bureaucracy stands as an obstacle against change regardless of whether that obstacle enjoys public or private status under the law. To an increasing extent private bureaucratic systems will have to become involved in helping to provide solutions to pressing socio-political needs,

---

[7] Again the Soviet Bloc nations must be excluded from this generalization, although even in this sector the influence of the transnational corporation has not been completely excluded. See especially Howard Pearlmutter, "Emerging East-West Ventures: The Trans-ideological Enterprise," *Columbia Journal of World Business* (September-October, 1969), pp. 39-50.

and to an equally increasing extent public bureaucracies will have to turn to these private systems for their help. The public-private distinction under these circumstances becomes artificial at the very least; within advanced societies the relevant distinction between bureaucratic systems in the future will have to be made in terms of a national-transnational dichtomy.

Conclusion

The primary purpose of this essay, as stated at the outset, has been to focus on that aspect of socio-political change which is critically related to and directly affected by, bureaucratic response to the external forces of change. Insofar as the future of this relationship is concerned, the projections advanced in the preceding pages are certainly not submitted as definitive proclamations. Instead, they are designed to suggest that established national bureaucratic responses are ineffective in responding to demands for broadscale change stemming from increasingly turbulent environments.

In addition, a persistence on the part of national bureaucratic systems to employ established solution procedures to new problems merely tends to compound the ineffectiveness of the bureaucratic response as well as the turbulence in the external environment. The demands for political, economic, social, and technological change have become transnational in scope. In many instances, these demands have created an autochthonous turbulence[8] which realistically cannot be expected to disappear spontaneously—except possibly by those individuals who view its eruption as a spontaneous event. Turbulence has become virtually the universal phenomenon of our time.

Ultimately, however, the national and transnational bureaucratic systems of the world emerge as the critical ingredients of the amalgam of the future. Given a projected state of permanent impermanence insofar as interpersonal and organizational relationships are concerned, bureaucratic systems become an important factor capable of providing some degree of cohesiveness to what Bennis and Slater refer to as highly temporary societies.[9]

Bureaucratic organizations cannot avoid assuming a key role in determining the direction and magnitude of the forces of change. The bureaucratic reaction can be positive or negative, responsive or anticipatory, consolidative or innovative. The basic premise of this essay has been that anything less than a fully comprehensive, innovative, and anticipatory approach to change will be insufficient in providing this critical amalgam to a highly temporary and impermanent future.

[8]For a more detailed discussion of environmental turbulence see F. E. Emery and E. L. Trist, "The Causal Texture of Organizational Environments," *Human Relations,* Vol. 18 (November, 1965), pp. 21-32.

[9]Warren Bennis and Philip Slater, *The Temporary Society* (New York: Harper and Row, 1968).

Applied Organization Change in Industry: Structural, Technical, and Human Approaches

In this reading, Leavitt delineates four broad categories regarding what is to be changed in an organization in order to improve its ability to function. The four variables, all of which interact to some degree, include: task, structure, technology (tools), and people (actors). In other words, any one of these variables is a major lever which can be pulled by the change agent or administrator in order to improve the socio-technical system. The author then provides a critical examination of each of these variables in order to give the reader an insight into positive and negative roles they play in the change process.

APPLIED ORGANIZATION CHANGE IN INDUSTRY: STRUCTURAL, TECHNICAL, AND HUMAN APPROACHES

Harold J. Leavitt

Carnegie Institute of Technology

This is a mapping chapter. It is part of a search for perspective on complex organizations; in this instance, through consideration of several classes of efforts to change ongoing organizations. Approaches to change provide a kind of sharp caricature of underlying beliefs and prejudices about the important dimensions of organizations. Thereby, perhaps, they provide some insights into areas of real or apparent difference among perspectives on organization theory.

To classify several major approaches to change, I have found it useful, first, to view organizations as multivariate systems, in which at least four interacting variables loom especially large: the variables of task, structure, technology, and actors (usually people). (See Fig. 1.)

Roughly speaking, "task" refers to organizational *raisons d'etre*—manufacturing, servicing, etc., including the large numbers of different, but operationally meaningful, subtasks which may exist in complex organizations.

By "actors" I mean mostly people, but with the qualification that acts usually executed by people need not remain exclusively in the human domain.

By "technology" I mean technical tools—problem-solving inventions like work measurement, computers, or drill presses. Note that I include both machines and programs in this category, but with some uncertainty about the line between structure and technology.

From *New Perspectives in Organization Research* edited by W. W. Cooper, H. J. Leavitt and M. W. Shelly II. Copyright © 1964 by John Wiley & Sons, Inc. By permission.

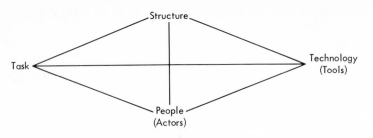

FIGURE 1.

Finally, by "structure" I mean systems of communication, systems of authority (or other roles), and systems of work flow.

These four are highly interdependent, so that change in any one will most probably result in compensatory (or retaliatory) change in others. In discussing organizational change, therefore, I shall assume that it is one or more of these variables that we seek to change. Sometimes we may aim to change one of these as an end in itself, sometimes as a mechanism for effecting some changes in one or more of the others.

Thus, for example, structural change toward, say, decentralization should change the performance of certain organizational tasks (indeed, even the selection of tasks); the technology that is brought to bear (e.g., changes in accounting procedures); and the nature, numbers, and/or motivation and attitudes of people in the organization. Any of these changes could presumably be consciously intended; or they could occur as unforeseen and often troublesome outcomes of efforts to change only one or two of the variables.

Similarly, the introduction of new technological tools—computers, for example—may effect changes in structure (e.g., in the communication system or decision map of the organization), changes in people (their numbers, skills, attitudes, and activities), and changes in task performance or even task definition, since some tasks may now become feasible of accomplishment for the first time.

Changes in the people and task variables could presumably branch out through the system to cause similar changes in other variables.

We can turn now to the central focus of this chapter, namely, a categorization and evaluation of several approaches to organizational change—approaches that differ markedly in their degree of emphasis and their ordering of these four variables.

Clearly most efforts to effect change, whether they take off from people, technology, structure, or task, soon must deal with the others. Human relators must invent technical devices for implementing their ideas, and they must evaluate alternative structures, classing some as consonant and some as dissonant with their views of the world. Structuralists must take stands on the kinds of human interaction that are supportive of their position, and the kinds that threaten to undermine it, etc.

Although I differentiate structural from technical from human approaches to organizational tasks, the differentiation is in points of origin, relative weightings, and underlying conceptions and values, not in the exclusion of all other variables.

This categorization must be further complicated by the fact that the objectives of the several approaches to organizational change are not uniform. All of them do share a considerable interest in improved solutions to tasks. But while some of the technical approaches focus almost exclusively on task solutions, that is, on the *quality* of decisions, some of the people approaches are at least as interested in performance of task subsequent to decisions. Although improved task solution serves as a common goal for all of these approaches, several carry other associated objectives that weigh almost as heavily in the eyes of their proponents. Thus some of the early structural approaches were almost as concerned with maintaining a power status quo as with improving task performance, and some of the current people approaches are at least as interested in providing organizations that fulfill human needs as they are in efficacious performance of tasks.

The several approaches are still further complicated by variations in the causal chains by which they are supposed to bring about their intended changes. Some of the structural approaches, for example, are not aimed directly at task but at people as mediating intervening variables. In these approaches one changes structure to change people to improve task performance. Similarly, some of the people approaches seek to change people in order to change structure and tools, to change task performance, and also to make life more fulfilling for people. We can turn now to the several varieties of efforts themselves.

The Structural Approaches

Applied efforts to change organizations by changing structure seem to fall into four classes. First, structural change has been the major mechanism of the "classical" organization theorist. Out of the deductive, logical, largely military-based thinking of early nonempirical organization theory, there evolved the whole set of now familiar "principles" for optimizing organizational performance by optimizing structure. These are deductive approaches carrying out their analyses from task backwards to appropriate divisions of labor and appropriate systems of authority. These early structural approaches almost always mediated their activities through people to task. One improves task performance by clarifying and defining the jobs of people and setting up appropriate relationships among these jobs. Operationally one worried about modifying spans of control, defining nonoverlapping areas of responsibility and authority, and logically defining necessary functions.

In retrospect, most of us think of these early approaches as abstractions, formal and legalistic, and poorly anchored in empirical data. They were also almost incredibly naive in their assumptions about human behavior. In fact, almost the only assumptions that were made were legalistic and moralistic ones:

that people, having contracted to work, would then carry out the terms of their contract; that people assigned responsibility would necessarily accept that responsibility; that people when informed of the organization's goals would strive wholeheartedly to achieve those goals.

The values underlying these early approaches were thus probably more authoritarian and puritanical than anything else. Order, discipline, system, and acceptance of authority seemed to be dominant values. The objective, of course, was optimal task performance, but within the constraints imposed by the hierarchy of authority.

In one variation or another, such structural approaches are still widely applied. It is still commonplace for consultants or organization planning departments to try to solve organizational problems by redefining areas of responsibility and authority, enforcing the chain of command, and so on.

A second widespread approach to structural change, allied to the first, somewhat more modern and sophisticated and somewhat narrower, too, is the idea of decentralization. The idea of changing organizations by decentralizing their structure was probably more an invention of the accounting profession than anyone else, though it has been widely endorsed by structuralists and by human relators too. Almost nobody is against it. Not too long ago, I heard the senior officer of one of the nation's largest consulting firms remind his large staff of young consultants that their firm was founded on the "bedrock principle of decentralization."

Decentralization affects the performance of tasks partially through its intervening effects on people. By creating profit centers, one presumably increases the motivation and goal-oriented behavior of local managers. One also adds flexibility so that variations in technology appropriate to the different tasks of different decentralized units now become more possible; so do subvariations in structure, and local variations in the use of people. Decentralization can be thought of as a mechanism for changing organizations at a meta level, providing local autonomy for futher change. Thus, within limits, decentralized units may further change themselves through the use of any one of the many alternatives available, and perhaps for this reason no group has questioned it, at least until the last couple of years.

Recently, two other structural approaches have shown up, but they have not yet reached a widespread level of application. One of them is best represented by Chapple and Sayles.* Theirs is a form of social engineering aimed at task, but via people. They seek to modify the behavior of people in order to improve task performance, but they do it by modifying structure, in this case, the flow of work. Out of the tradition of applied anthropology, they argue that planning of work flows and groupings of specialties will directly affect the morale, behavior, and output of employees. One of the failings of earlier structural models, in their view, is that the design of work was almost entirely determined by task and technical variables, and failed to take account of human social variables. They

*Cf., Eliot D. Chapple and Leonard R. Sayles, "Work Flow as the Basis of Organizational Design," reprinted in this volume, pp. 313-38.

provide illustrative cases to show that appropriate redesigning of work, in a social engineering sense, affects both human attitudes and output.

I cannot overlook in this discussion of structure the implications of a second approach—the research on communication networks. I know of no *direct* applications of this laboratory research to the real world, though it has some indirect influence on structural planning. In that research, variations in communication nets affect both routine and novel task performance rather significantly. The results suggest that appropriate communication structures might vary considerably within a complex organization, depending upon the type of task that any subunit of the organization undertakes. Thus for highly programmed repetitive tasks, highly centralized communication structures seem to operate most efficiently, but with some human costs. For more novel, ill-structured tasks, more wide-open communication nets with larger numbers of channels and less differentiation among members seem to work more effectively.

Technological Approaches to Organizational Change

My first entry in this technological category is Taylor's *Scientific Management*. Its birth date was around 1910, its father, Frederick W. Taylor. Its tools were work measurement tools. It bore none of the abstract deductive flavor of the structural approaches. From the classic programming of the labors of Schmidt, the immigrant pig-iron handler at Bethlehem, on to the more sophisticated forms of work measurement and analysis of succeeding decades, Taylorism has constituted a significant force in influencing task performance in American organizations.

Scientific Management, almost from its inception, took a position outside of the task, not of it. Taylor created a new technical skill—industrial engineering—and a new class of specialized practitioners—the industrial engineers. Theirs was a staff skill, a planning skill. They were the organizers and designers of work. The Schmidts were the doers.

Like the early structural approaches, Scientific Management was thus to a great extent ahuman, perhaps even inhuman. For in creating the separate planning specialist, it removed planning from its old location—the head of the doer of work. Many observers, both contemporary and subsequent, saw this phase of scientific management as downright demeaning of mankind. Taylor put his foot deeply into his mouth by saying things like this: "Now one of the very first requirements for a man who is fit to handle pig iron . . . is that he shall be so stupid and so phlegmatic that he more nearly resembles . . . the ox than any other type. . . . He must consequently be trained by a man more intelligent than himself."

But despite the flurry of congressional investigations and active counterattack by Taylor's contemporaries, Scientific Management grew and prospered, and radically changed structure, people, and the ways jobs get done. Indeed, it spread and flourished until no self-respecting manufacturing firm was without time-study men, methods engineers, work standards, piece rates, and job classification schemes.

The range of Scientific Management, however, was limited by its relatively simple tools to the programming of eye-hand and muscle jobs. Though Taylor and his fellows were ready to generalize their methods to almost any organizational problem, the methods themselves fell pretty short when applied to judgment and think-type jobs.

If one asks why Scientific Management flourished, several reasonable answers appear. The environment of the day, despite counterattacks by Upton Sinclair and others, was probably supportive. It was an environment of growth, expansiveness, and muscle flexing. Work in associated disciplines was supportive, too. Psychology, for example, was physiologically oriented, concerned with individual differences, and anxious to be treated as a science. Hence it, too, was measurement happy.[1] Finger dexterity tests meshed neatly with Taylor's motion study.

But most of all, Taylorism, like many other ideas, seemed to be carried by its own operational gimmicks—by its cheap, workable, easily taught techniques and methods.

Scientific Management receded into a relatively stable and undramatic background in the late 1930's and 1940's and has never made a real comeback in its original form. But the technological approaches were by no means dead. The development of operations research and the more or less contemporaneous invention and exploitation of computers have more than revived them.

I submit that operational operations research methods for changing organizational problem solving can be reasonably placed in the same category with Scientific Management. They have both developed a body of technical methods for solving work problems. They both are usually *external* in their approach, essentially separating the planning of problem-solving programs from the routine acting out of solutions. Operations research, too, is quickly developing, in its operational form, a new class of hot-shot staff specialists, in many ways analogous to the earlier staff efficiency man. What is *clearly* different, of course, is the nature of the techniques, although there may be larger differences that are not yet so clear.

The operations research and information processing techniques are turning out to be, if not more general, at least applicable to large classes of tasks that Scientific Management could not touch. Now, armed with linear programming methods, one can approach a task like media selection in an advertising agency, though it would have been nonsense to time study it.

[1] See for example, Bendix's account of the early enthusiasm of industrial psychologists. He quotes Hugo Munsterberg appraising the promise of industrial psychology in 1913: ". . . Still more important than the valued commercial profit on both sides is the cultural gain which will come to the total economic life of the nation, as soon as everyone can be brought to the place where his best energies may be unfolded and his greatest personal satisfaction secured. The economic experimental psychology offers no more inspiring idea than this adjustment of work and psyche by which mental dissatisfaction with the work, mental depression and discouragement, may be replaced in our social community by overflowing joy and perfect inner harmony."

But note the overall similarity: change the setting of the movie from Bethlehem, Pa., to Madison Avenue; the time from 1910 to 1962; the costuming from overalls to gray flannel suits; and the tasks from simple muscular labor to complex judgmental decisions. Turn worried laborer Schmidt into worried media executive Jones. Then replace Taylor with Charnes and Cooper and supplant the stopwatch with the computer. It is the same old theme either way—the conflict between technology and humanity.

A distinction needs to be drawn, of course, between operational operations research and other computer-based information-processing approaches, although they are often closely allied. "Management Science" hopefully will mean more than highly operational applications of specific techniques, and organizations are also being changed by simulation techniques and by heuristic problem-solving methods. Their impact has not yet been felt in anything like full force; but tasks, people, and structures are already being rather radically modified by them. In fact, one wonders if these task-directed efforts will not end up having at least as radical an impact on structure and on the role of humans as on task solutions themselves. For out of new information-processing methods we now begin to reconsider the bedrock issue of decentralization and to reconsider the permanency and primacy of human judgments for making certain classes of decisions. All the way round the organization, visible changes are being generated out of technical innovations.

Without delving further into the substance of these more recent technological approaches, it may be worth pointing up one other characteristic that they share with many of their predecessors—a kind of faith in the ultimate victory of *better* problem solutions over less good ones. This faith is often perceived by people-oriented practitioners of change as sheer naïveté about the nature of man. They ascribe it to a pre-Freudian fixation on rationality; to a failure to realize that human acceptance of ideas is the real carrier of change, and that emotional human resistance is the real roadblock. They can point, in evidence, to a monotonously long list of cases in which technological innovations, methods changes, or operations research techniques have fallen short because they ignored the human side of the enterprise. It is not the logically better solutions that get adopted, this argument runs, but the more humanly acceptable, more feasible ones. Unless the new technologist wises up, he may end up a miserable social isolate, like his predecessor, the unhappy industrial engineer.

Often this argument fits the facts. Operations research people can be incredibly naïve in their insensitivity to human feelings. But in another, more gracious sense, one can say that the technological approaches have simply taken a more macroscopic, longer view of the world than the people approaches. Better solutions do get accepted in the long run, because deeper forces in the economy press them upon the individual organization—competitive forces, mainly. Macroscopically these ahuman or people-last approaches may encounter bumps and grinds in the microcosms of the individual firm; but sooner or later, in the aggregate, human resistances will be allayed or displaced or overcome, and the steam drill must inevitably defeat John Henry.

The technological approaches assume some communication among firms, and between firms and the world; and they assume further that the demonstration of more economic solutions will eventually result in their adoption, though the road may be rough.

The technological approaches seem not only to predict the victory of cleaner, more logical, and more parsimonious solutions but also to *value* them. Failure of human beings to search for or use more efficient solutions is a sign, from this perspective, of human weakness and inadequacy. People must be teased or educated into greater logic, greater rationality. Resistance to better solutions is proof only of the poverty of our educational system; certainly it is not in any way an indication that "optimal" solutions are less than optimal.

The People Approaches

The people approaches try to change the organizational world by changing the behavior of actors in the organization. By changing people, it is argued, one can cause the creative invention of new tools, or one can cause modifications in structure (especially power structure). By one or another of these means, changing people will cause changes in solutions to tasks and performance of tasks as well as changes in human growth and fulfillment.

In surveying the people approaches, one is immediately struck by the fact that the literature dealing directly with organizational change is almost all people-oriented. Just in the last four or five years, for example, several volumes specifically concerned with organizational change have been published. All of them are people-type books. They include Lippitt, Watson, and Westley's *The Dynamics of Planned Change;* Lawrence's *The Changing of Organizational Behavior Patterns;* Ginsberg and Reilly's *Effecting Change in Large Organizations;* Bennis, Benne, and Chin's *The Planning of Change;* and Guest's *Organizational Change.*

This tendency to focus on the process of change itself constitutes one of the major distinguishing features of the people approaches. The technological and structural approaches tend to focus on problem-solving, sliding past the micro-processes by which new problem-solving techniques are generated and adopted.

Historically, the people approaches have moved through at least two phases. The first was essentially manipulative, responsive to the primitive and seductive question, "How can we get people to do what we want them to do?"

Although most of us identify such questions with borderline workers like Dale Carnegie, much of the early work (immediately post-World War II) by social scientists on "overcoming resistance to change" dealt with the same issues.

Carnegie's *How to Win Friends and Influence People* was first published in 1936, a few years ahead of most of what we now regard as psychological work in the same area. Like the social scientists that followed, Carnegie's model for change focused on the relationship between changer and changee, pointing out that changes in feelings and attitudes were prerequisites to voluntary changes in overt behavior. Carnegie proposes that one changes others first by developing a valuable (to the other person) relationship, and then using that relationship as a lever for bringing about the change one seeks. One does not attack with logic and criticism and advice. *A* offers *B* support, approval, a permissive atmosphere; and having thus established warm, affective bonds (invariably "sincere" bonds, too), *A* then requests of *B* that he change in the way *A* wishes, while *A* holds the relationship as collateral.

Though social scientists have tended to reject it out of hand, current research on influence processes suggests that the Carnegie model is not technically foolish at all, although we have disavowed it as manipulative, slick, and of questionable honesty.

The Carnegie model, moreover, has some current social scientific parallels. Thus Martin and Sims, for example, directly attack the issue of how to be a successful power politician in industrial organizations. They argue that dramatic skill, capacity to withhold certain kinds of information, the appearance of decisiveness, and a variety of other calculatedly strategic behaviors, appear to be effective in influencing behavior in organizational hierarchies.

In fact, Carnegie-like interest in face-to-face influence has finally become a respectable area of social scientific research. Several works of Hovland *et al.* on influence and persuasion provide experimental support for the efficacy of certain behavioral techniques of influence over others.

But if we move over into the traditionally more "legitimate" spheres of social science, we find that much of the work after World War II on "overcoming resistance to change" was still responsive to the same manipulative question. Consider, for example, the now classic work by Kurt Lewin and his associates on changing food habits, or the later industrial work by Coch and French. In both cases, *A* sets out to bring about a predetermined change in the behavior of *B*. Lewin sets out to cause housewives to purchase and consume more variety meats—a selling problem. Coch and French set out to gain acceptance of a preplanned methods change by hourly workers in a factory. In both cases the methodology included large elements of indirection, with less than full information available to the changees.

But whereas Dale Carnegie built warm personal relationships and then bargained with them, neither Lewin nor Coch and French are centrally concerned about intimate relationships between changer and changee. Their concern is much more with warming up the interrelationships among changees.

Thus 32 percent of Lewin's test housewives exposed to a group-decision method served new variety meats, as against only 3 percent of the women exposed to lectures. Lewin accounts for these results by calling upon two concepts: "involvement" and "group pressure." Lectures leave their audiences passive and unpressed by the group, whereas discussions are both active and pressing. Similarly, Coch and French, causing the girls in a pajama factory to accept a methods change, emphasize *group* methods, seeing resistance to change as partially a function of individual frustration, and partially of strong group-generated forces. Their methodology, therefore, is to provide opportunities for need satisfaction and quietly to corner the group forces and redirect them toward the desired change.

But it is this slight threat of stealth that was the soft spot (both ethically and methodologically) of these early people approaches to change, and this is the reason I classify them as manipulative. For surely no bright student has ever read the Coch and French piece without wondering a little bit about what *would* have happened if the change being urged by management just did not seem like a good idea to the "smaller, more intimate" work groups of Coch and French's "total participation" condition.

One might say that these early studies wrestled rather effectively with questions of affect and involvement, but ducked a key variable—power. Coch and French modified behavior by manipulating participation while trying to hold power constant. In so doing, the artistry of the "discussion leader" remained an important but only vaguely controlled variable, causing difficulties in replicating results and generating widespread discomfort among other social scientists.

Other contemporary and subsequent people approaches also avoided the power problem and encountered similar soft spots. The Western Electric counseling program that emerged out of the Hawthorne researches sought for change through catharsis, with a specific prohibition against any follow-up action by counselors—a "power-free" but eminently human approach. Later, users of morale and attitude surveys sought to effect change by feeding back anonymous aggregate data so that the power groups might then modify their own behavior. But the very anonymity of the process represented an acceptance of the power status quo.

It was to be expected, then, that the next moves in the development of people approaches would be toward working out the power variable. It was obvious, too, that the direction would be toward power equalization rather than toward power differentiation. The theoretical underpinnings, the prevalent values, and the initial research results all pointed that way.

But though this is what happened, it happened in a complicated and mostly implicit way. Most of the push has come from work on individuals and small groups, and has then been largely extrapolated to organizations. Client-centered therapy and applied group dynamics have been prime movers. In both of those cases, theory and technique explicitly aimed at allocating at least equal power to the changee(s), a fact of considerable importance in later development of dicta for organizational change.

Thus Carl Rogers describes his approach to counseling and therapy:

> This newer approach differs from the older one in that it has a genuinely different goal. It aims directly toward the greater independence and integration of the individual rather than hoping that such results will accrue if the counsellor assists in solving the problem. The individual and not the problem is the focus. The aim is not to solve one particular problem, but to assist the individual to grow.

At the group level, a comparable development was occurring, namely, the development of the T (for training) group (or sensitivity training or development group). The T group is the core tool of programs aimed at teaching people how to lead and change groups. It has also become a core tool for effecting organizational change. *T* group leaders try to bring about changes in their groups by taking extremely permissive, extremely nonauthoritarian, sometimes utterly nonparticipative roles, thus encouraging group members not only to solve their own problems but also to define them. The *T* group leader becomes, in the language of the profession, a "resource person," not consciously trying to cause a substantive set of changes but only changes in group processes, which would then, in turn, generate substantive changes.

Though the *T* group is a tool, a piece of technology, an invention, I include it in the people rather than the tool approaches, for it evolved out of those approaches as a mechanism specifically designed for effecting change in people.

In contrast to earlier group discussion tools, the *T* group deals with the power variable directly. Thus Bennis and Shepard comment:

> The core of the theory of group development is that the principle obstacles to the development of valid communication are to be found in the orientations toward authority and intimacy that members bring to the group. Rebelliousness, submissiveness or withdrawal as the characteristic responses to authority figures . . . prevent consensual validation of experience. The behaviors determined by these orientations are directed toward enslavement of the other in the service of the self, enslavement of the self in the service of the other, or disintegration of the situation. Hence, they prevent the setting, clarification of, and movement toward, group shared goals.

I offer these quotes to show the extent to which the moral and methodological soft spots of the early manipulative models were being dealt with directly in group training situations. These are not wish-washy positions. They deal directly with the power variable. Their objective is to transfer more power to the client or the group.

But these are both nonorganizational situations. For the therapist, the relationship with the individual client bounds the world. For the *T* group trainer, the group is the world. They can both deal more easily with the power variable than change agents working in a time-constrained and work-flow-constrained organizational setting.

At the organizational level, things therefore are a little more vague. The direction is there, in the form of movement toward power equalization, but roadblocks are many and maps are somewhat sketchy and undetailed. McGregor's development of participative Theory *Y* to replace authoritarian Theory *X* is a case in point. McGregor's whole conception of Theory *Y* very clearly implies a shift from an all-powerful superior dealing with impotent subordinates to something much more like a balance of power:

> People today are accustomed to being directed and manipulated and controlled in industrial organizations and to finding satisfaction for their social, egoistic and self-fulfillment needs away from the job. This is true of much of management as well as of workers. Genuine "industrial citizenship"—to borrow a term from Drucker—is a remote and unrealistic idea,

the meaning of which has not even been considered by most members of industrial organizations.

Another way of saying this is that Theory "X" places exclusive reliance upon external control of human behavior, while Theory "Y" [the theory McGregor exposits] relies heavily on self-control and self-direction. It is worth noting that this difference is the difference between treating people as children and treating them as mature adults.

Bennis, Benne and Chin specifically set out power equalization (PE) as one of the distinguishing features of the deliberate collaborative process they define as planned change: "A power distribution in which the client and change agent have equal, or almost equal, opportunities to influence" is part of their definition.

In any case, power equalization has become a key idea in the prevalent people approaches, a first step in the theoretical causal chain leading toward organizational change. It has served as an initial subgoal, a necessary predecessor to creative change in structure, technology, task solving, and task implementation. Although the distances are not marked, there is no unclarity about direction—a more egalitarian power distribution is better.

It is worth pointing out that the techniques for causing redistribution of power in these models are themselves power-equalization techniques—techniques like counseling and T group training. Thus both Lippitt *et al.* and Bennis *et al.* lay great emphasis on the need for collaboration between changer and changee in order for change to take place. But it is understandable that neither those writers nor most other workers in power equalization seriously investigate the possibility that power may be redistributed unilaterally or authoritatively (e.g., by the creation of profit centers in a large business firm or by coercion).

If we examine some of the major variables of organizational behavior, we will see rather quickly that the power-equalization approaches yields outcomes that are very different from those produced by the structural or technological approaches.

Thus in the PE models, *communication* is something to be maximized. The more channels the better, the less filtering the better, the more feedback the better. All these because power will be more equally distributed, validity of information greater, and commitment to organizational goals more intense.

Contrast these views with the earlier structural models which argued for clear but limited communication lines, never to be circumvented; and which disallowed the transmission of affective and therefore task-irrelevant information. They stand in sharp contrast, too, to some current technical views which search for optimal information flows that may be far less than maximum flows.

The PE models also focus much of their attention on issues of *group pressure, cohesiveness,* and *conformity.* The more cohesiveness the better, for cohesiveness causes commitment. The broader the group standards, the better. The more supportive the group, the freer the individual to express his individuality.

These, of course, are issues of much current popular debate. But as factors in effecting change, they are almost entirely ignored by the technical and most of the structural models. In their faith that best solutions will be recognized and in their more macroscopic outlook, until very recently at least, the technical and structural models did not concern themselves with questions of human emotionality and irrationality. If these were treated at all, they were treated as petty sources of interference with the emergence of Truth.

Evidence on this last question—the question of whether or not truth is obscured or enhanced by group pressures—is not yet perfectly clear. On the one hand, Asch has shown in his classic experiments that group pressures may indeed cause individuals to deny their own sense data. On the other hand, Asch himself has warned against interpreting this denial as an entirely emotional noncognitive process. When 10 good men and true announce that line A is longer than line B, and when the 11th man, still seeking truth, but himself seeing B as longer than A, still goes along with the group, he may do so not because he is overwhelmed by emotional pressure but because "rationally" he decides that 10 other good sets of eyes are more likely to be right than his own.

Moreover, some data from some recent experiments being conducted at Carnegie Tech and elsewhere[2] suggest that in-fighting and debate will cease rather rapidly within a group when a solution that is prominently better than other alternatives is put forth. This is to say that people use their heads as well as their guts; though at times in our history we have vociferously denied either one or the other.

Consider next the *decision-making* variable. Decision making, from the perspective of power equalization, is viewed not from a cognitive perspective, nor substantively, but as a problem in achieving committed agreement. The much discussed issues are commitment and consensual validation, and means for lowering and spreading decision-making opportunities.

Contrast this with the technical emphasis on working out optimal decision rules, and with the structuralist's emphasis on locating precise decision points and assigning decision-making responsibility always to individuals.

Summary

If we view organizations as systems of interaction among task, structural, technical, and human variables, several different classes of efforts to change organizational behavior can be grossly mapped.

Such a view provides several entry points for efforts to effect change. One can try to change aspects of task solution, task definition, or task performance by introducing new tools, new structures, or new or modified people or machines. On occasion we have tried to manipulate only one of these variables and discovered that all the others move in unforeseen and often costly directions.

We have more than once been caught short by this failing. The Scientific Management movement, for example, enamored of its measurement techniques,

---

[2]As reported in a personal communication from T. C. Schelling, 1961.

worked out efficient task solutions only to have many of them backfire because the same methods were also evoking human resistance and hostility. The human relations movement, I submit, is only now bumping into some of the unforeseen costs of building a theory of organization exclusively of human bricks, only to find that technological advances may obviate large chunks of human relations problems by obviating large chunks of humans or by reducing the need for "consensual validation" by programming areas formerly reserved to uncheckable human judgment.

Approaches with strong structural foci have also on occasion fallen into the one-track trap, changing structure to facilitate task solution only then to find that humans do not fit the cubbyholes or technology does not adapt to the new structure.

On the positive side, however, one can put up a strong argument that there is progress in the world; that by pushing structural or human or technical buttons to see what lights up, we are beginning gropingly to understand some of the interdependencies among the several variables. What we still lack is a good yardstick for comparing the relative costs and advantages of one kind of effort or another. We need, as Likert has suggested, an economics of organizational change.

If we had one, we could more effectively evaluate the costs of movement in one direction or another. Likert urges an economics of change because he believes the presently unmeasured costs of human resistance, if measured, would demonstrate the economic utility of organizational designs based on PE models. But such an economics might also pinpoint some of the as yet unmeasured costs of PE-based models. For the present state of unaccountability provides a protective jungle that offers quick cover to the proponents of any current approach to organizational change.

If I may conclude with a speculation, I will bet long odds that, as we develop such an economics, as we learn to weigh costs and advantages, and to predict second and third order changes, we will not move uniformly toward one of the approaches or another, even within the firm. We will move instead toward a melange, toward differentiated organizations in which the nature of changes becomes largely dependent on the nature of task. We have progressed, I submit; we have not just oscillated. We have learned about people, about structure, about technology; and we will learn to use what we know about all three to change the shape of future organizations.

References

Bennis, W. G., K. D. Benne, and R. Chin. *The Planning of Change.* New York: Holt, 1961.

Bennis, W. G. and H. A. Shepard. "A Theory of Group Development," in *The Planning of Change,* W. G. Bennis, K. D. Benne, and R. Chin. New York: Holt, 1961, p. 429.

Carnegie, D. *How To Win Friends and Influence People.* New York: Simon & Schuster, 1936.

Charnes, A. and W. W. Cooper. *Management Models and Industrial Applications of Linear Programming.* 2 vols. New York: Wiley, 1961.

Coch, L. and J. R. P. French. "Overcoming Resistance to Change," *Human Relations,* 1948, I, 512-33.

Ginsberg, E. and E. Reilly. *Effecting Change in Large Organizations.* New York: Columbia University Press, 1957.

Guest, R. H. *Organizational Change: The Effect of Successful Leadership.* Homewood, Ill.: Irwin, 1962.

Hovland, C., I. Janis, and H. Kelley. *Communication and Persuasion.* New Haven: Yale University Press, 1953.

Lawrence, P. *The Changing of Organizational Behavior Patterns.* Boston: Harvard University, Division of Research, 1958.

Lewin, K. "Group Decision and Social Change," in *Readings in Social Psychology,* G. E. Swanson, T. M. Newcomb, and E. L. Hartley (Eds.) (2nd ed.) New York: Holt, 1952, pp. 459-73.

Likert, R. *New Patterns of Management.* New York: McGraw-Hill, 1961.

Lippitt, R., Jeanne Watson, and B. Westley. *The Dynamics of Planned Change.* New York: Harcourt, Brace, 1958.

Martin, N. and J. R. Sims. "The Problem of Power," in *Industrial Man,* W. L. Warner and N. Martin (Eds.). New York: Harper, 1959, pp. 514-22.

McGregor, D. "The Human Side of Enterprise," in *The Planning of Change,* W. G. Bennis, K. D. Benne, and R. Chin. New York: Holt, 1961, p. 429.

Roethlisberger, F. J. and W. Dickson. *Management and the Worker.* Cambridge: Harvard University Press, 1939.

Rogers, C. R. *Counseling and Psychotherapy.* Boston: Houghton Mifflin, 1942, pp. 28-29.

Taylor, F. W. *Scientific Management.* New York: Harper, 1911.

Patterns of
Organization Change

Based upon a survey of eighteen studies of organizational change, Greiner's study provides information which helps answer the question as to what distinguishes a "successful" change program from an "unsuccessful" one. He first postulates three primary methods for initiating a change program: unilateral action; shared power; and delegated authority. Next, he describes what actually takes place within the unit destined for change prior to, during, and after application of each of the three approaches. This aspect of the change process is given skillful coverage by Greiner's enumeration and discussion of six phases which, he says, provide a "tentative explanatory scheme for viewing the change process as a whole, and also for considering specific managerial action steps within this overall process." Finally, he attempts to glance into the future by enumerating four positive actions to be taken.

Although Greiner himself labels this scheme tentative, its value is not diminished in the least thereby, for it represents a significant step forward in our search for one single integrated theory about the change process. Before a final theory of change can be expounded, many attempts at trial analytic frameworks for comprehending the introduction of change must be made.

PATTERNS OF
ORGANIZATION CHANGE

Larry E. Greiner
Harvard University

Today many top managers are attempting to introduce sweeping and basic changes in the behavior and practices of the supervisors and the subordinates throughout their organizations. Whereas only a few years ago the target of organization change was limited to a small work group or a single department, especially at lower levels, the focus is now converging on the organization as a whole, reaching out to include many divisions and levels at once, and even the top managers themselves. There is a critical need at this time to understand better this complex process, especially in terms of which approaches lead to successful changes and which actions fail to achieve the desired results.

Revolutionary Process

The shifting emphasis from small- to large-scale organization change represents a significant departure from past managerial thinking. For many years, change was regarded more as an evolutionary than a revolutionary process. The

Reprinted from Larry E. Greiner, "Patterns of Organization Change," *Harvard Business Review*, 45, No. 3, (May-June, 1967), 119-30. Used by permission. Copyright©1967 by the President and Fellows of Harvard College; all rights reserved.

AUTHOR'S NOTE: This article is part of a larger study on organizational development, involving my colleagues Louis B. Barnes and D. Paul Leitch, which is supported by the Division of Research, Harvard Business School.

evolutionary assumption reflected the view that change is a product of one minor adjustment after another, fueled by time and subtle environmental forces largely outside the direct control of management. This relatively passive philosophy of managing change is typically expressed in words like these:

> *Our company is continuing to benefit from a dynamically expanding market. While our share of the market has remained the same, our sales have increased 15% over the past year. In order to handle this increased business, we have added a new marketing vice president and may have to double our sales force in the next two years.*

Such an optimistic statement frequently belies an unbounding faith in a beneficent environment. Perhaps this philosophy was adequate in less competitive times, when small patchwork changes, such as replacing a manager here and there, were sufficient to maintain profitability. But now the environments around organizations are changing rapidly and are challenging managements to become far more alert and inventive than they ever were before.

Management Awakening

In recent years more and more top managements have begun to realize that fragmented changes are seldom effective in stemming the underlying tides of stagnation and complacency that can subtly creep into a profitable and growing organization. While rigid and uncreative attitudes are slow to develop, they are also slow to disappear, even in the face of frequent personnel changes. Most often these signs of decay can be recognized in managerial behavior that (a) is oriented more to the past than to the future, (b) recognizes the obligations of ritual more than the challenges of current problems, and (c) owes allegiance more to department goals than to overall company objectives.

Management's recent awakening to these danger signs has been stimulated largely by the rapidly changing tempo and quality of its environment. Consider:

Computer technology has narrowed the decision time span.

Mass communication has heightened public awareness of consumer products.

New management knowledge and techniques have come into being.

Technological discoveries have multiplied.

New world markets have opened up.

Social drives for equality have intensified.

Governmental demands and regulations have increased.

As a result, many organizations are currently being challenged to shift, or even reverse, gears in order to survive, let alone prosper.

A number of top managements have come around to adopting a revolutionary attitude toward change, in order to bridge the gap between a dynamic environment and a stagnant organization. They feel that they can no longer sit back and condone organizational self-indulgence, waiting for time to heal all wounds. So, through a number of means, revolutionary attempts are now being made to transform their organizations rapidly by altering the behavior and attitudes of their line and staff personnel at all levels of management. While each organization obviously varies in its approach, the overarching goal seems to be the same: to get everyone psychologically redirected toward solving the problems and challenges of today's business environment. Here, for example, is how one company president describes his current goal for change:

> *I've got to get this organization moving, and soon. Many of our managers act as if we were still selling the products that used to be our bread and butter. We're in a different business now, and I'm not sure that they realize it. Somehow we've got to start recognizing our problems, and then become more competent in solving them. This applies to everyone here, including me and the janitor. I'm starting with a massive reorganization which I hope will get us pulling together instead of in fifty separate directions.*

Striking Similarities

Although there still are not many studies of organization change, the number is growing; and a survey of them shows that it is already possible to detect some striking similarities running throughout their findings. I shall report some of these similarities, under two headings:

1. *Common approaches* being used to initiate organization change.
2. *Reported results*—what happened in a number of cases of actual organization change.

I shall begin with the approaches, and then attempt to place them within the perspective of what has happened when these approaches were applied. As we shall see, only a few of the approaches used tend to facilitate successful change, but even here we find that each is aided by unplanned forces preceding and following its use. Finally, I shall conclude with some tentative interpretations as to what I think is actually taking place when an organization change occurs.

Common Approaches

In looking at the various major approaches being used to *introduce* organization change, one is immediately struck by their position along a "power distribution" continuum. At one extreme are those which rely on *unilateral* authority. More toward the middle of the continuum are the *shared* approaches. Finally, at the opposite extreme are the *delegated* approaches.

As we shall see later, the *shared* approaches tend to be emphasized in the more successful organization changes. Just why this is so is an important question we will consider in the concluding section. For now, though, let us gain a clearer picture of the various approaches as they appear most frequently in the literature of organization change.

Unilateral Action

At this extreme on the power distribution continuum, the organization change is implemented through an emphasis on the authority of a man's hierarchical position in the company. Here, the definition and solution to the problem at hand tend to be specified by the upper echelons and directed downward through formal and impersonal control mechanisms. The use of unilateral authority to introduce organization change appears in three forms.

By Decree. This is probably the most commonly used approach, having its roots in centuries of practice within military and government bureaucracies and taking its authority from the formal position of the person introducing the change. It is essentially a "one-way" announcement that is directed downward to the lower levels in the organization. The spirit of the communication reads something like "today we are this way—tomorrow we must be that way."

In its concrete form it may appear as a memorandum, lecture, policy statement, or verbal command. The general nature of the decree approach is impersonal, formal, and task-oriented. It assumes that people are highly rational and best motivated by authoritative directions. Its expectation is that people will comply in their outward behavior and that this compliance will lead to more effective results.

By Replacement. Often resorted to when the decree approach fails, this involves the replacement of key persons. It is based on the assumption that organization problems tend to reside in a few strategically located individuals, and that replacing these people will bring about sweeping and basic changes. As in the decree form, this change is usually initiated at the top and directed downward by a high authority figure. At the same time, however, it tends to be somewhat more personal, since particular individuals are singled out for replacement. Nevertheless, it retains much of the formality and explicit concern for task accomplishment that is common to the decree approach. Similarly, it holds no false optimism about the ability of individuals to change their own behavior without clear outside direction.

By Structure. This old and familiar change approach is currently receiving much reevaluation by behavioral scientists. In its earlier form, it involved a highly rational approach to the design of formal organization and to the layout of technology. The basic assumption here was that people behaved in close agreement with the structure and technology governing them. However, it tended to have serious drawbacks, since what seemed logical on paper was not necessarily logical for human goals.

Recently attempts have been made to alter the organizational structure in line with what is becoming known about both the logics and nonlogics of human behavior, such as engineering the job to fit the man, on the one hand, or adjusting formal authority to match informal authority, on the other hand. These attempts, however, still rely heavily on mechanisms for change that tend to be relatively formal, impersonal, and located outside the individual. At the same time, however, because of greater concern for the effects of structure on people, they can probably be characterized as more personal, subtle, and less directive than either the decree or replacement approaches.

Sharing of Power

More toward the middle of the power distribution continuum, as noted earlier, are the shared approaches, where authority is still present and used, yet there is also interaction and sharing of power. This approach to change is utilized in two forms.

By Group Decision Making. Here the problems still tend to be defined unilaterally from above, but lower-level groups are usually left free to develop alternative solutions and to choose among them. The main assumption tends to be that individuals develop more commitment to action when they have a voice in the decisions that affect them. The net result is that power is shared between bosses and subordinates, though there is a division of labor between those who define the problems and those who develop the solutions.

By Group Problem Solving. This form emphasizes both the definition and the solution of problems within the context of group discussion. Here power is shared throughout the decision process, but, unlike group decision making, there is an added opportunity for lower-level subordinates to define the problem. The assumption underlying this approach is not only that people gain greater commitment from being exposed to a wider decision-making role, but also that they have significant knowledge to contribute to the definition of the problem.

Delegated Authority

At the other extreme from unilateral authority are found the delegated approaches, where almost complete responsibility for defining and acting on problems is turned over to the subordinates. These also appear in two forms.

By Case Discussion. This method focuses more on the acquisition of knowledge and skills than on the solution of specific problems at hand. An authority figure, usually a teacher or boss, uses his power only to guide a general discussion of information describing a problem situation, such as a case or a report of research results. The "teacher" refrains from imposing his own analysis or solutions on the group. Instead, he encourages individual members to arrive at their own insights, and they are left to use them as they see fit. The implicit assumption here is that individuals, through the medium of discussion about concrete situations, will develop general problem-solving skills to aid them in carrying out subsequent individual and organization changes.

By T-Group Sessions. These sessions, once conducted mainly in outside courses for representatives of many different organizations, are increasingly being used inside individual companies for effecting change. Usually, they are confined to top management, with the hope that beneficial "spill-over" will result for the rest of the organization. The primary emphasis of the T-group tends to be on increasing an individual's self-awareness and sensitivity to group social processes. Compared to the previously discussed approaches, the T-group places much less emphasis on the discussion and solution of task-related problems. Instead, the data for discussion are typically the interpersonal actions of individuals in the group; no specific task is assigned to the group.

The basic assumption underlying this approach is that exposure to a structureless situation will release unconscious emotional energies within individuals, which, in turn, will lead to self-analysis, insight, and behavioral change. The authority figure in the group, usually a professional trainer, avoids asserting his own authority in structuring the group. Instead, he often attempts to become an accepted and influential member of the group. Thus, in comparison to the other approaches, much more authority is turned over to the group, from which position it is expected to chart its own course of change in an atmosphere of great informality and highly personal exchanges.

Reported Results

As we have seen, each of the major approaches, as well as the various forms within them, rests on certain assumptions about what *should* happen when it is applied to initiate change. Now let us step back and consider what actually *does* happen—before, during, and after a particular approach is introduced.

To discover whether there are certain dimensions of organization change that might stand out against the background of characteristics unique to one company, we conducted a survey of 18 studies of organization change. Specifically, we were looking for the existence of dominant patterns of similarity and/or difference running across all of these studies. As we went along, relevant information was written down and compared with the other studies in regard to (a) the conditions leading up to an attempted change, (b) the manner in which the change was introduced, (c) the critical blocks and/or facilitators encountered during implementation, and (d) the more lasting results which appeared over a period of time.

The survey findings show some intriguing similarities and differences between those studies reporting "successful" change patterns and those disclosing "less successful" changes—i.e., failure to achieve the desired results. The successful changes generally appear as those which:

Spread throughout the organization to include and affect many people.

Produce positive changes in line and staff attitudes.

Prompt people to behave more effectively in solving problems and in relating to others.

Result in improved organization performance.

Significantly, the less successful changes fall short on all of these dimensions.

"Success" Patterns

Using the category breakdown just cited as the baseline for "success," the survey reveals some very distinct patterns in the evolution of change. In all, eight major patterns are identifiable in five studies reporting successful change, and six other success studies show quite similar characteristics, although the information contained in each is somewhat less complete. (See the Appendix page 62 for studies included in the survey.) Consider:

1. The organization, and especially top management, is under considerable external and internal pressure for improvement long before an explicit organization change is contemplated. Performance and/or morale are low. Top management seems to be groping for a solution to its problems.
2. A new man, known for his ability to introduce improvements, enters the organization, either as the official head of the organization, or as a consultant who deals directly with the head of the organization.
3. An initial act of the new man is to encourage a reexamination of past practices and current problems within the organization.
4. The head of the organization and his immediate subordinates assume a direct and highly involved role in conducting this reexamination.
5. The new man, with top management support, engages several levels of the organization in collaborative, fact-finding, problem-solving discussions to identify and diagnose current organization problems.
6. The new man provides others with new ideas and methods for developing solutions to problems, again at many levels of the organization.
7. The solutions and decisions are developed, tested, and found creditable for solving problems on a small scale before an attempt is made to widen the scope of change to larger problems and the entire organization.
8. The change effort spreads with each success experience, and as management support grows, it is gradually absorbed permanently into the organization's way of life.

The likely significance of these similarities becomes more apparent when we consider the patterns found in the less successful organization changes. Let us briefly make this contrast before speculating further about why the successful changes seem to unfold as they do.

"Failure" Forms

Apart from their common "failure" to achieve the desired results, the most striking overall characteristic of seven less successful change studies is a singular lack of consistency—not just between studies, but within studies. Where each of the successful changes follows a similar and highly consistent route of one step building on another, the less successful changes are much less orderly (see Appendix page 63 for a list of these studies).

There are three interesting patterns of inconsistency:

(1) The less successful changes begin from a variety of starting points. This is in contrast to the successful changes, which begin from a common point—i.e., strong pressure both externally and internally. Only one less successful change, for example, began with outside pressure on the organization; another originated with the hiring of a consultant; and a third started with the presence of internal pressure, but without outside pressure.

(2) Another pattern of inconsistency is found in the sequence of change steps. In the successful change patterns, we observe some degree of logical consistency between steps, as each seems to make possible the next. But in the less successful changes, there are wide and seemingly illogical gaps in sequence. One study, for instance, described a big jump from the reaction to outside pressure to the installation of an unskilled newcomer who immediately attempted large-scale changes. In another case, the company lacked the presence of a newcomer to provide new methods and ideas to the organization. A third failed to achieve the cooperation and involvement of top management. And a fourth missed the step of obtaining early successes while experimenting with new change methods.

(3) A final pattern of inconsistency is evident in the major approaches used to introduce change. In the successful cases, it seems fairly clear that *shared* approaches are used—i.e., authority figures seek the participation of subordinates in joint decision making. In the less successful attempts, however, the approaches used lie closer to to the extreme ends of the power distribution continuum. Thus, in five less successful change studies, a *unilateral* approach (decree, replacement, structural) was used, while in two other studies a *delegated* approach (data discussion, T-group) was applied. None of the less successful change studies reported the use of a *shared* approach.

How can we use this lack of consistency in the sequence of change steps and this absence of shared power to explain the less successful change attempts? In the next section, I shall examine in greater depth the successful changes, which, unlike the less successful ones, are marked by a high degree of consistency and the use of shared power. My intent here will be not only to develop a tentative explanation of the more successful changes, but in so doing to explain the less successful attempts within the same framework.

Power Redistribution

Keeping in mind that the survey evidence on which both the successful and the less successful patterns are based is quite limited, I would like to propose a tentative explanatory scheme for viewing the change process as a whole, and also for considering specific managerial action steps within this overall process. The framework for this scheme hinges on two key notions:

1. Successful change depends basically on a *redistribution of power* within the structure of an organization. (By *power,* I mean the locus of formal authority and influence which typically is top management. By *redistribution,* I mean a significant alteration in the traditional practices that the power structure uses in making decisions. I propose that this redistribution move toward the greater use of *shared* power.)

2. Power redistribution occurs through a *developmental process of change.* (This implies that organization change is not a black to white affair occurring overnight through a single causal mechanism. Rather, as we shall see, it involves a number of phases, each containing specific elements and multiple causes that provoke a needed *reaction* from the power structure, which, in turn, sets the stage for the next phase in the process.)

Using the survey evidence from the successful patterns, I have divided the change process into six phases, each of them broken down into the particular stimulus and reaction which appear critical for moving the power structure from one phase to another. Figure 1 represents an abstract view of these two key notions in operation.

Let us now consider how each of these phases and their specific elements make themselves evident in the patterns of successful change, as well as how their absence contributes to the less successful changes.

1. Pressure & Arousal

This initial stage indicates a need to shake the power structure at its very foundation. Until the ground under the top managers begins to shift, it seems unlikely that they will be sufficiently aroused to see the need for change, both in themselves and in the rest of the organization.

The success patterns suggest that strong pressures in areas of top management responsibility are likely to provoke the greatest concern for organization change.

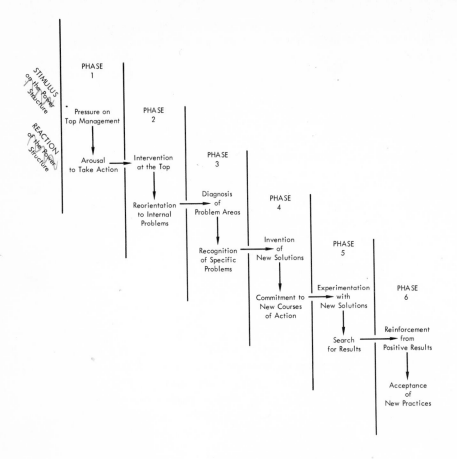

FIGURE 1. Dynamics of Successful Organization Change

These pressures seem to come from two broad sources: (1) serious environmental factors, such as lower sales, stockholder discontent, or competitor breakthroughs; and (2) internal events, such as a union strike, low productivity, high costs, or interdepartmental conflict. These pressures fall into responsibility areas that top managers can readily see as reflecting on their own capability. An excerpt from one successful change study shows how this pressure and arousal process began:

> *"Pressure" was the common expression used at all levels. Urgent telephone calls, telegrams, letters and memoranda were being received by the plant from central headquarters.... Faced with an increase in directives from above and cognizant of Plant Y's low performance position, the manager knew that he was, as he put it, "on the spot."* [1]

[1] Robert H. Guest, *Organization Change: The Effect of Successful Leadership* (Homewood, Illinois: The Dorsey Press, Inc., 1962), p. 18.

As this example points out, it is probably significant when both environmental and internal pressures exist simultaneously. When only one is present, or when the two are offsetting (e.g., high profits despite low morale), it is easier for top management to excuse the pressure as only temporary or inconsequential. However, when both are present at once, it is easier to see that the organization is not performing effectively.

The presence of severe pressure is not so clearly evident in the less successful changes. In one case, there was internal pressure for more effective working relations between top management and lower levels; yet the company was doing reasonably well from a profit standpoint. In another case, there was environmental pressure for a centralized purchasing system, but little pressure from within for such a change.

II. Intervention & Reorientation

While strong pressure may arouse the power structure, this does not provide automatic assurance that top management will see its problems or take the correct action to solve them. Quite likely, top management, when under severe pressure, may be inclined to rationalize its problems by blaming them on a group other than itself, such as "that lousy union" or "that meddling government."

As a result, we find a second stage in the successful change patterns—namely, intervention by an outsider. Important here seems to be the combination of the fact that the newcomer enters at the top of the organization and the fact that he is respected for his skills at improving organization practices. Being a newcomer probably allows him to make a relatively objective appraisal of the organization; entering at the top gives him ready access to those people who make decisions affecting the entire organization; and his being respected is likely to give added weight to his initial comments about the organization.

Thus we find the newcomer in an ideal position to reorient the power structure to its own internal problems. This occurs in the successful changes as the newcomer encourages the top managers to reexamine their past practices and current problems. The effect appears to be one of causing the power structure to suspend, at least temporarily, its traditional habit of presuming beforehand where the "real" problems reside. Otherwise, we would not find top management undertaking the third stage—identifying and diagnosing organization problems. We can see how an outsider was accomplishing this reorientation in the following comment by the plant manager in one successful change study:

> *I didn't like what the consultant told me about our problems being inside the organization instead of outside. But he was an outsider, supposedly an expert at this sort of thing. So maybe he could see our problems better than we could. I asked him what we ought to do, and he said that we should begin to identify our specific problems.*[2]

[2]From my unpublished doctoral dissertation, *Organization and Development* (Harvard Business School, June 1965).

Three of the less successful changes missed this step. Two of the three attempted large-scale changes without the assistance of an outsider, while the third relied on an outsider who lacked the necessary expertise for reorienting top management.

III. Diagnosis & Recognition

Here, we find the power structure, from top to bottom, as well as the newcomer, joining in to assemble information and collaborate in seeking the location and causes of problems. This process begins at the top, then moves gradually down through the organizational hierarchy. Most often, this occurs in meetings attended by people from various organization levels.

A *shared* approach to power and change makes itself evident during this stage. Through consulting with subordinates on the nature of problems, the top managers are seen as indicating a willingness to involve others in the decision-making process. Discussion topics, which formerly may have been regarded as taboo, are now treated as legitimate areas for further inquiry. We see the diagnosis and recognition process taking place in this example from one successful change study:

> The manager's role in the first few months, as he saw it, was to ask questions and to find out what ideas for improvement would emerge from the group as a whole. The process of information gathering took several forms, the principal one being face-to-face conversations between the manager and his subordinates, supervisors on the lower levels, hourly workers, and union representatives. Ideas were then listed for the agenda of weekly planning sessions. [3]

The significance of this step seems to go beyond the possible intellectual benefits derived from a thorough diagnosis of organization problems. This is due to the fact that in front of every subordinate there is evidence that (a) top management is willing to change, (b) important problems are being acknowledged and faced up to, and (c) ideas from lower levels are being valued by upper levels.

The less successful changes all seem to avoid this step. For example, on the one hand, those top managements that took a *unilateral* approach seemed to presume ahead of time that they knew what the real problems were and how to fix them. On the other hand, those that took a *delegated* approach tended to abdicate responsibility by turning over authority to lower levels in such a non-directive way that subordinates seemed to question the sincerity and real interest of top management.

IV. Invention & Commitment

Once problems are recognized, it is another matter to develop effective solutions and to obtain full commitment for implementing them. Traditional practices and

[3]Robert H. Guest, op. cit., p. 50.

solutions within an organization often maintain a hold that is difficult to shed. The temptation is always there, especially for the power structure, to apply old solutions to new problems. Thus, a fourth phase—the invention of new and unique solutions which have high commitment from the power structure—seems to be necessary.

The successful changes disclose widespread and intensive searches for creative solutions, with the newcomer again playing an active role. In each instance the newcomer involves the entire management in learning and practicing new forms of behavior which seek to tap and release the creative resources of many people. Again, as in the previous phase, the method for obtaining solutions is based on a *shared* power concept. Here the emphasis is placed on the use of collaboration and participation in developing group solutions to the problems identified in Phase III.

The potency of this model for obtaining both quality decisions and high commitment to action has been demonstrated repeatedly in research. In three successful changes, the model was introduced as part of the Phase III diagnosis sessions, with the newcomer either presenting it through his informal comments or subtly conveying it through his own guiding actions as the attention of the group turned to the search for a solution. In two other studies, formal training programs were used to introduce and to help implement the model. For all successful changes, the outcome is essentially the same—a large number of people collaborate to invent solutions that are of their own making and which have their own endorsement.

It is significant that none of the less successful changes reach this fourth stage. Instead, the seeds of failure, sown in the previous phases, grow into instances of serious resistance to change. As a result, top management in such cases falls back, gives up, or regroups for another effort. Because these studies conclude their reports at this stage, we are not able to determine the final outcome of the less successful change attempts.

V. Experimentation & Search

Each of the successful change studies reports a fifth stage—that of "reality testing" before large-scale changes are introduced. In this phase not only the validity of specific decisions made in Phase IV, but also the underlying model for making these decisions (*shared* power), falls under careful organization scrutiny. Instead of making only big decisions at the top, a number of small decisions are implemented at *all* levels of the organization. Further, these decisions tend to be regarded more as experiments than as final, irreversible decisions. People at all organization levels seem to be searching for supporting evidence in their environment—e.g., dollar savings or higher motivation—before judging the relative merits of their actions. This concern is reflected in the comment of a consultant involved in one successful change:

> As might be expected, there was something less than a smooth, un-resisted, uncomplicated transition to a new pattern of leadership and

organizational activity. Events as they unfolded presented a mixture of successes and failures, frustrations and satisfactions. . . . With considerable apprehension, the supervisors agreed to go along with any feasible solution the employees might propose.[4]

This atmosphere of tentativeness is understandable when we think of a power structure undergoing change. On the one hand, lower-level managers are undoubtedly concerned with whether top management will support their decisions. If lower-level managers make decisions that fail, or are subsequently reversed by top levels, then their own future careers may be in jeopardy. Or, on the other hand, if higher-level managers, who are held responsible for the survival of the firm, do not see tangible improvements, then they may revert to the status quo or seek other approaches to change.

Thus, with these experimental attempts at change and the accompanying search for signs of payoff, there begins a final stage where people receive the results and react to them.

VI. Reinforcement & Acceptance

Each of the studies of successful change reports improvements in organization performance. Furthermore, there are relatively clear indications of strong support for change from all organization levels. Obviously, positive results have a strong reinforcing effect—that is, people are rewarded and encouraged to continue and even to expand the changes they are making. We see this expansion effect occurring as more and more problems are identified and a greater number of people participate in the solution of them. Consider this comment by a foreman in one study:

> *I've noticed a real difference in the hourly workers. They seem a lot more willing to work, and I can't explain just why it is, but something has happened all right. I suppose it's being treated better. My boss treats me better because he gets treated better. People above me listen to me, and I hope, at least, that I listen to my people below me.*[5]

The most significant effect of this phase is probably a greater and more permanent acceptance at all levels of the underlying methods used to bring about the change. In each of the successful changes, the use of *shared* power is more of an institutionalized and continuing practice than just a "one shot" method used to introduce change. With such a reorientation in the decision-making practices of the power structure, it hardly appears likely that these organizations will "slip back" to their previous behavior.

[4]S. E. Seashore and D. G. Bowers, *Changing the Structure and Functioning of an Organization* (Ann Arbor: Survey Research Center, The University of Michigan, Monograph No. 33, 1963), p. 29.

[5]Robert H. Guest, op. cit., p. 64.

Looking Ahead

What is needed in future changes in organization is less intuition and more consideration of the evidence that is now emerging from studies in this area. While it would be unwise to take too literally each of the major patterns identified in this article (future research will undoubtedly dispel, modify, or elaborate on them), their overall import suggests that it is time to put to bed some of the common myths about organization change. As I see it, there are four positive actions called for.

1. *We must revise our egocentric notions that organization change is heavily dependent on a master blueprint designed and executed in one fell swoop by an omniscient consultant or top manager.*

   The patterns identified here clearly indicate that change is the outgrowth of several actions, some planned and some unplanned, each related to the other and occurring over time. The successful changes begin with pressure, which is unplanned from the organization's point of view. Then the more planned stages come into focus as top management initiates a series of events designed to involve lower-level people in the problem-solving process. But, even here, there are usually unplanned events as subordinates begin to "talk back" and raise issues that top management probably does not anticipate. Moreover, there are the concluding stages of experiencing success, partly affected by conscious design but just as often due to forces outside the control of the planners.

2. *We too often assume that organization change is for "those people downstairs," who are somehow perceived as less intelligent and less productive than "those upstairs."*

   Contrary to this assumption, the success patterns point to the importance of top management seeing itself as part of the organization's problems and becoming actively involved in finding solutions to them. Without the involvement and commitment of top management, it is doubtful that lower levels can see the need for change or, if they do, be willing to take the risks that such change entails.

3. *We need to reduce our fond attachment for both unilateral and delegated approaches to change.*

   The *unilateral* approach, although tempting because its procedures are readily accessible to top management, generally serves only to perpetuate the myths and disadvantages of omniscience and downward thinking. On the other hand, the *delegated* approach, while appealing because of its "democratic" connotations, may remove the power structure from direct involvement in a process that calls for its strong guidance and active support.

   The findings discussed in this article highlight the use of the more difficult, but perhaps more fruitful, *shared* power approach. As top managers join in to open up their power structures and their organizations to an exchange of influence between upper and lower levels, they may be unleashing new surges of energy and creativity not previously imagined.

4. *There is a need for managers, consultants, skeptics, and researchers to become less parochial in their viewpoints.*

For too long, each of us has acted as if cross-fertilization is unproductive. Much more constructive dialogue and joint effort are needed if we are to understand better and act wisely in terms of the complexities and stakes inherent in the difficult problems of introducing organization change.

Appendix: Survey of Studies

Those reporting "successful" organization changes include:

Robert R. Blake, Jane S. Mouton, Louis B. Barnes, and Larry E. Greiner, "Breakthrough in Organization Development," *Harvard Business Review,* November-December 1964, p. 133.

Robert H. Guest, *Organization Change: The Effect of Successful Leadership* (Homewood, Illinois, The Dorsey Press, Inc., 1962).

Elliott, Jaques, *The Changing Culture of a Factory* (New York, The Dryden Press, Inc., 1952).

A. K. Rice, *Productivity and Social Organization: The Ahmedabad Experiment* (London, Tavistock Publications, Ltd., 1958).

S. E. Seashore and D. G. Bowers, *Changing the Structure and Functioning of an Organization* (Ann Arbor, Survey Research Center, The University of Michigan, Monograph No. 33, 1963).

Those showing similar "success" patterns, but containing somewhat less complete information:

Gene W. Dalton, Louis B. Barnes, and Abraham Zaleznik, *The Authority Structure as a Change Variable* (Paper presented at the 57th meeting of the American Sociological Association, August 1962, Washington, D.C.).

Paul R. Lawrence, *The Changing of Organization Behavior Patterns: A Case Study of Decentralization* (Boston, Division of Research, Harvard Business School, 1958).

Paul R. Lawrence et al., "Battleship Y," *Organizational Behavior and Administration* (Homewood, Illinois, The Dorsey Press, Inc.), p. 328 (1965 edition).

Floyd C. Mann, "Studying and Creating Change: A Means to Understanding Social Organization," *Research in Industrial Human Relations,* edited by C. M. Arensberg et al. (New York, Harper and Brothers, 1957).

C. Sofer, *The Organization from Within* (London, Tavistock Publications, Ltd., 1961).

William F. Whyte, *Pattern for Industrial Peace* (New York, Harper and Brothers, 1951).

Included here are studies which reveal "less successful" change patterns:

Chris Argyris, *Interpersonal Competence and Organizational Effectiveness* (Homewood, Illinois, The Dorsey Press, Inc., 1962), especially pp. 254-257.

A. Gouldner, *Patterns of Industrial Bureaucracy* (Glencoe, Illinois, The Free Press, 1964).

Paul R. Lawrence et al., "The Dashman Company" and "Flint Electric," *Organizational Behavior and Administration* (Homewood, Illinois, The Dorsey Press, Inc.), p. 16 (1965 edition) and p. 600 (1961 edition).

George Strauss, "The Set-Up Man: A Case Study of Organizational Change," *Human Organization,* Vol. 13, 1954, p. 17.

A. J. M. Sykes, "The Effects of a Supervisory Training Course in Changing Supervisors' Perceptions and Expectations of the Role of Management," *Human Relations,* Vol. 15, 1962, p. 227.

William F. Whyte, *Money and Motivation* (New York, Harper and Brothers, 1955).

Theory and Method
in Applying Behavioral Science
to Planned Organizational Change

Functioning as change agents, behavioral scientists are playing an ever increasing role as the leading force in planning, initiating, and guiding organizational change. The resulting interface between the change agent and the client system is complex and filled with many subtleties.

In this selection, Bennis provides an exploration of some of the more critical issues in the change agent-client relationship, the ramifications of various strategies, and the methods available to the change agent in attempting to improve organizational effectiveness. Three broad types of change programs (training, consulting, and applied research) are discussed and two strategic, people-oriented change models (managerial grid and laboratory training) are focused upon. Bennis concludes with a forecast and some tentative generalizations regarding planned-change programs.

THEORY AND METHOD
IN APPLYING BEHAVIORAL SCIENCE
TO PLANNED ORGANIZATIONAL CHANGE[1]

Warren G. Bennis
Massachusetts Institute of Technology *

What we have witnessed in the past two or three decades has been called the "Rise of the Rational Spirit"—the belief that science can help to better the human condition (Merton & Lerner, 1951). The focus of this paper is on one indication of this trend: the emerging role for the behavioral scientist and, more specifically, the attempts by behavioral scientists to apply knowledge (primarily sociological and psychological) toward the improvement of human organizations.

The Emergence of the Action Role

Many signs and activities point toward an emerging action role for the behavioral scientist. The *manipulative standpoint,* as Lasswell calls it, is becoming distinguishable from the *contemplative standpoint* and is increasingly

*Warren G. Bennis is now the president of the University of Cincinnati.

Reproduced by special permission from *The Journal of Applied Behavioral Science,* "Theory and Method in Applying Behavioral Science to Planned Organizational Change," Warren G. Bennis, pp. 337-360. Copyright 1965 NTL Institute Publications.

[1] Drawn from keynote address presented at International Conference on Operational Research and the Social Sciences, Cambridge, England, September 1964.

ascendant insofar as knowledge utilization is concerned.[2] Evidence can be found in the growing literature on planned change through the uses of the behavioral sciences (Bennis, Benne, & Chin, 1961; Freeman, 1963; Zetterberg, 1962; Gibb & Lippitt, 1959; Leeds & Smith, 1963; Likert & Hayes, 1957; Glock, Lippitt, Flanagan, Wilson, Shartle, Wilson, Croker, & Page, 1960) and in such additions to the vocabulary of the behavioral scientist as action research, client system, change agent, clinical sociology, knowledge centers, social catalysts. The shift is also reflected in increased emphasis on application in annual meeting time of the professional associations or in the formation of a Center for Research on the Utilization of Scientific Knowledge within The University of Michigan's Institute for Social Research.

It is probably true that in the United States there is a more practical attitude toward knowledge than anywhere else. When Harrison Salisbury (1960) traveled over Europe he was impressed with the seeming disdain of European intellectuals for practical matters. Even in Russia he found little interest in the "merely useful." Salisbury saw only one great agricultural experiment station on the American model. In that case professors were working in the fields. They told him, "People call us Americans."

Not many American professors may be found working in the fields, but they can be found almost everywhere else: in factories, in the government, in underdeveloped countries, in mental hospitals, in educational systems. They are advising, counseling, researching, recruiting, developing, consulting, training. Americans may not have lost their deep ambivalence toward the intellectual, but it is clear that the academic intellectual has become *engagé* with spheres of action in greater numbers, with more diligence, and with higher aspirations than at any other time in history.

It may be useful to speculate about the reasons for the shift in the intellectual climate. Most important, but trickiest to identify, are those causative factors bound up in the warp and woof of "our times and age" that Professor Boring calls the *Zeitgeist.* The apparently growing disenchantment with the moral neutrality of the scientist may be due, in C. P. Snow's phrase, to the fact that "scientists cannot escape their own knowledge." In any event, though "impurity" is still implied, action research as distinguished from pure research does not carry the opprobrium it once did.

Perhaps the crucial reason for the shift in emphasis toward application is simply that we know more.[3] Since World War II we have obtained large bodies of research and diverse reports on application. We are today in a better position to assess results and potentialities of applied social science.

Finally, there is a fourth factor having to do with the fate and viability of human organization, particularly as it has been conceptualized as "bureaucracy." I use the term in its sociological, Weberian sense, not as a metaphor *a la* Kafka's

[2] For an excellent discussion of the "value" issues in this development, see Kaplan, A., *The Conduct of Inquiry.* San Francisco: Chandler, 1964, Chapter 10; and Benne, K. D., and Swanson, G. (eds.), "Values and Social Issues." *Journal of Social Issues,* 1960, 6.

[3] For a recent inventory of scientific findings of the behavioral sciences, see Berelson, B., and Steiner, G. A., *Human Behavior.* New York: Harcourt, Brace & World, 1964.

The Castle connoting "red tape," impotency, inefficiency, despair. In the past three decades Weber's vision has been increasingly scrutinized and censured. Managers and practitioners, on the one hand, and organizational theorists and researchers on the other, are more and more dissatisfied with current practices of organizational behavior and are searching for new forms and patterns of organizing for work. A good deal of activity is being generated.

The Lack of a Viable Theory of Social Change

Unfortunately, no viable theory of social change has been established. Indeed it is a curious fact about present theories that they are strangely silent on matters of *directing* and *implementing* change. What I particularly object to—and I include the "newer" theories of neo-conflict (Coser, 1956; Dahrendorf, 1961), neo-functionalism (Boskoff, 1964), and neo-revolutionary theories—is that they tend to explain the dynamic interactions of a system without providing one clue to the identification of strategic leverages for alteration. They are suitable for *observers* of social change, not for practitioners. They are theories of *change*, and not of *changing*.

It may be helpful to suggest quickly some of the prerequisites for a theory of changing. I am indebted here to my colleague Robert Chin (1961, 1963):

a. A theory of changing must include manipulable variables—accessible levers for influencing the direction, tempo, and quality of change and improvement.

b. The variables must not violate the client system's values.

c. The cost of usage cannot be prohibitive.

d. There must be provided a reliable basis of diagnosing the strength and weakness of conditions facing the client system.

e. Phases of intervention must be clear so that the change agent can develop estimates for termination of the relationship.

f. The theory must be communicable to the client system.

g. It must be possible to assess appropriateness of the theory for different client systems.

Such a theory does not now exist, and this probably explains why change agents appear to write like "theoretical orphans" and, more important, why so many change programs based on theories of social change have been inadequate. This need should be kept in mind as we look at models of knowledge utilization.

The Notion of Planned Change

Planned change can be viewed as a linkage between theory and practice, between knowledge and action. It plays this role by converting variables from the basic disciplines into strategic instrumentation and programs. Historically, the development of planned change can be seen as the resultant of two forces: complex problems requiring expert help and the growth and viability of the behavioral sciences. The term "behavioral sciences" itself is of post-World War II vintage coined by the more empirically minded to "safeguard" the social disciplines from the nonquantitative humanists and the depersonalized abstractions of the econometricists. The process of planned change involves a *change agent*, a *client system*, and the collaborative attempt to apply *valid knowledge* to the client's problems.[4]

Elsewhere I have attempted a typology of change efforts in which planned change is distinguished from other types of change in that it entails mutual goal setting, an equal power ratio (eventually), and deliberateness on both sides (Bennis et al., 1961, p. 154).

It may further help in defining planned change to compare it with another type of deliberate change effort, Operations Research. I enter this with a humility bordering on fear and a rueful sense of kinship in our mutual incapacity to explain to one another the nature of our work. There are these similarities. Both are World War II products; both are problem-centered (though both have also provided inputs to the concepts and method of their parent disciplines).[5] Both emphasize improvement and to that extent are *normative* in their approach to problems. Both rely heavily on empirical science; both rely on a relationship of confidence and valid communication with clients; both emphasize a *systems* approach to problems—that is, both are aware of interdependence within the system as well as boundary maintenance with its environment; and both appear to be most effective when working with systems which are complex, rapidly changing, and probably science-based.

Perhaps the most crucial difference between OR and planned change has to do with the identification of strategic variables, that is, with those factors which appear to make a difference in the performance of the system. Planned change is concerned with such problems as (1) the identification of mission and values, (2) collaboration and conflict, (3) control and leadership, (4) resistance and adaptation to change, (5) utilization of human resources, (6) communication, (7) management development. OR practitioners tend to select economic or engineering variables which are more quantitative, measurable, and linked to profit and efficiency. Ackoff and Rivett (1963), for example, classify OR problems under (1) inventory, (2) allocation, (3) queuing, (4) sequencing, (5) routing, (6) replacement, (7) competition, (8) search.

A second major difference has to do with the perceived importance of the relationship with the client. In planned change, the quality and nature of the relationship are used as indicators for the measure of progress and as valid sources of data and diagnosis. Undoubtedly, the most successful OR practi-

[4]For a fuller discussion, see Lippitt, R., Watson, J., and Westley, B., *The Dynamics of Planned Change.* New York: Harcourt, Brace & World, 1961; and Bennis et al., 1961.

[5]For a brilliant exposition on the contributions of applied research to "pure" theory, see Gouldner, A., "Theoretical Requirements of the Applied Social Sciences," in Bennis et al., 1961, pp. 83-95.

tioners operate with sensitivity toward their clients; but if one looks at what they *say* about their work, they are clearly less concerned with human interactions.

A third major difference is that the OR practitioner devotes a large portion of his time to research, to problem solving. The change agent tends to spend somewhat more time on implementation through counseling, training, management development schemes, and so forth. Fourth, planned-change agents tend to take less seriously the idea of the *system* in their approaches. Finally, the idea of an interdisciplinary team, central to OR, does not seem to be a part of most planned-change programs.

One thing that emerges from this comparison is a realization of the complexity of modern organization. Look through the kaleidoscope one way, and a configuration of the economic and technological factors appears; tilt it, and what emerges is a pattern of internal human relations problems. It is on these last problems and their effects upon performance of the system that practitioners of planned organizational change tend to work.

A Focus of Convenience

To develop what George Kelley refers to as a "focus of convenience" for planned organization change, I want to make two key aspects clearer: the notions of "collaborative relationships" and of "valid knowledge." I see the outcome of planned-change efforts as depending to some considerable extent on the relationship between client and agent. To optimize a collaborative relationship, there need to be a "spirit of inquiry," with data publicly shared, an equal freedom to terminate the relationship and to influence the other.

As to valid knowledge, the criteria are based on the requirements for a viable applied behavioral science research—an applied behavioral science that:

a. Takes into consideration the behavior of persons operating within their specific institutional environments;

b. Is capable of accounting for the interrelated levels (person, group, role, organization) within the context of the social change;

c. Includes variables that the policy maker and practitioner can understand, manipulate, and evaluate;

d. Can allow selection of variables appropriate in terms of its own values, ethics, moralities;

e. Accepts the premise that groups and organizations as units are amenable to empirical and analytic treatment;

f. Takes into account external social processes of change as well as interpersonal aspects of the collaborative process;

g. Includes propositions susceptible to empirical test focusing on the dynamics of change.

These criteria must be construed as an arbitrary goal, not as an existing reality. To my knowledge, there is no program which fulfills these requirements fully. In this focus of convenience, I have arbitrarily selected change agents working on organizational dynamics partly because of my greater familiarity with their work but also because they seem to fulfill the criteria outlined to a greater extent than do other change agents. My choice of emphasis is also based on the belief that changes in the sphere of organizations—primarily industrial—in patterns of work and relationship, structure, technology, and administration promise some of the most significant changes in our society. Indeed it is my guess that industrial society, at least in the United States, is more radical, innovative, and adventurous in adapting new ways of organizing than the government, the universities, and the labor unions, who appear rigid and stodgy in the face of rapid change. If space permitted, however, I would refer also to change agents working in a variety of fields—rural sociology, economics, anthropology—and in such settings as communities, hospitals, cultural-change programs.

Let us turn now to some of the "traditional" models of knowledge utilization.

Eight Types of Change Programs[6]

It is possible to identify eight types of change programs if we examine their strategic rationale: exposition and propagation, elite corps, human relations training, staff, scholarly consultations, circulation of ideas to the élite, developmental research, and action research.

I should like to look at each of these programs quickly and then refer to four biases which seem to me to weaken their impact.

Exposition and propagation, perhaps the most popular type of program, assumes that knowledge is power. It follows that the men who possess "Truth" will lead the world.

Elite corps programs grow from the realization that ideas by themselves do not constitute action and that a strategic *role* is a necessity for ideas to be implemented (e.g., through getting scientists into government as C.P. Snow suggests).

Human relations training programs are similar to the élite corps idea in the attempt to translate behavioral science concepts in such ways that they take on personal referents for the men in power positions.

Staff programs provide a source of intelligence within the client system, as in the work of social anthropologists advising military governors after World War II. The strategy of the staff idea is to observe, analyze, and to plan rationally (Myrdal, 1958).

---

[6]For a fuller exposition of these ideas, see my paper, "A New Role for the Behavioral Sciences: Effecting Organizational Change," *Administrative Science Quarterly,* 1963, 8, 125-165.

Scholarly consultation, as defined by Zetterberg (1962), includes exploratory inquiry, scholarly understanding, confrontation, discovery of solutions, and scientific advice to client.

Circulation of ideas to the elite builds on the simple idea of influencing change by getting to the people with power or influence.

Developmental research has to do with seeing whether an idea can be brought to an engineering stage. Unlike Zetterberg's scholarly confrontation, it is directed toward a particular problem, not necessarily a client, and is concerned with implementation and program. (I would wager that *little* developmental research is being done today in the behavioral sciences.)

Action research, the term coined by Kurt Lewin, undertakes to solve a problem for a client. It is identical to applied research generally except that in action research the roles of researcher and subject may change and reverse, the subjects becoming researchers and the researchers engaging in action steps.

These eight programs, while differing in objectives, values, means of influence, and program implications, are similar in wanting to use knowledge to gain some socially desirable end. Each seems successful or promising; each has its supporters and its detractors. Intrinsic to them all, I believe, is some bias or flaw which probably weakens their full impact. Four biases are particularly visible.

Rationalistic Bias: No Implementation of Program

Most of the strategies rely almost totally on rationality. But knowledge *about* something does *not* lead automatically to intelligent action. Intelligent action requires commitment and programs as well as truth.

Technocratic Bias: No Spirit of Collaboration.

Change typically involves risk and fear. Any significant change in human organization involves rearrangement of patterns of power, association, status, skills, and values. Some may benefit, others may lose. Thus change typically involves risk and fear. Yet change efforts sometimes are conducted as if there were no need to discuss and "work through" these fears and worries (e.g., F. W. Taylor's failure to consider the relationship between the engineer with the stopwatch and the worker, or Freud's early work when he considered it adequate to examine the unconscious of his patients and tell them what he learned—even to the extent of analyzing dreams by mail).

Individualist Bias: No Organization Strategy Is Involved

This refers to strategies which rely on the individual while denying the organizational forces and roles surrounding him. There is, however, simply no guarantee that a wise individual who attains power will act wisely. It may be that *role corrupts*—both the role of power and the role of powerlessness. In any event, there is no guarantee that placing certain types of people in management—or training them or psychoanalyzing them or making scientists of them—leads to more effective action. Scientists act like administrators when they gain power. And graduates of human relations training programs tend to act like non-alumni shortly after their return to their organizational base.

The staff idea, proposed by Myrdal, is limited by the unresolved tensions in the staff-line dilemma noted by students of organizational behavior and by the conflicts derived from the role of the intellectual working in bureaucratic structures. The élite strategy has serious drawbacks, primarily because it focuses on the individual and not the organization.

Insight Bias: No Manipulability

My major quarrel here is not with the formulation: insight leads to change, though this can be challenged, but with the lack of provision variables accessible to control. It is not obvious that insight leads directly to sophistication in rearranging social systems or making strategic organizational interventions. Insight provides the relevant variables for planned change as far as personal manipulation goes, but the question remains: How can that lead directly to the manipulation of external factors?

The Elements of Planned Organizational Change

In the October 7, 1963, edition of the *New York Times,* a classified ad announced a search for change agents. It read:

> *WHAT'S A CHANGE AGENT? A result-oriented individual able to accurately and quickly resolve complex tangible and intangible problems. Energy and ambition necessary for success . . .*

The change agents I have in mind need more than "energy and ambition." They are *professionals* who, for the most part, hold doctorates in the behavioral sciences. They are not a very homogeneous group, but they do have some similarities.

They are alike in that they take for granted the *centrality of work* in our culture to men and women in highly organized instrumental settings; in their concern with improvement, development, and measurement of *organizational effectiveness;* in their *preoccupation with people* and the process of human interaction; in their interest in changing the relationships, perceptions, and values of *existing personnel.* They may be members of the client system, arguing that inside knowledge is needed, or external agents, arguing that perspective, detachment, and energy from outside are needed. They intervene at different structural points in the organization and at different times.

Though each change agent has in mind a set of unique goals based on his own theoretical position and competencies as well as the needs of the client system, there are some general aims. In a paradigm developed by Chris Argyris (1962), bureaucratic values tend to stress the rational, task aspects of work and to ignore the basic human factors which, if ignored, tend to reduce task competence. Managers brought up under this system of values are badly cast to play the intricate human roles now required of them. Their ineptitude and anxieties lead to systems of discord and defense which interfere with the problem-solving capacity of the organization.

Generally speaking, the normative goals of change agents derive from this paradigm. They include: improving interpersonal competence of managers; effecting a change in values so that human factors and feelings come to be considered legitimate; developing increased understanding among and within working groups to reduce tensions; developing "team management"; developing better methods of "conflict resolution" than suppression, denial, and the use of unprincipled power; viewing the organization as an organic system of relationships marked by mutual trust, interdependence, multigroup membership, shared responsibility, and conflict resolution through training or problem solving.

Programs for Implementing Planned Organizational Change

Discussion here will focus on three broad types of change programs that seem to be most widely used, frequently in some combination: training, consultation, and research.

Training

Training is an inadequate word in this context, as its dictionary meaning denotes "drill" and "exercise." I refer to what has been called laboratory training, sensitivity or group dynamics training, and most commonly T-Group training.[7] The idea originated in Bethel, Maine, under the guidance of Leland Bradford, Kenneth Benne, and Ronald Lippitt, with initial influence from the late Kurt Lewin. The T Group has evolved since 1947 into one of the main instruments for organizational change. Bradford has played a central role in this development as director of the National Training Laboratories. Growth has been facilitated through the active participation of a number of university-based behavioral scientists and practitioners. Tavistock Institute has played a similar role in England, and recently a group of European scientists set up a counterpart to the National Training Laboratories.

The main objective at first was *personal change* or *self-insight.* Since the fifties the emphasis has shifted to *organizational development,* a more precise date being 1958, when the Esso Company inaugurated a series of laboratories at

---

[7]For a popular account of laboratory training, see Argyris, C., "T-groups for Organizational Effectiveness," *Harvard Business Review,* 1964, 42, 60-74. For a theoretical background, see Bradford, L. P., Gibb, J. R., and Benne, K. D. (eds.), *T-group Theory and Laboratory Method.* New York: Wiley, 1964; and Schein, E. H., and Bennis, W. G., *Personal and Organizational Change Via Group Methods.* New York: Wiley, 1965.

refineries over the country under the leadership of Blake and Shepard (Shepard, 1960).

Briefly, laboratory training unfolds in an unstructured group setting where participants examine their interpersonal relationships. By examining data generated by themselves, members attempt to understand the dynamics of group behavior, e.g., decision processes, leadership and influence, norms, roles, communication distortions, effects of authority on behavioral patterns, coping mechanisms. T-Group composition is itself a strategic issue. Thus the organization may send an executive to a "stranger laboratory" which fills a "seeding" function; "cousin laboratories" may be conducted for persons of similar rank and occupational responsibilities within the company but from different functional groups; "diagonal slices" may be composed of persons of different rank but not in the same work group or in direct relationship; and "family laboratories" may be conducted for functional groups. The more the training groups approach a "family," the more the total organization is affected.

Consulting

The change agent *qua* consultant, perhaps best exemplified in the work of the Tavistock Institute, operates in a manner very like the practicing physician or psychoanalyst: that is, he starts from the chief "presenting symptom" of the client, articulates it in such a way that causal and underlying mechanisms of the problem are understood, and then takes remedial action. Heavy emphasis is placed on the strategy of *role model* because the main instrument is the change agent himself. Sofer (1961) reveals this when he suggests that psychotherapy or some form of clinical experience is necessary preparation for the change agent. Argyris, as consultant, confronts the group with their behavior toward him as an analogue of their behavior *vis-à-vis* their own subordinates.

If the role of the consultant sounds ambiguous and vague, this probably reflects reality. Certainly in the consultant approach the processes of change and the change agent's interventions are less systematic and less programmed than in training or applied research programs. A word about the latter.

Applied Research

I refer here to research in which the results are used systematically as an *intervention*. Most methods of research application collect information and report it. Generally, the relationship ends there. In the survey-feedback approach, as developed primarily by Floyd Mann (1957) and his associates at The University of Michigan's Institute for Social Research, this is only the beginning. Data are reported in "feedback" meetings where subjects become clients and have a chance to review the findings, test them against their own experience, and even ask the researchers to test some of their hypotheses. Instead of being submitted "in triplicate" and probably ignored, research results serve to activate involvement and participation in the planning, collection, analysis, and interpretation of more data.

Richard Beckhard, too, utilizes data as the first step in his work as change agent (1966). In his procedure the data are collected through formal, non-structured interviews which he then codes by themes about the managerial activities of the client for discussion at an off-site meeting with the subjects.

It should be stressed that most planned-change inductions involve all three processes—training, consulting, researching—and that both agent and client play a variety of roles. The final shape of the change agent's role is not as yet clear, and it is hazardous to report exactly what change agents do on the basis of their reports. Many factors, of course, determine the particular intervention the change agent may choose: among these factors are ones pertaining to cost, time, degree of collaboration required, state of target system, and so on.

Strategic Models Employed by Change Agents

More often than not, change agents fail to report their strategy or to make it explicit. It may be useful to look at two quite different models that are available: one developed by Robert Blake in his "Managerial Grid" system, and one with which I was associated at an Esso refinery and which Chris Argyris evaluated some years later.

Blake has developed a change program based on his analytic framework of managerial styles (Blake, Mouton, Barnes, & Greiner, 1964). Figure 1 shows the grid for locating types of managerial strategies. Blake and his colleagues attempt to change the organization in the direction of "team management" (9, 9 or high concern for people and high concern for production). Based on experience with 15 different factories, the Blake strategy specifies six phases: off-site laboratory for "diagonal slice" of personnel; off-site program focused on team training for "family" groups; training in the plant location designed to achieve better integration between functional groups; goal-setting sessions for groups of 10 to 12 managers.

Blake and his colleagues estimate that these four phases may require two years or longer. The next two, implementing plans and stabilizing changes, may require an additional two years.

Figure 2 (Argyris, 1960) presents another strategy: a change program used in a large oil company to improve the functioning of one of its smaller refineries. A new manager was named and sent to a T-Group training session to gain awareness of the human problems in the refinery. The Headquarters Organizational Development staff then conducted a diagnosis through a survey and interview of the managerial staff (70) and a sample of hourly employees (40/350). About that time the author was brought in to help the headquarters staff and the new manager.

It was decided that a laboratory program of T Groups might be effective but

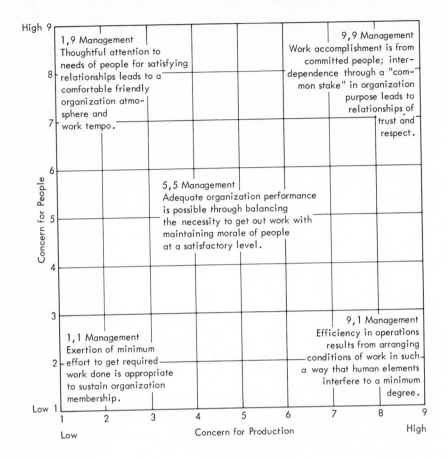

FIGURE 1. The Managerial Grid

premature, with the result that weekly seminars that focused on new developments in human relations were held with top management (about 20). A one-week laboratory training program followed for all supervisors in diagonal slices, and then another re-evaluation of needs was undertaken. Some structural innovations were suggested and implemented. During the last phase of the program (not shown in the figure), the Scanlon Plan was adapted and installed (incidentally, for the first time in a "process" industry and for the first time that a union agreed to the Plan without a bonus automatically guaranteed).

Though it cannot be said with any assurance that these two strategies are typical, it may be helpful to identify certain features: (a) *length of time* (Blake estimates five years; the refinery program took two years up to the Scanlon Plan); (b) *variety of programs* utilized (research, consulting, training, teaching, planning); (c) *necessity of cooperation* with top management and the parent organization; (d) approaching the organization *as a system* rather than as a collection of individuals; (e) *phasing program* from individual to group to inter-group to overall organization; (f) intellectual *and* emotional content.

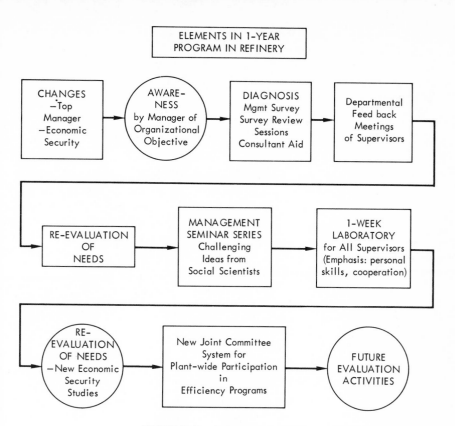

FIGURE 2. A Change Program

Power and the Role of the Change Agent

How and why do people and organizations change, and what is the nature and source of the power exerted by the change agent? We have to make inferences because change agents themselves tend to be silent on this. It is not *coercive power,* for the change agent generally does not have the ability to reward or punish. Moreover, he would prefer, at least intellectually, not to wield power at variance with his normative goals. Further, there is some evidence that coercive power is less durable than are other kinds of power, except under conditions of vigilant surveillance.

Traditional power? Almost certainly not. The change agent is, in fact, continually working without legitimization. *Expert power?* Possibly some, but it is doubtful whether his knowledge is considered "expert" enough—in the sense that an engineer or doctor or lawyer is seen as expert. *Referent or identification power?* Apparently so. Sofer, for example, attributes some influence to the client system's ability and desire to emulate the change agent. Still, this will vary from a considerable degree to not at all.

This leaves us with *value power* as the likeliest candidate of the possible sources of power. Most change agents do emit cues to a consistent value system.

These values are based on Western civilization's notion of a scientific humanism: concern for our fellow man, experimentalism, openness and honesty, flexibility, cooperation, democracy. If what I have said about power is correct, it is significant (at least in the United States) that this set of values seems to be potent in influencing top management circles.

Characteristics of Client System

For the most part, the client systems appear to be sub-systems of relatively large-scale international operations who find themselves in increasingly competitive situations, in rapidly changing environments, subjected to what have been called "galloping variables." Often the enterprise was founded through an innovation or monopolistic advantage which is thought to be in jeopardy.

Then there is some tension—some discrepancy between the ideal and the actual—which seems to activate the change program.

Finally, there is some faith in the idea that an intermediate proportion of organizational effectiveness is determined by social and psychological factors and that improvement here, however vague or immeasurable, may improve organizational effectiveness.

The Measurement of Effects

Until very recently, change agents, if they did any evaluation research at all, concentrated almost exclusively on attitudinal and subjective factors. Even so-called "hard" behavioral variables, like absentee rates, sickness and accident rates, and personnel turnover, were rarely investigated. Relating change programs to harder criteria, like productivity and economic and cost factors, was rarely attempted and never, to my knowledge, successful.

And again, the research that was conducted—even on the attitudinal measures—was far from conclusive. Roger Harrison attempted an evaluation study of Argyis' work and found that while there was a significant improvement in the individual executive's interpersonal ability compared with a control group, there was no significant "transfer" of this acuity to the real-life organizational setting. In short, there was a fairly rapid "fadeout" of effects obtained in T-Group training upon return to the organization (Harrison, 1962). This study also shows that new tensions were generated between those individuals who attended the training program and those who did not—an example of the lack of a *systems* approach. Shepard's evaluation on the Esso organization shows that the impact of laboratory training was greatest on personal and inter-personal learnings, but "slightly more helpful than useless" in changing the organization.

More recently, though, some studies have been undertaken which measure more meaningful, less subjective variables of organizational effectiveness. Blake, Mouton, Barnes, and Greiner (1964), for example, conducted an evaluation study of their work in a very large (4,000 employees) petrochemical plant. Not only did they find significant changes in the values, morale, and interpersonal behavior of the employees, but significant improvements in productivity, profits, and cost reduction. David (in press), a change agent working on a program that attempts to facilitate a large and complicated merger, attributed the following effects to the programs: increased productivity, reduced turnover and absenteeism, in addition to a significant improvement in the area of attitudes and subjective feelings.

While these new research approaches show genuine promise, much more has to be done. The research effort has somehow to equal all the energy that goes into developing the planned-change programs themselves.

Some Criticisms and Qualifications

The work of the change agents reported here is new and occurs without the benefit of methodological and strategic precedents. The role of the change agent is also new, its final shape not fully emerged. Thus it has both the advantage of freedom from the constraints facing most men of knowledge, and suffers from lack of guidelines and structure. Let us touch quickly on problems and criticisms facing the change agents.

Planned Change and Organizational Effectiveness

I can identify six dimensions of organizational effectiveness: legal, political, economic, technological, social, and personal. There is a good deal of fuzziness as to which of these change agents hope to affect, and the data are inconclusive. Argyris, who is the most explicit about the relationship between performance and interpersonal competence, is still hoping to develop good measures to establish a positive relationship. The connection has to be made, or the field will have to change its normative goal of constructing not only a *better* world but a more *effective* one.

A Question of Values

The values espoused indicate a way of *behaving and feeling;* for example, they emphasize openness rather than secrecy, collaboration rather than dependence or rebellion, cooperation rather than competition, consensus rather than individual rules, rewards based on self-control rather than externally induced rewards, team leadership rather than a one-to-one relationship with the boss, authentic relationships rather than those based on political maneuvering.

Are they natural? Desirable? Functional? What then happens to status or power drives? What about those individuals who have a low need for participation and/or a high need for structure and dependence? And what about those personal needs which seem to be incompatible with these images of man, such as a high need for aggression and a low need for affiliation? In short, what about those needs which can be best realized through bureaucratic systems? Or benevolent autocracies? Are these individuals to be changed or to yield and comply?

The problem of values deserves discussion. One of the obstacles is the emotional and value overtones which interfere with rational dialogue. More often than not, one is plunged into a polarized debate which converts ideas into ideology and inquiry into dogma. So we hear of "Theory X vs. Theory Y," personality vs. organization, democratic vs. autocratic, task vs. maintenance, human relations vs. scientific management, and on and on.

Surely life is more complicated than these dualities suggest, and surely they must imply a continuum—not simply extremes.

Lack of Systems Approach

Up to this point, I have used the term "organizational change" rather loosely. In Argyris' case, for example, organizational change refers to a change in values of 11 top executives, a change which was not necessarily of an enduring kind and apparently brought about some conflict with other interfaces. In most other cases of planned organizational change, the change induction was limited to a small, élite group. Only in the work of Blake and some others can we confidently talk about organizational change—in a systems way; his program includes the training of the entire management organization, and at several locations he has carried this step to include wage earners.

Sometimes the changes brought about simply "fade out" because there are no carefully worked out procedures to ensure coordination with other interacting parts of the system. In other cases, the changes have "backfired" and have had to be terminated because of their conflict with interface units. In any case, a good deal more has to be learned about the interlocking and stabilizing changes so that the total system is affected.

Some Generalizations

It may be useful, as peroration, to state in the most tentative manner some generalizations. They are derived, for the most part, from the foregoing discussion and anchored in experience and, wherever possible, in research and theory.

First, a forecast: I suspect that we will see an increase in the number of planned-change programs along the lines discussed here—toward *less* bureaucratic and *more* participative, "open system," and adaptive structures. Given the present pronounced rate of change, the growing reliance on science for the success of the industrial enterprise, the growing number of professionals joining these enterprises, and the "turbulent contextual environment" facing the firm, we can expect increasing demand for social inventions to revise traditional notions of organized effort.

As far as adopting and acceptance go, we already know a good deal.[8] *Adoption* requires that the *type* of change should be proven quality, easily demonstrable in its effects, and with information easily available. Its cost and accessibility to control by the client system as well as its value accord have to be carefully considered.

Acceptance also depends on the relationship between the change agent and the client system: the more profound and anxiety-producing the change, the more collaborative and closer relationship required. In addition, we can predict that an anticipated change will be resisted to the degree that the client system possesses little or incorrect knowledge about the change, has relatively little trust in the source of the change, and has comparatively low influence in controlling the nature and direction of the change.

What we know least about is *implementation*—a process which includes the creation of understanding and commitment toward a particular change and devices whereby it can become integral to the client system's operations. I will try to summarize the necessary elements in implementation:

(a) The *client system* should have as much understanding of the change and its consequences, as much influence in developing and controlling the fate of the change, and as much trust in the initiator of the change as is possible.

(b) The *change effort* should be perceived as being as self-motivated and voluntary as possible. This can be effected through the legitimization and reinforcement of the change by the top management group and by the significant reference groups adjacent to the client system. It is also made possible by providing the utmost in true volition.

(c) The *change program* must include emotional and value as well as cognitive (informational) elements for successful implementation. It is doubtful that relying solely on rational persuasion (expert power) is sufficient. Most organizations possess the knowledge to cure their ills; the rub is utilization.

(d) The *change agent* can be crucial in reducing the resistance to change. As long as the change agent acts congruently with the principles of the program and as long as the client has a chance to test competence and motives (his own and the change agent's), the agent should be able to provide the psychological support so necessary during the risky phases of change. As I have stressed again and again, the quality of the client-agent relationship is pivotal to the success of the change program.

[8]See in particular, Rogers, E. *The Diffusion of Innovations.* New York: Free Press, 1962; and Miles, M. (ed.), *Innovation in Education.* New York: Bureau of Publications. Teachers College, Columbia University, 1964.

References

Ackoff, R. L., and P. Rivett. *A Manager's Guide to Operations Research.* New York: Wiley, 1963, p. 34.

Argyris, C. *Organization Development: An Inquiry into the Esso Approach.* New Haven: Yale University, 1960.

Argyris, C. *Interpersonal Competence and Organizational Effectiveness.* Homewood, Ill.: Dorsey, 1962, p. 43.

Beckhard, R. "An Organization Improvement Program in a Decentralized Organization." *Journal of Applied Behavioral Science, 2:3-26.*

Bennis, W. G., K. D. Benne, and R. Chin (eds.). *The Planning of Change.* New York: Holt, Rinehart & Winston, 1961.

Blake, R. R., Jane S. Mouton, L. B. Barnes, and L. E. Greiner. "Breakthrough in Organization Development." *Harvard Business Review,* 42 (1964), 133-155.

Boskoff, A. "Functional Analysis as a Source of a Theoretical Repertory and Research Tasks in the Study of Social Change." in G. K. Zollschan and W. Hirsch, *Explorations in Social Change.* Boston: Houghton Mifflin, 1964.

Chin, R., "The Utility of System Models and Developmental Models for Practitioners." In W. G. Bennis, K. D. Benne and R. Chin (eds.). *The Planning of Change.* New York: Holt, Rinehart & Winston, 1961, pp. 201-214.

Chin, R. "Models and Ideas about Changing." Paper read at Symposium on Acceptance of New Ideas, University of Nebraska, November, 1963.

Coser, L. *The Functions of Social Conflict.* New York: The Free Press, 1956.

Dahrendorf, R. "Toward a Theory of Social Conflict." In W. G. Bennis, K. D. Benne, and R. Chin (eds.). *The Planning of Change.* New York: Holt, Rinehart & Winston, 1961, pp. 445-451.

David, G. "The Weldon Study: An Organization Change Program Based upon Change in Management Philosophy." In D. Zand (ed.). *Organization Development: Theory and Practice.* In press.

Freeman, H. E. "The Strategy of Social Policy Research." *The Social Welfare Forum* (1963), 143-160.

Gibb, J. R., and R. Lippitt (eds.). "Consulting with Groups and Organizations." *Journal of Social Issues,* 15 (1959).

Glock, C. Y., R. Lippitt, J. C. Flanagan, E. C. Wilson, C. L. Shartle, M. L. Wilson, G. W. Croker, and H. E. Page. *Case Studies in Bringing Behavioral Science Into Use.* Stanford, Calif.: Inst. Commun. Res., 1960.

Harrison, R. In C. Argyris, *Interpersonal Competence and Organizational Effectiveness.* Homewood, Ill.: Dorsey, 1962, Ch. 11.

Leeds, R., and T. Smith (eds.). *Using Social Science Knowledge in Business and Industry.* Homewood, Ill.: Irwin, 1963.

Likert, R., and S. P. Hayes, Jr. (eds.). *Some Applications of Behavioral Research.* Paris: UNESCO, 1957.

Mann, F. "Studying and Creating Change: A Means to Understanding Social Organization." *Research in Industrial Relations.* Ann Arbor: Industrial Relations Research Association, 1957, Publication No. 17.

Merton, R. K., and D. Lerner. "Social Scientists and Research Policy." In D. Lerner and H. D. Lasswell (eds.). *The Policy Sciences: Recent Developments in Scope and Method.* Stanford, Calif.: Stanford University Press, 1951.

Myrdal, G. *Value in Social Theory.* New York: Harper, 1958, p. 29.

Parsons, R. T. "Evolutionary Universals in Society." *American Sociological Review* 29 (1964), 339-357.

Salisbury, H. E. *To Moscow and Beyond.* New York: Harper, 1960, p. 136.

Shepard, H. "Three Management Programs and the Theory Behind Them." In *An Action Research Program for Organization Improvement.* Ann Arbor: Foundation for Research on Human Behavior, 1960.

Sofer, C. *The Organization from Within.* London: Tavistock, 1961.

Zetterberg, H. L. *Social Theory and Social Practice.* Totowa, N.J.: Bedminster, 1962.

The Change Process in Organizations: An Applied Anthropology Approach

Because most organizations can be logically viewed as dynamic and complex entities comprised of interrelated work flows, communications networks, control patterns, and formal authority relations, change within the system seems to be inherent. Although a manager might desire a unit which is both highly stable and productive, this is rarely the case in the "real world." Inasmuch as change is such an integral part of the workaday world, the author argues here that it is not a special, for-holidays-only activity.

In this exposition, Sayles discusses the manager's job as he endeavors to cope with the external pressures and internal problems which cause a shift from the "normal" equilibrium. He sees the job of the administrator as consisting of: (1) detecting disturbances or deviations in the system; (2) assessing the significance of the deviation; (3) taking corrective or stabilizing action (short-run change); (4) analyzing recurring or continuing sources of deviation and stress; (5) implementing long-run organizational structural change; (6) taking action to validate the change.

In general, Sayles believes that the key both to restoring a previous "normal" equilibrium of efficiency and production and to moving to a new and higher equilibrium of efficiency and production lies in the manipulation of the work flow, job design, technology, the authority structure, the reward-penalty system, and/or communication flows. This philosophy is a rather marked departure from the people-oriented approach advocated by Bennis in the previous reading.

THE CHANGE PROCESS
IN ORGANIZATIONS:
AN APPLIED ANTHROPOLOGY APPROACH

Leonard R. Sayles
Columbia University

Unfortunately, the subject of change in organizations (or of community or culture) is typically dealt with as a distinct, separate process, apart from the normal functioning of the system. Change is apparently viewed as something that is imposed on an unwilling, unresponsive audience or consumer. The problem of change, therefore, is usually one of gaining consent or acceptance through cajoling, force, participation, spotting the most likely sources of resistance and, occasionally, identifying gate-keepers or possible allies.

In other words, it is the difficulty of *introducing change* into a resistant system which has captured the attention of most students of the subject. However, if one observes the behavior of managers or leaders it will be noted that this aspect of the problem does not account for a significant amount of the total amount of time and energy expended on administration. Our purpose here, then, is to broaden the analysis to include the total process of change. This means viewing change as an intimate, integral part of the administrator's task of managing—really *stabilizing*—a system of human relations. Change, then is not a special, for holidays only, activity. It is part and parcel of the normal administrative process of assessing how the system is operating, determining where *significant* deviations are occurring, identifying the source of the disturbances, taking administrative actions to eliminate the source of the instability (what we

Reprinted from Leonard R. Sayles, "The Change Process in Organizations: An Applied Anthropology Approach," *Human Organization,* XXI, No. 2 (1962), 62-67; 82-85. By permission of the author and The Society for Applied Anthropology.

will call short-run change) and, finally, where the disturbance or deviation is recurring—the introduction of "long-run" change and its implementation and control.

What follows is an exposition of the stages in this process and their interrelationship. This analysis also represents our view of the job of the administrator in operational or interactional terms. It is an effort to depart from subjective, unquantifiable variables that have usually been associated with the analysis of all management processes (not just change) often quasi-psychological variables like the degree of personal security or sensitivity of the leader, the degree of "consideration" he generates and his ability to give assignments which equate authority and responsibility (parenthetically, a most unrealistic and unlikely possibility).

One last point to the introduction and approach. It is naive to assume that the administrator-leader suddenly commits himself to the accomplishment of change and then devotes all his efforts to this objective. Change must be accomplished simultaneously with the continued operations of an organization or system of work relationships. There is no "breathing spell," typically, where the organization can go all-out in the effort to pull itself up by its boot straps. This, of course, is another reason for considering change as part of the total organizational process.

The Paradox: Change and Stability

Paradoxically, the manager's job is to accomplish both stability and change. In order to maximize both the productivity of the processes under his jurisdiction and maintain high motivation among subordinates (which in turn facilitates productive efforts), he must endeavor to minimize the frequency with which the patterns of work flow and coordination are disturbed. In fact, the frequency with which such actual or potential interruptions to the work patterns occur, as we have described in a recent book,[1] are the prime determinants of the work load of the manager. It is the development and maintenance of work flow routines which is his major objective, and these "predictable and repeated patterns of interaction" are the source of morale or the absence of debilitating stress and its concomitant: destructive emotional reaction (what we have called compensatory behavior).[2]

> In a situation requiring cooperative endeavors, whether it is a work group, employees and managers, or staff and line officials, each tries to develop a stable pattern of work, of interaction. When these stable patterns are disturbed, individuals experience stress or an uncomfortable feeling of pressure and dissatisfaction. A breakdown in the flow creates opposition as the individuals struggle to restore it. The expected responses

[1] Eliot D. Chapple and Leonard R. Sayles, *The Measure of Management*, Macmillan, New York, 1961, pp. 46-68.

[2] *Ibid.*, pp. 114-141.

from the individuals in the sequence prove inadequate, and new coordination problems arise.

The regularities of actions and interactions disappear when this stress occurs, and erratic variation takes over. The difference is obvious between a smoothly running operation and one with a problem. Under stress, people react emotionally, and, because more than one individual is involved, the reactions usually conflict with each other.

Thus, a vicious circle is established. Something happens in the work situation that causes the relationship of individuals to change or to depart from the normal pattern. This creates a stress, either of opposition or nonresponse, that is further complicated by higher levels of supervision and staff specialists whose unexpected interactions, i.e., outside the usual organization pattern, irritate the disturbed work-flow relations. People get upset; they become angry with each other and, depending on their individual characteristics, react temperamentally. These personality conflicts have direct ramifications in the work process because the emotional reactions change the pattern of contact and interaction. Joe is angry with Bill, so he does not check with him before starting a new experimental run. Consequently, a special test that should have been included in the run is left out, and the whole thing has to be done over. To complete the circle, these emotional disturbances damage the work-flow sequence, which causes additional personality stresses.[3]

But, of course, as we "sophisticated" observers know, the achievement of this stability—which is the manager's objective—is a never-to-be-attained ideal. He is like a symphony orchestra conductor—endeavoring to maintain a melodious performance in which the contributions of the various instruments are coordinated and sequenced, patterned and paced—while the orchestra members are having various personal difficulties, stage hands are moving music stands, alternating excessive heat and cold is creating audience and instrument problems, and the sponsor of the concert is insisting on irregular changes in the music to be played.

In other words, the manager faces constant internal and external interruptions. As we shall see, some of these require mere palliatives—readjustments—in order to bring the system of relationships back to stability, for example, a disciplinary action (which is one type of change). Other disturbances require more drastic action if the system is to be stabilized, for example, the introduction of new methods or personnel as a result of a change in market conditions or the demands of some other part of the organization.

Presumably we might call this a moving equilibrium. External pressures and internal problems require constant "change," but the manager endeavors to accomplish this as he returns the system to equilibrium.

Detecting Disturbances or Deviations

Thus, an important element in the manager's job is the detection of disturbances or deviations in the system of human relationships which comprise his

[3]*Ibid.,* pp. 37-38.

work flows. This is the control function of the manager: developing methods of detection whereby he can assess and appraise how and where he should devote his managerial efforts, perhaps supplemented by the assistance of other specialists.

We need to be aware that a manager's scarcest resource is (or ought to be) his own time and energy, and that of other members of management. Therefore, he needs to devote his attention to what are indeed problems and avoid spending time in areas which are functioning well.

How does the manager "check" or control? He looks at statistical reports of quality, quantity, turnover, and what have you. He "inquires around" as to how people are doing and he endeavors to "sense" when people are acting differently. Unfortunately, some of this is usually done intuitively and there is little systematic attention to an integrated control system.[4] In a well-developed theory of organization change, we would expect to set forth the actual pattern of control: how frequently and with whom or what the manager checks. We would also expect to see an integrated series of controls involving technical measures of performance (e.g. quality, quantity, etc.) embodied in relatively automatic data processing systems combined with measures of organizational relationships.

Among others, F. L. W. Richardson, Jr., has shown that one can interrelate variations in the technical performance of a system with variations in the human relations dimensions.[5] In other words, there are correlations between such things as output and changes in internal work group interactions, manager-subordinate interactions and subordinate-outside group interactions. These provide the new materials of an effective and objective monitoring system. The manager need not be able to "smell trouble."

Assessing the Significance of the Deviation

The next step in the process is the manager's assessment of the significance of the deviations he is observing. It is likely that Parkinson's Law could be stated more realistically in terms of managers making work for themselves and others by going into action to deal with a problem that is not a problem—in other words, to introduce a change in a system which is operating within *expected limits of variation.*

The mathematical statisticians have begun to work on just this problem—noting that management can introduce serious instabilities into inventory maintenance systems, that is, can really amplify variations—by endeavoring to over-correct for variation. We see the same thing in human relations terms—where the supervisor contacts his own subordinates and others to discuss

---

[4]There has been inadequate attention paid to the development of a theory of systems control outside of some of the recent efforts of the mathematical statisticians. Eliot Chapple is also concerned with this problem, and his remarks may concentrate on this area.

[5]F. L. W. Richardson, *Talk, Work, and Action,* Monograph No. 3, Society for Applied Anthropology, 1961.

"mutual problems," where the contact itself creates the problem, and none existed before. The foolishness is never detected, of course, because the endeavor to over-correct the system *does create a problem* which in turn justifies the supervisor's attention and energy expenditure.

Of course, the opposite is the more traditionally identified difficulty; the failure to detect quickly enough or to move quickly enough to quench a real fire. Thus the manager requires as part of his control apparatus a theory of significant differences which will enable him to place certain "limits" on the occurrence or amplitude of the phenomenon he is observing. This requires a knowledge of the limits on normal or expected variation, given the nature of the system. He then hoards his managerial actions for the significant deviations in the system—and avoids becoming himself a source of upset where none existed before.

It may be well to repeat here that this theory of change encompasses deviations or disturbances in the system that are imposed by superior fiat or environmental change as well as internal malfunctioning. We would expect that instabilities from the "outside" would be transmitted through his contacts with his own superior and other managers as well as through the flows of relationship in which his subordinates participate with "outsiders" in their job activities.

From the point of view of organization design and the specification of managerial actions, it thus becomes possible to set forth explicitly (and thus control and check the performance of) managerial surveillance actions. These would include operationally definable patterns for what to check, how and how often, as well as techniques of data analysis to ascertain significant differences. This becomes another step in the process of making managerial actions less art and intuition and more science, but within the realm of human relationships. For example, we can distinguish those checks that require the manager to initiate, those initiated to him, and those that come from reports. All, however, require organizational analyses, that is, a knowledge of the time dimensions of the work-flow system which are to be controlled, prior to the elaboration of the "checking" and "evaluation" procedures.

Corrective or Stabilizing Action

In moving toward a science of administration we would view the next task of the manager in the control-change sequence as taking corrective actions where significant deviations have been revealed. Here, too, we can be explicit about the interaction pattern required. These are the "short-run" changes. This area is the one usually encompassed by the human relations literature when it deals with getting a behavior change. This means the traditional techniques of order-giving, criticism, discipline, training, communication and persuasion (of course, we would insist that these can all be described in operational, interaction terms).[6]
We can, in fact, write sequences of remedial action which the supervisor takes

[6]Cf. Chapple and Sayles, *op cit.,* pp. 48-64.

(or should take) in endeavoring to bring the work flow system back to a stable state. Some of these patterns involve outside contacts as well which may serve to bring the system back to normal. For example, the unsatisfactory pacing of the activities of a service department may be creating internal problems. The manager may move through his superior or other channels in seeking to bring the tempo of these activities more in alignment with his needs. Or additional personnel may have to be secured through recruitment channels or permission to work overtime secured from higher management in order to adjust to pressures for increased output. From the point of view of the organization as a whole, the manager operating these controls also must be required to alert his manager and others who may be affected by the departures from equilibrium of his system. This enables them to take complementary actions to avoid having the disturbance spread from the jurisdiction of this manager through the entire organization. All of these actions can be prescribed and quantified interactionally.

Analyzing Recurring or Continuing Sources of Deviation and Stress

Some of the problems with which the supervisor must cope will not be solved by the administrative actions to which we have referred. These are the ones we distinguish as recurring problems. They are the cause of comments like this:

> I am always having to go down to engineering and have a battle over specifications—hardly a week goes by in which there isn't an argument here and probably a big meeting as well.

Some are not recurring, they are just never solved. We have referred to these in our recent book as "spiralling" or cumulating deviations.[7] Figuratively an initial source of infection in the organizational system "spreads" to other flows and these, in turn, may react back on the original source, thus adding to the disturbance at that point. These are the so-called major crises or explosions. In either case the detection by the supervisor that such a problem exists should bring into action additional remedial measures.

The first of these may well be an investigatory pattern. After all, these are the problems which consume inordinate amounts of supervisory time and create major losses to the organization. Their occurrence suggests that some more significant and far reaching change is required than an adjustment in the attention or the immediate activity pattern of the supervisor. So-called staff groups, or consultant-specialists, unfortunately even task force committees, may be used to assess the situation. They come into action, or should be mobilized only when the controls maintained by the manager identify this type of problem or when the auditing mechanisms of the staff group themselves so indicate. It is well to note at this point that large, complex organizations frequently assign to

---

[7]*Ibid.*, p. 161.

staff groups the responsibility for accumulating some of the data that the manager uses for control purposes.[8]

As part of the investigatory process, the manager needs to be intellectually aware of the likely structural sources of stubborn instability. At some future time control mechanisms may be developed which will identify the source as well as the problem. The applied anthropologist has contributed a great number of "classic cases" for such analysis:

1. Heavily "unbalanced" interaction patterns such as some of the jobs in Whyte's restaurants,[9] and as exhibited by poor supervisors and conflict-laden union-management relations.[10]

2. Unstable or irregular patterns (e.g. Whyte's time-study-man analysis[11]), also other staff positions.

3. Contacts where there is an inadequate frequency of contact (e.g. see Sayles discussion of "Erratic Groups"[12] and Tavistock studies of the Longwall coal-getting method[13] and the Indian Weaving Shed).[14]

The applied anthropologist has identified these as typical sources:

1. Locations where the manager's jurisdiction has been poorly conceived such that "unit work flows" are broken by the organization. These are interrelated work positions between which a constant "rhythm" needs to be maintained, that is the parameters of the flow are identical.

2. Service groups outside of these flows which become "scarce resources."

3. Work positions where the requirements of the job are incompatible with personality of the incumbent.

4. Employees in positions which have undergone transformations to which they have not yet adjusted (e.g. the "succession" problem, the change

[8]The so-called staff-line problem is usually the result of a failure to organize on this basis. Staff groups go into action and initiate to the supervisor in areas and at times when the supervisor has not agreed there is a significant deviation. Then his dealing with the staff itself becomes a stressful relationship and a time-consuming one. In turn, this is partially the result of the failures of traditional administrative management theory in conceptualizing the staff "role." Apart from its audit functions the staff ought to be measured on its success in bringing deviating systems back to equilibrium—which, in turn, would minimize their conflicts with line managers. For a fuller discussion of this problem see G. Strauss and L. Sayles, *Personnel,* Prentice-Hall, Englewood Cliffs, N.J., 1960, pp. 399-417.

[9]William F. Whyte, *Human Relations in the Restaurant Industry,* McGraw-Hill, New York, 1948.

[10]William F. Whyte, *Pattern for Industrial Peace,* Harper & Bros., New York, 1951.

[11]William F. Whyte, *Money and Motivation,* Harper & Bros., New York, 1955

[12]Leonard R. Sayles, *Behavior of Industrial Work Groups,* Wiley, New York, 1958, pp. 78-79.

[13]E. L. Trist and E. W. Bamforth, "Social and Psychological Consequences of the Longwall Method of Coal-getting," *Human Relations,* IV (1951), 8.

[14]A. K. Rice, "Productivity and Social Organization in an Indian Weaving Shed," *Human Relations,* VI (1953), 297-329.

in "status" and power of the nurse or the first line supervisor, and see also the many examples in H. O. Ronken and P. R. Lawrence, *Administering Changes*).[15]

5. "Men in the middle."

6. The impact of organizational innovations such as staff groups or incentives.

This then is an interim requirement for the change process—technical diagnoses of potential organizational trouble spots which can drain managerial time and energy. Beyond the diagnosis the manager has a great deal of work to do. This is the implementation process.

Usually we find that the manager must spend a great deal of time convincing superiors in the organization that a structural or "long-run" change is necessary, even before he gets an opportunity to engage in the difficult job of establishing the change in the organization. Many managers—or leaders—are kept so busy "putting out fires" that they never take on the job of seeking to find the source of recurring blazes. In a sense a rather great capital investment, in terms of time and energy, is necessary to provide a more permanent solution. The manager must take time away from his regular activities to undertake lengthy "selling" contacts with superiors and others plus the major problems of coping with affected subordinates. Many lack the energy and the ability to do this, and this is the major reason why "change" is not introduced at an appropriate rate in the organization, *not* the recalcitrance of subordinates, unions and habits!

Implementing the Change

The traditional human relations literature has also concentrated on the problem of gaining acceptance for structural changes. Here is where one reads about participation and timing, the use of informal leaders, etc. Arensberg, however, again from the point of view of the applied anthropologist, has provided the only clearly operational description of the implementing process.[16]

1. First an increase in managerial initiative to subordinates.

2. Opportunity for increased inter-worker contacts (presumably informal group activity).

3. Followed by an increase in redressive contacts or initiations to the manager (and in turn the manager must be prepared time-wise to accept these).

4. Rewarding managerial responses to these subordinate initiations (often

[15]Harvard University, Division of Research, Graduate School of Business Administration, Boston, 1952.

[16]Cf. Conrad Arensberg and Geoffrey Tootell, "Plant Sociology: Real Discoveries and New Problems," in Mirra Komarovsky (ed.), *Common Frontier of the Social Sciences,* The Free Press, Glencoe, Illinois, 1957.

the change period is such a hectic one that time is not available for this step).

In our terminology both (2) and (3) represent compensatory behavior—reactions of the individuals to the stress of changed jobs, managerial contact patterns, etc.

Again these are time consuming patterns of administration and detract from the other commitments of the supervisor. In addition, the organization typically may neglect the more formalized accommodation patterns identified by the anthropologist as easing major dislocations in human patterns of interaction. We have in mind the *rites de passage* and symbolic ceremonies which the community has evolved for such crises.

Validating the Change

The manager cannot afford to assume that a change he has introduced has actually become part of the operating system. We know that human relations systems tend to return to previous equilibria when pressures are removed which have shifted them away from that position. However, it would be a mistake to assume that all changes are imposed on "comfortable" equilibria, although these are the ones which are grist for the case writers. There are many situations in which people are under substantial stress and tension; the organization is not providing them with personal satisfactions, and they welcome change. Whether initially welcomed or not, the manager must utilize methods of appraisal to validate that the change has become stabilized. Essentially this means checking to see that the flow, sequence and coordinating patterns are as planned.

Organization Change vs. Conversion

It should now be evident that the applied anthropologist's theory of change and administration encompasses both traditional methods of persuasion and influence, usually emphasized in social psychological terms but operationally definable in behavioral, interaction terms, and more long-run or permanent alterations in the organizational constraints. In another work we have chosen to call the former "conversion" by which we meant simply that the manager seeks to convince or persuade a subordinate to shift his behavior in some way and thus eliminate a source of disturbance.[17]

Obviously, this type of administrative activity is important and constantly used. It is involved in the giving of brief orders and lengthy disciplinarian sessions. But the administrator who relies solely on this type of change is ignoring one of the most important parts of his job: seeking out and remedying the persisting and compounding problems. These require, as we have endeavored

[17]Chapple and Sayles, *op. cit.*

to illustrate, the introduction of changes in the organizational constraints: the flow of work, the components of jobs, the incumbents on jobs, the structure of authority, the incentives and even the controls themselves that are used.

Conclusion

We have endeavored to write an operational description of the change process as an integral part of the manager-leader's day-to-day administrative activities. This analysis lends itself to behavioral quantification and objective validation so that the organization can provide for change within its structure and appraise the success of its members in carrying forth these patterns. Rather than a "last straw," when all else has failed, change, in the applied anthropologist's view, can precede serious crises. Further, administrators can be trained in terms of unambiguous behavioral skills to carry forth such programs.

In our view, the process of change has consisted of these interrelated sequences of managerial action:

1. Specific organizational and technical checks (of prescribed characteristics and frequency) on the stability of the system under the jurisdiction of the manager.
2. Established criteria for evaluating significant deviations from the desired stable state.
3. Prescribed administrative patterns of corrective action to bring the system back to equilibrium. (Short-run change)
4. Appraisals of recurring or continuing instabilities in the system with provision for staff (or specialist) assistance in investigating potential structural sources of organization stress and remedial measures.
5. Administrative patterns for implementing "long-run" organizational structural change.
6. Administrative action to validate the change.

We have purposely ignored the usual shibboleths about starting at the top of the organization and getting "grass roots" support, etc., etc. In our view of change as part of every manager's operational job requirement, this pattern is repeated at each level with adjustments in controls to view the processes below. There is no starting or ending point as such—change is an integral and essential part of all organizational behavior.

What is the implication for this description of the change process in organizations for the growing social concern with the impact of large hierarchical structures or initiative and creativity? It would seem to me that this type of analysis presents a far different prognosis for the role of the individual than the usual political science view of delegated and strictly delimited authority or the psychologists' emphasis on palliatives to reduce the sting of hierarchical power.

In our recent research we have viewed the actual behavior of managers in a very large organization and we find that their organizational positions give them much "leeway" in utilizing their personality skills and energies in meeting the challenges of constant restabilization requirements and the need to initiate to introduce change. The notion that the lower level manager deals passively as a transmitter of orders from higher ups and a feedback mechanism, reporting what is going on below, is just not reality, except where the manager's personality is inadequate to taking the initiative. We would not want, however, to minimize the number in the latter category.

When the organization is viewed as a complex series of interlocking patterns of human relationships, work flow patterns and control patterns, the opportunity for the individual to innovate and shape his own environment becomes apparent. Creativity and innovation are a product of the individual's ability to extract the time and energy from the "fire fighting" preoccupations of the moment, in order to modify the pressures and stresses which are being showered on himself and on his subordinates. The hierarchy is no barrier to this—it is, as it has been in every culture—the challenge to the able.

part II

FEEDBACK AND INFLUENCE: SEEDS FOR A THEORY OF CHANGING

In Part II our attention turns to an exposition of the literature regarding certain philosophies, techniques, and variables that can be distilled into a theory of changing behavior.

The information presented here does not proffer a simple prescription of "do's and don'ts" for the change agent or administrator; rather, it provides a way of thinking about, and attacking, this extremely touchy problem. Before designing a change program to alter behavior, the change agent needs some "principles" to guide him if he is to maximize his chance of succeeding.

Some of the factors of major importance in developing a theory of changing are: (1) the use of feedback, both negative and positive; (2) the role of coercion and force; (3) the compliance theory of Herbert C. Kelman; (4) the influence model of Kurt Lewin, which is comprised of unfreezing, change (by identification and/or internalization), and refreezing.

Floyd C. Mann's essay, "Studying and Creating Change: A Means to Understanding Social Organization," which is the lead article in this portion of the book, shows the inadequacies of the traditional management development approach for producing meaningful change in behavior. Mann then presents a detailed discussion of his interesting method for altering behavior which has as its hub the collection, feedback, and discussion of organizational data to relevant people. Among other things, it demonstrates the powerful role of feedback relative to changing. Alton C. Bartlett, in "Changing Behavior Through Simulation: An Alternate Design to T-Group Training," chronicles the specifics of a multiphase program for influencing a behavior change first, which will then spawn a congruent attitude change if the individual perceives the new behavior as more successful.

The third selection, "Management Development as a Process of Influence" by Edgar H. Schein, reports the particulars of the unfreezing-change-refreezing technique of influence and demonstrates its application to management development. The following paper, "Influence and Organizational Change" by Gene W. Dalton, presents a general model for modifying behavior that expands the scope of Kurt Lewin's three-step model. The last essay, "Toward a Theory of Changing Behavior: An Elaboration on the Role of Influence and Coercion" by Alton C. Bartlett and Thomas A. Kayser, links the previous material into a unified whole and draws some conclusions with respect to the state of the art of changing.

Studying and Creating Change: A Means to Understanding Social Organization

At the time this material was written, systematic research studies concerning the introduction and implementation of organizational change were in their infancy. Most attempts to alter behavior and improve organizational performance revolved around the traditional "classroom" supervisory training programs. Typically, these were comprised of workshops and seminars or conferences relying almost exclusively upon lectures, interspersed on occasion with role playing or discussion, plus some assorted visual aids.

Mann begins by citing several empirical studies that tested the effectiveness of the so-called "classroom" approach. The conclusion reached is that these programs are ineffective as a means of bringing about lasting change in interpersonal behavior "back home" in the work environment.

The author then shifts to a detailed discussion of the organizational feedback method for changing patterns of relationships between superiors and subordinates. Seven implications from a field study using the technique are then outlined. These implications should be examined carefully by the reader inasmuch as several of the other articles presented in this book (most notably those by Schein, Bartlett, Dalton, Sheldon Davis, plus Blake and Mouton) appear to draw upon these findings.

Mann concludes his paper by summarizing the differences between the organizational feedback method and the "classroom" approach.

STUDYING AND CREATING CHANGE: A MEANS TO UNDERSTANDING SOCIAL ORGANIZATION[1]

Floyd C. Mann
University of Michigan

Social organizations are functioning entities with interdependent structures and processes. They are not fixed, static structures, but rather continuously moving patterns of relationships in a much larger field of social activity. To understand what their essential elements and dimensions are, what it is that gives an organization its unity, it is necessary to study and create social change within organizational settings.

Relatively little is known about organizational change. Social scientists stress the study of the dynamic in social systems, but few[2] accept the risks involved to gain the knowledge and skills needed to create and measure changes in functioning organizations. This is not surprising, for research within large-scale organizations is at such an early stage that the social scientist knows little about how (1) to gain access to these research sites, (2) to initiate and sustain organizational change, and (3) to measure such changes. We have only begun the

Reprinted from Arensberg *et al., Research in Industrial Human Relations* (N.Y.: Harper & Row, Publishers, Incorporated, 1957), chap. 10, pp. 146-167. Reprinted by permission of the Industrial Relations Research Association and the author.

[1]Drs. Rensis Likert; Daniel Katz, Robert Kahn, and Norman R. F. Maier have made especially helpful suggestions concerning the organization and presentation of this material. They can, of course, in no way be held responsible for the shortcomings which remain.

[2] For an account of a conspicuous exception to this, see N. C. Morse and E. Reimer, "The Experimental Manipulation of a Major Organizational Variable," in *Journal of Abnormal and Social Psychology* (1956).

systematic codification of the working knowledge and skills necessary for the researcher to get into, and maintain himself within, the social science laboratories of functioning organizations.[3] Systematic, quantitative measurement of change processes in complex organizational settings is in its infancy. Longitudinal studies are rare—social scientists seldom attempt to obtain more than a single "before" and "after" measurement and are often content to try and decipher findings from *ex post facto* study designs. The actual steps and skills necessary to initiate and sustain changes within an organization are not only relatively unknown, but there is even some suspicion that knowledge of social action and an ability to engineer change are not appropriate for the social scientist.

While social scientists are not spending any sizable proportion of their time in learning how to change interpersonal and intergroup relations in functioning organizations, a wide variety of practitioners are. These include at the one extreme the consultants or the "operators" who take over organizations which are failing and rebuild them, and at the other extreme, the "human relations" trainers. Most of these men know very little theoretically about processes of organizational, attitudinal, and behavioral change, but they do know a great deal intuitively about the problems of changing people in an organization. This is especially true of the training men.

This suggests that there should and can be a closer working relationship between those concerned with actually *changing* organizational structure and processes and those researchers concerned with *understanding* organizational change. Social scientists have not begun to take advantage of their opportunities for learning about organizations from those in the "practicing professions"—those who are *doing*.[4] Observations and systematic measurements around the practitioner's efforts to alter systems of relationships in organizations can provide the researcher with valuable insights into the dynamics of organization. Gaps in knowledge become excruciatingly apparent; new sources of data and problems for research emerge. In turn, social scientists can contribute to practitioners by helping them assess what effect their actions as change agents have. Most practitioners—and especially those trainers who are concerned with changing the human relations skills of supervisors—have very little systematic, and no quantitative, evidence on the success of their efforts to create changes in individuals or organizations. It seems clear that there is a broad basis for cooperation here. Systematic studies of the work of those attempting to change the way things are done in an organization may contribute to our understanding of social organizations. And developments in measurement and the procedures used by researchers to understand organizations better may contribute to the working knowledge of trainers and others in the "practicing professions."

In this chapter we will focus on the description and evaluation of several

[3]F. Mann and R. Lippitt, eds., "Social Relations Skills in Field Research," *Journal of Social Issues,* VIII, No. 3 (1952).

[4]Donald Young, "Sociology and the Practicing Professions," *American Sociological Review,* XX (December 1955), pp. 641-648.

different types of procedures designed to change interpersonal and intergroup relations in complex organizations. We will first look at two human relations training programs whose effects have been systematically and quantitatively studied Then we will describe briefly the development and evaluation of a change procedure with which we are experimenting to increase the understanding, acceptance, and utilization of survey research findings. At the close of the chapter these two specific types of procedures for creating change in organizational settings are contrasted as a first step in identifying facets of change processes which merit greater experimentation and in providing insights into the structure and functioning of organizations.

Changing Interpersonal Relations through Training Supervisors

Recurrent opportunities for social scientists to study a change process within an organizational setting are provided by human relations training programs for supervisors. As change procedures, these programs are formal, rational, purposeful efforts to alter institutional behavior. In contrast to the day-to-day attempts of management to bring about change, they are bounded in time and organizational space, and are thus easily studied intensively.

Because of the several historical developments described [elsewhere], management by the late forties began to be convinced that training might be useful for their supervisors, and there has since been a wholesale adoption of human relations programs. While there was and still is a remarkable range in the content, methods, and settings of these programs, nearly all of them have centered around improving supervisory skills in dealing with people—either as individuals or in face-to-face groups. They are frequently directed at teaching the supervisor how to work with an employee as an individual, occasionally at working with employees as members of a small group, but only rarely at understanding and working within the complex social system of the large corporation or factory. Another way of saying this is that the courses have drawn heavily from psychology, to a lesser extent from social psychology, and usually not at all from sociology.

There are no commonly agreed-upon ways by which these programs can be described. The following headings are, however, useful: objectives, content, methods, setting, training leader, and training unit. For example, the objectives of these programs are usually very general and quite ambitious: "to assist supervisors in developing the skills, knowledge, and attitudes needed to carry out their supervisory responsibilities," or "to improve morale, increase production, and reduce turnover." Their contents usually include human nature, personality, motivation, attitudes, and leadership, and other information about relevant psychological principles and research findings may also be included. More often than not the methods of training are some variant of the "lecture-discussion method." The settings are frequently in a classroom away from the job. The trainers are generally staff men whom the trainee did not know before the training; the trainees, first-line supervisors or foremen meeting with other supervisors from other parts of the organization.

Few systematic, quantitative studies have been made to investigate the effectiveness of these programs.[5] This is not to say that there has been no interest in evaluation. Any review of the literature will indicate many such attempts and many testimonials about the relative advantages of different procedures of training. Mahler and Monroe[6] reported a number of "evaluative studies" after reviewing the literature and conducting a survey of 150 companies known to have training programs. While these studies almost without fail acclaim the many benefits of such training, few of them meet more than a fraction of the requirements necessary for a rigorous test of the basic underlying assumptions.

What are these assumptions? In general, they are that training supervisors in human relations will result in changes in the supervisors' attitudes and philosophy, that these changes will be reflected in their behavior toward employees on the job, that this changed behavior will be seen by the employees, and that they will in turn become more satisfied with their work situation, then more highly motivated, and, ultimately, more productive workers.

While there is a good deal of evidence that human relations training programs do meet part of these assumptions—e.g., they do appear to change the verbal veneer of supervisors—there are few scientifically rigorous, quantitative studies which have demonstrated that these changes in what supervisors *know* affect their attitudes and behavior as seen or experienced by their subordinates. Few studies show that human relations training of supervisors is related to changes in the attitudes or productivity of employees under those supervisors.

It is not possible to make a complete review of these studies here. A review of the findings from several recent, major evaluative studies will, however, provide a good deal of evidence concerning the effectiveness of certain types of training programs. The findings will certainly emphasize the need for more systematic, quantitative research to assess the most effective combinations of content, methods, settings, training units, and trainers.

The Canter-Tyler Studies

In 1949, Canter[7] developed a human relations training course for first-line supervisors in the home offices of a large insurance company. The three objectives of the course were "(1) to establish facts and principles concerning

[5] A nonquantitative, but extraordinarily thorough and insightful, study of foreman training was made by A. Zaleznik, *Foreman Training in a Growing Enterprise* (Boston: Graduate School of Business Administration, Harvard University, 1951).

[6] W. R. Mahler and W. H. Monroe, *How Industry Determines the Need for and Effectiveness of Training,* Personnel Research Section Report 929 (Washington: Department of the Army, 1952).

[7] R. R. Canter, "A Human Relations Training Program," *Journal of Applied Psychology,* XXXV (February 1951), pp. 38-45.

psychological aspects of behavior and group functioning to enable supervisors to become more competent in their knowledge and understanding of human behavior; (2) to increase supervisors' capacities for observing human behavior; and (3) to present personality adjustment concepts to aid in integration of achievements made in the first two objectives." This training was designed to provide a foundation of information on which to build later through additional practice and "technique" training. Specific content was primarily psychological: human nature, personality, motivation, attitudes, leadership, and group structure. Method was lecture-discussion. The training occurred in the conference rooms of the company; Canter himself was the trainer. The trainees were eighteen supervisors whose superiors had participated in a preliminary run for executives. The course was presented in ten two-hour weekly sessions.

To determine the influence of this training, Canter employed a battery of paper-and-pencil questionnaires and tests which were given before and after training to two groups of supervisors: an experimental group of eighteen from one department who received the training, and a control group of eighteen from two other departments who did not receive training. The two groups were similar in type of work performed, age (about thirty), education (thirteen years), and proportion of men and women. While the control group had more years of service with the company (7.5 and 4.6 respectively) and higher mean scores on a mental alertness test, the statistical technique used in the final analysis did not require prematched individuals or groups.

Six tests, yielding a total of twelve separate scores, were used. (1) General Psychological Facts and Principles; (2) "How Supervise"; (3) General Logical Reasoning; (4) Social Judgment Test; (5) Supervisory Questionnaire; and (6) Test for Ability to Estimate Group Opinion. The major findings were that the trained supervisors obtained mean scores on all tests better than would have been predicted on the basis of the performance of the untrained group alone. For five out of the twelve measures, the differences were statistically significant at the 5 per cent level; for two other measures, differences were significant at the 10 per cent level. Other important conclusions were that trained supervisors became more similar in abilities measured by the tests and more accurate in estimating the opinions of employees in their departments, but not their sections. It was also found that those holding highest scores initially gained the most on all measures except the Test of Ability to Estimate Group Opinion, where the opposite result was obtained.

While Canter assumed in his design that cognitive training—i.e., an ability to understand human relations concepts and principles—would have to precede any behavioral training in supervisory skills, practices, and attitudes, Tyler[8] designed a companion study to measure any changes in employee morale which might be attributed to this training. Her morale surveys indicated improvement in employee morale scores for *both* the experimental and control departments. Morale improved by an average of 11 points per section (range 2-25 points) in

[8]B. B. Tyler, "A Study of Factors Contributing to Employee Morale" (Master's thesis, Ohio State University, 1949).

five of seven sections in the experimental group, and decreased slightly in two others. "In the control groups, morale increased in eight of the nine sections by an average of 14 points (range 5-32 points). The decrease in the other section was seven points. The only category which showed a somewhat consistent change among sections was 'supervision' on which scores for over half of the sections decreased." After warning the reader of the possible effect of the before-test experience, she notes: "Undoubtedly, the difference in change in morale between the control and the experimental groups is not large enough to be significant" (page 47). Canter, however, points out that in Tyler's study "morale was quite high initially, which might account for the lack of any improvement in the experimental department over the control."

The strength of the Canter-Tyler studies is that they used both *before* and *after* measures for experimental and control groups. Canter's use of multiple criteria against which to evaluate the various sub-goals of the training program is also noteworthy. The use of Tyler's perceptual and employee morale measures in conjunction with Canter's attitudinal and cognitive measures permits an evaluation of the course's effectiveness at two levels: the supervisor's intent, and his on-the-job performance. The findings from this combination of studies make it obvious that classroom learning does not guarantee the translation of such learning into job performance. It should be remembered, however, that Canter did not set out to change supervisors' skills and practices, but only their understanding of human relations concepts and ideas.

Fleishman-Harris Studies

Working with the education and training staff of a large company manufacturing trucks and farm machinery, Fleishman[9] developed a study design and a battery of research instruments for measuring the continuing effectiveness of leadership training. The general objectives of this training[10] were to change understanding, attitudes, habits, and skills of foremen by giving them solid foundation in four basic areas of industrial knowledge. These areas were personal development, human relations, economics, and company operations. The method was primarily lecture-discussion. The training staff included full-time instructors, former supervisors, and part-time university faculty. The training was given to foremen who were taken from a wide variety of operations and plants and sent to a central school in Chicago for two weeks of eight-hours-a-day intensive development.

To determine the effects of this course on foremen from one motor-truck plant who had taken this training, Fleishman employed an *ex post facto* design with four groups of about thirty each. One group had not received the training; the other three had, 2-10, 11-19, and 20-29 months earlier. The groups were

[9]Edwin A. Fleishman, "Leadership Climate, Human Relations Training, and Supervisory Behavior," *Personnel Psychology,* VI (Summer 1953), pp. 205-222.

[10]Charles L. Walker, Jr., "Education and Training at International Harvester," *Harvard Business Review,* XXVII (September 1949), pp. 542-558.

alike on a number of background characteristics: age (early forties), education (eleven years), length of service (sixteen years), supervisory experience (seven years), size of work group (about twenty-eight), and supervisory experience with present work group (six years). Seven paper-and-pencil questionnaires were used to obtain opinion, expectation, and perceptual data about leadership practices from the trainees, their superiors, and their subordinates. This battery gave Fleishman an opportunity to investigate the differences between supervisory beliefs as reported by the foreman himself and supervisory practices as reported by his employees, and to explore the interaction of training effects with the supervisor's "leadership climate." Each questionnaire contained two independent leadership dimensions which had been identified by factor analysis: "consideration"—the extent to which the supervisor was considerate of the feelings of employees; and "initiating structure"—the extent to which the supervisor defined or facilitated group interactions toward goal attainment.

The results obtained by giving attitude questionnaires to foremen on the first and last days of their training in Chicago provide evidence of how the topics stressed in this leadership training affected these two dimensions. The results obtained from these before and after measures showed a significant increase in "consideration" (.05 level) and an even more marked decrease in "initiating structure" (.01 level). The on-the-job effects of the training, however, appeared to be "minimal." "The training did not produce any kind of permanent change in either the attitudes or behavior of the trained foremen." The employees under the most recently trained foremen actually saw them as *less* considerate than the employees under the untrained foremen saw their superiors. This statistically significant finding was supported by other trends toward more structuring and less consideration by those foremen who had the training. Thus, while the human relations approach was stressed in the course and understood at least well enough to be registered as an opinion change on a paper-and-pencil questionnaire, it was not evident in what trained foremen said they did, or what their employees saw them doing in the actual work situation.

The most important variable found to affect leadership was the climate within which the foreman worked. In fact, the kind of superior under whom the foreman operated seemed "more related to the attitudes and behavior of the foremen in the plant than did the fact that they had or had not received the leadership training."

These results, showing that the training was not meeting its objective of making foremen more human-relations oriented in the plant, left two alternatives open: redesign the course, or initiate an intensive criterion study relating supervisory behavior to group effectiveness. The latter alternative was chosen, and Harris [11] designed a study in the same plant to investigate (1) the relationship between these two dimensions of leadership behavior and various measures of work efficiency, and (2) the effects of a training course planned as a brief

[11]E. F. Harris, "Measuring Industrial Leadership and Its Implications for Training Supervisors" (Doctoral thesis, Ohio State University, 1952).

refresher for the central school training in Chicago. It is the findings from this second objective in which we are primarily interested here.

The course, lasting one week, was given at a small nearby college. The effects were evaluated by field experimental design with before and after measures for experimental and control groups. Two groups of thirty-one foremen were established through matching on a number of variables, including length of time since attending the central school (almost three years), scores on before measures (including leadership climate), and other personal factors. One group was given the training. Questionnaires, similar to Fleishman's, were used to obtain information from employees and foremen about the foremen's attitudes and behavior.

Harris used several different methods of analyzing his findings. His most rigorous method indicated there were no statistically significant differences in the foremen's own leadership attitudes or the workers' descriptions of their foremen's behavior—before and after this additional refresher course. The only significant difference he found was a decrease in the degree to which the foremen in the *control* group showed structuring in their leadership behavior as described by their employees. Building on Fleishman's gradual decreases in structuring and increases in consideration the longer the foreman is back on the job, Harris suggests this finding might be interpreted to mean that the refresher course may have "tended to retard a general decrease in structuring."

Harris and Fleishman[12] in analyzing the data from both of their studies in the same plant have uncovered one finding which tends to qualify the general, completely negative conclusion of their findings regarding the effectiveness of this training. This finding concerns the stability of leadership patterns of individual foremen who did not have the training in contrast to those foremen who had the training. They find there is *less* stability in the pre-post measures for the foremen who had the training than for those foremen who did not have training. This suggests that the courses had markedly different effects on different foremen, and that "large individual shifts in scores occur in both directions." They conclude that their research findings show no significant changes in *group* means among trained foremen and that future research should be directed toward investigating personal and situational variables which interact with the effects of training.

At best, these two studies suggest that this type of training has little or no general effect on the behavior of foremen in the plant. At worst, they suggest that the unanticipated consequences of separating foremen from their work groups and making them keenly aware of their role in management more than offset the anticipated consequences of making the foremen more considerate of employees as human beings. Fleishman's finding that *leadership climate* appeared to be a better predictor than *training* of foremen's plant attitudes and behavior underscores the importance of considering the constellation of expecta-

[12]E. F. Harris and E. A. Fleishman, "Human Relations Training and the Stability of Leadership Patterns," *Journal of Applied Psychology*, XXXIX (February 1955), pp. 20-25.

tion patterns in which the trainee is embedded. Training which does not take the trainee's regular social environment into account will probably have little chance of modifying behavior. It may very well be that human relations training—as a procedure for initiating social change—is most successful when it is designed to *remold the whole system of role relationships of the supervisor.*[13]

The findings from these four studies suggest that trainers, researchers, and others interested in social change need to rethink what forces are necessary to create and sustain changes in the orientation and behaviors of peoples in complex systems of relationships. There is a good deal of evidence that management and trainees are enthusiastic about these training courses in general. Management's enthusiasm may be an index of whether the training will continue, but it does not indicate whether training is achieving changes in behavior. And while trainee satisfaction and acceptance may be important as an antecedent to learning, these factors do not indicate whether the training will produce attitudinal and, more significantly, on-the-job behavioral changes.

It should be stressed that the criterion which has been used here for measuring the effects of human relations training is not easily met. There is ample quantitative evidence in the preceding studies that supervisors' information about, and verbal understanding of, human relations principles can be increased. There is much less evidence that these courses have an effect on the trainee's on-the-job behavior as seen by those working under him. And the hard fact remains that there are no quantitative studies which indicate that these courses in leadership affect workers' job satisfactions or motivations.

Feedback: Changing Patterns of Relationships between Superiors and Subordinates by Using Survey Findings

Long-range interest in the actual varying of significant variables in organizations has necessitated that members of the Human Relations Program of the Institute for Social Research, University of Michigan, not only study existing programs for training and changing people in organizations, but that we *develop* new techniques for changing relationships, and that we learn how to *measure* the effects of such changes within organizations. As a result, we have invested a good deal of professional effort in exploring the effectiveness of different procedures for changing attitudes, perceptions, and relationships among individuals in complex hierarchies without changing the personnel of the units. The latter is an important qualification, for we have found that the changes in subordinates' perceptions and attitudes which follow a change in supervisory personnel are frequently of a much larger order than those generated by training or other procedures for changing the attitudes or behavior of incumbents.

---

[13]For a full account of these two studies combined, see E. A. Fleishman, E. F. Harris, and H. E. Burtt, *Leadership and Supervision in Industry* (Columbus: Personnel Research Board, Ohio State University, 1955).

One procedure which we developed and subsequently found to be effective in changing perceptions and relationships within organizations has been called "feedback." This change process evolved over a period of years as we[14] tried to learn how to report findings from human relations research into organizations so that they would be understood and used in day-to-day operations. Work began on this process in 1948 following a company-wide study of employee and management attitudes and opinions. Over a period of two years, three different sets of data were fed back: (1) information on the attitudes and perceptions of 8000 nonsupervisory employees toward their work, promotion opportunities, supervision, fellow employees, etc.; (2) first- and second-line supervisor's feelings about the various aspects of their jobs and supervisory beliefs; and (3) information from intermediate and top levels of management about their supervisory philosophies, roles in policy formation, problems of organizational integration, etc. We had several aims in this exploratory phase: (1) to develop through first-hand experience an understanding of the problems of producing change; (2) to improve relationships; (3) to identify factors which affected the extent of the change; and (4) to develop working hypotheses for later, more directed research.

The process which finally appeared to maximize the acceptance and utilization of survey and research findings can be described structurally as an interlocking chain of conferences. It began with a report of the major findings of the survey to the president and his senior officers, and then progressed slowly down through the hierarchical levels along functional lines to where supervisors and their employees were discussing the data. These meetings were structured in terms of organizational "families"[15] or units—each superior and his immediate subordinates considering the survey data together. The data presented to each group were those pertaining to their own group or for those subunits for which members of the organizational unit were responsible.

Members of each group were asked to help interpret the data and then decide what further analyses of the data should be made to aid them in formulating plans for constructive administrative actions. They also planned the introduction of the findings to the next level. The meetings were typically led by the line officer responsible for the coordination of the subunits at a particular level. Usually, a member of the Survey Research Center and the company's personnel staff assisted the line officer in preparing for these meetings, but attended the meetings only as resource people who could be called upon for information about the feasibility of additional analyses.

These meetings took place in the office of the line supervisor whose organiza-

[14]A number of people contributed to the design of this feedback process during its developmental phase. They included Sylvester Leahy, Blair Swartz, Robert Schwab, and John Sparling from the Detroit Edison Company, and Rensis Likert, Daniel Katz, Everett Reimer, Frances Fielder, and Theodore Hariton from the Survey Research Center.

[15]F. Mann and J. Dent, "The Supervisor: Member of Two Organizational Families," *Harvard Business Review*, XXXII (November-December 1954), pp. 103-112.

tional unit was meeting, or in the department's own small conference room. All of the survey findings relative to each group were given to the leader and the members of his organizational unit; they decided what to consider first, how fast to work through each topic, and when they had gone as far as they could and needed to involve the next echelon in the process.

This feedback change procedure was developed in an organization where a great amount of effort had already been invested in the training of management and supervisors. During the war the company had participated in the various J-programs sponsored by the War Manpower Commission, and more important, during the several years we were experimentally developing the feedback process, Dr. Norman R. F. Maier was working with all levels of management to improve their understanding of human relations and supervision.[16] The supervisors with whom we were working to increase their understanding of their own organizational units therefore had a great deal of training in the application of psychological principles to management.

Our observations of the feedback procedure as it developed suggested that it was a powerful process for creating and supporting changes within an organization.[17] However, there was no quantitative proof of this, for our work up to this point had been exploratory and developmental.

A Field Experiment in Accounting Departments.

In 1950, when eight accounting departments in this same company asked for a second attitude and opinion survey of their seventy-eight supervisors and eight hundred employees, we [18] had an opportunity to initiate the steps necessary to measure the effects of this organizational change process. The questionnaires used in this resurvey were similar to those used in 1948 and provided the basis for a new cycle of feedback conferences. The general plan for the handling of these new resurvey data was to let everyone in the departments—employees and department heads—see the over-all findings for eight accounting departments combined as soon as they were available, and then to work intensively on their use in *some* departments, but not in others until there had been a third survey.

While our objective was to test the effectiveness of the basic pattern of feedback developed during the preceding two years, we encouraged department heads and their supervisors to develop their own variations for reporting data to their units and maximizing their use in the solution of problems. After the all-department meetings had been concluded, the chief executive of the accounting departments held a meeting with each department head in the experimental

[16]For a thorough description of this training, see N. R. F. Maier, *Principles of Human Relations* (New York: Wiley, 1952).

[17]F. Mann and R. Likert, "The Need for Research on Communicating Research Results," *Human Organization,* XI (Winter 1952), pp. 15-19.

[18]F. Mann and H. Baumgartel, *The Survey Feedback Experiment: An Evaluation of a Program for the Utilization of Survey Findings,* Survey Research Center, University of Michigan, mimeographed, 1954, 8 pp.

group. At this meeting, the findings for the department head's unit were thoroughly reviewed. The findings included comparisons of (1) changes in employee attitudes from 1948 to 1950, (2) attitudes in that department with those in all other departments combined, and (3) employees' perceptions of supervisory behavior with supervisory statements about their behavior. Department heads were encouraged to go ahead with feedback meetings as soon as they felt ready, tentative next steps were discussed, and assistance from the researchers and the company personnel staffs was assured. Four departments launched feedback activities which were similar to each other in purpose but somewhat different in method. The programs varied in duration (13-33 weeks), in intensity (9-65 meetings), and in the extent to which nonsupervisory employees were involved in the process. During the eighteen months that these differences were unfolding, nothing was done in two of the remaining four departments after the first all-department meetings. This was done so they might be available as "controls." Changes in key personnel eliminated the remaining two departments from any experimental design.

A third survey of attitudes was conducted in these departments in 1952 after the natural variations in the feedback programs had run their courses. In 1950 and 1952 surveys were then used as "before" and "after" measurements, the four departmental programs as "experimental variations," with the two inactive departments as "controls."

Our findings indicate that more significant positive changes occurred in employee attitudes and perceptions in the four experimental departments than in the two control departments. This was based on two measures of change: (1) a comparison of answers to sixty-one identical questions which were asked in 1950 and 1952, and (2) a comparison of answers to seventeen "perceived change" questions in which employees had an opportunity to indicate what types of changes had occurred since the 1950 survey. In the experimental group, a fourth of the sixty-one items shows relative mean positive changes, significant at the .05 level or better; the change for another 57 per cent of the items was also positive in direction, but not statistically significant. Major positive changes occurred in the experimental groups in how employees felt about (1) the kind of work they do (job interest, importance, and level of responsibility); (2) their supervisor (his ability to handle people, give recognition, direct their work, and represent them in handling complaints); (3) their progress in the company; and (4) their group's ability to get the job done. The seventeen perceived-change items were designed specifically to measure changes in the areas where we expected the greatest shift in perceptions. Fifteen of these showed that a significantly higher proportion of employees in the experimental than in the control departments felt that change had occurred. More employees in the experimental departments saw changes in (1) how well the supervisors in their department got along together; (2) how often their supervisors held meetings; (3) how effective these meetings were; (4) how much their supervisor understood the way employees looked at and felt about things, etc. These indicate the extent to which the feedback's effectiveness lay in increasing understanding and communication as well as changing supervisory behavior.

Comparisons of the changes among the four experimental departments showed that the three departments which had the two feedback sessions with their employees all showed positive change relative to the control departments. The change which occurred in the fourth was directionally positive, but it was not significantly different from the control departments. In general, the greatest change occurred where the survey results were discussed in both the departmental organizational units *and* the first-line organizational units. The greater the involvement of all members of the organization through their organizational families—the department heads, the first-line supervisors, *and* the employees—the greater the change.

Implications of These Findings

The basic elements of this feedback process described above are not new. They involve (1) the orderly collection of information about the functioning of a system, and (2) the reporting of this information into the system for (3) its use in making further adjustments.

Work by Hall[19] and others who have had considerable practical experience with the use of information about a system for creating change show a similarity in both action steps and basic approach. This suggests there are certain psychological and sociological facts which must be taken into consideration in attempting to change the attitudes and behavior of an *individual* or a *group of individuals* in an *organizational setting*.

1. Attitudes and behavior of an individual are functions of both basic personality and social role. *Change processes need to be concerned with altering both the forces within* an individual and the forces in the *organizational situation* surrounding the individual.
2. Organizations, as systems of hierarchically ordered, interlocking roles with rights and privileges, reciprocal expectations, and shared frames of reference, contain tremendous forces for stability or change in the behavior of individuals or subgroups. Change processes need to be designed to harness these forces for creating and supporting change. *As forces already in existence, they must first be made pliable, then altered or shifted, and finally made stable again to support the change.*
3. Essentially, unilateral power and authority structures underlie the hierarchical ordering of organizational roles. *Expectations of the superior are therefore more important forces for creating change in an individual than the expectations of his subordinates.* Also those with a direct authority relationship—line superiors—have more influence than those without direct authority—staff trainers.
4. The attitudes, beliefs, and values of an individual are more firmly grounded in the groups which have continuing psychological meaning

[19]Milton Hall, "Supervising People—Closing the Gap Between What We Think and What We Do," *Advanced Management*, XII (September 1947), pp. 129-135.

to him than in those where he has only temporary membership. The supervisor's role of interlocking the activities of two organizational units requires that he have continuing membership in two groups: (a) the organizational unit directed by his superior in which he is a subordinate along with his immediate peers; and (b) the organizational unit for which he is responsible. *Change processes designed to work with individual supervisors off the job in temporarily created training groups contain less force for initiating and reinforcing change than those which work with an individual in situ.*

5. Information about the functioning of a system may introduce a need for change. This is especially true when the new data are seen as objective and at variance with common perceptions and expectations. Change processes organized around objective, new social facts about one's own organizational situation have more force for change than those organized around general principles about human behavior. *The more meaningful and relevant the material, the greater the likelihood of change.*

6. Involvement and participation in the planning, collection, analysis, and interpretation of information initiate powerful forces for change. Own facts are better understood, more emotionally acceptable, and more likely to be utilized than those of some "outside expert." *Participation in analysis and interpretation helps by-pass those resistances which arise from proceeding too rapidly or too slowly.*

7. Objective information on direction and magnitude of change— knowledge of results—facilitates further improvement. *Change processes which furnish adequate knowledge on progress and specify criteria against which to measure improvement are apt to be more successful in creating and maintaining change than those which do not.*

Comparison of "Classroom" Human Relations Training and Organizational Feedback

This is only a partial listing of the points with which a scientifically based technology of social change in organizational settings will have to be concerned. Our conceptualization and the identification of the relevant individual and organizational variables and their interrelationship is at a primitive stage. The systematic quantitative investigation of the effectiveness of different change procedures has scarcely begun. Even at this early date, however, a comparison between the structure and process of feedback and "classroom" human relations training as two different types of change procedures may be a useful exercise. It may help identify variables or facets of change processes which merit greater experimentation and investigation both by the practitioners and by those researchers interested in organizational change. By a "classroom" human relations program we mean a training which would consist of a series of class-room-like meetings in which supervisors from many different points of the organization meet to listen to a presentation of psychological principles which a trainer from the personnel department thinks they ought to know about and be ready to use on the job after a brief discussion following the training. This kind of training experience differs from the feedback process in a number of respects. These differences are stated to keep the comparisons reasonably brief and to sharpen the contrasts.

1. What are the objectives?

   "Classroom" Training—Improve supervisor-subordinate relations through changing the supervisors' understanding of human behavior, attitudes, and skills.

   Organizational Feedback—Improve organizational functioning through changing understanding, attitudes, and behavior among all members of the organization.

2. What is the setting in which change is being attempted?

   "Classroom" Training—Trainees are taken off the job and out of the network of interpersonal relationships in which they normally function for training in an "encapsulated"[20] classroom-like situation.

   Organizational Feedback—Change is attempted as a regular part of the day's work in established organizational relationships.

3. What is the informational content?

   "Classroom" Training—General psychological principles of human behavior, case materials, or data from outside the training group and often the organization, only occasionally using problems from the group's own experience.

   Organizational Feedback—Objective quantitative information about attitudes, beliefs, and expectations of the trainees themselves, or the subordinates in their own organization.

4. What is the method?

   "Classroom" Training—Lectures, presentations, films, skits, and occasionally role-playing followed by discussion on how to apply what has been learned back on the job.

   Organizational Feedback—The progressive introduction of new information about the problems within the groups for which the trainees are responsible. Group discussions of the meaning and action implications of the findings, followed by group decisions on next steps for changing or handling the situation.

5. Who are the trainees?

   "Classroom" Training—First-line supervisors and foremen whose superiors may have, but more often have not, had the course.

[20]M. Haire, "Some Problems of Industrial Training," *Journal of Social Issues,* IV, No. 3 (1948), pp. 41-47.

Organizational Feedback—Everyone in the organization from the top down[21]—the president, top management, intermediate and first-line supervision, *and* employees.

6. What is the training unit?

"Classroom" Training—An aggregate or collection of individual supervisors from different departments throughout the organization. A functional conglomerate without continuing psychological meaning for the individuals. Frequently seen as a "group" simply because the individuals are in close spatial proximity to one another.

Organizational Feedback—An organizational unit whose members have an organizational function to perform and whose members (a superior and his immediate subordinates) have continuing psychological meaning perceptually and behaviorally to one another as a team or family.

7. Who is the change agent?

"Classroom" Training—An outsider—an expert, a staff man—who has no direct, continuing authority or power over the trainee and few recurrent opportunities to reinforce the training.

Organizational Feedback—The organizational unit's line supervisor, who is given some help through pre- and postmeeting coaching by the expert outsider.

8. How is the pace or rate of change set?

"Classroom" Training—The trainer sets the pace, attempting to gear the training to the average trainee's ability to comprehend and assimilate the material.

Organizational Feedback—The members of the group move from one topic to another as they are ready for the next step.

9. How long does the change process continue?

"Classroom" Training—A fixed number of days or weeks, seldom less than 16 or more than 80 hours.

Organizational Feedback—No fixed length of time, the change procedure usually continues over a period of months—6 to 24 months.

10. How much tension is there?

"Classroom" Training—Usually relatively little; most trainees feel they already know a good deal about human behavior and how others feel.

Organizational Feedback—Frequently considerable, as objective information and particularly the differences between supervisory beliefs and practices come into a focus so sharp that complacency is shattered and the security about what is social reality is shaken.

[21] N. R. F. Maier, "A Human Relations Program for Supervision," *Industrial and Labor Relations Review,* I (April 1948), pp. 443-464.

11. What assumptions are made about attitudes and how they are changed?[22]

"Classroom" Training—The primary assumption is that the trainee does not know certain facts, that his previous organization of relevant information will be altered when he understands the new facts. Attitudes are seen as a function of the range of information available to the trainee; they are changed by altering cognitive structure.

Organizational Feedback—Here the assumptions are that the trainee already has satisfying ways of seeing things and relating to others, that attitudes and behavior can be changed only by altering their motivational bases. Norms of psychologically relevant groups are seen as more important determinants of attitudes than cognitive processes.

12. How is effectiveness of the change measured?

"Classroom" Training—Usually by informal comments of trainees, occasionally by interviews or questionnaires with the traineees after the training.

Organizational Feedback—By changes in employees' perception of their supervisor's behavior.

The differences drawn between these two types of procedures for creating change in an organizational setting may not be as marked as presented here. Human relations training programs do vary tremendously from company to company and from time to time. There is no single pattern. Since we know little about the frequency of different species of human relations training programs, the specific mix of content, method, setting, etc., which we used as the basis of our contrast may no longer be found in organizations. Our comparison aimed to emphasize the extent to which various characteristics of change processes vary on the basic dimension of *motivation for change.*

Different contents, different methods, different settings, different training units, and different change agents contain different motivational impacts for change. What constitutes the most effective combination for changing behavior in organizations is not known. Few practitioners have really done any bold experimenting; almost none have combined measurement and experimenting to search for the most significant dimensions and variables in change processes. This is an area in which there is a great need for social experimentation and social invention.

In the social sciences, as in the physical sciences, invention plays a crucial role. Inventions in social technology—skills and processes for creating change—and innovations in measurement both contribute speedily to progress in understanding social phenomena. The responsibility of experimenting with different methods of measuring change and with new procedures for investigating the

---

[22]I. Sarnoff and D. Katz, "The Motivational Bases of Attitude Change," *Journal of Abnormal and Social Psychology*, XLIX (January 1954), pp. 115-124.

interrelationship of functioning organizational processes rests heavily with the students of social organization. The rate at which knowledge about organization is developed will probably be closely correlated to the rate at which we try new approaches to the study of problems in this area.

Changing Behavior through Simulation: An Alternate Design to T-Group Training

This study introduces a multiplicity of tools and describes ways in which to utilize them in designing and presenting management development programs intended to encourage changes in behavior. It effectively illustrates that: (1) T-groups are not the only way to make available what Winn calls "opportunity for expansion in depth,"[1] and (2) the conceptual parameter of the "cultural islands"[2] can be broadened with favorable results. It also reveals some effective pedagogical techniques for use in a change program.

Of utmost importance is the author's analysis of what he sees as a major conceptual dilemma: should change efforts be directed at altering attitudes or behaviors? Most of the literature from professional change agents, whether they are theorizing or merely reporting, talks in terms of changing attitudes.[3] Even granting that this is the ultimate objective, however, one is still left with the question of whether or not it would be easier to change behavior first. Is not

---

[1] Alexander Winn, "Social Change in Industry: From Insight to Implementation," *The Journal of Applied Behavioral Science,* II, No. 2 (1966), 174 and *passim.*

[2] See, for example, Ronald Lippit, Jeanne Watson, and Bruce Westley, *The Dynamics of Planned Change* (New York: Harcourt, Brace, Jovanovich, Inc., 1958), p. 111, and Douglas McGregor, *The Human Side of Enterprise* (New York: McGraw-Hill Book Company, 1960), p. 223.

[3] See, for example, Edgar H. Schein, "Management Development as a Process of Influence," reprinted as the next selection in this volume, pp. 135-52.

approaching change through behavior rather than attitudes more in keeping with the available theories about resistance to change? The author says yes, illustrates one way to accomplish it, and subsequently reports on the substantial results of the change program. [4]

---

[4]For a further elaboration of the change program and the results, see Alton C. Bartlett, "Changing Behavior as a Means to Increased Efficiency," reprinted in Part III of this volume, pp. 234-53.

CHANGING BEHAVIOR THROUGH SIMULATION:

An Alternate Design to T-Group Training

Alton C. Bartlett
University of South Florida

As will clearly be seen from the following excerpts, taken from interviews with over 80 top management people, some express serious doubts or reservations about T-group training.[1]

> *It's* group psychotherapy. *I don't want my decisionmakers to* have to *expose themselves to unstructured* attacks *on their psyches. Just can't believe it is right to* force *people to subject themselves to such a* possible psychological *threat, and, it is no damn good on a* voluntary *basis where some participate in laboratory training and some don't, especially since those who really need it don't go.* Leaderless, no content *training is a waste of time. Such training away from home is* too expensive *for us to afford, unless it can be* statistically proven *it does indeed have a highly* significant *impact on more* efficiency *in terms of* planning, decision making, reduced costs *and* higher profits. *No report yet has satisfied me that what they supposedly learn away is ever* carried home *and* used effectively, over time! (Italics stand for respondent inflection as heard on tape recorder.)

Reprinted from Alton C. Bartlett, *Training and Development Journal*, XXI, No. 8 (August 1967), 38-52, by permission of the American Society for Training and Development and the author.

[1] This does not mean that I agree with their perceptions. The fact is that it is immaterial. It does not matter what is correct. Correct is what they believe it to be! I am being responsive to their reality.

It is important to note that they are not alone. Many "qualified" academicians have also raised questions on a variety of different points.[2]

This article offers hope for the corporation which is uncomfortable exposing executives to what it perceives as a traumatic experience. It says, T-groups are not the *only* way to "make opportunity for expansion in depth" available.[3] It describes an alternate (other than T-group) training design for improving individual manager's "interpersonal competence."[4] It reports success, in 300 to 500-employee organizations.[5] Individuals do come to *own* the conceptual tools of the behavioral sciences, and they do carry information and attitudes away from the laboratory, back to the work place. They also demonstrate improved performance on their job, and facilitate a significant increase in productivity and quality, a reduced absenteeism/turnover problem, plus cost reduction which vastly improves the profit picture.[6]

Objectives and Assumptions

1. Fundamental to this design is the assumption that: *it is easier to change behavior than attitudes!* Why launch a direct onslaught upon the latter when they will follow if the former is changed?

2. Man may say (but he seldom believes) he doesn't "know it all."

3. Unless currently under extreme pressure from authority figures, man (drawing on his entire past experience) will recall favorable examples as proof that he does a fine job in dealing with and understanding people.

4. Man's attitudes concerning human behavior are deeply ingrained. He possesses an *"attitudinal" sound barrier* which must be penetrated

[2]Cf., George Odiorne. "The Trouble with Sensitivity Training," *Training Directors Journal,* Oct. 1963; John E. Drotning, "Sensitivity Training Doesn't Work Magic," *The Management of Personnel Quarterly,* Summer 1968, Vol. 7, No. 2, pp. 14-20. *Business Week,* "Where Executives Tear Off The Masks," Sept. 3, 1966, pp. 76-83; Wendell W. Wolfe, "Human Relations Laboratory Training: Three Questions," *Journal of Business,* Oct. 1966, pp. 512-515; John E. Drotning, "Sensitivity Training: Some Critical Questions," *Personnel Journal,* Vol. 45, No. 10, November 1966, pp. 604-606.

[3]See Alexander Winn. "Social Change in Industry: From Insight to Implementation," *The Journal of Applied Behavioral Science,* Vol. 2, No. 2, Apr.-June, 1966, p. 174 and passim.

[4]The definition of this term is that of Chris Argyris, "Explorations in Interpersonal Competence—I." *The Journal of Applied Behavioral Science,* Vol. 1, No. 1, Jan.-Mar., 1965, p. 59.

[5]It should be noted that William P. Gellerman, Assistant Professor, N.Y.S.S.I.L.R., Cornell University, New York City Extension, has used portions of a similar design in a much larger organization with apparent good results.

[6]For a detailed exposition see Alton C. Bartlett, "Changing Behavior as a Means to Increased Efficiency," *The Journal of Applied Behavioral Science,* Vol. 3, No. 3, 1967, pp. 381-411.

before behavioral changes can occur. He must be "unfrozen," then changed.[7]

5. If someone engages you in theoretical discussions about human behavior, not grounded in your frame of reference, you may see them as interesting or even useful but, you certainly will be guilty of "selective exposure and awareness" plus "perceptual defense."[8]

6. The usual lectures and conferences which (at best) spoon feed neatly manageable bites of "wisdom" are not nearly powerful enough to break through an "attitudinal" sound barrier.

7. Lasting changes as a result of conventional classroom methods are quite unlikely: their impact is temporary. Permanent changes call for utilizing unconventional methods.

8. One unconventional method for changing behavior, strong enough to pierce the "attitudinal" sound barrier, is *simulation*. This involves, under the guise of skill training, having subjects (*Ss*) practice *doing* differently (in a laboratory situation). As they are given rewards for *doing* differently, their attitudes will (absent pressure) tend to soften.

9. Next, their conventional behaviors will be experienced as inadequate, and they will start to change by the mechanism of "identification."[9]

10. By gradually changing the organization's structure and reward system to keep pace with the changes in behavior being simulated, behavior on the job will also change by "internalization."[10] As it changes, if favorable feedback and payoff continue to be received for change, their attitudes will also adapt. There will then be a "refreezing."[11]

The Training Design

The primary vehicle, intended to carry most of the burden down the long road to improved interpersonal competence, is a training program ostensibly to improve communications. There are several reasons.

To begin with, improvement in interpersonal competence is partially dependent upon a free flowing dialogue between all principals. It is important, therefore, to focus everyone's attention upon fundamentals of communication like to whom, why, where, when, what, and how. While informal skills ought to be upgraded early, formal skills must be.

[7]Kurt Lewin. "Frontiers in Group Dynamics: Concept, Method, and Reality in Social Science," *Human Relations,* Vol. 1, 1947, pp. 5-42.

[8]For definition see Bernard Berelson and Gary L. Steiner, *Human Behavior,* Harcourt, Brace, World, 1964, pp. 100-102.

[9]Edgar H. Schein. "Management Development as a Process of Influence," *Industrial Management Review,* Vol. 2, No. 2, May, 1961, p. 62.

[10]Ibid.

[11]Kurt Lewin, op. cit.

Secondly, communication is a neutral subject in the sense that it is devoid of "content."[12] The focus is entirely on "process."[13] Though this design also calls for introducing a number of conceptual tools, it is important that none of them are specifically related to the company's policies and procedures. Usage of material of this nature allows the change agent (CA) to be an expert in *how*, not, a judge of *what*. This is conducive to the rapid creation of a climate of trust between CA and *Ss*. Said climate could be vital, for example, if there were expectations of much frustration, uncertainty, or bitterness among participants. It could facilitate their unloading problems and achieving catharsis.

A third reason is that since the purpose is to increase everyone's capacity to work effectively with others, a practical and painless method, in what will be seen as a natural site, has to be devised. *Simulation* in an in-house laboratory is herein proposed to satisfy both of these and at the same time: (a) accomplish goals similar to those of a T-group, while; (b) recognizing and being responsive to objections similar to the ones above. Consider the reasoning behind this proposal.

A Practical and Painless Method

Skill training in communications, where *Ss* would continually get to practice "listening and telling,"[14] will lend itself naturally to broadening their frame of reference and perceptions related to human behavior. Interpersonal competence will be developing as a by-product of *doing* differently: (a) while practicing new behaviors they will be receiving descriptive nonevaluative feedback as to how well they are doing; (b) rewards will flow for more empathic, creative, open behavior from both CA and peers, and; (c) the intimidating specter of failure, as new risk taking actions are tried, is not present because the emphasis is on learning a skill, not the ancillary behaviors.

A Natural Site

Now there are clearly some distinct advantages to employing the concept of the "cultural island" in terms of being away from the daily grind

> ... *in order to train adults in new patterns of interpersonal behavior it is desirable to* remove *them from their* standard *environments and place them in* special *environments where they are free to innovate, practice, and test new behaviors. (my italics)*[15]

[12]George Strauss and Leonard Sayles, *Personnel,* Prentice-Hall, Inc., 1960, p. 242.
[13]Ibid.
[14]Alexander Winn. "Training in Administration and Human Relations," *Personnel,* Vol. 30, Sep., 1953, pp. 139-149.
[15]Ronald Lippitt, Jeanne Watson, and Bruce Westley. *The Dynamics of Planned Change,* Harcourt, Brace, World, 1958, p. 111.

There are disadvantages too. Often a firm cannot spare whole days, let alone weeks, from any number of their supervisor's work time. Perhaps they cannot justify the cost of travel, rooms, meals, plus salaries. To the heads of many small, highly-competitive firms, these are legitimate obstacles.[16] Even more important, from a broad viewpoint, one certainly cannot even try to carry newly-learned behaviors back to the job while away from it. Ultimately, however, comes the question as to how one (or a dozen for that matter) manager, returning with even evangelical fervor from two weeks exposure to a T-group, can be expected to have very much lasting impact on organizational climate? If he tells others what he experienced (and most cannot articulate this well) peers are unlikely to understand, and suppose they did, could this cause them to demonstrate a new pattern of behavior? If he engages in the same open, risk taking behavior back home, as the T-group climate may elicit, many will view him as "some kind of a nut"! If he encourages others to join him, he (and in many cases they) may lose his job for starting an insurrection.[17]

To counteract such disadvantages, what could be a more obvious and natural laboratory for changing behavior than a classroom where communications skills are being worked on? When you are simulating new behaviors every day in class, and then going back to work, it is easy and normal to try them out while they are fresh in your mind. Where reactions are favorable to new methods, and this program improves the kind of behavior that will make them so, there is an immediate reward which cannot help but enhance the transference of new patterns of behavior from classroom simulation to the real world of the job.

To summarize the third reason, the training design attempts to set up a modified form of cultural island within the plant. Programs are

> ... *conducted in locations which are psychologically if not geographically remote from everyday life.*[18]

To illustrate, one conference room can be turned over completely to the program, making absolutely certain by words and deeds that this is their private sanctuary: a place apart. To assist in this, make sure regular company business is *not* conducted there during this time, never let any supervisor be taken away from the laboratory to attend to matters of business (the point is that this program is of equal importance), and make sure whatever goes on in the room is *not* carried away and reported to superiors.[19]

---

[16]This is not an academic theory. Over 50 heads of small firms have agreed to intensive in-depth interviews, lasting from one to two hours, concerning these and other considerations about training.

[17]This entire analysis represents a synthesis of the reflection from former T-group *Ss* who have experienced precisely these kinds of end results and problems when they returned home from a cultural island.

[18]Douglas McGregor. *The Human Side of Enterprise,* McGraw-Hill Book Co., 1960, p. 223.

[19]Naturally, CA can, and will, report aggregate behavior, sentiments, and norms. No individual, however, should be identified or singled out by name as having said or done any particular thing.

Remember, an attempt is being made to introduce change from the top down, through all levels of management *at once*. To accomplish this, continuing classes using simulated behavior are run, which will be taken in turn each day by each different level of supervision. Certainly this will affect: (a) their interactions, sentiments, norms, activities, and symbols[20]; (b) the formal, informal, and nonformal social structure,[21] and; (c) the existing technology[22] in the work place each successive day. It is meant to! Unless you close the plant down, such an all encompassing change has to be undertaken in the work place during regular operations.

Finally, a last reason for electing communications training is that it seemed desirable to provide the means by which *Ss* may develop their own new guidelines to fit their own new behavior. Where do they want the formal channels of communication to be? Conference leadership training, as a sub-part of communication, is a practical way for this and other guidelines to be studied, discussed, and established while they are purportedly mastering the skills of the "good" conference leader. This is also how they get considerable practice thinking and acting within the framework of decision making, but with no threat of punishment for failure. It develops more confidence, certainty, attention to process, and responsibility for when they are back in the day-to-day life of the real organization. Let a loser feel free to try to win and he gets confident.

Case Method Techniques

The two major techniques selected to best provide simulation are the case method and role playing. Of course, these would be supplemented, as appropriate, by other techniques such as specially created "spot lectures" of 150 to 400 words, the Pigor *incident process*,[23] and other meaningful exercises on occasion to portray an essential fact or clue.[24]

A series of case problems and incidents can be developed which consist of factual, uninterpreted accounts of problems which have taken place within the organization. Earliest ones can include a description of what happened (what people did, said, and thought), real in every detail but, of course, disguised to render identification impossible.[25] Later cases should get increasingly vague and

[20]These concepts are used in the sense that William F. Whyte, *Money and Motivation,* Harper & Brothers, 1955, pp. 191-193, uses them.

[21]Robert Dubin. *The World of Work,* Prentice-Hall, Inc., 1958.

[22]By technology is meant the whole gamut covered in Leonard R. Sayles, *Behavior of Industrial Work Groups,* Wiley, 1958.

[23]Paul Pigors and Faith Pigors. *The Incident Process: Case Studies in Management, Series I. Supervisory Problems,* Bureau of National Affairs, Inc., Washington, D.C., 1955, and *Cases in Human Relations: The Incident Process,* McGraw-Hill, 1961.

[24]Cf. Harold·J. Leavitt. *Managerial Psychology,* 2nd ed., The University of Chicago Press, 1964, pp. 141-145.

[25]Set this company's real interaction situations in government, hospital, restaurant, university, or any other organization, with the different argot, job titles, and structures. Situations will thus be familiar to *Ss,* but not identifiable, and they will be real.

sketchy so that *Ss* will have to project much of their own frame of reference into them. The CA usually discovers a considerable number of Ss who are unable to define company policy while in this phase. Frequently, during a discussion of a case, *Ss* can be asked to act out what they are saying. The other roles required can best be acted out by the CA as he knows best how to structure the situation to get the desired result. Here is where *Ss* get the first glimmer of their interpersonal deficiencies in not being "socially sensitive and behaviorally flexible."[26] Note they experience it; they are not told or scolded.

Role Playing Techniques

Interaction situations, adapted in advance from real ones that took place in this company, and which are *loaded* with emotional elements, can be introduced. The two basic roles are *interviewer (Ier)* and *interviewee (Iee)*. The former is the important role. *Ier* should get minimal coaching and little time to prepare. Set the scene with him out of the room! The latter role requires a stooge, "programmed" to give the appropriate response (reward), only if the *Ier* shows facile interpersonal competence. Whenever the *Ier* deviates, the *Iee* does not give him any reward, in fact, he lies, crys, talks incessantly, yells, clams up, or usurps role of *Ier*. In other words, part of the learning comes from peers observing *Iers*, but this cannot happen unless the *Iee* is carefully coached. Experience seems to suggest that the *Iee* should: (a) be given his fact sheet several days in advance, at which time the mood should be established, so he will have time to study and think his part through; (b) be carefully coached again in front of the whole class before bringing the *Ier* in and setting him up.

It is extremely important that these role play situations are never allowed to be seen as a win/lose encounter. The point must be repeatedly stressed in giving pre role play instructions that these are only being done to provide a basis for discussion and it is to be expected that the *Ier* will have a tough time: the deck is stacked against him on purpose, and everyone must be allowed to see this as the coaching is done in front of them. Consider excerpts from consensus of S's after training: "since we believe no one's job, or income, is hanging on the outcome, since we learn our boss will not find out, and since we perceive it as a situation which appears far removed from our own job and company, we view this as a *safe environment.*"

In sum, opportunities for growth are provided *Ss* as: (a) *interviewers,* where they have an opportunity in this safe environment to test a variety of approaches to real situations encountered every day in their jobs; (b) *interviewees,* where they have a chance to experience such broad differences between autocratic, demanding, unsure, emphatic, risk taking, creative, open, and other types of bosses, and; (c) *observers,* where they have a chance to watch and analyze actual interactions between two people in a work oriented situation, and to speculate what they would do if it were their turn "on camera."

[26]Robert Tannenbaum. "Dealing with Ourselves before Dealing with Others," *Office Executive,* Vol. 32, No. 8, Aug., 1957, pp. 29-30.

Two Tape Recorders

One tape recorder is used only during role playing, discussions of cases, or mock conferences. It provides for instant playback that allows diagnosis, analysis, and prescription of alternative courses of action while it is still fresh in *Ss* minds. The second runs continuously each session so everything is captured for later review. It is very important to re-record[27] tapes in such a way as to render all voices unrecognizable though understandable. *Ss* are then free to borrow them to play again so as to heighten learning through recall. This can be more conducive to learning than some of real life. For the most part a real encounter is over before one has time to gather his wits about him. There is no way to bring the episode back to see it as it really happened. Either one is left to walk away muttering when he said you're fired, I should have said you can't fire me, I quit, or, as it becomes ancient history most of us embellish our performance until at long last we distinctly remember how we put him in his place so he'll never forget it.

The advantage offered by simulation exercises is that anyone may bring up any number of ideas that might have worked, and they can be acted out and replayed on the spot, and later, for comparison with former tactics. Now all this amounts to is trial and error, but this is known to be a most effective way for learning complex behavioral skills and what effects they have on others.

Preserving Anonymity

To assure *Ss* that their behavior will not become known to their superiors, fish, bird, and animal names can be affixed to name tags and distributed to each *S* at the opening session. Between using names no way connectable to the *S,* and re-recording tapes so no one connected with the firm ever hears the originals, *Ss* believe they are protected. The CA also establishes from the outset, however, that he owns the tapes, and in addition, demonstrates how a re-recorded tape sounds.

Implementation: Stage One—Perception

The initial step, after warmup, is to cause each *S* to recognize that what he sees is not simply "what is," but is rather, a product of what is in his brain acting upon a picture received from his eyes. In short, the mind sees; the eyes only send information to the brain for interpretation. Each one's brain, in turn, is conditioned by all of one's socio-politico-psychological-economic environment and experience.

[27]This involves transferring the recorded material from one recorder to dictating equipment at a "slightly different speed," and then, at another speed, transferring it onto yet another tape recorder.

To insure that this message breaks through their attitudinal sound barrier, several different illusory devices can be introduced.[28] The CA has used a stencil cutout of the letters SLY in capitals on a full sheet of white paper, in white. Managerial *Ss* have been 96% (289/300) unable to "see" the letters because they said, "they assumed that they were looking at dark letters on a light background," which (based upon a lifetime of experience) they expected.[29] When told the background is dark, the letters light, their eyes refocus and they report "seeing it" at once. Another strong eye opener is Leavitt's picture of the two women.[30] These, and a myriad of others, all serve another purpose (tension relaxer) too.

While the majority will claim they "see it" right away, someone always admits he doesn't make anything out. This triggers hurried glances and furtive whispers. Then *Ss* begin to buzz and openly show each other what they see. Many, who claimed at first to "see it" can clearly be heard on the tape, later, saying such things as:

> *Oh! Now I see it. Well I'll be. Ha Ha! Clever? Hmmm! Ha! Ho! Huh!*
> *Isn't that the darndest thing? My God I felt my eyeballs snap when you*
> *pointed it out for me. I really couldn't see it. I don't see it yet! Show me.*

Experience has shown the impact of this is tremendous, and it should not be necessary to note the purpose is not to entertain, but to get a conceptual understanding of perception. It may be unorthodox, but it works. The first session starts with this because the balance of the material draws upon it, and only because it leads off is there such a strong overtone of hokum.

Frame of Reference

This concept is presented in the form of a paper and pencil exercise. It grows quite naturally out of perception. *Ss* are given two tasks: (a) make a 6 from IX by adding only one more line; (b) using no more than four lines, connect three rows of three dots. Despite the care that is taken *not* to convey a frame of reference, *Ss* indicate later they felt as if they *had to* stick with what they perceived as a given frame of reference. They say, IX, like a Roman Numeral, seems to call for a straight line; the nine dots appear as a square, and suggest no line should be drawn outside of it. Since the *IX* can *only* be made into a 6 by adding a crooked line (SIX), and you must go outside of the dots to connect them, only slightly over 4 per cent ever accomplish the task.[31]

[28] Cf., Berelson & Steiner, op. cit., pp. 87-131; R. L. Gregory, *Eye and Brain,* London: World University Library, 1966; S. Tolansky, *Optical Illusions,* London: Pergamon Press, 1966.

[29] No significant difference is found with 877 graduate and undergraduate students who have been confronted with this.

[30] Harold J. Leavitt, op. cit., p. 29.

[31] Of over 500 management *Ss* given this exercise, 455 tried to stay within the (perceived) box, and 435 have tried to stick with a straight line. Of these, 325 and 313

To repeat, the purpose of such exercises is to send a concrete message about perception and frame of reference which can be reintroduced whenever appropriate. The CA needs only make a comment such as:

> *Remember, some people just cannot see that old woman . . . you are searching within those nine dots for a solution again, or, trying to get (SIX) the hard way? . . .*

and the *S* will smile or chuckle as he recalls how he handled the exercise or (as sometimes happens) how he didn't "see" SLY for over two weeks. Of prime importance, though, he will remember the message about perception.

> *What a set of words, or a particular action, means to you or me depends upon our "frame of reference." That is, if my way of thinking or looking at things is different from yours, I will get a different meaning from the same communication . . . . To develop a* common understanding, *it would be* necessary *for at least* one *of this pair to* learn the other's . . . *way of looking at things.*[32] (my italics)

Time can be spent having *Ss* practice on three or four line "caselets"[33] where they can learn either to: (a) get into the other fellow's frame of reference; (b) get him to join theirs, or; (c) both move to some neutral ground. At this stage the first one is definitely encouraged.

The Plurality of Self

A matrix may be drawn for the alternates of our "self."[34] This one introduces *Ss* to at least four possibilities. Self A is known to me and everyone else (I wear glasses). Self B is known to me but not to others (I abhor both art and opera, but pretend to care when a colleague treats me by letting me see or hear his favorites). Self C is unknown to me yet everyone coming in close face-to-face

TABLE 1
Four Alternates of "Self"

	Known to Others	Unknown to Others
Known to Me	Self A	Self B
Unknown to Me	Self C	Self D

respectively, expressed some feeling that I had cheated when I went outside the box and wrote SIX.

[32] Adapted from Lester Tarnopol. "Attitudes Block Communications," *Personnel Journal,* Vol. 37, No. 9, Feb. 1959, pp. 325-328.

[33] Cf., Strauss and Sayles, op. cit., pp. 234-235, for examples.

[34] This model utilizes the concept of the *Jo-Hari Window* attributable to Joseph Luft (Jo) and Harrington Ingham (Hari). See "Healthy Interactions a Composite Clinical Picture," *Journal of General Psychology,* Vol. 57, 1957, pp. 241-246; also, *Journal of Social Psychology,* Vol. 39, 1954, pp. 293-297.

contact with me knows and conceals from me that (I have bad breath). Self D is unknown to me and all others too. (How many times have we said, I was shocked or I had no idea X was like that? Well, remember, X had no idea he was like that either, because had he only realized it, he could have sought help.)

Since the focus of this change program will be on Self B and C, some technique has to be devised to cause each S to examine his own carefully, without being allowed to become unduly frightened at such an early stage. One technique the CA often uses involves the introduction (via a story) of a friend who really exists. He can become a sort of surrogate: effective for introducing ideas.[35]

The story notes this friend always has the Ss he trains "write out one or two things about their Self B on a piece of paper, anonymously, and give it to him." At this point, instead of telling what the friend learns, CA writes the results on a sheet of paper which he folds, and gives to a high status S to hold. "To better demonstrate," CA then asks each S to do what the friend's Ss do. Papers are gathered and read aloud without comment. The S, holding what the CA had written, is now asked to read it aloud. The CA wrote, "over 60% usually indicate in one way or another that they have a feeling of insecurity or inadequacy."[36]

The point almost makes itself: most managerial groups, no matter how high the level, will respond in a similar manner. CA can now ask Ss to "look around the room at your peers."

> Do you realize that over two out of three of your peers in this room feel this way, and admit it? Perhaps more secretly feel this way! This is true all the way up in your firm. Imagine the improved atmosphere if you all started leveling with each other when you are unsure, instead of bluffing, blustering, and trying to conceal your uncertainty.

In this spot lecture, CA can also restate the prime objectives are to: (a) give each one the opportunity to openly admit we do not always have answers; (b) provide the time and a place to seek to find answers; (c) experiment with being open, giving and getting descriptive nonevaluative feedback, taking risks, and; (d) to do this with confidence because there is no longer a need to be afraid of being punished, ridiculed, or found out for doing so. The CA always has talked openly of his uncertain self at this moment, too.

Illustrating the Importance of Feedback

Have Ss select one S who is good with technical material (engineer) to help in a demonstration. Seated at the front of the room, with his back to the group,

[35]Note, for best results, keep their attention on the friend and his technique, like you are letting them in on something confidential.

[36]CA has utilized this approach with 178 Ss in management training and development, or change, programs for presidents, functional staff experts, top line managers, and foremen of well-known, and obscure, profitable, and unprofitable, firms. Over two out of every three Ss have voiced similar feeling no matter which level they represent! Ronald Lippitt, "The Collusion of Ignorance," *Trans-action*, Vol. 1, No. 2, Jan., 1964, offers a fine discussion

and given a sheet with a number of like geometric objects arranged in a specific spatial way,[37] S is asked to describe (with no verbal or visual clues from other Ss) what he sees while they try to create an exact replica. The results are anything but a duplication of what he sees. This is repeated with a second S who is allowed to face Ss and receive yes or no responses, only, from them. These copies will be better. Finally, a tnird S repeats this but he is allowed complete freedom, visually and verbally, to interact. Now practically all Ss are able to draw a facsimile of the original. Important points about feedback can be stressed.

Communication often is *much* faster if feedback is eliminated, but it is *much* more effective in obtaining superior performance, even if *much* slower, when feedback is allowed.

Improving Communication: Stage Two

Far more is meant by improving communication than just writing clear memos. Managers must master oral communication. They need to know, in addition to how to communicate, what, where, when, why, and to whom!

When to Communicate and Why

The transition can be smooth. What happens as a result of poor, or no, exchanges of verbal and visual information has already been demonstrated. The use of a before and after type of approach (similar to the two-part "Case of the Extra Half Plum"),[38] in which Ss hear carefully staged prerecordings of what is *bad*, then *good*, nondirective interviewing technique, paves the way for discussing the whole matter of communication.

How to Communicate

The natural breaks between class sessions must be utilized to assign outside readings. By the time they reach this point, Ss need to feel at home with several concepts including: "active listening,"[39] "empathy,"[40] "defensive communication,"[41] "masterminding,"[42] "premature judgment,"[43] and "probe,"[44] to

---

which suggests that people do not realize how others feel and are afraid or ashamed to admit how they feel. This is exactly what this CA has found.

[37]Harold J. Leavitt, op. cit., pp. 141-145.

[38]Cited in Strauss and Sayles, op. cit., pp. 235-237 and attendant answer book.

[39]Carl B. Rogers and Richard E. Farson, "Active Listening," in Bergen and Haney (eds.), *Organizational Relations and Management Action,* McGraw-Hill, 1966, pp. 61-76.

[40]Robert N. McMurry. "Empathy: Management's Greatest Need," *Advanced Management,* Vol. 18, No. 7, July, 1953, pp. 6-11, 34.

[41]Jack R. Gibb. "Defensive Communication," *Journal of Communication,* Vol. XI, No. 3, Sep., 1961, pp. 141-148.

name but a few.[45] Since they do read about them out of class, too, considerable time can be spent in class to allow them to *own* these concepts. Exercises, spot lectures, case problems, role playing, and reports of findings from additional research will all assist in this undertaking, and much can be accomplished with anecdotal material also.

To Whom to Communicate, What, and Where

A never ending source of amazement is how much less common agreement is found among supervision as to where they are supposed to go to provide information, what to tell, and to whom to tell it, than textbooks, based on the idea of a rational man, would have us believe. Most Ss really do believe they know, until they are confronted with specific situations. A recent change program uncovered a company's Table of Organization (report to, structure) set up in such a manner that when certain types of communication were issued through the normal distribution system, seven second level supervisors, with 30% of the work force reporting to them, would not hear of the order and thus could not pass it on.

It is vitally necessary, therefore, to allow Ss time to work out and understand the formal channels of communication: what do they say, and where do they say it, to tell whom: (a) there is a shortage of a scarce material? (b) you are unable to meet specifications? (c) of an easier way to do something? (d) about an employee with halitosis? (e) of a personal problem adversely affecting your work? (f) that hot order the president said must go out today isn't going? Role playing is invaluable for this, and so is the mock conference designed to allow practice in conducting an effective conference. Ss actually decide the answers while using these problems only to practice learning how to decide.

A Final Word about Role Playing

Despite the protestations of many that role playing is little more than a game, or, just isn't real life, the evidence (this CA finds) is quite the opposite.[46]

---

[42]Strauss and Sayles; op. cit., p. 233.

[43]Ibid., p. 232.

[44]Robert L. Kahn and Charles F. Cannell. *The Dynamics of Interviewing,* Wiley, 1957, pp. 203-232.

[45]Other readings include Carl Rogers and F. J. Roethlisberger, "Barriers and Gateways to Communication," *Harvard Business Review,* Vol. 30, No. 4, July, 1952, pp. 46-52; Robert Tannenbaum, op. cit., pp. 29-30; Solomon E. Asch, "Opinions and Social Pressure, *Scientific American,* Nov., 1955, pp. 31-34, and; Richard S. Crutchfield, "Conformity and Character," *American Psychologist,* Vol. X, 1955, pp. 191-198.

[46]As Herbert C. Kelman, "Deception in Social Research," *Trans-action,* Vol. 3, No. 5, Jul.-Aug., 1966, p. 24, says: "In general the results of role-playing experiments have been very encouraging."

Granted there is a brief moment of self-consciousness when Ss show off or laugh nervously. Some even try a finesse, asking much like the method actor might, about the motivation of the part.

Handle this, however, and they will throw themselves into their part so completely that they lose their inhibitions and assume their real life identity. That is, as they begin to dig in, they get anxious to show how well they can do, and they pull out all the stops. This means they handle interviewees in the normal manner including browbeating, pleading, yelling, or passing the buck. Whether 1,9; 1,1; 5,5; 9,1; or 9,9 managers, this is where they will drop the facade and show their true colors.[47]

A vice president, while playing the role of a production foreman, was trying to get an employee (actually his own boss) to work overtime on Saturday. The employee, coached not to agree for Saturday, but to jump at Friday night or Sunday, provided the interviewer (using the proper tools supposedly learned) listened, showed he understood, and offered the alternatives himself. Interviewee was not to volunteer, hint, or make it easy. After one of the worst exhibitions of authoritarian pressure possible, including masterminding, arguing, and thinly veiled threats, with no attention to the employee or any alternate solution, the VP lost control. He became red-faced, began screaming and pounding on the table, and finally fired the employee in a tirade

> *I'm not mad. I never get mad (louder). You wait, I.ll fix it so you never get another day's work, damn it! I tried to be fair about this, see both sides, can't you see my point of view? We both have a job to do. I'm doing mine; you have to do yours tomorrow. That's an order! You say you won't? Alright, you're fired!*

Conclusion

This has been a description in some detail of a program the CA has used on a number of occasions. It will help improve the interpersonal competence of a corporation's managers. The design is intended specifically to do this while also being attentive to certain reservations expressed in some quarters about the T-group approach. It must be noted:

1. It will not help unless properly introduced from the top down, through all levels at once, with a simultaneous, but gradual, change in both pay-off structure and organizational climate.
2. It will not help everyone. Some will feel threatened. Some will consider quitting.
3. It should not be used until, and unless, top management is ready to

---

[47] These managerial styles are fully developed in R. R. Blake and J. S. Mouton, *The Managerial Grid,* Gulf Publishing Co., 1964, especially pp. 18-211.

accept open, risk taking, creative, emphatic behavior on the part of subordinates and to act in a similar manner toward them.

Assuming these essentials are understood, and acceptable, however, this program will do the job. Behavior can be, and has been, changed by the technique called *simulation.* [48]

[48] Alton C. Bartlett, op. cit.

Management Development as a Process of Influence

This article is one of the more widely read pieces in the area of organizational change. In it, Edgar Schein presents a concise discussion of the prerequisites to positive and lasting behavior change and an introduction to Kurt Lewin's famous three-step influence model of unfreezing, change, refreezing. The model's applicability is illustrated by a series of examples in both business and non-business settings. Regarding the use of this model in business organizations, Schein convincingly argues that the influence process, as opposed to traditional management development programs (seminars, workshops, conferences, special projects, and so forth), is a far more effective method for changing employee attitudes in a meaningful way.

MANAGEMENT DEVELOPMENT AS A PROCESS OF INFLUENCE[1]

Edgar H. Schein
Massachusetts Institute of Technology

The continuing rash of articles on the subject of developing better managers suggests, on the one hand, a continuing concern that existing methods are not providing the talent which is needed at the higher levels of industry and, on the other hand, that we continue to lack clear-cut formulations about the process by which such development occurs. We need more and better managers and we need more and better theories of how to get them.

In the present paper I would like to cast management development as the problem of how an organization can influence the beliefs, attitudes, and values (hereafter simply called attitudes) of an individual for the purpose of "developing" him, i.e. changing him in a direction which the organization regards to be in his own and the organization's best interests. Most of the existing conceptions of the development of human resources are built upon assumptions of how people learn and grow, and some of the more strikingly contrasting theories of management development derive from disagreements about such assumptions.[2] I

Reprinted from "Management Development As a Process of Influence," by Edgar H. Schein. Used by permission of the *Industrial Management Review* of M.I.T., Vol. 2, No. 2, (May 1961).

[1]I am greatly indebted to Warren Bennis and Douglas McGregor, whose helpful comments on the first draft of this paper have helped me to refine many of the ideas in it.

[2]An excellent discussion of two contrasting approaches—the engineering vs. the agricultural—deriving from contrasting assumptions about human behavior can be found in McGregor, 1960, Chapter 14.

will attempt to build on a different base: instead of starting with assumptions about learning and growth, I will start with some assumptions from the social psychology of influence and attitude change.

Building on this base can be justified quite readily if we consider that adequate managerial performance at the higher levels is at least as much a matter of attitudes as it is a matter of knowledge and specific skills, and that the acquisition of such knowledge and skills is itself in part a function of attitudes. Yet we have given far more attention to the psychology which underlies change in the area of knowledge and abilities than we have to the psychology which underlies change in attitudes. We have surprisingly few studies of how a person develops loyalty to a company, commitment to a job, or a professional attitude toward the managerial role; how he comes to have the motives and attitudes which make possible the rendering of decisions concerning large quantities of money, materials, and human resources; how he develops attitudes toward himself, his co-workers, his employees, his customers, and society in general which give us confidence that he has a sense of responsibility and a set of ethics consistent with his responsible position, or at least which permit us to understand his behavior.

It is clear that management is becoming increasingly professionalized, as evidenced by increasing emphasis on undergraduate and graduate education in the field of management. But professionalization is not only a matter of teaching candidates increasing amounts about a set of relevant subjects and disciplines; it is equally a problem of preparing the candidate for a role which requires a certain set of attitudes. Studies of the medical profession (Merton, Reader, and Kendall, 1957), for example, have turned their attention increasingly to the unravelling of the difficult problem of how the medical student acquires those attitudes and values which enable him to make responsible decisions involving the lives of other people. Similar studies in other professions are sorely needed. When these are undertaken, it is likely to be discovered that much of the training of such attitudes is carried out implicitly and without a clearly formulated rationale. Law school and medical schools provide various kinds of experiences which insure that the graduate is prepared to fulfill his professional role. Similarly, existing approaches to the development of managers probably provide ample opportunities for the manager to learn the attitudes he will need to fulfill high level jobs. But in this field, particularly, one gets the impression that such opportunities are more the result of intuition or chance than of clearly formulated policies. This is partly because the essential or pivotal aspects of the managerial role have not as yet been clearly delineated, leaving ambiguous both the area of knowledge to be mastered and the attitude to be acquired.

Existing practice in the field of management development involves activities such as: indoctrination and training programs conducted at various points in the manager's career; systematic job rotation involving changes both in the nature of the functions performed (e.g. moving from production into sales), in physical location, and in the individual's superiors; performance appraisal programs including various amounts of testing, general personality assessment, and counseling both within the organization and through the use of outside consultants; apprenticeships, systematic coaching, junior management boards, and special projects to facilitate practice by the young manager in functions he will have to perform later in his career; sponsorship and other comparable activities in which a select group of young managers is groomed systematically for high level jobs (i.e. made into "crown princes"); participation in special conferences and training programs, including professional association meetings, human relations workshops, advanced management programs conducted in business schools or by professional associations like the American Management Association, regular academic courses like the Sloan programs offered at Stanford and MIT, or liberal arts courses like those offered at the University of Pennsylvania, Dartmouth, Northwestern, etc. These and many other specific educational devices, along with elaborate schemes of selection, appraisal, and placement, form the basic paraphernalia of management development.

Most of the methods mentioned above stem from the basic conception that it is the responsibility of the business enterprise, as an institution, to define what kind of behavior and attitude change is to take place and to construct mechanisms by which such change is to occur. Decisions about the kind of activity which might be appropriate for a given manager are usually made by others above him or by specialists hired to make such decisions. Where he is to be rotated, how long he is to remain on a given assignment, or what kind of new training he should undertake, is masterminded by others whose concern is "career development." In a sense, the individual stands alone against the institution where his own career is concerned, because the basic assumption is that the institution knows better than the individual what kind of man it needs or wants in its higher levels of management. The kind of influence model which is relevant, then, is one which considers the whole range of resources available to an organization.

In the remainder of this paper I will attempt to spell out these general themes by first presenting a conceptual model for analyzing influence, then providing some illustrations from a variety of organizational influence situations, and then testing its applicability to the management development situation.

A Model of Influence and Change

Most theories of influence or change accept the premise that change does not occur unless the individual is *motivated* and *ready* to change. This statement implies that the individual must perceive some need for change in himself, must be able to change, and must perceive the influencing agent as one who can facilitate such change in a direction acceptable to the individual. A model of the influence process, then, must account for the development of the motivation to change as well as the actual mechanisms by which the change occurs.

It is usually assumed that pointing out to a person some of his areas of deficiency, or some failure on his part in these areas, is sufficient to induce in him a readiness to change and to accept the influencing agent's guidance or recommendations. This assumption may be tenable if one is dealing with deficiencies in intellectual skills or technical knowledge. The young manager can see, with some help from his superiors, that he needs a greater knowledge of economics, or marketing, or production methods, and can accept the suggestion that spending a year in another department or six weeks at an advanced management course will give him the missing knowledge and/or skills.

However, when we are dealing with attitudes, the suggestion of deficiency or the need for change is much more likely to be perceived as a basic threat to the individual's sense of identity and to his status position vis-à-vis others in the organization. Attitudes are generally organized and integrated around the person's image of himself, and they result in stabilized, characteristic ways of dealing with others. The suggestion of the need for change not only implies some criticsm of the person's image of himself, but also threatens the stability of his working relationships because change at this level implies that the expectations which others have about him will be upset, thus requiring the development of new relationships. It is not at all uncommon for training programs in human relations to arouse resistance or to produce, at best, temporary change because the expectations of co-workers operate to keep the individual in his "normal" mold. Management development programs which ignore these psychological resistances to change are likely to be self-defeating, no matter how much attention is given to the actual presentation of the new desired attitudes.

Given these general assumptions about the integration of attitudes in the person, it is appropriate to consider influence as a process which occurs over time and which includes three phases:

(1) *Unfreezing:*[3] an alteration of the forces acting on the individual, such that his stable equilibrium is disturbed sufficiently to motivate him and to make him ready to change; this can be accomplished either by increasing the pressure to change or by reducing some of the threats or resistances to change.

(2) *Changing:* the presentation of a direction of change and the actual process of learning new attitudes. This process occurs basically by one of two mechanisms: (a) *identification*[4]—the person learns new attitudes by identifying with and emulating some other person who holds those attitudes; or (b) *internationalization*—the person learns new attitudes by being placed in a situation where new attitudes are demanded of him as a way of solving problems which confront him and which he cannot avoid; he discovers the new attitudes essentially for himself, though the situation may guide him or make it probable that he will discover only those attitudes which the influencing agent wishes him to discover.

(3) *Refreezing:* the integration of the changed attitudes into the rest of the personality and/or into ongoing significant emotional relationships.

In proposing this kind of model of influence we are leaving out two important cases—the individual who changes because he is *forced* to change by the

[3]These phases of influence are a derivation of the change model developed by Lewin (1947).

[4]These mechanisms of attitude change are taken from Kelman (1958).

agent's direct manipulation of rewards and punishments (what Kelman calls "compliance") and the individual whose strong motivation to rise in the organizational hierarchy makes him eager to accept the attitudes and acquire the skills which he perceives to be necessary for advancement. I will ignore both of these cases for the same reason—they usually do not involve genuine, stable change, but merely involve the adoption of overt behaviors which imply to others that attitudes have changed, even if they have not. In the case of compliance, the individual drops the overt behavior as soon as surveillance by the influence agent is removed. Among the upwardly mobile individuals, there are those who are willing to be unfrozen and to undergo genuine attitude change (whose case fits the model to be presented below) and those whose overt behavior change is dictated by their changing perception of what the environment will reward, but whose underlying attitudes are never really changed or refrozen.

I do not wish to imply that a general reward-punishment model is incorrect or inappropriate for the analysis of attitude change. My purpose, rather, is to provide a more refined model in terms of which it becomes possible to specify the differential effects of various kinds of rewards and punishments, some of which have far more significance and impact than others. For example, as I will try to show, the rewarding effect of approval from an admired person is very different in its ultimate consequences from the rewarding effect of developing a personal solution to a difficult situation.

The processes of unfreezing, changing, and refreezing can be identified in a variety of different institutions in which they are manifested in varying degrees of intensity. The content of what may be taught in the influence process may vary widely from the values of Communism to the religious doctrines of a nun, and the process of influence may vary drastically in its intensity. Nevertheless there is value in taking as our frame of reference a model like that proposed and testing its utility in a variety of different organizational contexts, ranging from Communist "thought reform" centers to business enterprises' management development programs. Because the value system of the business enterprise and its role conception of the manager are not as clear-cut as the values and role prescriptions in various other institutions, one may expect the processes of unfreezing, changing, and refreezing to occur with less intensity and to be less consciously rationalized in the business enterprise. But they are structurally the same as in other organizations, One of the main purposes of this paper, then, will be to try to make salient some features of the influence of the organization on the attitudes of the individual manager by attempting to compare institutions in which the influence process is more drastic and explicit with the more implicit and less drastic methods of the business enterprise.

Illustrations of Organizational Influence

Unfreezing

The concept of unfreezing and the variety of methods by which influence targets can be unfrozen can best be illustrated by considering examples drawn from a broad range of situations. The Chinese Communists in their attempt to inculcate Communist attitudes into their youth or into their prisoners serve as a good prototype of one extreme. First and most important was the removal of the target person from those situations and social relationships which tended to confirm and reinforce the validity of the old attitudes. Thus the targets, be they political prisoners, prisoners of war, university professors, or young students, were isolated from their friends, families, and accustomed work groups and cut off from all media of communication to which they were accustomed. In addition, they were subjected to continuous exhortations (backed by threats of severe punishment) to confess their crimes and adopt new attitudes, and were constantly humiliated in order to discredit their old sense of identity.

The isolation of the target from his normal social and ideological supports reached its height in the case of Western civilians who were placed into group cells with a number of Chinese prisoners who had already confessed and were committed to reforming themselves and their lone Western cell mate. In the prisoner of war camps such extreme social isolation could not be produced, but its counterpart was created by the fomenting of mutual mistrust among the prisoners, by cutting off any supportive mail from home, and by systematically disorganizing the formal and informal social structure of the POW camp (by segregation of officers and non-commissioned officers from the remainder of the group, by the systematic removal of informal leaders or key personalities, and by the prohibition of any group activity not in line with the indoctrination program) (Schein, 1960, 1961).

The Chinese did not hesitate to use physical brutality and threats of death and/or permanent non-repatriation to enforce the view that only by collaboration and attitude change could the prisoner hope to survive physically and psychologically. In the case of the civilians in group cells, an additional and greater stress was represented by the social pressure of the cell mates who would harangue, insult, revile, humiliate, and plead with the resistant Westerner twenty-four hours a day for weeks or months on end, exhorting him to admit his guilt, confess his crimes, reform, and adopt Communist values. This combination of physical and social pressures is perhaps a prototype of the use of coercion in the service of unfreezing a target individual in attitude areas to which he is strongly committed.

A somewhat milder, though structurally similar, process can be observed in the training of a nun (Hulme, 1956). The novice enters the convent voluntarily and is presumably ready to change, but the kind of change which must be accomplished encounters strong psychological resistances because, again, it involves deeply held attitudes and habits. Thus the novice must learn to be completely unselfish and, in fact, selfless; she must adapt to a completely communal life; she must give up any source of authority except the absolute authority of God and of those senior to her in the convent; and she must learn to curb her sexual and aggressive impulses. How does the routine of the convent facilitate unfreezing? Again a key element is the removal of the novice from her accustomed routines, sources of confirmation, social supports, and old relationships. She is physically isolated from the outside world, surrounded by others who are undergoing the same training as she, subjected to a highly demanding and fatiguing physical regimen, constantly exhorted toward her new role and punished for any evidence of old behaviors and attitudes, and subjected to a whole range of social pressures ranging from mild disapproval to total humiliation for any failure.

Not only is the novice cut off from her old social identity, but her entry into the convent separates her from many aspects of her physical identity. She is deprived of all means of being beautiful or even feminine; her hair is cut off and she is given institutional garb which emphasizes formlessness and sameness; she loses her old name and chronological age in favor of a new name and age corresponding to length of time in the convent; her living quarters and daily routine emphasize an absolute minimum of physical comfort and signify a total devaluation of anything related to the body. At the same time the threat associated with change is minimized by the tremendous support which the convent offers for change and by the fact that everyone else either already exhibits the appropriate attitudes or is in the process of learning them.

If we look at the process by which a pledge comes to be a full-fledged member of a fraternity, we find in this situation also a set of pressures to give up old associations and habits, a devaluation of the old self by humiliations ranging from menial, senseless jobs to paddling and hazing, a removal of threat through sharing of training, and support for good performance in the pledge role. The evangelist seeking to convert those who come to hear him attempts to unfreeze his audience by stimulating guilt and by devaluating their former selves as sinful and unworthy. The teacher wishing to induce motivation to learn sometimes points out the deficiencies in the student's knowledge and hopes at the same time to induce some guilt for having those deficiencies.

Some of the elements which all unfreezing situations have in common are the following: (1) the physical removal of the influence target from his accustomed routines, sources of information, and social relationships; (2) the undermining and destruction of all social supports; (3) demeaning and humiliating experience to help the target see his old self as unworthy and thus to become motivated to change; (4) the consistent linking of reward with willingness to change and of punishment with unwillingness to change.

Changing

Once the target has become motivated to change, the actual influence is most likely to occur by one of two processes. The target finds one or more models in his social environment and learns new attitudes by identifying with them and trying to become like them; or the target confronts new situations with an experimental attitude and develops for himself attitudes which are appropriate to the situation and which remove whatever problem he faces. These two processes—*identification* and *internalization*—probably tend to occur together in most concrete situations, but it is worthwhile, for analytical purposes, to keep them separate.[5]

---

[5]Both are facilitated greatly if the influence agent saturates the environment with the new message or attitude to be learned.

The student or prisoner of the Chinese Communists took his basic step toward acquiring Communist attitudes when he began to identify with his more advanced fellow student or prisoner. In the group cell it was the discovery by the Western prisoner that his Chinese cell mates were humans like himself, were rational, and yet completely believed in their own and his guilt, which forced him to re-examine his own premises and bases of judgment and led him the first step down the path of acquiring the Communist point of view. In other words, he began to identify with his cell mates and to acquire their point of view as the only solution to getting out of prison and reducing the pressure on him. The environment was, of course, saturated with the Communist point of view, but it is significant that such saturation by itself was not sufficient to induce genuine attitude change. The prisoner kept in isolation and bombarded with propaganda was less likely to acquire Communist attitudes than the one placed into a group cell with more reformed prisoners. Having a personal model was apparently crucial.

In the convent the situation is essentially comparable except that the novice is initially much more disposed toward identifying with older nuns and has a model of appropriate behavior around her all the time in the actions of the others. It is interesting to note also that some nuns are singled out as particularly qualified models and given the appropriate name of "the living rule." It is also a common institution in initiation or indoctrination procedures to attach to the target individual someone who is labelled a "buddy" or "big brother," whose responsibility it is to teach the novice "the ropes" and to communicate the kinds of attitudes expected of him.

In most kinds of training and teaching situations, and even in the sales relationship, it is an acknowledged fact that the process is facilitated greatly if the target can identify with the influence agent. Such identification is facilitated if the social distance and rank difference between agent and target are not too great. The influence agent has to be close enough to the target to be seen as similar to the target, yet must be himself committed to the attitudes he is trying to inculcate. Thus, in the case of the Chinese Communist group cell, the cell mates could be perceived as sharing a common situation with the Western prisoner and this perception facilitated his identification with them. In most buddy systems, the buddy is someone who has himself gone through the training program in the recent past. If the target is likely to mistrust the influence attempts of the organization, as might be the case in a management-sponsored training program for labor or in a therapy program for delinquents in a reformatory, it is even more important that the influence agent be perceived as similar to the target. Otherwise he is dismissed as a "company man" or one who has already sold out, and hence is seen as someone whose message or example is not to be taken seriously.

Internalization, the discovery of attitudes which are the target's own solutions to his perceived dilemmas, can occur at the same time as identification. The individual can use the example of others to guide him in solving his own problems without necessarily identifying with them to the point of complete imitation. His choice of attitude remains ultimately his own in terms of what works for him, given the situation in which he finds himself. Internalization is only possible in an organizational context in which, from the organization's point of view, a number of different kinds of attitudes will be tolerated. If there is a "party line," a company philosophy, or a given way in which people have to feel about things in order to get along, it is hardly an efficient procedure to let trainees discover their own solutions. Manipulating the situation in such a way as to make the official solution the only one which is acceptable can, of course, be attempted, but the hazards of creating real resentment and alienation on the part of the individual when he discovers he really had no choice may outweigh the presumed advantages of letting him think he had a choice.

In the case of the Chinese Communists, the convent, the revival meeting, the fraternity, or the institutional training program, we are dealing with situations where the attitudes to be learned are clearly specified. In this kind of situation, internalization will not occur unless the attitudes to be learned happen to fit uniquely the kind of personal problem the individual has in the situation. For example, a few prisoners of the Communists reacted to the tremendous unfreezing pressures with genuine guilt when they discovered they held certain prejudices and attitudes (e.g. when they realized that they had looked down on lower class Chinese in spite of their manifest acceptance of them). These prisoners were then able to internalize certain portions of the total complex of Communist attitudes, particularly those dealing with unselfishness and working for the greater good of others. The attitudes which the institution demanded of them also solved a personal problem of long standing for them. In the case of the nun, one might hypothesize that internalization of the convent's attitudes will occur to the extent that asceticism offers a genuine solution to the incumbent's personal conflicts.

Internalization is a more common outcome in those influence settings where the direction of change is left more to the individual. The influence which occurs in programs like Alcoholics Anonymous, in psychotherapy or counseling for hospitalized or incarcerated populations, in religious retreats, in human relations training of the kind pursued by the National Training Laboratories (1953), and in certain kinds of progressive education programs is more likely to occur through internalization or, at least, to lead ultimately to more internalization.

Refreezing

Refreezing refers to the process by which the newly acquired attitude comes to be integrated into the target's personality and ongoing relationships. If the new attitude has been internalized while being learned, this has automatically facilitated refreezing because it has been fitted naturally into the individual's personality. If it has been learned through identification, it will persist only so long as the target's relationship with the original influence model persists unless new surrogate models are found or social support and reinforcement is obtained for expressions of the new attitude.[6]

---

[6]In either case the change may be essentially permanent, in that a relationship to a model

In the case of the convent such support comes from a whole set of expectations which others have of how the nun should behave, from clearly specified role prescriptions, and from rituals. In the case of individuals influenced by the Chinese Communists, if they remained in Communist China they received constant support for their new attitudes from superiors and peers; if they returned to the West, the permanence of their attitude change depended on the degree of support they actually received from friends and relations back home, or from groups which they sought out in an attempt to get support. If their friends and relatives did not support Communist attitudes, the repatriates were influenced once again toward their original attitudes or toward some new integration of both sets.

The importance of social support for new attitudes was demonstrated dramatically in the recent Billy Graham crusade in New York City. An informal survey of individuals who came forward when Graham called for converts indicated that only those individuals who were subsequently integrated into local churches maintained their faith. Similar kinds of findings have been repeatedly noted with respect to human relations training in industry. Changes which may occur during the training program do not last unless there is some social support for the new attitudes in the "back home" situation.

The kind of model which has been discussed above might best be described by the term "coercive persuasion." The influence of an organization on an individual is coercive in the sense that he is usually forced into situations which are likely to unfreeze him, in which there are many overt and covert pressures to recognize in himself a need for change, and in which the supports for his old attitudes are in varying degrees coercively removed. It is coercive also to the degree that the new attitudes to be learned are relatively rigidly prescribed. The individual either learns them or leaves the organization (if he can). At the same time, the actual process by which new attitudes are learned can best be described as persuasion. In effect, the individual is forced into a situation in which he is likely to be influenced. The organization can be highly coercive in unfreezing its potential influence targets, yet be quite open about the direction of attitude change it will tolerate. In those cases where the direction of change is itself coerced (as contrasted with letting it occur through identification or internalization), it is highly unlikely that anything is accomplished other than surface behavioral change in the target. And such surface change will be abandoned the moment the coercive force of the change agent is lessened. If behavioral changes are coerced at the same time as other unfreezing operations are undertaken, actual influence can be facilitated if the individual finds himself having to learn attitudes to justify the kinds of behavior he has been forced to exhibit. The salesman may not have an attitude of cynicism toward his customers initially. If, however, he is forced by his boss to behave as if he felt cynical, he might develop real cynicism as a way of justifying his actual behavior.

---

or surrogate can last indefinitely. It is important to distinguish the two processes, however, because if one were to try to change the attitude, different strategies would be used depending upon how the attitude had been learned.

Management Development:
Is It Coercive Persuasion?

Do the notions of coercive persuasion developed above fit the management development situation? Does the extent to which they do or do not fit such a model illuminate for us some of the implications of specific management development practices?

Unfreezing

It is reasonable to assume that the majority of managers who are being "developed" are not ready or able to change in the manner in which their organization might desire and therefore must be unfrozen before they can be influenced. They may be eager to change at a conscious motivation level, yet still be psychologically unprepared to give up certain attitudes and values in favor of untried, threatening new ones. I cannot support this assumption empirically, but the likelihood of its being valid is high because of a related fact which is empirically supportable. Most managers do not participate heavily in decisions which affect their careers, nor do they have a large voice in the kind of self-development in which they wish to participate. Rather, it is the man's superior or a staff specialist in career development who makes the key decisions concerning his career (Alfred, 1960). If the individual manager is not trained from the outset to take responsibility for his own career and given a heavy voice in diagnosing his own needs for a change, it is unlikely that he will readily be able to appreciate someone else's diagnosis. It may be unclear to him what basically is wanted of him or, worse, the ambiguity of the demands put upon him combined with his own inability to control his career development is likely to arouse anxiety and insecurity which would cause even greater resistance to genuine self-assessment and attitude change.[7] He becomes preoccupied with promotion in the abstract and attempts to acquire at a surface level the traits which he thinks are necessary for advancement.

If the decisions made by the organization do not seem valid to the manager, or if the unfreezing process turns out to be quite painful to him, to what extent can he leave the situation? His future career, his financial security, and his social status within the business community all stand to suffer if he resists the decisions made for him. Perhaps the most coercive feature is simply the psychological pressure that what he is being asked to do is "for his own ultimate welfare." Elementary loyalty to his organization and to his managerial role demands that he accept with good grace whatever happens to him in the name of his own career development. In this sense, then, I believe that the business organization has coercive forces at its disposal which are used by it in a manner comparable to the uses made by other organizations.

---

[7] An even greater hazard, of course, is that the organization communicates to the manager that he is not expected to take responsibility for his own career at the same time that it is trying to teach him how to be able to take responsibility for important decisions!

Given the assumption that the manager who is to be developed needs to be unfrozen, and given that the organization has available coercive power to accomplish such unfreezing, what mechanisms does it actually use to unfreeze potential influence targets?

The essential elements of unfreezing are the removal of supports for the old attitudes, the saturation of the environment with the new attitudes to be acquired, a minimizing of threat, and a maximizing of support for any change in the right direction. In terms of this model it becomes immediately apparent that training programs or other activities which are conducted in the organization at the place of work for a certain number of hours per day or week are far less likely to unfreeze and subsequently influence the participant than those programs which remove him for varying lengths of time from his regular work situation and normal social relationships.

Are appraisal interviews, used periodicially to communicate to the manager his strengths, weaknesses and areas for improvement, likely to unfreeze him? Probably not, because as long as the individual is caught up in his regular routine and is responding, probably quite unconsciously, to a whole set of expectations which others have about his behavior and attitudes, it is virtually impossible for him to hear, at a psychological level, what his deficiencies or areas needing change are. Even if he can appreciate what is being communicated to him at an intellectual level, it is unlikely that he can emotionally accept the need for change, and even if he can accept it emotionally, it is unlikely that he can produce change in himself in an environment which supports all of his old ways of functioning. This statement does not mean that the man's co-workers necessarily approve of the way he is operating or like the attitudes which he is exhibiting. They may want to see him change, but their very expectations concerning how he normally behaves operate as a constraint on him which makes attitude change difficult in that setting.

On the other hand, there are a variety of training activities which are used in management development which approximate more closely the conditions necessary for effective unfreezing. These would include programs offered at special training centers such as those maintained by IBM on Long Island and General Electric at Crotonville, N. Y.; university-sponsored courses in management, liberal arts, and/or the social sciences; and especially, workshops or laboratories in human relations such as those conducted at Arden House, N. Y., by the National Training Laboratories. Programs such as these remove the participant for some length of time from his normal routine, his regular job, and his social relationships (including his family in most cases), thus providing a kind of moratorium during which he can take stock of himself and determine where he is going and where he wants to go.

The almost total isolation from the pressures of daily life in the business world which a mountain chateau such as Arden House provides for a two-week period is supplemented by other unfreezing forces. The de-emphasis on the kind of job or title the participant holds in his company and the informal dress remove some of the symbolic or status supports upon which we all rely. Sharing a room and bath facilities with a roommate requires more than the accustomed exposure of private spheres of life to others. The total involvement of the participant in the laboratory program leaves little room for reflection about the back home situation. The climate of the laboratory communicates tremendous support for any efforts at self-examination and attempts as much as possible to reduce the threats inherent in change by emphasizing the value of experimentation, the low cost and risk of trying a new response in the protected environment of the lab, and the high gains to be derived from finding new behavior patterns and attitudes which might improve back home performance. The content of the material presented in lectures and the kind of learning model which is used in the workshop facilitates self-examination, self-diagnosis based on usable feedback from other participants, and rational planning for change.[8]

The practice of rotating a manager from one kind of assignment to another over a period of years can have some of the same unfreezing effects and thus facilitate attitude change. Certainly his physical move from one setting to another removes many of the supports to his old attitudes, and in his new job the manager will have an opportunity to try new behaviors and become exposed to new attitudes. The practice of providing a moratorium in the form of a training program prior to assuming a new job would appear to maximize the gains from each approach, in that unfreezing would be maximally facilitated and change would most probably be lasting if the person did not go back to a situation in which his co-workers, superiors, and subordinates had stable expectations of how he should behave.

Another example of how unfreezing can be facilitated in the organizational context is the practice of temporarily reducing the formal rank and responsibilities of the manager by making him a trainee in a special program, or an apprentice on a special project, or an assistant to a high ranking member of the company. Such temporary lowering of formal rank can reduce the anxiety associated with changing and at the same time serves officially to destroy the old status and identity of the individual because he could not ordinarily return to his old position once he had accepted the path offered by the training program. He would have to move either up or out of the organization to maintain his sense of self-esteem. Of course, if such a training program is perceived by the trainee as an indication of his failing rather than a step toward a higher position, his anxiety about himself would be too high to facilitate effective change on his part. In all of the illustrations of organizational influence we have presented above, change was defined as being a means of gaining status—acceptance into Communist society, status as a nun or a fraternity brother, salvation, etc. If participants come to training programs believing they are being punished, they typically do not learn much.

The above discussion is intended to highlight the fact that some management development practices do facilitate the unfreezing of the influence target, but that such unfreezing is by no means automatic. Where programs fail, therefore, one of the first questions we must ask is whether they failed because they did not provide adequate conditions for unfreezing.

[8]Although, as I will point out later, such effective unfreezing may lead to change which is not supported or considered desirable by the "back home" organization.

Turning now to the problem of the mechanisms by which changes actually occur, we must confront the question of whether the organization has relatively rigid prescribed goals concerning the direction of attitude change it expects of the young manager, or whether it is concerned with growth in the sense of providing increasing opportunities for the young manager to learn the attitudes appropriate to even more challenging situations. It is undoubtedly true that most programs would claim growth as their goal, but the degree to which they accomplish it can only be assessed from an examination of their actual practice.

Basically the question is whether the organization influences attitudes primarily through the mechanism of identification or the mechanism of internalization. If the development programs stimulate psychological relationships between the influence target and a member of the organization who has the desired attitudes, they are thereby facilitating influence by identification but, at the same time, are limiting the alternatives available to the target and possibly the permanence of the change achieved. If they emphasize that the target must develop his own solutions to ever more demanding problems, they are risking that the attitudes learned will be incompatible with other parts of the organization's value system but are producing more permanent change because the solutions found are internalized. From the organization's point of view, therefore, it is crucial to know what kind of influence it is exerting and to assess the results of such influence in terms of the basic goals which the organization may have. If new approaches and new attitudes toward management problems are desired, for example, it is crucial that the conditions for internalization be created. If rapid learning of a given set of attitudes is desired, it is equally crucial that the conditions for identification with the right kind of models be created.

One obvious implication of this distinction is that programs conducted within the organization's orbit by its own influence agents are much more likely to facilitate identification and thereby the transmission of the "party line" or organization philosophy. On the other hand, programs like those conducted at universities or by the National Training Laboratories place much more emphasis on the finding of solutions by participants which fit their own particular needs and problems. The emphasis in the human relations courses is on "learning how to learn" from the participant's own interpersonal experiences and how to harness his emotional life and intellectual capacities to the accomplishment of his goals, rather than on specific principles of human relations. The nearest thing to an attitude which the laboratory staff, acting as influence agents, does care to communicate is an attitude of inquiry and experimentation, and to this end the learning of skills of observation, analysis, and diagnosis of interpersonal situations is given strong emphasis. The training group, which is the acknowledged core of the laboratory approach, provides its own unfreezing forces by being unstructured as to the content of discussion. But it is strongly committed to a method of learning by analysis of the member's own experiences in the group, which facilitates the discovery of the value of an attitude of inquiry and experimentation.

149

Mutual identification of the members of the group with each other and member identifications with the staff play some role in the acquisition of this attitude, but the basic power of the method is that the attitude of inquiry and experimentation *works* in the sense of providing for people valuable new insights about themselves, groups, and organizations. To the extent that it works and solves key problems for the participants, it is internalized and carried back into the home situation. To the extent that it is learned because participants wish to emulate a respected fellow member or staff member, it lasts only so long as the relationship with the model itself, or a surrogate of it, lasts (which may, of course, be a very long time).

The university program in management or liberal arts is more difficult to categorize in terms of an influence model, because within the program there are usually opportunities both for identification (e.g., with inspiring teachers) and internalization. It is a safe guess in either case, however, that the attitudes learned are likely to be in varying degrees out of phase with any given company's philosophy unless the company has learned from previous experience with a given course that the students are taught a point of view consistent with its own philosophy. Of course, universities, as much as laboratories, emphasize the value of a spirit of inquiry and, to the extent that they are successful in teaching this attitude, will be creating potential dissidents or innovators, depending on how the home company views the result.

Apprenticeships, special jobs in the role of "assistant to" somebody, job rotation, junior management boards, and so on stand in sharp contrast to the above methods in the degree to which they facilitate, indeed almost demand, that the young manager learn by watching those who are senior or more competent. It is probably not prescribed that in the process of acquiring knowledge and skills through the example of others he should also acquire their attitudes, but the probability that this will happen is very high if the trainee develops any degree of respect and liking for his teacher and/or supervisor. It makes little difference whether the teacher, coach, or supervisor intends to influence the attitudes of his trainee or not. If a good emotional relationship develops between them, it will facilitate the learning of knowledge and skills, and will, at the same time, result in some degree of attitude change. Consequently, such methods do not maximize the probability of new approaches being invented to management problems, nor do they really by themselves facilitate the growth of the manager in the sense of providing opportunities for him to develop solutions which fit his own needs best.

Job rotation, on the other hand, can facilitate growth and innovation provided it is managed in such a way as to insure the exposure of the trainee to a broad range of points of view as he moves from assignment to assignment. The practice of shifting the developing manager geographically as well as functionally both facilitates unfreezing and increases the likelihood of his being exposed to new attitudes. This same practice can, of course, be merely a convenient way of indoctrinating the individual by sending him on an assignment, for example, "in order to acquire the sales point of view from Jim down in New York," where higher management knows perfectly well what sort of a view Jim will communicate to his subordinates.

Refreezing

Finally, a few words are in order about the problem of refreezing. Under what conditions will changed attitudes remain stable, and how do existing practices aid or hinder such stabilization? Our illustrations from the non-industrial setting highlighted the importance of social support for any attitudes which were learned through identification. Even the kind of training emphasized in the National Training Laboratories programs, which tends to be more internalized, does not produce stable attitude change unless others in the organization, especially superiors, peers, and subordinates, have undergone similar changes and give each other stimulation and support, because lack of support acts as a new unfreezing force producing new influence (possibly in the direction of the original attitudes).

If the young manager has been influenced primarily in the direction of what is already the company philosophy, he will, of course, obtain strong support and will have little difficulty maintaining his new attitudes. If, on the other hand, management development is supposed to lead to personal growth and organizational innovation, the organization must recognize the reality that new attitudes cannot be carried by isolated individuals. The lament that we no longer have strong individualists who are willing to try something new is a fallacy based on an incorrect diagnosis. Strong individuals have always gained a certain amount of their strength from the support of others, hence the organizational problem is how to create conditions which make possible the nurturing of new ideas, attitudes, and approaches. If organizations seem to lack innovators, it may be that the climate of the organization and its methods of management development do not foster innovation, not that its human resources are inadequate.

An organizational climate in which new attitudes which differ from company philosophy can nevertheless be maintained cannot be achieved merely by an intellectual or even emotional commitment on the part of higher-ranking managers to tolerance of new ideas and attitudes. Genuine support can come only from others who have themselves been influenced, which argues strongly that at least several members of a given department must be given the same training before such training can be expected to have effect. If the superior of the people involved can participate in it as well, this strengthens the group that much more, but it would not follow from my line of reasoning that this is a necessary condition. Only some support is needed, and this support can come as well from peers and subordinates.

From this point of view, the practice of sending more than one manager to any given program at a university or human relations workshop is very sound. The National Training Laboratories have emphasized from the beginning the desirability of having organizations send teams. Some organizations like Esso

Standard have created their own laboratories for the training of the entire management complement of a given refinery, and all indications are that such a practice maximizes the possibility not only of the personal growth of the managers, but of the creative growth of the organization as a whole.

Conclusion

In the above discussion I have deliberately focused on a model of influence which emphasizes procedure rather than content, interpersonal relations rather than mass media, and attitudes and values rather than knowledge and skills. By placing management development into a context of institutional influence procedures which also include Chinese Communist thought reform, the training of a nun, and other more drastic forms of coercive persuasion, I have tried to highlight aspects of management development which have remained implicit yet which need to be understood. I believe that some aspects of management development are a mild form of coercive persuasion, but I do not believe that coercive persuasion is either morally bad in any *a priori* sense nor inefficient. If we are to develop a sound theory of career development which is capable of including not only many of the formal procedures discussed in this paper, but the multitudes of informal practices, some of which are more and some of which are less coercive than those discussed, we need to suspend moral judgments for the time being and evaluate influence models solely in terms of their capacity to make sense of the data and to make meaningful predictions.

References

Alfred, T. M. *Personal Communication,* 1960.

Hulme, K. *The Nun's Story.* Boston, Little, Brown, 1957.

Kelman, H. C. "Compliance, Identification, and Internalization: Three Processes of Attitude Change." *Conflict Resolution,* 1958, *2,* 51-60.

Lewin, K. "Frontiers in Group Dynamics: Concept, Method and Reality in Social Sceince." *Human Relations,* 1947, *I,* 5-42.

McGregor, D. *The Human Side of Enterprise.* New York, McGraw-Hill, 1960.

Merton, R. K., Reader, G. G., and Kendall, Patricia L. *The Student-Physician.* Cambridge, Mass., Harvard University Press, 1957.

National Training Laboratory in Group Development: *Explorations in Human Relations Training: An Assessment of Experience, 1947-1953.* Washington, D.C., National Educational Association, 1953.

Schein, E. H. *Brainwashing.* Cambridge, Mass., Center for International Studies, M.I.T., 1961.

Schein, E. H. "Interpersonal Communication, Group Solidarity, and Social Influence" *Sociometry,* 1960, *23,* 148-161.

Influence and
Organizational Change

There is a paucity of explicit models *pertaining to the process of organizational change. Although the model presented by Dalton in this reading is not an integrated one, it certainly does order one's thinking about the change process in general and also provides a solid base for further debate and research.*

Using data from five rather successful change programs and Kurt Lewin's three-step change model, Dalton details his sequential model for induced change. He notes that two conditions—tension within the system and intervention of a prestigious influencing agent—are important antecedents for the successful initiation of change.

Next, he elaborates the elements of his change model: (1) setting objectives (movements from general to specific goals); (2) altering social ties (breaking up old interaction patterns and forming new ones); (3) building-self-esteem (movement from low to high self-esteem); and (4) internalizing motives (external motive for change becomes internalized motive for change).

Dalton's paper concludes with a brief examination of the technical, moral, and social implication of the model.

INFLUENCE AND
ORGANIZATIONAL CHANGE

Gene W. Dalton
Harvard University

During the last few years a new term, Organizational Development, has been rapidly finding its way into the organization charts of American corporations. Because of the recency of this phenomenon it is sometimes difficult to ascertain the extent to which the activities carried out under this title are old activities being carried out under a new name or a new set of activities aimed at an old but increasingly urgent problem. But one fact does emerge: there is an increasing number of men in these organizations whose primary function is to foster change. This has always been part of the job of a manager and often a significant part, but now there is an increasing number of men in the organizations who are essentially specialists in the process of organizational change.

Almost inevitably, a part of the requirement of this new role will be an ability to be explicit about the change process itself, for the O.D. specialist will be an advisor and helper more often than an initiator. In this role of counselor, he will

Reprinted from *Organizational Behavior Models,* Comparative Administration Research Institute Series No. 2, copyright 1970 by the Bureau of Economic and Business Research, Kent State University. Reprinted by permission.

Professor Dalton's paper is published with the special permission of the Comparative Administration Research Institute (CARI), a research unit in the Center for Business and Economic Research at Kent State University. For CARI contributions in organizational change, interested readers should refer to the recent CARI volume titled *Functioning of Complex Organizations: Contextual, Environmental, and Socio-Cultural Explanations,* published by the Kent State University Press.

need a framework or model for both thinking and talking about the means by which individuals and groups are influenced to change their behavior in organizations. A model has a number of uses. It can help order the available data and clarify discussion. It can provide some much-needed categories so that similarities between similar acts can be highlighted. It can point out the multiple functions which some act performs without forcing us to talk about everything at once.

For several years my colleagues and I have been studying an organization in which a new director of a research and development center set out to change the behavior of a substantial number of managers and engineers. We observed his efforts over time and attempted to measure their effects. Over a period of a year and a half it became increasingly evident that he had been successful in influencing one part of the men but had had little effect on the others. This result both baffled and challenged us. In our attempt to understand the difference, we examined the studies we could find which described instances where someone had successfully influenced others to change their behavior. From the analysis of these studies and of our own data we constructed an elementary model of the influence process in organizational change. I am proposing that it may serve as a useful point of departure for those engaged in organizational development, as well as for those of us who study organizational life.

Organizational and Individual Change

First I should clarify what I mean by organizational change. As used here, the term refers to any significant alteration of the behavior patterns of a large part of the individuals who constitute that organization. I make a point of this because students of organizations, in their efforts to characterize an organization as a system or organism, too often lose sight of the fact that the "behavior" of an organization is made up of the actions and interactions of the individuals in it. We read so frequently about an organization "adapting" to market shifts, economic conditions, and scientific discoveries that we slide over the internal processes by which an organization does that adapting. The biological analogy of an organism adapting to its environment can be dramatic and conceptually helpful, but students of organizations typically make only partial use of the analogy. They stop at this generalized level of explanation and fail to follow their biologist colleagues, whose concepts they have borrowed, to the next step of examining the internal processes by which the system adapts.

Our focus will be on the response within the organization to factors in its environment. Typically, one or more individuals in the organization see something in the environment which calls for different behavior on the part of the members of the organization. He (or they) then tries to move others in the organization to make this change in their behavior. This is fundamentally an influence process and it is the process I shall be representing here. The primary data chosen for illustration comes from our own study plus studies of change in organizational settings by Guest,[1] Seashore and Bowers,[2] Jaques,[3] and Blake, Mouton, Barnes and Greiner,[4] and was all focused on the internal change process.

Some of the best reported studies of the influence process, however, were made in non-organizational settings: experimental studies of attitude change, individual and group psychotherapy, religious conversion, and so-called thought reform. In deciding whether to draw from these, I was faced with the question as to whether studies of individual change materially can aid our understanding of organizational change and my answer was affirmative. Certainly, membership in a formal organization places the individual within a potent influence network and any explanation of changes in his behavior and attitudes must take this network into account. But we must not allow ourselves to presume that behavior in formal organizations is discontinuous from human behavior elsewhere. The object of change in planned change programs is the behavior and attitudes of individuals. Within an organization, these attitudes and actions form an inextricable part of larger formal and informal systems but the workings of social processes ultimately take place as intrapersonal and interpersonal processes.

Sequencing

In our study of the events at the Nampa Development Center, one of the first things we noted was the importance of time. Often the most significant fact about a given event was that it followed other events or that it created a condition which influenced subsequent events. This is also the one point on which other students of change agree—that behavioral and attitudinal change takes place in sequential steps or phases.

Probably the most fruitful conception of the change process, judging from the frequency of its use by others and by the research it has stimulated, is the three-step model advanced by Kurt Lewin:[5] unfreezing the system which is operating in a given pattern, moving to a new pattern, and refreezing into this new pattern. Lewin postulated that systems tend to operate in a given pattern or at a given level as long as there is a relative balance of forces acting on the system.

A sequential model serves a number of functions. It provides a dimension along which to order events and draws attention to events and conditions at the boundaries of the phenomena under examination. Too often, I think, those of us

---

[1] R. A. Guest, *Organizational Change* (Illinois: Richard D. Irwin, Inc.)

[2] S. E. Seashore and D. G. Bowers, *Changing the Structure and Functioning of an Organization,* Monograph, No. 33 (Ann Arbor, Michigan: University of Michigan, 1963).

[3] E. Jaques, *The Changing Culture of a Factory* (London: Tavistock Publications Ltd., 1951).

[4] R. R. Blake, J. S. Mouton, L. B. Barnes and L. E. Greiner, "Breakthrough in Organizational Development," *Harvard Business Review* (November-December 1964).

[5] K. Lewin, "Group Decision and Social Change," *Readings in Social Psychology,* edited by T. M. Newcomb and E. L. Hartley, 1947.

managing or studying organizations tend to be historical in our approach. For example, in our own study, when we conceived of "unfreezing" broadly, we were led to examine not only the unsettling effects of the director's changes in the organizational structure, but also the conditions in the organization at the time he became director and the events leading up to them. Using this one dimension, time, we could characterize the change process at the Center, where successful, as follows:

TABLE 1

Unfreezing		*Change*	*Refreezing*
Tension and the need for change was experienced within the organization.	Change was advocated by the new director.	Individuals within the organization tested out the proposed changes.	New behavior and attitudes were either reinforced and internalized, or rejected and abandoned.

Subprocesses

So far, so good. Time is important and a sequential model such as Lewin's is useful in pointing to the tendency toward orderly movement related to prior events. But, as we compared the successful attempts to exert influence, it also became obvious that there was not one process at work but several, all moving simultaneously. Where influence was successful, changes occurred not only in the way an individual related to the influencing agent, but also to his co-workers and to himself. As interaction patterns were dissolving and reforming, changes were taking place within the individuals involved, changes in their feelings about themselves and in the objectives they sought.

We identified four major subprocesses that tended to characterize successful change in our own study and in the other empirical studies of change we examined.

The four subprocesses are characterized by movement:

away from:	*and*	*toward:*
generalized goals		specific objectives
former social ties built around previous behavior patterns		new relationships which support the intended changes in behavior and attitudes
self-doubt and a lowered sense of self-esteem		a heightened sense of self-esteem
an external motive for change		an internalized motive for change

A Model for Induced Change

If we combine these four subprocesses with our notion of sequencing, we arrive at the diagram in Table 2. Following this diagram, we shall look at the two antecedent conditions which were present in each case of successful planned change examined. Then we shall look separately at each of the four subprocesses pictured.

Internal Tension as an Antecedent Condition

At the risk of stating a truism, let me point out that one of the most important conditions necessary for the successful initiation of change is a sense of tension or a felt need for change among those who are the targets of influence. In nearly every instance in the studies reviewed where one person or group successfully influenced the behavior of others, those influenced were experiencing a more-than-usual amount of tension or strain.

In our own study, a major project on which many of the men had worked for years had just been discontinued and the technology sold to a competitor. The decision by top management not to manufacture or market the product, which had been announced just prior to the new director's appointment, had generated a sense of disappointment and frustration at the Center, since many had come to identify their own future with the success of the project. The men were also concerned about the falling prices of their division's major product and at the Center's apparent lack of success in recent years at translating their technical capabilities into dramatic new products.

Guest, in his three-year study of leadership and organizational change in an automobile assembly plant, reported that before the arrival of the new production manager who succeeded in "turning the plant around" from the least to the most efficient plant in the Division, there was great tension. Labor grievances were high, turnover was twice that in other plants and the plant was under constant pressure from Division Headquarters.[6]

Seashore and Bowers, in their study of an ultimately successful change effort by a consulting-research team from the University of Michigan, reported that in the year prior to the interventions of the team, "Banner (the company) dropped to a very marginal profit position . . . . Waste, service, and quality of problems arose . . . . There was a sense of things getting out of control, a feeling shared and expressed by many non-managerial people."[7]

Elliot Jaques, in his pioneering study of social and technical change in the Glacier Metal Company, reported the impact of a crisis which resulted in a large number of lay-offs and "great anxiety about job security." "The procedure adopted (to handle the lay-offs) had lessened some of the morale problems—but it did not and could not remove everyone's anxiety about job security."[8] Jaques, in fact, concluded that a necessary factor in allowing for a working

[6]R. H. Guest, op. cit., pp. 17-39.
[7]S. E. Seashore, and D. G. Bowers, op. cit., p. 11.
[8]E. Jaques, op. cit., pp. 45-48.

TABLE 2

A Model of Induced Change

Tension Experienced within the System	Intervention of a Prestigious Influencing Agent	Individuals Attempt to Implement the Proposed Changes	New Behavior and Attitudes Reinforced by Achievement, Social Ties and Internalized Values – Accompanied by Decreasing Dependence on Influencing Agent
	Generalized Objectives Established	Growing Specificity of Objectives – Establishment of Sub-Goals	Achievement and Resetting of Specific Objectives
Tension within Existing Social Ties	Prior Social Ties Interrupted or Attenuated	Formation of New Alliances and Relationships Centering Around New Activities	New Social Ties Reinforced Altered Behavior and Attitudes
Lowered Sense of Self-Esteem	Esteem-Building Begun on Basis of Agent's Attention and Assurance	Esteem-Building Based on Task Accomplishment	Heightened Sense of Self-Esteem
	External Motive for Change	Improvisation and Reality-Testing	Internalized Motive for Change
	(New Schema Provided)		

159

through of group problems was a "problem severe and painful enough for its members to wish to do something about it."

Blake, Mouton, Barnes and Greiner, describing a major organizational change effort featuring a training program, noted the presence of great tension in the Sigma plant prior to the training consultant's arrival at the plant. A merger had taken place, bringing the plant under a new headquarters staff, and a serious problem arose over the "use of Sigma manpower on construction work of new projects." When the headquarters staff began to "prod Sigma," the plant management "became defensive" and, according to one of the managers at headquarters, "some of our later sessions became emotional." "Strained relations between different departments and levels within the plant "began to develop."[9] Greiner reported that "plant morale slipped badly, insecurity arose and performance slumped," while a manager within the plant reported that: "Everything seemed to get out of control."[10]

This uniformity was also evident in other settings where there was a successful attempt to influence attitudes and behavior. The religious convert usually is experiencing self-doubt and guilt before he gives careful heed to the missionary or revivalist. A need for change is already felt by the person who walks into the Christian Science reading room or the revivalist tent. Certain organizations, such as Alcoholics Anonymous, whose central aim is to induce specific behavioral change, refuse to admit anyone unless he is consciously experiencing distress. An applicant to A.A. must openly admit the failure of previous individual efforts and his need for help.[11] Jerome Frank suggests that in psychotherapy the presence of prior emotional distress is closely related to the results of the treatment. He argues as follows:

> The importance of emotional distress in the establishment of a fruitful psychotherapeutic relationship is suggested by the facts that the greater the over-all degree of expressed distress, as measured by a symptom check list, the more likely the patient is to remain in treatment, while conversely two of the most difficult categories of patients to treat have nothing in common except lack of distress.[12]

Even in Chinese "thought-reform" prisons, where the interrogator had the power to induce new stresses, the presence of internal tension prior to imprisonment appears to have been a crucial factor in the prisoners' susceptibility to induce an attitude change. Schein and his associates, who studied the Chinese thought-reform program as it was reported by American civilian prisoners in Chinese prisons assigned a crucial role to the sense of guilt experienced by the individual.

[9] R. R. Blake, J. S. Mouton, L. B. Barnes, and L. E. Greiner, op. cit.

[10] L. E. Greiner, "Antecedents of Planned Organizational Change," *The Journal of Applied Behavioral Science*, Vol. 3, No. 1 (1967), p. 62.

[11] O. H. Mowrer, *The New Group Therapy* (Princeton, New Jersey: Van Nostrand Co., 1964).

[12] J. Frank, *Persuasion and Healing* (New York: Schocken Books, 1963).

They reported that "if the prisoner-to-be was susceptible to social guilt, he was particularly vulnerable to the pressure of the cellmates in a group cell."[13]

It is important to note that these are qualitatively different situations, in many ways, from industrial settings; Alcoholics, Communist prisoners, and psychiatric patients share an emotional distress and lack of control over their own actions which differentiate them from men working in industrial organizations. But as in the industrial studies, attempts to influence behavior have a high probability of success only when the individuals have been experiencing internal stress.

In an organization, of course, the need for change isn't experienced uniformly throughout the organization and its locus helps determine the methods used to effect change. If the tension is felt primarily by those at the top of the authority structure but not by those below, change efforts will be exerted through the existing authority structure. Resistance usually takes the form of circumvention and token compliance. If, on the other hand, the tension exists at the bottom of the legitimate power structure, but not at the top, attempts to change the organization take the form of a revolt and an attack on the existing authority structure, as in campus riots and wildcat strikes. The extent and locus of tension also help determine outcomes. In our own study, two groups, the Senior Scientists and Junior Managers, were relatively more frustrated than others at the Center and it was among the men in these two groups that the new Director found the greatest acceptance of the changes he proposed.

Authority and Prestige of the Influencer

The forces for change represented by tension and the desire for change must be mobilized, however, and given direction, while forces acting to resist change in a given direction must be overcome, neutralized, or enlisted. In an organization, unless there is to be protracted resistance, someone must gain the acceptance and possible support of individuals not seeking change and even those who feel threatened by it.

A second prerequisite for successfully induced change, therefore, appears to be that the initiation come from a respected and, ideally, a trusted source. The persons being influenced need confidence that the change can, in fact, be effected, and a large part of this confidence comes initially from their confidence in the power and judgment of the influencing agent. When men are unsure of their capacity to cope effectively with the situation, they identify with someone whom they perceive as having the knowledge or power to successfully cope with it and who states *where* they need to change. As such, he is then placed in a position where his expectations can become "self-fulfilling prophesies."[14]

[13]E. H. Schein, et al., *Coercive Persuasion* (New York: W. W. Norton and Co., 1961), p. 167.

[14]R. Rosenthall, and L. F. Jacobsen, *Scientific American* (April, 1968).

In the organizational studies reviewed, successful attempts to change either were initiated by the formal head of the organizational unit involved or were given his strong support. In Guest's study, the initiator was the new plant manager who brought with him a strong reputation for success in his previous position. Furthermore, it quickly became obvious to the other employees that he had the support of the district management.[15] (Pelz reported that upward influence with one's own superior was a necessary condition for influence with subordinates.)[16] Jaques also had the active support of the Managing Director of Glacier Metals.[17]

The changes at the "Banner Corporation"[18] were initiated by the highest official at the plant. He gained support from Rensis Likert and brought in an agent from the Survey Research Center who carried with him the prestige of the University as well as the authority of an experienced manager. The change effort at the Sigma plant had a similar dual sponsorship, receiving active support from the Plant Manager and a consultant, Robert Blake, who "had an impressive reputation with the management in other parts of (the headquarters company)."[19] (As a contrast to these successful change efforts, consider for a moment the many ineffectual training programs for first and second line supervisors in which the top management group did not participate and therefore never fully understood or supported.)

Non-organizational studies show the same link between prestige and influence: individuals tend to believe and do those things suggested by authoritative, prestigeful sources.[20] Goalsetting studies reported by Mace indicated that setting goals for individuals and associating these goals with prestigeful authorities like "scientific progress" or "the advancement of research" tended to have a favorable effect on performance.[21]

Studies of operant conditioning of verbal behavior, where one person reinforces certain verbal signals emitted by another person, indicate that when the conditioner has some prestige or power in the subjects' eyes, the influence tends to be stronger and more consistent. Students were more consistently influenced by their instructors, for example, than by fellow students. (Of course, this was several years ago. Perhaps today instructors over 30 may not enjoy the same influence.)

Another area of study focusing on the persuasive influence of a prestigeful figure is faith-healing and the so-called "placebo effect" on medicine. Jerome Frank reports that even healers regarded by the community as charlatans or

[15] R. H. Guest, op. cit., pp. 42, 108.

[16] D. C. Pelz, "Influence: A Key to Effective Leadership in the First-Line Supervisor," *Personnel,* Vol. 29 (1952), pp. 209-217.

[17] Jaques, E., op. cit., pp. 1-23.

[18] S. W. Seashore, and D. G. Bowers, op. cit., pp. 10-15.

[19] R. R. Blake, J. S. Mouton, L. B. Barnes, and L. E. Greiner, op. cit., p. 146.

[20] C. J. Hovland, I. L. Janis, and H. Kelley, *Communication and Persuasion: Psychological Studies of Opinion Change* (New Haven: Yale University Press, 1953).

[21] C. A. Mace, "Satisfaction in Work," *Occupational Psychology,* Vol. 22 (1948), pp. 5-12.

quacks were able, in some instances, to bring about change and symptom relief among persons who regarded them as sources of authority and power. Their success appeared to rest on their ability to evoke the patient's expectancy of help. In medical treatment, the fact that relief and healing can be brought about solely by the patient's expectation of help from the physician, is demonstrated by experiments verifying the so-called "placebo effect." In these studies, the doctor administers a pharmacologically inert substance to the patient rather than an active medication. Since the placebo is inert, its beneficial effects derive from the patient's confidence in the doctor's prescription and in the institutions of science and medicine which he represents. There is evidence that placebos can have marked physiological effects. Studies have shown that their use has been accompanied by healing of tissue damage ranging from warts to peptic ulcers. A similar effect is the "hello-goodbye" effect in psychotherapy. Patients who merely had contact with a prestigeful (in their eyes) psychiatrist improved significantly over the individuals in a control group who were placed on a waiting list and did not see a psychiatrist. In fact, these minimal contact patients showed almost as much improvement of certain kinds as a third group who underwent prolonged treatment.[22]

Even in thought-reform prisons, there is some suggestion that interrogators or cellmates with higher education and intelligence as this was perceived by the prisoner, were more likely to be able to influence the prisoner than were those whom he "looked down on."[23] Statistical evidence on American prisoners of war in Korea show the small proportion (about 15%) of the prisoners who were classified as collaborators came primarily from low status positions in American society,[24] and therefore among the group most likely to see their interrogators and discussion leaders as prestigeful persons. In one of the most graphic accounts by a prisoner who successfully resisted influence by his interrogators, Gonzales reports that he never came to think of his interrogators as authorities in any real sense nor in any way superior to himself except that they were more numerous than he.[25] There is, of course, abundant evidence in our own study and elsewhere to refute a claim that any change initiated by a high status person will be successful. The process of change is more complex than that. But prestige and power on the part of the initiator seems to be a necessary, if not sufficient, condition for introducing large-scale change in any system. Where the person planning to initiate change does not already possess prestige and power in the organization, as Loomis has pointed out, it is his first task to develop "social capital" for himself, i.e., to build his reputation and power in the social system he intends to change.[26]

[22] J. Frank, op. cit.

[23] E. H. Schein, et al., op. cit.

[24] J. Segal, "Correlates of Collaboration and Resistance Behavior Among U.S. Army's POW's in Korea," *Journal of Social Issues,* Vol. 13, pp.31-40.

[25] V. Gonzales, and J. Gorkin, *El Campesino: Life and Death in Soviet Russia* (New York: Putnam, 1952).

[26] C. P. Loomis, "Tentative Types of Directed Social Change Involving Systematic Linkage," *Rural Sociology,* Vol. 24, No. 4 (December, 1959).

Subprocesses

Now let us turn from the conditions which precede and facilitate change to an examination of the change process itself. The subtleties and interdependencies of the process, of course, are difficult and, in many ways, impossible to represent or describe because the phenomena occur simultaneously and are "of a piece." But as is shown in the diagram, we were able to distinguish four major subprocesses, all of which seemed to proceed simultaneously in those instances where individuals and groups were influenced to change their behavior and where these new behavior patterns persisted. Movement along each of these four streams characterized the Junior Managers and Senior Scientists at Nampa but were either absent or restricted among the other men at the Center whose behavior and attitude changed least.

Movement along each of these streams, where present, appeared to follow a consistent pattern or direction, and while each seemed distinct and separable, movement along all four appeared to occur simultaneously. The first two of these deal with changes in shared objectives and relationships, while the last two concern changes within the individual.

Movement Toward Specific Objectives

The first pattern which consistently seems to characterize successful attempts to bring about behavioral and attitudinal change is a movement from generalized goals toward specific and concrete objectives. As the change progresses, the targets take on greater immediacy and concreteness; one of the clearest signals that a new pattern of behavior will not be established and maintained is the objectives' remaining general and non-specific. In the Nampa Center the changes outlined for all the groups began at a very general level. The Junior Managers, for example, were told they were to take on more responsibility for the administration of their groups and to "plan the technical work" for their groups. The Senior Managers were told to spend at least half their time doing long-range planning. Soon afterward, the Junior Managers were asked to prepare budget requests for their groups. Later they were given responsibility for performing a specific technical objective and a target date was set for completion, and soon they were working out a week-by-week projected schedule. The assignment given the Senior Managers to do long-range-planning, however, remained essentially at that level of generality, with neither the Director nor the Senior Managers working out intermediate or sub-objectives. Fifteen months later, of course, it was the Junior and not the Senior Managers whose attitudes and behavior had changed in the intended direction.

In each of the other studies, whenever someone successfully influenced another person or group of persons to change their behavior or attitudes, movement toward greater specificity of goals was a prominent feature. Sometimes the person initiating the change set the sub-goals, sometimes those being influenced set them; most often it was a joint or alternating arrangement. But the consistent element was that someone set concrete subgoals and the behavior change moved along step-by-step. Guest reported that the new manager at Plant Y began by outlining a "few general goals" such as better planning. He set up meetings for discussing general problems, but attention was steadily brought to focus on improving specific areas, such as accounting methods and inspection procedures.[27] Jaques' report of a three-year period of change in the Glacier Metal Company described how the project team worked successfully with councils and management groups at various levels and departments throughout the organizations. The process followed in their work with each group showed remarkable consistency—beginning with the general goals of "understanding their difficulties," moving to a goal of understanding their own "here-and now" relationships and finally heading toward the resolution of specific problems or the writing of a new constitution.[28]

The Plant Manager's initially announced objective at "Banner Corporation" was to introduce "participation management" into the organization. After several months, four sub-goals were explicitly stated as a way of implementing the overall goal:

(a) increased emphasis on the work group, as a functioning unit,
(b) more supportive behavior from supervisors,
(c) greater employee participation in decision-making, and
(d) increased interaction among and influence among work group members.

A series of meetings with all the supervisors in the experimental department followed in which the objective became more and more operational in the minds of the supervisors. Finally, these intermediate goals were translated into more specific goals, such as bringing the employees into the decisions about a new shift rotation scheme.[29] The changes reported by Blake, et al. at the Sigma refinery followed in an identical pattern.[30] Beginning with a training program in which the objectives for the participants were the general goals of understanding the concepts and assessing their own present management style. Other meetings followed in which the objectives were to explore ways to transfer the new concepts and personal learning of the Seminars to the operations of their own group. The objective became even more concrete as the men consciously tried to use some of their new problem-solving methods in working out a program for reducing utility costs and in negotiating a difficult union-management contract.

Outside organizational settings, the most carefully conceptualized example of this aspect of the change process is found in the descriptions of the therapeutic process. At the beginning of the relationship between the patient and the

[27]R. H. Guest, op. cit.

[28]E. Jaques, op. cit.

[29]S. E. Seashore, and D. G. Bowers, op. cit.

[30]R. R. Blake, J. S. Mouton, L. B. Barnes, and L. E. Greiner, op. cit.

therapist, the mutually understood objective is usually relatively general in character: to help the patient to operate more effectively in his environment, to find relief from serious distress, or to achieve an understanding of the patient's problems and their causes. Explorations may begin by looking at the patient's past behavior, his relationships outside therapy, and his feelings about these. But nearly all schools of therapy agree that as the relationship continues, the patient comes to show his feelings and behavior towards the therapist similar to those making trouble for him outside therapy. The examination of these concerete specific events acted out in their own relationship is undertaken as a means of achieving the more general objective.[31] Religious conversion begins with the goals of total repentence and "casting off the old man for the new," but where the conversion has lasting effects, this general goal moves toward the specific objectives of giving up certain practices, making contributions, or proselyting others. Then as an individual makes small behavioral commitments in a certain direction, he justifies and rationalizes these acts by accepting values and explanations which reduce dissonance between these acts and his self-image. He becomes his own socializing agent. Even in the thought-reform prisons, the early demand of the interrogator for confession of guilt narrows and focuses to the objective of producing a written document confession of specific "criminal acts" which the interrogator will accept.

Altering Old Relationships and Establishing New Social Ties

The second pattern which seemed to characterize successful change was the loosening of old relationships and the establishment of new social ties which support the intended changes in attitude and behavior. Old behavior and attitudes are often deeply imbedded in the relationships which have been built up over the years, and as long as the individuals involved maintain these relationships unaltered, changes are unlikely to occur. By the same token, new behavior patterns are most readily and firmly established when they are conditions of regular membership in a new group, for group members exercise the most powerful tool for shaping behavior, selective reinforcement of responses with immediate rewards.

In other studies this was the dimension of the change process that has been most explicitly recognized: the beliefs, attitudes, and activities of a person are closely related to those of his reference groups. New attitudes and new activity patterns are most likely to be established when an individual becomes associated with a new reference group.[32] Certainly, not all of an individual's former associations will counteract an intended change, nor will new groups formed in a change situation always work in the direction that the influencing agent intends, but in general, any significant changes in activities or attitudes include some movement from old object relationships toward new ones.

[31]J. I. Stein, *Contemporary Psychotherapies* (Glencoe, Illinois: Free Press, 1961).

[32]B. Berelson, and G. A. Steiner, *Human Behavior: An Inventory of Scientific Findings* (New York: Harcourt, Brace, 1964).

Behavioral scientists did not orginate the ideas that an alteration of old relationships facilitates change in individuals or groups. Most influencing institutions in our society separate the individual whom they wish to influence from his regular social contacts and routines. Convents, monasteries, and prisons tend to make this a total separation, and educational institutions make the same separation to a lesser degree by their physical distance from home and a demanding work load. Perhaps the best reported study of this is the work done by Newcomb at Bennington College. During their four years at the College, the girls tended to take on the attitudes of the faculty and student leaders, and to relinquish those of their parents.[33] The individuals' greater susceptibility to influence when he is separated from social contacts which support his current beliefs was ingeniously demonstrated by the famous Asch experiments: when subjects were placed in a situation where no other person agreed with the subject's own judgments, a third of the subjects came to doubt their own perceptions to the extent that they reported seeing what the others reported in over half the trials. Yet, if only one person in the group confirmed a subject's own perception, his resistance to social pressure was significantly increased.[34] Rice, in his study of change in a textile weaving mill in India, found some confirmation for his argument that this need for removal from previous contacts applied also to groups where the group was the focus of the change. Otherwise the prior social relationships continued to support the behavior patterns and attitudes which the change program was trying to alter.[35]

Breaking up or loosening former social ties may act to unfreeze an individual or group, but this alone provides no assurance that any resulting changes will be in a given direction or that they will have any permanency. Establishing new relationships which reward the desired behaviors and confirm the modified attitudes also seem to be essential. Otherwise, there will be an active seeking to return to former activities and attitudes and to the relationships which supported and reinforced them.

In our study of the Nampa Center, all the men in the experimental sections reported some disruption of their former relationships. Changes in job requirements and work schedules broke up former important interaction patterns in all the groups, but there was a sharp difference among the groups in the extent to which new relationships were established. The men in the groups which eventually changed most were assigned to new decision-making committees with their peers from other parts of the company. When decisions were made in the groups there were strong pressures from the other members of the group to defend these decisions even in dealings with the Senior Managers. The men who even-

[33]T. M. Newcomb, "Attitude Development as a Function of Reference Groups: The Bennington Study," *Readings in Social Psychology,* E. E. Macoby, T. M. Newcomb, and E. L. Hartley, eds. (New York: Holt, Rinehart, and Winston, Inc., 1958). See also E. Schein, et al., op. cit., pp. 270-271.

[34]S. E. Asch, "Effects of Group Pressure Upon the Modification and Distortion of Judgments," *Groups, Leadership, and Men,* H. Geutzkow, ed. (Pittsburgh: Carnegie Press, 1951).

[35]A. K. Rice, *Productivity and Social Organization: The Ahmedabad Experiment* (London: Tavistock, 1953).

tually changed least, on the other hand, established no new relationships. Their previous ties were attentuated, but they formed no new relationships which might have pulled them more deeply into new patterns of activities and beliefs.

One of the most interesting studies illustrating this phenomenon was the follow-up study of an International Harvester Company training program emphasizing human relations skills which the investigators categorized as "consideration." Tested before and after the two-week training program, the foremen's attitude test scores showed an immediate increase on "consideration," but, over time, the scores shifted until these foremen actually scored lower in consideration than did a control group who had not been trained. Only those foremen whose immediate superiors scored high' on consideration continued to score high themselves. The other foreman, whose superiors did not place a high value on consideration, returned to a pattern very close to that of their chief. Daily interaction completely negated the effect of the training program. The foremen's ties had been interrupted only during the two week training period. Then they returned to a situation where the most significant relationship was with their own supervisors. No continuing new relationships had been established which would act to confirm and reinforce any attitude changes begun in the training program.[36]

A study which differs in important ways from the International Harvester study, yet confirms its findings, is the Barnes and Greiner investigation of the effects of Blake's organization development program at the Sigma oil refinery. At Sigma the management and staff members at all levels of the plant went through an initial training program during which men were taken out of their regular work groups and placed among relative strangers. They then returned to their old work groups, as in the International Harvester program, but with the difference that their superiors and colleagues had also been through the same training experience. In addition, a second series of meetings was held in which the teams who worked together jointly examined their own operations and made mutual commitments to change. A follow-up study revealed that the program had had an impact on the plant's operations and on the behavior and attitudes of some of the men but, again, not all. In this case, 92% of the supervisors who were rated as most changed by their subordinates worked in groups where a majority of their colleagues were also rated as "most improved" by their subordinates, while only 26% of the supervisors rated as "least improved" worked in such groups. In fact, it appeared to the investigators that even the presence of only one "least improved" cynic was enough to have a strong dampening effect, since 60% of the "most improved" supervisors worked in settings where there were no "least improved" colleagues whatsoever.[37] As in the Nampa and International Harvester studies, there was no behavioral change unless relationships changed to support the new behavior. The Sigma study, however, differs in one significant way: the major reinforcing relationships in the

[36]E. A. Fleishman, E. J. Harris, and H. E. Butte, *Leadership and Supervision in Industry* (Columbus, Ohio: Personnel Research Board, Ohio State University, 1945).

[37]R. R. Blake, J. S. Mouton, L. B. Barnes, and L. E. Greiner, op. cit., pp. 154, 155.

refinery study were with the same people with whom they had worked before. The parties to the relationship had not changed, but the relationships had. This, of course, has important implications for an administrator who wishes to maintain his work teams intact, but hopes to alter behavior and attitudes in these groups. Still, the major point to be made here is that unless the relationships change, behavioral change is more difficult.

Some of the other studies involved an actual break-up of former associations, while in others the parties did not change, but the relationships between those parties did. Guest, in his study of a successful change, reported a high incidence of personnel shifts breaking up old social ties and established new relationships which supported the new behavior patterns. There were few discharges, but a program of planned and deliberate lateral transfers and promotions was instituted. Only 25% of the plant's supervisors held the same job throughout the period studied. Moreover, the Plant Manager set up a new pattern of interactions through an increased use of meetings.

The scope and function of the meetings established by the new manager stood in marked contrast to those of the earlier period: there were more of them, they were regularly scheduled, they covered a wider range of activities, more people took part in them. . . .[38]

Relationships in these meetings were established around new attitudes and behaviors, and support and reinforcement for the new behavior patterns came from these ties.

The studies reported by Jaques and by Seashore and Bower, however, focused on changes in the nature of the existing relationships. Jaques found that at Glacier Metals a number of new relationships had been established around the new activities (new worker-management committees, etc.) but the primary thrust of the research team's efforts was to alter the expectations and the reinforcement patterns in the existing relationships. This came primarily through what they termed "role clarification" and "working through." Role clarification consisted of a joint examination of the several roles members were expected to play in the group and in the organization as well as the achievement of a common set of expectations about the new ways in which those roles were to be filled. Jaques described "working through" as a serious attempt to voice the unrecognized difficulties, often socially taboo, which have been preventing the group from going ahead with whatever task it may have had. The research team's focus on "working through" was not to aid in the solution of any one problem but to alter the relationship and the manner of working together. Jaques' underlying thesis was that, "Once a group has developed insight and skill in recognizing forces related to status, prestige, security, . . . (etc.) these forces no longer colour subsequent discussion nor impede progress to the same extent as before."[39]

[38]R. H. Guest, op. cit., p. 45.
[39]E. Jaques, op. cit., p. 307.

The most vivid example of new social interactions acting to bring about the intended change itself is in the "struggle sessions" in thought reform prisons. In some reform prisons on the Chinese mainland, western prisoners were placed in cells with a group of "advanced" prisoners, who had already made confessions or were in the process. These prisoners, who themselves were taking on the reformed attitudes, and who were given to know that the progress of the entire cell was dependent on the performance of the least-reformed member, exerted strong pressures (accusations, browbeating) on their new member. The potency of this pressure from fellow prisoners was so pronounced that Schein concluded it was the single most effective device used to influence the prisoners to confess and change attitudes.[40] The Communist prison struggle groups are an extreme form of a group influencing a new member to assume new behaviors and attitudes, but the same process goes on in all groups with lowered intensity. The entering member is required to demonstrate adherence to the norms and values of the group to a greater extent, even, than established members.[41]

The establishment of new social ties for confirmation and reinforcement of changes already begun also has traditionally been a part of evangelistic programs. John Wesley organized his converts into small units of twelve or less. This small group, with a chosen leader, met together weekly to tell of their experiences. The leader visited a member each week to collect dues and to verify the sincerity of his conversion. Quarterly, each member was reassigned a ticket of membership admitting him to sacrament meetings. Backsliding was watched carefully and even three or four absences could bring the loss of his ticket and expulsion from the Society.[42]

The importance of the establishment of new social relationships which confirm and support change begun probably is best illustrated by examining change attempts where new ties are not established. Following a Billy Graham crusade in New York City, an informal survey of individuals who came forward and converted during the Crusade found that only those who were subsequently integrated into local churches maintained their faith. For others, the conversion became merely a temporary and lapsed response.[43]

There are those who lay complete stress on group membership and social pressure in explaining the change process. Such explanations seem incomplete, and that is obviously not our position here, but movement along this dimension appears to be a necessary if not sufficient condition for inducing significant and lasting behavioral change.

Heightening Self-Esteem

Changes in self-esteem on the part of the person being influenced also appear to be an integral part of the process. Interestingly, a movement toward greater

[40]E. Schein, op. cit., p. 193.

[41]G. C. Homans, *The Human Group* (New York: Harcourt, Brace and Co., 1950).

[42]W. Sargent, *Battle for the Mind* (Garden City, New York: Doubleday, 1957).

[43]E. Schein, op. cit., p. 282.

self-esteem seems to be a facilitating factor not only in the establishment of new patterns of thought and action, but also in the unfreezing of old patterns. The abandonment of previous patterns of behavior and thought is easier when an individual is moving toward an increased sense of his own worth. The movement along this continuum is away from a sense of self-doubt toward a feeling of positive worth—from a feeling of partial inadequacy toward a confirmed sense of personal capacity. The increased sense of one's own potential is evident throughout this continuum, not merely at the end. This may seem a paradox, but the contradiction is more apparent than real.

As noted earlier, one of the preconditions for successful change is the experience of stress within the system. Though stress is usually present even before the intervention of the change agent, the agent himself can play an extremely important role in challenging the individual's sense of adequacy. His means of doing this may be explicit or implicit. The negative diagnosis may be openly stated as when the religious revivalist points to the prospective proselyte's indulgent life and he calls him to repentance. The older members at an A.A. meeting may confront the alcoholic with the fact that he is destroying himself and his family. The Communist prison interrogator may insist on the prisoner's "criminal acts against the people." On the other hand, the negative diagnosis may be communicated implicitly by the agent's acting to introduce change in the object system, such as a psychotherapist embarking on a program of treatment after he has had exploratory talks with the patient.

In organizational change, we also find both patterns. A new executive may himself confront the members of the organization with the inconsistencies and inefficiencies in their operations as he did in the Nampa case. An outside consultant, however, will more often seek a confrontation among the members of the organization. For example, Robert Blake, in working with the management of the Sigma plant, suggested an initial meeting between plant managers and the headquarters staff, at which the problems uncovered "shocked" the plant management. From this meeting came the impetus to design a development program in which each of the members of the supervisory group was likewise confronted by others' perceptions of his behavior.[44] Jaques and the research team at Glacier Metals worked with the staff in their meetings, helped them to "express feelings which they had been suppressing sometimes for years." Many, for the first time, were able to assess the consequences of some of their behavior.[45]

On the other hand the manager of the plant studied by Guest entered into a situation where the men had already had abundant evidence of the unsatisfactory consequences of their behavior. He felt it necessary only to acknowledge this evidence.

In the first meeting with all supervision he put forward what he called "a few basic goals" for the organization in terms of expected efficiency

---

[44]R. R. Blake, J. S. Mouton, L. B. Barnes, and L. E. Greiner, op. cit., p. 141.
[45]E. Jaques, op. cit., p. 306.

and quality. He stated candidly to the group that Plant Y had a bad reputation. He said he had heard that many members of the group were not capable of doing their jobs. He said he was "willing to prove that this was not so, and until shown otherwise, I personally have confidence in the group." [46]

In each of these instances, the manager or consultant signaled that the men needed to change; that their former performance was not adequate or appropriate. How, then, does this kind of action foster a heightened sense of worth? The men cannot help feeling they are of some worth, receiving this much attention from someone whom they respect. He is making an investment in them. Even though he is communicating a negative evaluation of their present behavior or attitudes, he is also indicating that he has higher expectations. He is saying, in effect, that he respects their potential. Finally, when he communicates his negative diagnosis he also offers hope implying that there is a better way and that he knows that better way. The effect on self-esteem is negative at this point in that the attention received derives from their past inadequacy—their need to change. But it is positive in that it lays a foundation for a new beginning, and promise of better results in the future.

For instances of successful change, there is a movement toward increased self-regard as the person finds himself capable of making the changes in behavior. He experiences a sense of accomplishment, a relief from tension, and a reintegration around a new pattern of activity and thought. The Junior Managers at Nampa, for example, had the opportunity to assume new roles and take on new tasks. As they accomplished these tasks, which had been previously performed by their superiors, they gained a new confidence rooted in their own achievements.

This gain in self-esteem was evident in each of the studies. Early in each of the organizational studies, managers began listening to their subordinates and responding to them. In each case subordinates began taking on responsibilities and participating in decisions that had been withheld from them in the past. The confidence gained from success in these early attempts led to further steps. In Guest's study, men expressed an increasing feeling of competence. ("Just gradually we learned how to do the job.") and confidence in their future ("The foreman knows that he's got the staff, he's going to be recognized and promoted."). Toward the end of the period studied, the "promotion" theme was mentioned often in the interviews, while only three years earlier none had expressed the hope of advancing.[47] At the Sigma Refinery, studied by Barnes and Greiner, a new set of programs for increasing productivity and improving costs was confidently and successfully carried out.[48] At Glacier, Jaques reported that increased confidence and self-esteem was demonstrated in a capacity to tackle formerly taboo problems with considerably less anxiety.

---

[46]R. A. Guest, op. cit., p. 42.

[47]R. A. Guest, op. cit., p. 60.

[48]R. R. Blake, J. S. Mouton, L. B. Barnes, and L. E. Greiner, op. cit., p. 144-145.

The study of the Banner Company, conducted by Seashore and Bower, is perhaps the most interesting of the four concerning this factor, in that managers and consultants were explicit about the need for increased self-esteem. The consultants set a goal to build "supportive supervisory behavior," which they defined as increasing "the extent to which subordinates (at all levels) experienced positive, ego-sustaining relations with superiors and peers whenever they undertook to act in ways which would promote their common goals."[49] Paradoxically, it was at Banner where increased confidence was most difficult to attain, as the early attempts at supervisory support became the focus of misunderstanding and illwill. The supervisors attempted in good faith to be "supportive" but often found no way to link this up to accomplishment. Undiscriminating support not only failed to build self-esteem, but actually undermined it. This factor, plus a deteriorating economic situation and some formal organizational blocks controlled by higher management, retarded progress to the point where the representative from the Survey Research Center proposed a suspension of the field work. It was only after a reorganization, allowing the plant greater freedom, that the latent gains from the early change efforts began to produce the spiraling achievement and confidence that increased plant productivity.

The best-known study demonstrating that a heightening of self-worth is an integral part of the influence process comes from the Relay Assembly Test Room Experiments begun in 1924 by the Western Electric Company at their Hawthorne works. The tests, of course, were initially designed to examine the "relation of quality and quantity of illumination to efficiency in industry," but the baffled experimenters found that productivity increased in their "test groups" and "control groups" in almost equal magnitude. They were obtaining greater efficiency, but it apparently was not "illumination that was making the difference!" Further study, this time experimentally varying rest pauses and working hours, again revealed no simple correlation between the experimentally imposed changes and rate of output. Production rose steadily even when the experimental conditions were returned to their original condition. This time, however, the experimenters took careful note of other factors, one of which was the experimenters' influence on the girls to increase productivity. Ostensibly, the experiment had not been an attempt to change behavior, and the experimenters disclaimed any conscious desire to influence the girls toward increased production. The superintendent's notes concerning the first meeting held with the girls indicated that great care was taken to convince them that the purpose of the test was not to boost production:

> *The group were assured that the test was not being set up to determine the maximum output, and they were asked to work along at a comfortable pace and particularly not to attempt to see how much they could possibly do.*[50]

[49]Seashore and Bowers, op. cit., p. 53.

[50]J. F. Roethlisberger, and W. J. Dickson, *Management and the Worker* (Cambridge, Mass.: Harvard University Press, 1939), p. 33.

But in fact the girls received signals which conveyed an exactly opposite message.[51] The superintendent's next words were:

If increased output resulted from better or more satisfactory working conditions, both parties would be the gainers.[52]

Increased productivity *was* what interested the experimenters! The girls could see that it was the production output which was being recorded so meticulously and subjected to such careful scrutiny.[53]

In retrospect the treatment the girls were given seems almost perfectly designed to increase their sense of self-esteem. A new supervisor who was promoted to department chief became the test observer and he treated them very differently from their previous superior. The observer and the experimenters made every effort to obtain the girls' whole-hearted cooperation for each change, consulting them about each change and even canceling some change which did not meet with their approval. The girls' health, well-being, and opinions were the subject of genuine concern. Investigators spent full time recording and analyzing their output and the Superintendent of the Inspection Branch visited the room frequently, accompanied by an intermittent stream of industrial psychologists and university professors. Each of the girls became a valued member of a cohesive and cooperative group, and as their efficiency increased, so did their sense of confidence.

The experimenters had sought to hold all factors constant except those which were explicitly manipulating in each period. In their attempts to provide an optimal climate for objective research, however, the things which were changed most were the very factors most likely to facilitate change. Each of the conditions and processes so far described was present. (1) The girls, in a new and unfamiliar situation, were initially tense and unsure; (2) persons holding great prestige in the girls' eyes introduced the change; (3) initially the objective which the researchers sought was vague and unclear to the girls, but, judging from the reports, it became increasingly clear to the girls that the search had a specific objective—to find ways to increase productivity; (4) the girls were separated from their former associates and formed a new group built around new activities and attitudes; (5) finally the experimenters created conditions which gave the girls a greater sense of importance and worth. The Relay Assembly Test Room Experiments Series have been cited by many writers to illustrate many things,

---

[51]Committee on Work in Industry, National Research Council, *Fatigue of Workers: Its Relation to Industrial Production* (New York: Reinhold Publishing Corporation, 1941), pp. 56-66.

[52]F. J. Roethlisberger, and W. J. Dickson, op. cit., p. 33.

[53]There seems little doubt that the girls received this message whether the experimenters were consciously trying to convey it or not. Studies have shown that even when one person in a close interpersonal relationship is trying to be "non-directive," the other person's behavior can still be strongly influenced by the subtle signals of approval and disapproval which the first person unintentionally gives.

E. J. Murray, "A Content Analysis Method for Studying Psychotherapy," *Psychological Monographs,* Vol. 70 (1956), p. 420.

but whatsoever else it demonstrates, it provides us with a carefully reported instance of influence and induced change with increasing self-esteem—an integral part of that process.

Internalization

Internalization of the motive for change was the fourth part of the influence process. The motivating force toward a particular change originates outside the individuals to be influenced. They may be actively searching for more adequate behavior, but the actual kind or direction of the change originates outside. Someone else introduces the plan, the scheme, the interpretation, the suggestion or the idea. Where the new behavior patterns are to become lasting, however, the individuals involved must internalize or come to "own" the rationale for the change.

Internalization occurs as an individual finds the ideas and the prescribed behavior intrinsically rewarding in helping him to cope with external and internal stresses. He adopts the new behavior because he sees it as useful for the solution of a problem or because it is congenial to his own orientation.[54] In the Nampa Center as well as in the historical and experimental settings mentioned earlier, internalization seemed to consist of three elements:

(1) provision of a new cognitive structure

(2) application and improvisation

(3) verification through experience

Provision of a New Cognitive Structure

To judge from the studies examined, the first step in the internalization process is the influencing agent's introduction of a new conceptual framework. The new framework may be restricted to a way of conceiving of a limited set of phenomena or it may be far-reaching in its attempt to explain the totality of a

---

[54]We are very close here to Kelman's formulation of identification. (See "Processes of Opinion Change," *Public Opinion Quarterly,* Spr. '61. And "Compliance, Identification and Internalization, Thru Processes of Attitude Change," *Journal of Conflict Resolution,* Vol. II, No. 1 (March, 1958).)

Kelman, however, argues that internalization is not a necessary part of the influence process. An individual, he reasons, may adopt a new behavior pattern through *compliance,* not because he believes in the content, but in order to gain a specific reward or avoid some anticipated punishment. Or he may, through *identification,* accept influence in order to establish or maintain a relationship with another person or group. This distinction between compliance, identification, and internalization can be made conceptually, but in complex interpersonal relations, in which social influence is being exerted over an extended period of time, neither compliance to external demands nor identification with new reference groups appears to operate successfully without internalization of content on the part of the persons being influenced. Certainly in the Nampa situation, it would be difficult to explain the changes we have noted in terms of compliance or identification alone.

person's experience. In either case, the individual is given a new means for reordering the information he has about himself and his environment. Implicit in the framework are relationships of acts to outcomes so that certain ends call for certain behavior. The framework also provides a language which not only communicates the cognitive structure, but creates an "associative net"[55] by which the individual can relate the events in his own life to the new scheme. Once an idea has been acquired, it serves as a discriminative stimulus and increases the probability that a wide range of relevant behaviors will occur.[56]

This provision of a new cognitive structure by the person seeking to exert influence was a part of all the organizational change studies examined. The new director in our study spent a considerable amount of time differentiating his views of authority from those which underlay the manner in which the Nampa Center had been administered before. At the Banner Corporation, the Plant Manager and the consultants agreed that the first step was to "provide the plant management group of fourteen people with a thorough grounding in the concepts and research basis for participation management." A series of seminars was agreed upon partly "to explore the concepts" and to "outline a conceptual scheme."[57] At the Piedmont Oil Refinery, a training program which emphasized a conceptual scheme developed by Robert Blake, called the Management Grid, initiated the change providing the managers at the plant with new ways of conceiving of their experiences and actions.[58] In other instances, such as the automobile assembly plant studied by Guest, the new scheme was not presented so formally. The new manager met with the plant in various meetings and told them "what he believed in." He outlined in writing a long-range program and he set up a series of regular meetings to examine their operations. Gradually, the men were brought to "a greater awareness of how the total organization 'fitted together'."[59]

The introduction of a new conception of experience as a part of the internalization process is even more apparent in non-organizational settings. The religious evangelist presents a world view which explains events in terms of spiritual force and points to the relationships of man's actions to this force. The Communistic prison interrogator advances a world view which interprets events as part of a struggle between "progress" and "reaction." From this world view proceeds a prescription of "progressive" and "reactionary" behavior. Different forms of psychotherapy provide a conception of health and sickness that enables the patient to reconceive of his life and supplies him a consistent way of interpreting his experiences.

[55]D. C. McClelland, "Toward a Theory of Motive Acquisition," *American Psychologist* (May, 1965).

[56]A. H. Brayfield, "Human Resources Development," *American Psychologist,* Vol. 23, No. 7 (July, 1968).

[57]S. E. Seashore, and D. G. Bowers, op. cit., pp. 11-12.

[58]R. R. Blake, J. S. Mouton, L. B. Barnes, and L. E. Greiner, op. cit.

[59]R. A. Guest, op. cit., p. 111.

Introduction of a new cognitive structure is not sufficient for internalizing to take place, however. The individual must, in some way, "make it his own." Our data suggests that he must actively participate in trying to understand the scheme and apply it to his own problems. Where internalization occurs, typically the guidelines are general enough that the person being influenced is forced to improvise. Thus the new cognitive structure has to be amplified and integrated into the individual's existing thought patterns. King and Janis demonstrated the effectiveness of improvisation for inducing opinion change in an experiment with college students.[60] Three groups of male students were presented a written document concerning the induction of graduating college students into the military service, a topic of personal importance to them. Men in one group were asked only to study the statement. Men in a second group were asked to read it aloud with as much effect as possible so that the statement could be tape-recorded and played to judges. Those in the third group were asked to read the statement, then to role-play the part of an advocate of the views stated in the paper. Results of questionnaires filled out several months before and immediately after the experiment showed that only the group who had had to improvise showed a significant opinion change. Moreover, the experimenters' analysis showed that the difference between the groups could not be attributed to closer attention to the written statement nor higher satisfaction with their performance.

In the studies at Banner, Piedmont, and Guest's auto assembly plant, the supervisors had to improvise to make the suggested ideas operational in their own departments. At Banner, the managers and supervisors had to build on their own ideas in order to implement "participation management" in their own part of the plant. At Piedmont, the men had an idea at the end of the training session about the aims of "9.9" management, but they had to improvise to apply the ideas to their own unique situation. At the auto assembly plant studied by Guest the supervisors were impressed by the way the new manager treated them and by his use of meetings to gather the relevant information and to plan the work. But they had to take his pattern, modify it, and improvise to make the new approach work for them.

Schein and his associates reported that in the Chinese thought reform prisons, the prisoners were kept under extreme pressure to make a confession of their guilt.[61] But they were not told what the content of the confession was to be. The prisoner had to supply the material for the confession himself. He was only told repeatedly to stop holding back and to make a complete confession. Only then would there by any promise that the pressure would cease. His task was to

[60]B. King, and I. Janis, "Comparison of the Effectiveness of Improvised Vs. Non-Improvised Role Playing in Producing Opinion Change," *Human Relations,* Vol. 9, pp. 177-186.

[61]E. Schein, et al., op. cit., p. 136.

produce a confession which would demonstrate to the satisfaction of his captors his complete and unqualified acceptance of the Communist scheme of things. To do this he had to improvise with material from his own experience. Usually, completely fabricated confessions were condemned and rejected. For an acceptable selection and interpretation of this material he had to look for cues from his interrogator, his fellow prisoners who had successfully confessed, and from the controlled mass media. The prisoner had to try repeatedly to demonstrate he had come to interpret the events in his life in terms of the constructs of his captors. Having had to use these constructs to analyze his own life experiences, the prisoner found the communistic world view less implausible and foreign.

Verification through Experience

Testing a new scheme through one's own experience is probably the most important of the three elements of internalization, and it is too often overlooked in the rush to examine the irrational aspects of the influence process. The individual adopts the attitude or behavior and gives it meaning independent of the original source only as he finds it valid in working with his own problems. He must test it against the world as he perceives that world.

At Nampa the Junior Managers were told that they would be the contact men for their projects with Research and Sales, and before long they were assigned to committees with important and urgent tasks with these men. In approximately the same manner, the Senior Scientists were given an open-ended assignment: to make themselves more useful to the line projects. Soon afterward they were assigned to committees where the task was to plan and execute line projects. Specific organizational mechanisms were provided by the Director to help both groups achieve their objectives, and thus they consistently found their experience coinciding with their expectations.

For the other two groups the situation was very different. The Senior Managers' assignment to do long-range technical planning was no more open-ended than the assignments given the two groups just discussed, but no mechanisms were established to implement this difficult assignment. Moreover, the Senior Managers could see that the Director was not in the same power position to support them in their role as long-range planners that he was for the Junior Managers and Senior Scientists in their new roles.

Though the situation for the Junior Scientists was different, the net result was the same. The Director did have the power to support his assertion that the changes would give the Junior Scientists more responsibility and autonomy, but he provided no specific organizational mechanisms to help bring this about.

At Banner, experimenters first introduced participative management in an industrial engineering project; efficiency rose and morale remained high. So later they set up an experimental department and again the early results were close enough to those anticipated that the superintendents in the plant chose to extend the new management methods to other departments. At Plant Y the supervisors tried new methods of running their departments and produced better results. Following the new manager's lead in holding regular meetings, they found it possible to coordinate their efforts better. They took chances, made mistakes, and were not fired. In recommending technical changes they found each change gave them "that much more chance to think ahead so we won't get in the hole next time." At Sigma the management at the plant drew heavily on the approaches developed in the Grid Laboratory sessions in deciding how to handle a manpower reduction, and the results were so encouraging that they sought to use the approach on more of their operating problems.

In each of the above instances, the new scheme found confirmation in the individual's experience, but there is also the other side of the coin. One of the striking outcomes of the Chinese thought-reform program among western prisoners is that, among most returned prisoners, it did *not* produce long-range ideological changes independent of the external support provided in the prison setting. Only a very few former prisoners maintained an espousal of the ideological position "taught" in the prison after they had had time to re-evaluate the prison experience and had new sources of information which they could check. What would have happened to these prisoners had they returned to a Communist society is impossible to say, but where the viewpoint of his captors failed to find validation in the prisoner's experience after the prison experience, it was not internalized. Of course, in those areas where the Chinese captors' scheme *did* continue to be congruent with their experience, the change in the ex-prisoners' attitudes and behavior continued to be affected.[62]

In one sense, this part of the internalization process may be termed reality-testing, but this is not to say that uniform views of reality prevail. Indeed, an individual's perception of reality may be distorted, but for an individual to integrate the new construct into his system of beliefs he must validate it through his perception of reality.

Implications

So much for the model itself, what are its implications? For those who have a major interest in organizational change, a model such as this raises three kinds of issues:

(1) technical
(2) moral
(3) social

By the term technical, I refer simply to the issues concerning how someone can do his task more effectively. In this vein, even an elementary paradigm like this shows the utility of such a device to a practitioner. If nothing else, it serves as a check list forcing him to ask himself what he has neglected. For example, the importance of tension and the recognition by those involved that some

[62]E. Schein, et al., op. cit., pp. 157-166.

change is required would seem to be nothing beyond common sense. But how often is it ignored by the managers or by the organizational development staff man who is eager to demonstrate the utility of his methods? It is my hope that better models will keep the organizational development specialist from becoming a victim of the "law of the instrument!" (i.e. if you give a boy a hammer, he'll find things to hit) and push him toward an improvement of his diagnostic skills.

The near-necessity that the change be introduced or supported by those with power and respect has been learned many times the hard way by those in management training. Although a chief executive's actual participation may not be necessary or in some cases even desirable, his understanding and support can be vital. A full recognition of this feature of organizational change processes may lead the O.D. staff man to spend more time as a counselor to the line executive and less time in training sessions. The line manager may accomplish more using means available to him than the staff specialist can with many times the effort. But, this will require those engaged in organizational development work to educate themselves not only in training methods but also in the creative design of formal structures, and in the behavioral effects of information and measurement systems.

Movement toward increasingly specific goals, while seeming the most obvious, is, from my observation, probably the dimension on which most change efforts flounder. General goals, often widely and genuinely shared, too frequently die for the lack of the crucial idea as to how the first few concrete steps can be taken. Laboratory training often provides a first useful step, but the steps which can help an individual or a group translate the goal from there into daily job performance arise only from planning and creative collaboration of the parties involved.

The use of laboratory training methods has made a major contribution to organizational change in providing a means, however imperfect, of changing relationships without requiring that work teams be broken up or that change wait upon shifts in personnel. But, more needs to be learned about the use of groups to support and reinforce change and experimentation. Work by Schein[63] and others suggests that there is much to be learned about helping individuals use entrance into and exits from organizational units with greater understanding in order to maximize their own effectiveness and freedom.

At an intuitive level, we all understand the part self-esteem plays in change, but the message from the learning theorists about the superior effectiveness of positive reinforcement as a teaching strategy has yet to be utilized fully. Concerning internalization, it is my opinion that as we improve our models of behavioral change, we will become even more impressed with the importance of the cognitive constructs. The constructs now used more widely by those in industry (such as McGregor's X and Y) benefit from the impact which a dichotomy provides, but they also suffer from the polarization it induces. In my

[63]E. Schein, "Organizational Socialization and the Profession of Management," *Industrial Management Review* (Winter, 1968).

opinion, we need new constructs and have been living on the conceptual capital of a prior decade for some time.

The moral issues raised by the use of some explicit representation of the influence process probably are heightened by citing examples drawn from clearly coercive instances of influence as I have done here. In one sense, this is a semantic issue. "Influence" as a descriptive term may cause concern while "leadership" would have an opposite effect. But, there is more here than semantics. Manipulation does occur. Anyone who deals with others in a responsible position is in danger of becoming manipulative. His only effective means of coping with this danger is an intelligent awareness of his own actions and motives and an openness in his dealings with others. A refusal to examine his aims and the processes in which his actions play a part can do no more than serve as a psychological defense against some guilt he may feel. We are all in the business of influencing others. It is not our understanding or consciousness which presents the real moral issues, but our motives and methods. These can be better scrutinized when made explicit.

The social implications primarily are potential rather than actual. Given the swiftness of technological change, it seems imperative that we understand and learn to manage the social change which must accompany it. From scientific invention until the manufacture of the product, the time lag for photography was 112 years. The telephone took half that time—56 years. That period for the transistor was only 5 years, and the integrated circuit went into production in 3 years. This technological pace is becoming increasingly unforgiving of those who fail to anticipate and remain abreast. Organizations, groups, and individuals which do not change rapidly enough must be shunted aside and, at best, placed under some disguised form of care-taking. Even if (in our abundance) we can afford this economically, there is an increasing intolerance in our society, particularly among the young, with our failure to change our organizations to keep pace with shifts in the environment and our failure to keep all segments of our population in the swift mainstream. They impatiently demand that we plan for and cope with change more effectively and humanely—now. These demands cannot be completely dismissed as naive, for within almost all our organizations are individuals who are aware of the environmental shifts and who have some vision of the required behavioral changes. Management's challenge is to translate that awareness to effective action. The implication for students of organizations, it seems to me, is that mine should be only one of an increasing number of attempts to become explicit about the process by which planned change takes place.

Toward a Theory of Changing Behavior: An Elaboration on the Role of Influence and Coercion

This article was written especially for use with the collection of readings in this book. It represents a "working paper" of our thoughts of the moment as we attempt to hammer out one possible application of some of the tools, concepts, and theories which seem to permeate the literature related to change and changing. [1]

In our comments, it should be noted, we have explicitly *opted for an inte-*

[1] Among these are included the three-step model ("unfreezing, changing, and refreezing") from Kurt Lewin, "Frontiers in Group Dynamics: Concept, Method and Reality in Social Science," *Human Relations,* I (1947), 5-42; "supportive climate" from Jack R. Gibb, "Defensive Communication," *Journal of Communication,* XI, No. 3 (September 1961), 141-48; "social sensitivity, behavioral flexibility and feedback" from Robert Tannenbaum, "Dealing with Ourselves before Dealing with Others," *Office Executive,* XXXII, No. 8 (August 1957), 29-30, 35; "empathy" from Robert N. McMurry, "Empathy: Management's Greatest Need," *Advanced Management,* XVIII, No. 7 (July 1953), 6-11, 34; "active listening" from Carl R. Rogers and Richard Farson, "Active Listening," in *Organizational Relations and Management Action,* ed. Garret L. Bergen and William V. Haney (New York: McGraw-Hill Book Company, 1966), pp. 61-76; "interaction product" from Robert R. Kahn and Charles F. Cannell, *The Dynamics of Interviewing* (New York: John Wiley & Sons, Inc., 1963); "nonsupport" from Robert Albanese, "Overcoming Resistance to Stability," *Business Horizons,* reprinted in this volume; "coercive persuasion" from Edgar H. Schein "Management Development as a Process of Influence," reprinted in this volume; "*n* Ach" from David C. McClelland, "Business Drive and National Achievement," *Harvard Business Review,* July-August 1962, plus "Achievement Motivation Can be Developed," *Harvard Business Review,* November-December 1965; and a myriad of others, including a solid base from both motivation and learning theory.

grated changing process that utilizes ingredients from what we see as the "structural," the "behavioral," and the "technological" schools of thought about changing. We have taken this approach because we most certainly believe that people's behavior is shaped by structure, technology, task, and environment, as well as by other people.[2] *It is our belief, then, that the ultimate theory of changing will have to be what might be termed a total systems approach in which each of the components—representing in this case the structural, behavioral, and technological approaches and the research findings associated with them—is merged together into one approach. Before such a theory can emerge, much work needs to be done in reconciling all of the many conflicting claims and contradictory reports which abound in the rather vast literature of change and changing which is scattered quite extensively throughout a variety of academic disciplines.*

[2]For an excellent, brief overview of these approaches to change see, Harold J. Leavitt, "Applied Organization Change in Industry: Structural, Technical, and Human Approaches," reprinted in this volume. See also, Harold J. Leavitt, "Applied Organizational Change in Industry: Structural, Technological, and Humanistic Approaches," in J. G. March, ed., *Handbook of Organizations* (Chicago: Rand-McNally & Co., 1964); Leonard R. Sayles, *Behavior of Industrial Work Groups: Prediction and Control* (New York: John Wiley & Sons, Inc., 1958); Elliot Jaques, *The Changing Culture of a Factory* (London: Tavistock Publication, Ltd., 1951); Frederick G. Lesieur, ed., *The Scanlon Plan: A Frontier in Labor-Management Cooperation* (New York and Cambridge: Wiley and The Technology Press, 1958); William F. Whyte, *Money and Motivation* (New York: Harper & Row, Publishers, Inc., 1955); Robert T. Golembiewski, *Behavior and Organization: O & M and the Small Group* (Chicago: Rand McNally & Co., 1965); Warren G. Bennis, *Changing Organizations* (New York: McGraw-Hill Book Company, 1966); Leland P. Bradford *et al., T-Group Theory and Laboratory Method* (New York: John Wiley & Sons, Inc., 1964); Edgar H. Schein and Warren G. Bennis, *Personal and Organizational Change through Group Methods: The Laboratory Approach* (New York: John Wiley & Sons, Inc., 1966).

TOWARD A THEORY OF CHANGING BEHAVIOR: AN ELABORATION ON THE ROLE OF INFLUENCE AND COERCION

Alton C. Bartlett
University of South Florida

Thomas A. Kayser
University of South Florida

We do not presume to know all of the answers required for a definitive theory of changing. We undoubtedly do not even know all of the questions. Yet progress is being made and the leading edge of knowledge is continually being moved forward. It is our hope that this paper will help in this evolutionary process.

Commencing the Change Process

A Look at Forced Unfreezing

Our thoughts begin with the "unfreezing" stage.[1] Hitting a *square* ice cube with a hammer undoubtedly results in many small fragments and, if you will, a sort of "humpty-dumpty" type problem. Certainly there is no more square ice cube, and if our goal were to change it into a *round* ice cube we would have failed.

By Alton C. Bartlett, Professor and Chairman, Management Department, and Thomas A. Kayser, Instructor of Management, both faculty from the College of Business Administration, University of South Florida. This original article was written especially for this collection of readings.

[1] Kurt Lewin, "Frontiers in Group Dynamics: Concept, Method and Reality in Social Science," *Human Relations,* I (1947), 5-42, proposes three stages in the change process: "unfreezing, changing, and refreezing." See also Edgar H. Schein, "Management Development as a Process of Influence," reprinted in this volume, pp. 135-52.

We believe it is usually this way with people too. That is, *force or pressure to get people to change either their attitudes or their behavior rarely results in a permanent change in the desired direction.* Of course, numerous qualifications and exceptions must be made before this statement can be allowed to stand.

Some Examples of Forced Changes in Behavior

To begin with, we all can recount situations where behavioral changes have come about simply as a result of changes in law, rules and regulations, policies, or codes which specify penalties for noncompliance as well as from the more blatant forms of coercion, such as violence or threat of violence. Examples include: (1) the modification or alteration in the pattern of race relations in the south between 1950 and 1970; (2) the transformation in labor-management relations from open hostility to creative collective bargaining, partly as a result of legislative and judicial mandates between, say, 1932 and 1935, plus the continuing influence of the N.L.R.B. after that; and (3) the obvious behavioral changes in Russia between 1925 and 1935, and in China between 1960 and 1972.

Let us examine several models relating to forced change.

Models of Forced Behavioral Change

The most extreme method of accomplishing a lasting change by force involves simply killing everyone who does not agree with the change. Clearly one can effectively negate dissent by eliminating all dissenters. An approach such as this is not unknown in war. In fact, if we substitute the words *mass firing* for *mass killing,* it is not unknown in corporate circles either—especially when a new manager takes over. This is a rather foolproof way to ensure that a change will be permanent. A slightly less extreme method replaces mass extermination of resistors with the application of massive amounts of physical punishment or unusual psychological tortures.[2] We will not belabor this point, for it seems clear that changes—in behavior at least—can be forced. However, even under the conditions just described, most of these changes in behavior would not be permanent if the law, threat, or force were withdrawn. Consider, if you will, the following example.

In Florida, during the 1972 primary elections, one of the premier issues was the so-called forced busing question. The matter was placed on the ballot and over 80 percent of those voting in the primaries voted against forced busing. Yet, because of the laws and court interpretations the busing continues, for the vote had no legal force at all. Although no one can be certain, it seems—on the basis of that straw ballot—that if Congress passed a law making forced busing optional within each state, forced busing would be halted in Florida even before the ink was dry on the paper.

[2] Cf. Edgar H. Schein, *Brainwashing* (Cambridge, Mass.: Center for International Studies, M.I.T., 1961).

Thus, the crux of the matter is that if a change in *behavior alone* is attained through intimidation or force, it usually will not be sustained when the instruments of threat or violence are withdrawn. Of course, situations may arise in which individuals who are forced to change their behavior subsequently discover that the new behavior works to their advantage, and so they also change their attitudes, thus internalizing the new behavior as part of their life style. Notice, however, that both their *behavior* and their *attitudes* were changed. This is the critical point, for changing requires an alteration of two elements: attitudes and behavior. Coercion, threat, or violence may well result in a perceived change in behavior, but there is nothing to guarantee a corresponding attitude change. Let us return therefore to the beginning of the change process and consider an alternative to forced unfreezing—namely, what we shall call *self-motivated unfreezing.*

A Look at Self-Motivated Unfreezing

Suppose, instead of hitting a square ice cube with a hammer, we expose it to a gradual and gentle heat. Would not the unfreezing occur in this instance without destruction? At least, while it is in liquid form it still could be refrozen into a square ice cube and, of even more importance, it also could be reshaped (changed) before refreezing.

Our point, then, is that the unfreezing process can—and should—be gradual and gentle. It must move slowly but steadily, as appropriate for each participant, toward the condition Albanese termed "nonsupport."[3] In essence, the client system is being provided feedback which allows it to compare and contrast the appropriateness or effectiveness of its behavior with that of "significant others"—whether peers or the change agent. During this time the climate should be conducive to openness, growth, risk taking, giving and receiving descriptive, nonevaluative feedback, and experimentation—in short, supportive of changing one's behavior rather than threatening.[4]

Ordinarily this process takes place in a cultural island setting where the normal distractions and status cues are minimized. Frequently the vehicle is some form of sensitivity training such as a T-Group. It is hard to quarrel with this approach, for it has proved to be a powerful technique. As with any other method for changing behavior, however, there are some legitimate problems

[3]Robert Albanese, "Overcoming Resistance to Stability," reprinted in this volume, pp. 410-22.

[4]For a thorough discussion of this and an elaboration of these concepts, see Chris Argyris, "Explorations in Interpersonal Competence–I," *The Journal of Applied Behavioral Science,* I, No. 1 (January-March 1965), 59, and also *Interpersonal Competence and Organizational Effectiveness* (Homewood, Ill.: R. D. Irwin, Inc. and the Dorsey Press, 1965).

associated with it.[5] Certainly it is not the only way and if the appropriate tools, concepts, and theories are properly incorporated in the design, we feel there are very practical, equally powerful alternatives available to the change agent.[6]

Kelman's Concept of "Compliance"

There is one last point to be considered before we move beyond the unfreezing stage. We have been wrestling, so far, with *forced* versus what we called *self-motivated* unfreezing, but there is at least one other common kind of behavior change that a change agent may encounter. This is what Kelman calls "compliance."[7] Compliance comes into play because some people are willing to do or say anything to get ahead; some people have an obsession with feeling important; some people want everyone in their "public" to think they are a nice guy; some people seek recognition from a particular "significant other"; some strive mightily to become accepted memebers of some high status group; some simply do not want to get involved.

It is the chameleonlike behavior changes associated with these phenomena that make the changing process even more complex than it otherwise would be. Just because you see a changed behavior pattern and/or hear people verbalize different thoughts does not mean that a permanent change has taken place. It may mean, instead, that what you are seeing and hearing is what they think you want to see and hear, and they have decided it is easier to humor you and give you what you want than to struggle.

Changing Behavior

What Makes a Person Want to Change?

Once unfreezing is accomplished, the subject(s) are ready for the changing process. At this stage—as in the prior one—self-motivation is the key variable. The premise upon which our whole approach rests is that the person to be

[5]Cf. Robert J. House, "T-Group Training: Good or Bad?" *Business Horizons,* XII (December 1969), 69-77; John E. Drotning, "Sensitivity Training: Some Critical Questions," *Personnel Journal,* XLV, No. 10 (November 1966), 604-6. For a somewhat different approach see Alton C. Bartlett, "Changing Behavior Through Simulation: An Alternate Design to T-Group Training," reprinted in this volume, pp. 118-34.

[6]For one such design see Alton C. Bartlett, "Changing Behavior as a Means to Increased Efficiency," reprinted in this volume, pp. 234-53; see also R. R. Blake, *et al.,* "Breakthrough in Organizational Development," reprinted in this volume, pp. 254-89.

[7]H. C. Kelman, "Compliance, Identification, and Internalization: Three Processes of Attitude Change," *Conflict Resolution,* II, No. 1 (March 1958), 51-60, and "Processes of Opinion Change," *Public Opinion Quarterly* (Spring 1961). See also, Gene W. Dalton, "Influence and Organizational Change," *Organizational Behavior Models,* Comparative Administration Research Institute Series No. 2 (Kent State University. Bureau of Economic and Business Research, 1970), pp. 97 and passim, especially footnote 54, pp. 107-8, reprinted in this volume, pp. 153-81

changed must be motivated and ready to change. The client system must: (1) see a need for change; (2) be able to change; and (3) perceive the change agent as one who can assist in bringing about the change in a direction acceptable to the client. This is much too superficial a use of the concept of motivation, however. We really need to inquire as to how people become motivated.

Motivation Cannot Be Forced

Strictly speaking, you cannot make a person be motivated any more than you can force a permanent change in attitude. In both cases the initiative must come from within the self. Fortunately, (1) *an unfilled need is a motivator;* (2) *the desire to learn or change does occur as a result of a feeling of inadequacy or a need to do better, and* (3) *this felt need can be created or intensified.*

It is at this point that we cross the theoretical bridge between the essence of "nonsupport,"[8] which we explored in the unfreezing stage, and "coercive persuasion."[9] For while there are wide latitudes in terms of both the direction and speed of the changing step, depending upon the needs of the client system and the change agent's *change design,* one can "give motivation a little push." By the time you push, the prospective changes should already have been involved in numerous task-related activities and interactions as part of the change program. In the main, they have encountered both nonempathic and empathic behavior; observed both behavioral flexibility and inflexibility; talked to both nonlisteners and active listeners. They also have watched some people succeed quite easily in accomplishing assigned tasks while others, perhaps including themselves, have performed rather poorly or have failed altogether. They have, then, been experiencing nonsupport. At this point the change agent can utilize some coercive persuasion. This begins, simply, with the change agent providing a model of behavior which the subject(s) can emulate *if they wish.* Schein suggests that people can form new behavior patterns by the process of either "identification or internalization."[10]

Identification

Identification can be described as mimicking the behavior of some other person who is either respected and trusted or whose behavior is not inconsistent with one's own. At the precise moment in time when the behavior one usually would employ in a given situation has been called into question as ineffective, there is a tremendous need to grasp for an alternative. If the change agent has presented an emulative model, the subject may well try it. Should the new behavior work better than the old one, we have the beginnings of the process of changing.

[8] Albanese, *op. cit.*

[9] Schein, "Management Development as a Process of Influence," reprinted in this volume, p. 135-52.

[10] *Ibid.*

By itself, however, identification usually results in temporary change only. When the person you emulate is no longer around, or the situation you are faced with is one you have never seen handled by the person you copy, you probably revert to an old behavior type.

Internalization

The key technique to obtain internalization is not threat, but rather a *reward-punishment climate* quite different from the one most of us are used to. After all, the system most of us live and work in uses a rigid structure based upon preplanned, prescribed, conforming behavior. Rewards are given for doing as told—without question or challenge—and the "yes-man" is king. Sanctions are imposed for asking why or how.

Internalization calls for a climate conducive to growth and change, however. People are encouraged to feel free to find out who they are, and then to be themselves. They are allowed to satisfy their own needs. Exploring new ideas, self introspection, and experimenting with new behaviors is the *in* thing to do: that is what gets rewarded. When changes come about due to internalization, they become permanent.

In a sense, we have just described the ideal learning climate for any educational institution.[11] Even in the more structured, formalized learning situations, the discussion leader (teacher) needs to become, if you will, a conductor of a symphony orchestra. This means he interprets the music and usually selects which pieces to play. In addition he also establishes the rhythm, controls the tempo, and enhances the rendition with his own special syncopation. But the music still must come from the musicians (students). The conductor (teacher) can hardly expect his concert to include "There'll Be Some Changes Made" if his orchestra (students) only knows—or wants to play—"Auld Lang Syne" or "Yesterday."

Learning is a very private process. So is changing. Understanding this is mandatory if one is to perform effectively as a change agent. As we continually review and update our study of the literature as well as engage in action research, we become increasingly aware that altering behavior is a tricky business. So is changing attitudes. Both require careful planning, an extensive knowledge of theory, a thorough grasp of the literature, plenty of experience, and an error-free performance at every step.

It seems important, before shifting our focus to the last stage, that we stress one point again. Schein did not feel that coercive persuasion was in any way morally bad. Neither do we. This is, however, because we believe in an emphasis upon *persuasion* rather than *coercion*. We absolutely reject the idea of forced change. We are comfortable with persuasion because few people can be really hoodwinked for very long into holding attitudes contrary to their total life styles or frames of reference.

[11]Cf. John Holt, *How Children Learn* (New York: Pittman Publishing Company, 1967); Don M. Flournoy & Associates, *The New Teachers* (San Francisco: Jossey-Bass, Inc., 1972).

The Most Critical Stage

Although it may be truly a moot point to select one of Lewin's three steps as the most important, we nevertheless explicitly opt for step three: refreezing. The reason is, simply, that we believe the other two steps can be—and frequently are—completely negated or neutralized at this point. Even if the unfreezing and changing steps have been performed with care and show very positive results, the effects of them will all be lost unless genuine support for the new behavior and attendant attitudes is provided for in the everyday work environment.

For any change to "take," it must be "locked in" by the very strong backing of key managerial people up and down the hierarchy. In addition, the structure and climate of the formal organization must provide continuous rewards for the new behavior mode. This is why change programs frequently fail to produce the desired results. Suppose the ABC Company sends Barney to a five-day, live-in laboratory session at some remote ski resort and he changes in the desired direction. What happens when he returns to the same old job, same old red tape, and same old miserable boss? The best guess is that Barney will revert to what he was before he went away. Either that, or he will be so out of phase that he will get fired or quit.

Thus, it would seem that if the ABC Company wants Barney's new, T-Group-induced behavior to last, it also must alter the technology and job design, rules, reward-punishment structure, and style of leadership of Barney's boss. Moreover, these changes must be accomplished before Barney returns, for it is then he needs the maximum supportive climate.

The real test as to whether changes in behavior will result in the corresponding attitude changes—and thus become permanent—is the test of time. What happens after the change agent withdraws? What happens if the new behavior is challenged. What happens when the client system faces sudden, unexpected adversity? Do we see a return to the old ways, or creative, resourceful, dynamic behavior which not only deals with the crisis but also goes beyond what the change agent was able to "transmit"? If the former takes place, all was for naught; if the latter occurs, then success can be proclaimed.

We are, of course, aware that the preceding paragraphs call for a virtually impossible response from any organization in a short time like a year—let alone two weeks, which might be average for a T-Group experience to last. Impossible, that is, unless the change efforts are designed: (1) to take place over an extended period of time (two years is probably a minimum); and (2) to entail a gradual evolution of not only the behavior and attitudes of the people in it, but of the structure and technology of the organization as well.

Such a change program will require an integrated theory that draws from and incorporates all that is relevant from the literature of whatever field it may be and whatever preferences the change agent may have in terms of a design for change.

part III

CHANGE STRATEGIES IN ACTION: METHODS AND RESULTS

Part III brings together a variety of "action research" field studies that detail the specific methods and techniques for instituting organizational change. This is applied research. The first section contains material concerned with attempts to alter organizational direction by launching a direct attack on individual behavior. We have categorized these articles under the heading "The Organization Development Approach."

Relative to philosophy, the proponents of the organization development (O.D.) approach, or the behavioral approach as it is often called, assert that real organizational change occurs only if there is a shift in values, beliefs, and attitudes of the employees who must make it work. By referring back to our conceptual model in the first article of Part I, the reader will see that the behavioralists advocate transformations in the personal system. They argue that the organization structure, and the jobs within it, will be altered automatically by the employees whose attitudes, values, and beliefs have been changed.

Client-centered applied group dynamics, where power is redistributed or equalized and individual growth and development is encouraged, forms the nucleus of the O.D. approach. Programs for doing this embrace opening strong two-way communications channels, utilizing genuine participative decision making (i.e., shared power), forming group goals, and tapping group resources to solve organizational problems. Specific training methods applying the behavioral philosophy include, in order of increasing structure, T-Groups, confrontation groups, simulation, and managerial grid programs.

The behavioral approach can operate on any of three levels: (1) the individual level, which is involved with changing the person's perceptions, motivation, learning, and maturing mechanisms; (2) the interpersonal level, which is involved with improving competence in two-person (primarily superior/subordinate) relationships; and (3) the small group level, which is concerned with enhancing cooperation and working relations of the unit as a whole.

Paul C. Buchanan's essay, "Laboratory Training and Organization Development," initiates the O.D. section. It is not a change program per se, but is included to provide the reader with a survey of laboratory training and O.D. and to make the next three selections more meaningful. These papers, "An Organic Problem-Solving Method of Organizational Change" by Sheldon A. Davis, "Changing Behavior as a Means to Increased Efficiency" by Alton C. Bartlett, and "Breakthrough in Organization Development" by Robert R. Blake, Jane S. Mouton, *et al.*, represent various ways of impelmenting the O.D. approach to altering organizational behavior.

The second section of Part III is comprised of four studies characterizing the structural method for changing behavior. As contrasted with the behavioral approach, the main focus here is on altering the environment around the individual so as to lead ultimately to a change in behavior. For this reason it is sometimes called the indirect approach to change and obtains its prime support from the ranks of the classical organization theorists.

For altering the course of an organization by this method, three basic tactics are available. First, jobs can be redesigned so as to enlarge and enrich them. Among other things, this entails minimizing job overlap; restructuring content to build in greater creativity, variety of duties, responsibility, and so forth; reducing the span of control; and improving coordinating devices. Second, workflow can be viewed as the central nervous system of the work process, with people and jobs rearranged or modified to ameliorate the flow of work. This is often labeled the social engineering approach. Third, the organization structure can be manipulated to provide a decentralized environment; this entails pushing the final decision-making powers down to lower levels in the hierarchy and gives individuals at lower levels more autonomy. It also gets decisions made closer to the point of action, provides greater flexibility and tactical mobility, improves the speed of decision making, and increases the likelihood that subordinates will demonstrate initiative and incentive.[1]

The Louis E. Davis article, "The Design of Jobs," is a fine piece showing the positive relationship between job redesign and behavioral change. This is followed by the Eliot D. Chapple and Leonard R. Sayles selection, "Work Flow as the Basis for Organization Design," which presents three change programs detailing improved task performance by utilizing the natural flow of work as the foundation and modifying the flow of jobs accordingly. The reading by Elaine Cumming, I. L. W. Clancey, and John Cumming, "Improving Patient Care through Organizational Changes in the Mental Hospital," pertains to the betterment of organizational attitudes and functioning through direct changes in the organization structure and policy as well as in the nursing hierarchy. The Nancy

[1] These advantages of decentralization were excerpted from Anthony G. Athos and Robert Coffey, *Behavior in Organizations: A Multidimensional View* (Englewood Cliffs, N.J.: Prentice-Hall, Inc., 1968), p. 229.

C. Morse and Everett Reimer study, "The Experimental Change of a Major Organizational Variable," which completes this section, demonstrates the positive effect on job satisfaction and productivity by moving from a centralized to decentralized structure to give lower-level personnel more independence in making final decisions.

In studying these articles, the reader should be aware that even though this section is divided into two parts we are not trying to set up an either/or choice between the two basic methods. There are advantages as well as drawbacks to each approach. As Glueck states:

> ... the structuralists contend that structural change is adequate to bring organization change. They criticize behavioral change methods as taking too long, costing too much, having "fade out," and leading to ethical problems. (Is it the organization's right to attempt to change an employee's personality.) The behavioralists contend that real long-term change comes only with their methods. They contend that structural change alone leads to more apparent than real results that are not long lasting and not effective.[2]

For this reason, it should not be a matter of choosing between the behavioral (people) approach and the structural (things) approach; rather, it should be a matter of the CA distilling the information presented here and blending *both* approaches into a viable change program.[3]

[2]William F. Glueck, "Organization Change in Business and Government," *Academy of Management Journal,* XII (December 1969), 443.

[3]For the interested reader who wants to pursue material beyond this text, there are many other fine studies detailing change strategies in action. Under the O.D. approach one might examine several recent and excellent books in the Addison-Wesley series on O.D., namely: *Organization Development: Strategies and Models* by Richard Beckhard; *Organization Development: Its Nature, Origins, and Prospects* by Warren G. Bennis; *Building a Dynamic Corporation through Grid Organization Development,* by Robert R. Blake and Jane S. Mouton. In addition, comprehensive treatment of the topic is found in: Chris Argyris, *Intervention Theory and Method: A Behavioral Science View* (Reading, Mass.: Addison-Wesley Publishing Company, 1970); and Chris Argyris, *Management and Organizational Development* (New York: McGraw-Hill Book Company, 1971). A few excellent articles on the behavioral approach include: Robert T. Golembiewski and Stokes B. Currigan, "Planned Change in Organization Style Based on the Laboratory Approach," *Administrative Science Quarterly* (March 1970), pp. 79-93; Alexander Winn, "Social Change in Industry: From Insight to Implementation," *The Journal of Applied Behavioral Science,* II, No. 2 (April-June 1966), 170-84; Michael G. Blansfield, "Depth Analysis of Organizational Life," *California Management Review,* V, No. 2 (Winter 1967), 29-42; Richard Beckhard, "An Organization Improvement Program in a Decentralized Organization," *The Journal of Applied Behavioral Science,* II, No. 1 (January-March 1966), 3-25. With respect to the structural approach as a change strategy, the reader might examine: Arthur J. Kover, "Reorganization in an Advertising Agency: A Case Study of a Decrease in Integration," *Human Organization,* XXII, No. 4 (Winter 1963), 252-59; Kilburn Le Compte, "Organizational Structures in Transition," as it appears in Albert H. Rubenstein and Chadwick J. Haberstroh, eds., *Some Theories of Organization* (Homewood, Ill.: Richard D. Irwin, Inc., and the Dorsey Press, 1966), pp. 309-24; Paul R. Lawrence, *The Changing of Organizational Behavioral Patterns: A Case Study of Decentralization* (Boston: Division of Research, Harvard Business School, 1958); Jonathan A. Slesinger and Ernest Harburg, "Organizational Change and Executive Behavior," *Human Organization,* XXVII, No. 2 (Summer 1968), 95-109; A. K. Rice, *Productivity and Social Organization: The Ahmedabad Experiment* (London: Tavistock Publication, Ltd., 1958); S. E. Seashore and D. G. Bowers, *Changing the Structure and Functioning of an Organization,* Monograph No. 33 (Ann Arbor, Michigan: University of Michigan, 1963); Shigeru Kobayashi, "The Creative Organization—A Japanese Experiment," *Personnel* (December 1970).

Laboratory Training and Organization Development

Paul C. Buchanan's essay is really the foundation article for the next three selections. It provides the reader with the relevant background material for understanding and critically assessing the effectiveness of laboratory training as a means for altering behavior. Drawing from the existing empirical evidence, the author presents a cogent discussion of the value and impact of laboratory training by exploring six prime topics: (1) problems of research design for evaluating effectiveness; (2) theory development regarding what takes place inside a T-Group; (3) kinds of learning that transpire; (4) factors that increase learning by participants; (5) types of individual influenced; and (6) the use of laboratory training in organizational development programs. The article concludes with a four-point summary of the literature.

LABORATORY TRAINING AND ORGANIZATION DEVELOPMENT

Paul C. Buchanan

Yesheva University

This paper reviews studies published between 1964 and May 1968 on laboratory training in human relations and its use in attempts to enhance the effectiveness of organizations. After some of the difficulties in conducting such research in this area are considered, findings are examined as they relate to five issues in the design and the application of laboratory training. These findings are also compared with findings from a similar review reported by the author four years ago.

A systematic review of the literature on the effectiveness of laboratory training in industry (Buchanan, 1965) resulted in the following conclusions:

1. Laboratory training is effective as a means of facilitating specifiable changes in individuals in the industrial setting.

2. It has been used effectively in some programs of organizational development, but not in others.

3. Behavioral scientists associated with the National Training Laboratories are actively engaged in subjecting their theories and methods to systematic analysis, and in developing strategies for organization development.

Paul C. Buchanan is associate professor of education and coordinator of doctoral programs in school administration in the Ferkauf graduate school of humanities and social studies at Yeshiva University.

Reprinted from *Administrative Science Quarterly*, XIV, No. 3 (Sept. 1969), 466-80. Reprinted by permission of the *Administrative Science Quarterly* and the author.

4. Some of these strategies, now being studied systematically, are showing exciting results.

The purpose of this paper is to bring the earlier review up to date and to broaden the focus from industry to all types of organizations.

Interest in laboratory training in human relations has expanded significantly. For example, in 1968, National Training Laboratories were conducting 20 percent more sessions than in the previous year; sensitivity training has become a common activity in workshops and teacher institutes in the field of education; and the number of professionals in the National Training Laboratories has increased from 159 in 1963 to 289 in 1968.

Research on laboratory training has also expanded. There have been 68 technical articles or books which pertain to some aspect of laboratory training published since the earlier review (Buchanan, 1965). In a bibliography of research prepared by Durham and Gibb (1960), 49 studies were listed for the period 1947-1960, and 76 for the period 1960-1967. Undoubtedly the best single source of background information on the topic up to 1965 is the book by Schein and Bennis (1965).

Studies on laboratory training during the past four years deal with (1) the methodology of evaluation, (2) theory development, (3) kinds of learning brought about in the laboratories, (4) factors influencing learning in the laboratories, (5) types of individuals who learn from laboratory training, and (6) laboratory training in organization development.

Methodology of Evaluation

The methodology of evaluation continues to be a major problem, yet several recent studies indicate progress.

General Variables in Methodology

House (1967) classified the variables relevant to the problem of evaluation into four categories: objectives of the training, initial states of the learner, initial states of the organization, and methods of inducing change in the learner. Then, considering the methods as input variables, the objectives of the laboratory training as output variables, and the initial states of both the participants and the organization as moderators, he generated a paradigm of relationships that highlighted the issues in planning and assessing organizational development efforts and outlined a specific assessment design to illustrate the paradigm. The result is a clear presentation of relevant types of variables and their inter-connectedness, a paradigm that is applicable to the design and assessment of any change in the "person dimension" (Leavitt, 1965) of organization performance. House's study also makes clear that neither the design nor the assessment of any training program is likely to be effective if it does not take into account variables in the *situation* as well as variables in the *person*, a finding highlighted earlier by Fleishman *et al.* (1955), but still often ignored. Equally important, House shows how theory can be used to make it possible for evaluation studies to contribute to a systematic body of knowledge. However, his paradigm is more adequate in providing for moderator than for output variables. As moderators he lists "the nature of the primary work group," "the formal authority system" of the organization, and "exercise of authority by superior"; yet he doesn't list these organization factors as output variables: he lists only changes in knowledge, skill, attitude, and job performance. But it is on the assumption that such changes in the participant will result in changes in the output of the work unit to which the learner belongs that organizations support training. As important as House's work is, therefore, it omits some important variables.

Problems of Design

While House dealt with general problems of design and evaluation, Harrison (1967) has made a thoughtful analysis of some specific issues. First, as he points out, it is seldom possible to assign participants randomly to the treatment and a control group. Usually participants are either self-selected, or are assigned for administrative or other organizational reasons (the personnel officer wants them to attend; they are part of a unit that is to participate; etc.) where control-groups are used for assessment studies. They are usually selected *post hoc* and with little information available about their similarity to the treatment group. For example, in the studies of Bunker (1965) and Bunker and Knowles (1967), control subjects were nominated by participants, and no data are given for the basis of this nomination, about the experiences the controls had during the period covered by the assessment, or the reasons why participants had attended the laboratory and the controls had not. Only two of the studies reviewed in this paper meet requirements for appropriate control groups (Deep, Bass, and Vaughan, 1967; Schmuck, 1968).

But there is an added difficulty in using a control group which Harrison discusses: the fact that being a member of a group influences expectations and thereby introduces bias, if perceptions of behavior are used as criteria. Because of these difficulties, Harrison encourages (and utilizes) assessment designs that examine the relation between (predicted) processes of training and outcomes from training.

A second problem is that of when assessment measures after laboratory training should be taken to obtain a valid evaluation of the impact of training. As Harrison points out, until one knows the pattern of the impact, he doesn't know what kinds of changes to look for and when. For example, the immediate effect on participants may be uncertainty, discomfort, and experimentation, which may then give way to confidence, new behavior patterns, and stabilization. If this were the case, then measures taken only at the end of the training would be very misleading.

Related to the issue of timing of evaluation is that of whether assessment should focus on predicted and/or desired outcomes (what Harrison calls a normative approach), or should be more like a net to catch whatever influences may be apparent. Harrison also discusses difficulties in assessing change on metagoals of laboratory training.

Because of variability in the designs of programs which are called laboratory training it is difficult to specify and apply a design that can be replicated or meaningfully compared with other training methods. As Harrison (1967:6) says, ".... we do not yet have adequate enough theory about the effects of different elements of training design even to permit us to classify laboratories according to design."

Miles (1965a, 1965b), for many years an innovator of evaluation designs, met many of the requirements of House's paradigm and Harrison's emphasis on examining process variables. More recently he and his associates have used theory in increasing the rigor of assessment designs (Miles *et al.*, 1965 and 1966; Benedict *et al.*, 1967). This method which they called a "clinical-experimental approach," has five components: (1) It calls for a clear division of labor between the researcher responsible for assessment, and the change agents responsible for participants. (2) Data are collected both clinically (running account of events before, during, and following the interventions) and experimentally (by pre-planned and periodic measurements of the treatment and a control group. (3) The investigators make theory-based general predictions about the impact that the training is likely to have on specific variables of the organization. (4) The change agent obtains information from the participants, and on this basis formulates specific training activities; then he makes short-range predictions about the variables which the intervention would affect. (5) Careful attention is given to the tactical assessment design. (Miles uses a design involving treatment and control groups and several post-training measurements.) In the study reporting their attempt to use this design (Benedict *et al.*, 1967) the investigators were not completely successful in meeting their methodological prescriptions; problems arose around keeping the research members and change agents from influencing each other (especially through the exchange of data); and there was questionable similarity between the treatment and the control groups. Even so, the approach of Miles and associates represents a significant improvement in evaluating change efforts.

The study of Marrow *et al.* (1967) is of special significance, partly because it exploited the availability of two large organizations with known similarity and with known "states of health." As in Miles' design, the change agents and the researchers constituted two separate teams. Measurements of human factors and management practices were repeated for both the treatment and the control organization. In addition, economic data were also obtained and systematically analyzed in relation to both short-range and longer-range impact on a number of variables. Further elaboration of the measure used is provided by Likert (1967).

Greiner's study of a grid-based organizational-development project was another methodological advance, in that in addition to the researchers' not being part of the change-agent team, information was obtained about conditions that preceded and in fact apparently led to the intervention (Greiner, 1965; Blake *et al.*, 1964).

Many of the studies reviewed have attempted, as Harrison and House suggest, to examine hypothesized relations among independent, intervening, and dependent variables (Rubin, 1967 a, b; Harrison, 1966; Kolb *et al.,* 1968; French *et al.,* 1966; Deep *et al.,* 1967; and Friedlander, 1967); Yet in many the basis on which the predicted connection between the training and the measured outcome is not specified (Bunker and Knowles, 1967; Byrd, 1967). Equally important, many do not provide theoretical links between the expected change and improvement in performance on the job.

The practice of assessing the extent of change attributed to a training program by asking participants and their associates to describe any changes they have noted during a specified time after the training (Bunker, 1965; Bunker and Knowles, 1967) has obvious weaknesses such as the demand it makes on memory. But comparisons of responses to questionnaires obtained before and after training also present difficulties. One problem is that the standard of reference used by the respondent may itself be influenced significantly by the training. For example, Blake and Mouton (1968) required participants to rank themselves as to grid styles before and at the end of the seminar, and one of the expected outcomes from the seminar was to increase the use of the "9,9," style by participants. The data (Blake and Mouton 1968:52) from measures before and after the seminar show a *decrease* of around 32 in the percentage of participants who saw themselves having 9,9 as their most characteristic style. And it is a common experience in groups where questionnaires are used to help the group diagnose and assess its progress on, say, openness, to find no increase or actually a decrease on ratings of openness at the same time that members state (and demonstrate) that they are becoming more open with each other.

There is also the problem of test sensitization, which can influence the responses of a control group. Friedlander (1967:305), in interpreting his data which revealed a decrease in effectiveness of the control group, noted:

> The first administration of the [Group Behavior Inventory] queried comparison group members with blunt questions on sensitive issues which they were unprepared to confront at that time. But after six months of observing those inadequacies that did occur, expectations and standards of the leadership role became clearer. Since current leadership practice did not conform to these expectations, comparison group members now perceived significantly greater inadequacies in the rapport and approachability of their chairman.

To the extent that a decrease occurs in the responses of the comparison group after the laboratory training, statistically significant differences between the treatment and the control group will lead to inaccurate conclusions about the impact of the training upon the treatment group. (They will look better due to an apparent decrease in the control group.) It appears that any measurement scheme involving perceptions are subject to error; therefore greater effort to devise other kinds are much needed.

Some additional shortcomings in the design of the assessment studies reviewed are:

1. In several evaluation procedures, changes noted were given equal weight, even though they appeared to vary greatly in importance (i.e., "listens more" was equivalent in the scoring system to "conducts more effective staff meetings").

2. Results from one study could not be compared with results from other studies, since the training programs evaluated varied in length, in the specific design, in the occupational mix of participants, and in the age and sex of participants. Also, the studies varied in the variables examined, the instrument used to assess change in a given variable, and the time at which measures were gathered after the training period. Thus a body of self consistent knowledge is slow to develop.

3. Where laboratory training was part of an organization development program (Blake and Mouton, 1968; Marrow *et al.*, 1967; Miles *et al.*, 1966), it was difficult to know how much any change effected was due to the laboratory training and how much to other circumstnaces (Greiner, 1965, 1967).

One must conclude, then, that even though much work has been done to devise more effective evaluation designs, the major shortcomings have not been overcome. This means that the findings summarized below are based on inadequate design and can only be tentative.

Theory Development

In 1964 eight fellows of the National Training Laboratories presented their views on what happens in a T-group. Several important theoretical papers dealing with this issue have appeared since that time.

Theories

Hampden-Turner (1966) developed "an existential learning theory" which he used to integrate findings from three empirical studies of T-group effectiveness. His theory involved a "developmental spiral," wherein he hypothesized that the participant's initial quality of cognition, clarity of identity, and extent of self-esteem would result in his ordering his experience. This ordering in the context of a T-group, leads the participant to risk his competence in interacting with another person; the reaction of the other person stimulates the participant to a new integration of his experiences. This in turn leads to changes in the quality of the participant's cognition, clarity of identity, and extent of self-esteem, and to a repetition of the cycle.

Harrison (1965) formulated a "cognitive model for interpersonal and group behavior" which was intended as a framework for research, and which he later used as a basis for forming training groups (Harrison and Lubin, 1965) and for designing laboratories (Harrison and Oshry, 1965). Harrison sees learning resulting when a participant's way of construing events is "up-ended" by confrontation with other participants who construe the same event differently, and when the participant also feels sufficiently supported by others that he is able to work through the consequences of the distrubing confrontation. This theory clearly has value as a basis for designing training experiences, and there is considerable support for the belief that the type of learning (change) it emphasizes is important. For example, Harvey (1966) has detected several differences in behavior of people who are high on abstract (versus concrete) thinking, a difference which appears to be compatible with Harrison's emphasis on cognitive structure.

Argyris (1965) stated a theory of individual learning from which he derived implications for designing laboratories. Criticism from several fellows of the National Training Laboratories (Argyris, 1967) should dispel any belief that the National Training Laboratories have become complaisant as a result of their present rapid growth and popularity. Argyris also utilized his theory to identify variables in terms of which change could be assessed, devised measures of these variables, and tested his theory (Argyris, 1965).

Clark and Culbert hypothesized that self-awareness develops as a function of mutually congruent therapeutic relations between participants and trainers (Clark and Culbert, 1965).

Schein and Bennis (1965) set forth a theory of learning through laboratory training which consists of a cyclical interplay of a dilemma or disconfirming experience, attitude change, new behavior, new information and awareness, leading to additional change, new behavior, etc.

Smith (1966) formulated and tested a complex theory of learning based on Kelman's model of influence. Bass (1967) made a critique of T-group theory and concluded that the kinds of learning emphasized can be dysfunctional to job performance. As partial evidence for this view, he cites a study (Deep *et al.* 1967) in which it was found that intact T-groups performed less effectively on a business game than groups composed of members from different T-groups. (In the study by Deep *et al.* (1967), the T-group met without trainers and were conducted in what is called "instrumented" laboratory training.)

Laboratory Training and the Improvement of Organizational Performance

Several people have formulated systematic theories about the use of laboratory training in improving the functioning of organizations. Perhaps the most important are those of Blake and Mouton (1964, 1968) in regard to industrial organizations, and Miles and associates (1966) in regard to schools. Blake and Mouton (1968) deal wholly with their plan for organizational development and with guidelines for implementing the plan. Although the basic concepts of planned change which they present are similar to those conceptualized by Lippitt, Watson, and Westley (1958) the value of the study lies in its technology: Blake and Mouton have devised and tested concrete and theoretically sound methods for implementing the concepts.

Miles and his associates (1966) built upon the survey-feedback strategy of planned change and made a special effort to determine empirically the way in which intervention (or input), intervening, and output variables were interrelated, especially in school systems.

Several other writers have formulated theories about organizations, which are congruent with the value of laboratory training and which emphasize laboratory training as a means of improving the functioning of organizations (Shepard, 1965; McGregor, 1967; Bennis, 1966; Davis, 1967; Schein and Bennis, 1965).

Greiner (1967) speculates systematically about "antecedents to planned change," asking why the Blake-Mouton interventions had the impact they did. He was able to identify "how the consultants made use of roots put down in the unplanned stages many years before [the beginning of the consultant-planned change] to build top management support for Managerial Grid training," and he relates specific events that occurred during the organization development program to these historic roots. His study thus integrates imaginative observation, survey findings, and theory derived from a variety of related fields into a coherent and nonpolemic theory of organization change. He emphasizes the importance of the historical development of an organization in attempts to change it, a conclusion also reached by Sarason (1966) in his statement that the outcome of a *current* change effort is highly influenced by the outcome of *earlier* change efforts. Failure to cope effectively with the organization's earlier experiences with changes also appeared to be one of the reasons for the limited impact of a change project in a recent study (Buchanan, 1968).

From this brief overview of recent theoretical developments, it appears that the primary focus has been on how an individual learns in T-groups, and on processes of planned organizational development. Much less attention has been given to the processes of *group* development. Only two studies (Lakin and Carson, 1964; Psathas and Hardert, 1966) attempted to explore patterns of group development.

Kinds of Learning

Persistence of Learning

In summarizing findings from studies of laboratory training it seems appropriate, first, to consider whether the learning from laboratory training persists. Two studies bear on this question. Schutz and Allen (1966) gathered information on the FIRO-B (Fundamental Interpersonal Relations Orientation—Behavioral) questionnaire from participants (and a control group) at the beginning, the end, and six months after a two-week laboratory. They found that participants changed during the training, and that the changes continued after the training. Harrison (1966) collected information from 76 participants at the beginning, a few weeks after, and a few months after they took part in a laboratory. He concluded that there was a change in the predicted direction at both follow-up periods, but that the difference became significant only between the end of the training and the second follow-up measure; thus the training appeared to be progressive. These findings are consistent with those of Bunker and Knowles (1967), who found significant changes in participants (as compared with a control group) 10–12 months following training. Also, Morton and Bass (1964), in a study of 97 participants, found a marked increase in motivation to improve their performance at the end of the laboratory and substantial changes in job performance in a follow-up 12 weeks later. French *et al.* (1966) also found further changes in participants' self-concepts following the laboratory.

Types of Learning

The next question to be explored concerns what is learned. Here it is difficult to categorize the findings, since researchers rarely look for the same results; and when they do, they typically use different measures, except for the retrospective "behavior change description questionnaire" developed by Miles (1965a) and Bunker (1965) and used in at least three studies.

Reduction of Extreme Behavior

Two studies produce findings, similar in this respect to an earlier study by Boyd and Ellis, which suggest that laboratory training changes people selectively, depending upon their personality. Schutz and Allen (1966) found that (as measured by FIRO-B) very dominant participants become less dominant, while very submissive participants become more assertive. Using the same instrument, Smith (1964) found that his experimental subjects (108 students in 11 training groups) changed significantly more in the direction of a better match between what they *expected* and what they *wanted* on both the control and the affection scales of FIRO-B. Some of the findings of Bunker can also be interpreted as an indication that reduction of abrasive or otherwise undesirable behaviors occurred. Such studies raise the possibility that laboratory training produces other-directed behavior; but Kassajian (1965) found no change in laboratory participants on an instrument which purported to measure other-directedness.

Openness, Receptivity, Awareness, Tolerance of Differences. Changes such as these are most consistently found following laboratory training (and are, of course, among the most commonly stated objectives). Such changes apparently result even from short laboratories. Bunker and Knowles (1967), Morton and Wight (1964), Rubin (1967), Morton and Bass (1964), Schutz and Allen (1966), Smith (1966), and Kolb *et al.* (1968) all report this kind of learning. Such changes probably occurred in the other studies also, but the measures used did not relate to this kind of change.

Operational Skills. This category includes behavior like listening, encouraging the participation of others, use of new techniques, solicitation of feedback, etc. Outcomes of this sort were reported by Bunker and Knowles (1967), Schutz and Allen (1966), Morton and Wight (1964), Sikes (1964), De Michele (1966), and Schmuck (1968).

Because of its design, the study by Schmuck is worth further comment. He studied a four-week laboratory for 20 classroom teachers, where the design included T-groups, problem-solving exercises, and practice in using instruments and procedures for diagnosing classroom problems. Then before the laboratory ended, each teacher formulated specific plans for the following year, applying what she had learned. Follow-up meetings were held bimonthly from September through December. He also met weekly with another set of teachers from the same large school system (and apparently with random assignment of teachers to the two groups), from September to December, covering the same material as in the laboratory except for the T-group work (and of course with much less total time). He found marked differences in the two groups as to the number of practices the participants tried out in their classrooms (5 to 17 by laboratory participants compared with 1 to 2 by the seminar participants), and in the *esprit de corps* among the teachers as indicated by the contacts they made with each other during the fall. What is more significant, he found improvement in the classrooms of the laboratory participants (as compared to both the seminar participants and a small control group), in that the students perceived themselves as having more influence in the class, as being better liked and an integral part of a friendship group in the class, and as being helpful to each other.

Cognitive Style. Examples of this type of outcome are findings by Blake *et al.* (1965) that union and managerial participants reflected predicted differential shifts on a managerial grid questionnaire. Harrison (1966) found shifts on the Role Repertory Test from the use of concrete-instrumental toward inferential-expressive modes of thought. Oshry and Harrison (1966) found that many laboratory participants viewed their work environment more humanly and less impersonally, saw themselves more as a significant part of their work problems, and saw more connection between the meeting of interpersonal needs and the effectiveness of their work.

In some studies, however, changes that were expected were not found. Bowers and Soar (1961) found no differences between a group of 25 teachers who took part in half-day training sessions over a three week period and a control group, with respect to their use of group processes in their classrooms during the following academic year. This contrasts with Schmuck's finding significant carry-over into the classrooms (but his intervention consisted of four weeks full time, with systematic follow-up during the fall). Bunker (1965) found no differences between his laboratory participants and controls in initiative and assertiveness. Sikes (1964) failed to find predicted differences between laboratory graduates and a control group in their accuracy in predicting the responses of other members in a discussion group. And Oshry and Harrison (1966) predicted, but did not find, significant changes in sensitivity to the interpersonal needs of others or in the importance attributed to the interpersonal needs of others, when participants returned to their jobs.

Where does laboratory training effect change? There is clear evidence that personal growth results for most participants—they feel better about themselves, have new insights, and consider the training one of the important experiences in their life. Furthermore, participants continually report improvement in their family relations as a result of the experience (Winn, 1966). The value of the laboratory experience for job performance, however, is less convincing: fewer extreme behaviors, greater openness and self-awareness, increased operational skills, and new alternatives for viewing situations. These seem small advances compared to the powerful forces that maintain a status quo in organizations. But what such change does represent is an increased readiness for "next steps."

Factors Influencing Learning

Several recent studies deal with factors that increase learning by participants in the laboratory training; those dealing with the value of laboratory training for organizational development are discussed later.

Group Composition

Perhaps the most clear-cut results have emerged regarding the effects of group composition which have been examined in terms of personality and organizational membership of participants. (Harrison (1965:418–9) theorizes about personality factors as follows:

> The process of learning is best facilitated when the individual is placed in a learning situation where either the structure produces dissonance or a significant number of others will act, feel, and perceive in ways which create sharp, clear dissonance for the learner or are contrary to his values. The dissonance must, however, be meaningful to the learner in that the alternatives presented by the others have some anchoring points within his current cognitive systems regarding himself and his interpersonal relationships. . . . we propose that a degree of polarization be created on important issues within the group. This polarization provides the battlefield on which learning by the explorations of opposites can take place. "However, if the individual is exposed only to confrontation and dissonance, he is apt to react in extreme ways. . . . For our learning model to operate, the individual should find in the group some relationships which serve as a refuge and support. Persons with similar cognitive systems, values, and perceptions can provide this support and protection against the destructive efforts of a purely confronting experience. This supportive climate is the castle in our analogy.

After reviewing relevant literature, Harrison concluded that personality variables relevant to obtaining his conditions in the formation of groups were of three types: activity-passivity, high-low affect, and negative-positive affect. He found empirical confirmation of his theory, in that groups homogeneous or mixed on one or more of these variables differed predictably in the way the groups functioned and in the kind of learning. More specifically he concluded (1965:431):

1. Learning is facilitated by a group climate which provides support for one's cognitive, emotional, and behavioral orientation and at the same time confronts one with meaningful alternatives to those orientations.

2. Group climate can be manipulated by relatively crude selection procedures.

3. The models and the research findings reviewed here can be applied to the diagnosis of wide ranges of interpersonal learning difficulties and to the design of learning groups which will provide favorable conditions of support and confrontation. A study by Smith (1966) seems to support Harrison's findings about the importance of personality mix of participants.

Morton and Wight (1964) studied differences in organizational membership. They conducted three instrumented laboratories within a company with groups composed so that participants in six of the D-groups (the designation for T-groups in instrumented laboratories) were all from one department, and all members had direct superior-subordinate relations with others in the group; whereas participants in the other six D-groups did not have direct superior-subordinate relationships, and were from separate units of the plant. The three laboratories were conducted according to the same design. On the basis of critical events (critical event was defined as "anything that has happened since the laboratory which would not have occurred had their been no training") obtained from 90 percent of the participants three months after the laboratories, they (1964:35-36) concluded that

Participants from the more homogeneous groups reported a significantly greater proportion of critical events. In areas of personal responsibility such as supervisor responsibility for his subordinates, his responsibility for individual problem solving, for . . . listening, . . . and sensitivity for what was taking place, there was no significant difference in the frequencies with which incidents were reported. When the problems exceeded the limits of the customary personal responsibility and involved the kind of responsibility that results in highly effective team working relations, the homogeneous . . . groups far exceeded the heterogeneous trained groups in the frequencies with which these critical incidents were reported. The post-training activities of the participants have led them into some difficulties. The nature of the difficulties have varied with the homogeneity of the groups. Those who trained in the less homogeneous groups are reporting less accomplished and more resistance of a personal nature. The members of the homogeneous groups, . . . are reporting the greatest number of organizational barriers to applying what they have learned. Whereas the heterogeneous trained groups found their greatest barriers within their primary work group, among those who have not been in the training, the homogeneous trained group report their greatest difficulty in problem solving with those outside their department who have not received training.

These findings must be considered tentative, however, since variables other than the D-group composition could account for the differences between the two types of groups. For example, the report does not make clear the circumstances under which so many members from one department participated in the laboratories; it may have been the supervisor's enthusiasm rather than the D-group composition which accounted for the change. It is also possible that the differences in outcome occurred because many people from the same department had a similar training experience (i.e., participating in a laboratory) rather than that they were in the same D-groups.

Duration of Laboratory

A third variable apparently making a difference in learning outcome is the duration of the laboratory training. Bunker and Knowles (1967) compared the outcomes from two three-week and two two-week summer sessions conducted by National Training Laboratories. They found that the three-week laboratories "fostered more behavioral changes" than the two-week ones; that is, more participants in the three-week ones made changes "toward more pro-active and interactive behavior," while changes made by the two-week participants were in the area of increased receptiveness (i.e., listening, sensitivity, etc.) However, they noted that the laboratories were similar in the amount of time spent in T-groups, but differed greatly in the time devoted to problems relating to their work; thus the differential impact could be due to the design, or interaction between the design and duration, rather than to duration alone. The question of duration merits more study since costs are closely related to duration and almost every study indicates that the trained group shows change.

Trainer Behavior

Interaction effects between trainer and participant orientation on the FIRO-F questionnaire were found to have differential impact upon the "laboratory learning climate" (Powers, 1965) and upon kinds of learning (Smith, 1966). Bolman (1968) also studied the relation of trainer behavior-openness, congruence, and consistency (as judged by participants) to learning by participants. Although the results were inclusive, he succeeded in isolating dimensions of trainer behavior and a way of measuring them. Culbert examined the differential impact of "more" and "less" self-disclosing trainer behavior in two T-groups, and found that although trainer behavior differed as planned, the groups attained the same level of self-awareness (Culbert, 1968).

Goal-setting and Feedback

Several studies have been conducted to examine the effects of goal-setting and feedback. Kolb et al. (1968) introduced a procedure in T-groups, by which each participant set a specific change goal for himself and was encouraged to work to meet his goal; then they varied the amount of feedback received during the training, and they attempted to heighten each participant's commitment to the goals he set. They found that differences in both the extent of commitment and in the amount of feedback influenced learning. French, et al. (1966) also found that the greater the amount of feedback, the greater the extent of change on self-selected change goals. And Harrison (1966) found that the amount of change in cognitive orientation was significantly related to ratings by participants of how other participants reacted to and utilized feedback during T-group sessions. Those who made it easy for others to give feedback, and who tested the validity of feedback by seeking more, showed the most change. Thus it appears that provision for participants to obtain and utilize feedback is an important factor in laboratory design.

In summary, then, it appears that the climate which develops in the training group, and the kind and/or extent of learning which occurs, are influenced by the personality mix of the participants, the organizational relationships of the participants, and the way the design utilizes feedback. Studies regarding the effect of duration of the laboratory and of trainer behavior are inconclusive.

Type of Laboratory Training and Job Improvement

The question of whether the greatest improvement on the job results from laboratories which focus almost wholly on personal growth or from those which include personal growth organizational problems, and planning for changes on the job has not been studied with sufficient rigor for meaningful conclusions to be drawn. Bunker and Knowles related their data to the issue; but since the laboratories that they studied varied in duration as well as in the proportion of time spent in T-groups, the differences they found cannot be attributed to the design alone.

Wilson *et al.* (1968) reported results from a follow-up on two 6-day "off-site" laboratories one of which utilized "the traditional sensitivity approach described by Weschler" and the other Morton's version of an instrumented laboratory. Six months after the instrumented laboratory and 18 months after the "sensitivity" laboratory, a very high and similar proportion of participants of the two laboratories reported that the experience was of value to them as individuals; participants of the instrumented laboratory showed significantly greater improvement as managers, as members of a team, in building team effort in their organizations, and in communicating with others in the work setting. Although the study design was a weak one, as the authors note, the findings were consistent with their predictions.

There are not studies comparing laboratory training with rational training (Ellis and Blum, 1967), "motive acquisition" training (McClelland, 1965), or other forms of training; yet there is certainly a need for such studies.

Types of Individual Influenced

Personality and Organization Variable

In one of the more thorough analyses of learning processes and outcomes, Miles (1965) explored 595 relations among criterion, home organization, treatment, and personal variables. He found significant relations between on-the-job change and sex (males change more), job security (as measured by years as a school principal, the more secure participant changed more), and power (as measured by number of teachers supervised, the more powerful changed more). He did not find significant differences between on-the-job change and age, ego strength (as measured by Barron's scale), flexibility (as measured by Barron's scale), need affiliation (as measured by French's test of insight), a combination of these personality variables, autonomy on the job (as measured by frequency of meetings with superior), perceived power in his work situation, perceived flexibility of his organization, and a combination of these three organizational variables. On the other hand, he found that several of these variables were significantly related to the participant's behavior during the training (specifically to the extent to which he became more communicative, and to the trainer's rating of the extent to which participants changed), and such behavior was in turn related to on-the-job changes.

Unfortunately, there are few replications of Miles' studies. No other study examines age or sex as a factor in learning from laboratories. With respect to personality, Rubin (1967) found that anomy (which as predicted was itself unaffected by laboratory training) significantly influenced the extent of change in self-awareness, which was a factor in the extent of change in acceptance of others. Harrison (1966) found no significant relation between prelaboratory scores on an instrument measuring concrete-instrumental versus inferential-expressive orientation and extent of change as indicated by comparing pre-training with post-training scores on this instrument. He also found no relation between the prelaboratory scores on this instrument and the participants' reactions to feedback during the laboratory—a finding which seems surprising if Harrison's theory about the importance of cognitive orientation is accurate.

In a study of classroom teachers, Bowers and Soar (1961) found that an increase in the teachers' use of group processes in the classroom following training was greatest for teachers (a) who were well adjusted and (b) who used group methods before receiving the training. Harrison and Oshry (1965) found that people who were seen as changing most in a T-group were those who were described by colleagues as open to the ideas of others, were accepting of others, and listened well. These two studies suggest that laboratory training develops the participant's interpersonal style further rather than reversing it.

There is rather strong evidence that participants who become involved in the T-group learn more than those who are ranked low on involvement (Bunker, 1965; Harrison and Oshry, 1966). Although Miles did not find the relation between involvement and on-the-job change to be significant, he did find involvement significantly related to trainer ratings of the participants' effectiveness in the group, which was in turn significantly related to on-the-job change. Perhaps involvement in the training group is a function of the amount of dissonance produced—or of having "a castle and a battlefield," as Harrison suggests.

The direction that research should take, in the tradition of Miles' study, is exemplified by Smith (1966). Using a complex model of training based on Kelman's model of influence, and four separate measures of learning, Smith explored the relations among group climates (as indicated by the mix of participant orientation, trainer styles, and types of influence underlying the trainer-participant interaction process) and types of learning. He found support for his predictions that (a) the compliant learning pattern, found among groups with authority-oriented participants and trainers, showed highest learning in diagnostic ability, and (b) the internalizing learning pattern, found in groups with data-oriented participants and people-oriented trainers, showed the greatest favorable changes on FIRO scores and on interpersonal awareness. (This study was based on 31 T-groups, but since the laboratories varied in duration, and the participants in age and occupational background, it is difficult to know the extent to which extraneous factors clouded the findings.)

Influence of Background

Bunker and Knowles (1967) found that human relations laboratory participants from religious and governmental organizations showed significant change after a three-week laboratory but not after a two-week one; whereas participants from industry, education, and social service changed significantly after a two-week session, but the differences between the two-week and the three-week sessions were not significant. However, in this study the data on participants' background did not permit more than rough groupings, so little confidence can be placed in the findings.

In summary, these studies provide some support for the prediction that sex, job security, organizational power, anomy of the participant, trainer-participant interaction patterns, the openness of the participant, and the participant's involvement in the T-group make a difference in how much the participant learns; but clearly this is a topic which merits much more systematic exploration.

Laboratory Training in Organization Development

The evidence rather clearly indicates that laboratory training has a predictable and significant impact on most participants; yet it is also clear that from the standpoint of organizational improvement, laboratory training by itself is not enough. Several researchers have addressed themselves to facilitating "transfer of learning" (Winn, 1966, Bass, 1967, Oshry and Harrison, 1966.) Bass has identified eight different approaches currently being tried as a means of increasing transfer. In varying degrees, these methods involve including in the training people and/or activities associated with participants on the job, while still retaining a focus on behavior in the laboratory. Laboratory training systematically undertaken throughout the company, using combinations of stranger, work, and interface groups, was a major intervention in the program at the Space Technology Laboratories (Davis, 1967), in Non-Linear Systems (Kuriloff and Atkins, 1966), and in a division of Alcan (Winn, 1966). And the indications are that in all three companies the development efforts were effective.

In several strategies, however, laboratory training is one component of a multiphased program, as in Harwood Manufacturing Company's revitalization of Weldon (Marrow, *et al.* 1967), in Beckhard's work (1966) with a large hotel company, in Blake's and Mouton's work (1968), and in several projects in school systems (Buchanan, 1968; Miles *et al.*, 1966). In all of these cases of organization development, it is difficult to assess how important the laboratory training was in the impact of the total program (and of course it is equally difficult to assess the effectiveness of the total program itself). In an attempt to learn (Buchanan, 1967) what characterized effective programs of organization development eight successful programs and three unsuccessful ones were examined in the hope of finding some crucial variable. The use of laboratory training (or any other formal training) was not a crucial variable. Neither of the two cases (Guest, 1962; Jaques, 1951) where there was the clearest evidence of success involved formal training. One of the variables that did emerge as crucial was the introduction of new and more fruitful concepts for diagnosing current problems of the organization and setting improvement goals. Having new concepts for diagnosing current practices seemed to provide members of the organization with a means of getting from symptoms to variables which provided leverage for change; having new concepts for setting targets was important in working out clear ideas of potentiality and in developing dissonance and thus motivation for change. Information which has become available since that study was made is consistent with the conclusion about the development of new concepts as a crucial issue in organization development. In a project of organization development, analysis of the case reports on work done with two schools indicated that in the more effective of the two projects much more time was given to developing new concepts and the skills of key participants before diagnosis and planning for system change was undertaken (Buchanan, 1968). In the school system where there was more change, the superintendent had participated in a laboratory conducted by National Training Laboratories, and he and the key members of the system took part in a one-week laboratory of their own. In the other system, the superintendent did not have prior laboratory experience, and he and his key staff had a two-day laboratory of their own. In two other cases of organizational development where there was little evidence of effectiveness (Benedict *et al.*, 1967; Miles *et al.*, 1966), diagnosis of current conditions in the system was undertaken before any effort was made to develop new concepts. In contrast, Blake and Mouton (1968) continually stress the understanding of grid theory and the development of skills required in its application as an essential first step in each phase of their strategy. They begin by exposing the key person in the treatment organization to the managerial grid concept and to alternative styles of management and their implications. This is followed by familiarizing a representative sample of participants with the same concepts. Then all members of management are exposed to the same concepts, and only then are needs diagnosed and improvement goals set by individuals and teams for themselves and for the total organization. A case study recently reported by Bartlett

(1967), in which the development effort appeared to be successful, also involved development of new concepts and skills as the first step in the program.

Cognitive Changes

Quite clearly formal training is one effective means for developing cognitive changes as an opening step in organizational development. At the same time, it is also clear that there are other means of creating cognitive changes. The question, then, is whether laboratory training and, in fact, what *kind* of laboratory training provides the most useful concepts and skills for organizational development. Answers to this question can be sought from two courses: from theories about effective organization functioning, and from outcomes of organizational development programs that utilize different methods for introducing new concepts and skills. Although the latter method would be more convincing, at this time there is little such information available. One must therefore look to theory for support of the utility of laboratory training as a means of providing relevant cognitive changes in participants in programs of organizational development. Blake and Mouton have made a case for laboratory training based on grid theory; Shepard, Likert, Argyris, Bennis, and McGregor have provided relevant theory in the case of non-grid laboratory training; and Miles has systematically sought empirical data relevant to the question as it pertains to school systems.

One can summarize this review of the literature as to the value of laboratory training as follows:

1. It facilitates personal growth and development, and thus can be of value to the individual who participates.

2. It accomplishes changes in individuals which according to several theories are important in effecting change in organizations and in effectively managing organizations.

3. One study, in which an instrumented laboratory was compared with sensitivity training, provides some indication that more organizational change resulted from the instrumented approach.

4. The findings from this literature search are compatible with the conclusions reached in a similar review made four years ago (Buchanan 1965).

References

Argyris, Chris. "Explorations in interpersonal competence—I and II." *Journal of Applied Behavioral Science,* I:58-83; 255-269, 1965.

——, "On the future of laboratory education." *Journal of Applied Behavioral Science,* 3:153-183, 1967.

Bartlett, Alton C., "Changing behavior as a means to increased efficiency." *Journal of Applied Behavioral Science,* 3:381-403, 1967.

Bass, Bernard M. "The anarchist movement and the T-group." *Journal of Applied Behavioral Science* 3:211-226, 1967.

Benedict, Barbara, Paula Calder, Daniel Callahan, Harvey Hornstein, and Matthew B. Miles. "The clinical-experimental approach to assessing organizational change efforts." *Journal of Applied Behavioral Science,* 3:347-380, 1967.

Bennis, Warren G. *Changing Organizations.* New York: McGraw-Hill, 1966.

Beckhard, Richard. "An organization improvement program in a decentralized organization." *Journal of Applied Behavioral Science,* 2:3-26, 1966.

——, "The confrontation meeting." *Harvard Business Review,* 45:1·49-155, 1967.

Blake, Robert R., and Jane S. Mouton. *The Managerial Grid.* Houston: Gulf, 1964.

——, "Some effects of managerial grid seminar training on union and management attitudes toward supervision." *Journal of Applied Behavioral Science,* 2:387-400, 1966.

——, *Corporate Excellence through Grid Organization Development.* Houston: Gulf, 1968

Blake, Robert R., Jane S. Mouton, Lewis B. Barnes, and Larry E. Greiner. "Breakthrough in organization development." *Harvard Business Review,* 42:133-155, 1964.

Blake, Robert R., Jane S. Mouton, and Richard L. Sloma. "The union management intergroup laboratory: strategy for resolving intergroup conflict." *Journal of Applied Behavioral Science,* 1:25-57, 1965.

Bolman, Lee. "The Effects of Variations in Educator Behavior on the Learning Process in Laboratory Human Relations Education." Doctoral dissertation, Yale University, 1968.

Bowers, N. D., and R. S. Soar. "Evaluation of laboratory human relations training for classroom teachers. Studies of human relations in the teaching-learning process: V. final report." Columbia: University of South Carolina, 1961.

Buchanan, Paul C. "Evaluating the effectiveness of laboratory training in industry." *In Explorations in Human Relations Training and Research,* Report No. 1. Washington: National Training Laboratories, 1965.

——, "Crucial issues in organizational development." In Goodwin Watson (ed.), *Change in School Systems.* Washington: National Training Laboratories, 1967.

——, *Reflections on a Project in Self-renewal in Two School Systems.* Washington: National Training Laboratories, 1968.

Bugental, James, and Robert Tannenbaum. "Sensitivity training and being motivation." *Journal of Humanistic Psychology,* III: 76-85, 1963.

Bunker, Douglas R. "Individual applications of laboratory training." *Journal of Applied Behavioral Sciences,* I: 131-148, 1965.

Bunker, Douglas R., and Eric S. Knowles. "Comparison of behavioral changes resulting from human relations training laboratories of different lengths." *Journal of Applied Behavioral Science,* 3:505-524, 1967.

Byrd, Richard E. "Training in a non-group." *Journal of Humanistic Psychology,* VII: 18-27, 1967.

Clark, James, and Samuel A. Culbert. "Mutually therapeutic perception and self-awareness in a T-group." *Journal of Applied Behavioral Science,* I:180-194, 1965.

Culbert, Samuel A. "Trainer self-disclosure and member growth in two T-groups." *Journal of Applied Behavioral Science,* 4:47-73, 1968.

Davis, Sheldon A. "An organic problem-solving method of organizational change." *Journal of Applied Behavioral Science,* 3:3-21, 1967.

Deep, S., Bernard Bass, and James Vaughan. "Some effects on business gaming of previous quasi-T-Group affiliations." *Journal of Applied Psychology,* 51:426-431, 1967.

De Michele, John H. "The Measurement of Rated Training Changes Resulting from a Sensitivity Training Laboratory of an Overall Program in Organization Development." Doctoral dissertation, New York University, 1966.

Ellis, Albert, and Milton Blum. "Rational training: a new method of facilitating management and labor relations." *Psychological Reports,* 20:1267-1284, 1967.

Fleishman, Edwin A., E. F. Harris, and H. E. Burtt. *Leadership and Supervision in Industry.* Columbus: Bureau of Educational Research, Ohio State University, 1955.

French, J. R. P., J. J. Sherwood, and D. L. Bradford. "Change in self-identity in a management training conference." *Journal of Applied Behavioral Science,* 2:210-218, 1966.

Friedlander, Frank. "The impact of organizational training laboratories upon the effectiveness and interaction of ongoing groups." *Personal Psychology,* 20:289-308, 1967.

Greiner, Larry E. "Organization Change and Development: A Study of Changing Values, Behavior, and Performance in a Large Industrial Plant." Doctoral dissertation, Harvard Business School, 1965.

——, "Antecedents of planned organization change." *Journal of Applied Behavioral Science,* 3:51-86, 1967.

Guest, Robert. *Organizational Change.* Homewood, Ill.: Dorsey, 1962.

Hampden-Turner, C. M. "An existential 'learning theory' and the integration of T-group research." *Journal of Applied Behavioral Science,* 2:367-386, 1966.

Harrison, Roger, "Group composition models for laboratory design." *Journal of Applied Behavioral Science,* I:409-432, 1965.

——, "Cognitive change and participation in a sensitivity training laboratory." *Journal of Consulting Psychology,* 30:517-520, 1966.

———, "Problems in the design and interpretation of research on human relations training." *Explorations in Human Relations Training and Research,* Report No. 1. Washington: National Training Laboratories, 1967.

Harrison, Roger, and B. Lubin. "Personal style, group composition, and learning." *Journal of Applied Behavioral Science,* 1:286-301, 1965.

Harrison, Roger, and Barry Oshry. "The design of one-week laboratories." In E. H. Schein and W. G. Bennis (eds.), *Personal and Organizational Growth through Group Methods:* 98-106. New York: Wiley, 1965.

———, *The Impact of Laboratory Training on Organizational Behavior: Methodology and Results.* Working paper, National Training Laboratories, 1966.

Harvey, O. J. *Experience, Structure, and Adaptability.* New York: Springer, 1966.

House, Robert J. " 'T-group' training: some important considerations for the practicing manager." *New York Personnel Management Association Bulletin,* 21:4-10, 1965.

———, "Manager development: a conceptual model, some propositions, and a research strategy for testing the model." *Management Development: Design, Evaluation & Implementation.* Ann Arbor: University of Michigan, 1967.

Jaques E. *The Changing Culture of a Factory.* London: Tavistock, 1951.

Kassarjian, H. "Social character and sensitivity training." *Journal of Applied Behavioral Science,* 1:433-440, 1965.

Knowles, Eric S. "A bibliography of research—since 1960." *Explorations in Human Relations Training and Research,* Report No. 2. Washington: National Training Laboratories, 1967.

Kolb, D. A., S. K. Winter, and D. E. Berlew. "Self-directed change: two studies." *Journal of Applied Behavioral Science,* 4:453-471, 1968.

Kuriloff, A., and S. Atkins. "T-group for a work team." *Journal of Applied Behavioral Science,* 2:63-93, 1966.

Lakin, M., and R. Carlson. "Participant perception of group process in group sensitivity training." *International Journal of Group Psychotherapy,* 14:116-122, 1964.

Leavitt, H. "Applied organizational change in industry: structural, technological, and humanities approaches." In James G. March (ed.), *Handbook of Organizations:* 1144-1170. Chicago: Rand McNally, 1965.

Likert, Rensis. *The Human Organization.* New York: McGraw-Hill, 1967.

Lippitt, Ronald, Jeanne Watson, and Bruce Westley. *The Dynamics of Planned Change.* New York: Harcourt, Brace and World, 1958.

McClelland, David C. "Toward a theory of motive acquisition." *American Psychologist,* 20:321-333, 1965.

McGregor, Douglas. *The Professional Manager.* New York: McGraw-Hill, 1967.

Marrow, A., D. Bowers, and S. Seashore, *Participative Management.* New York: Harper and Row, 1967.

Medow, Herman. "Sensible non-sense." *Journal of Applied Behavioral Science,* 3:202-203, 1967.

Miles, M. B. "Learning processes and outcomes in human relations training: a clinical-experimental study." In E. H. Schein and W. G. Bennis (eds.), *Personal and Organizational Growth through Group Methods:* 244-254. New York: Wiley, 1965.

——, *Methodological Problems in Evaluating Organizational Change: Two Illustrations.* Working paper, Columbia University, 1965.

Miles, M. B., J. R. Milavsky, D. Lake, and R. Beckhard. *Organizational Improvement: Effects of Management Team Training in Bankers Trust.* Unpublished monograph, Bankers Trust Company, New York, 1965.

Miles, M. B., P. Calder, H. Hornstein, D. Callahan, and S. Schiavo. *Data Feedback and Organizational Change in a School System.* Working paper, Columbia University, 1966.

Morton, R. B., and B. M. Bass. "The organizational training laboratory." *Training Directors Journal,* 18:2-18, 1964.

Morton, R. B., and A. Wight. *A Critical Incidents Evaluation of an Organizational Training Laboratory.* Working paper, Aerojet General Corporation, 1964.

Oshry, B., and R. Harrison. "Transfer from 'here-and-now' to 'there-and-then': changes in organizational problem diagnosis stemming from T-group training." *Journal of Applied Behavioral Science,* 2:185-198, 1966.

Powers, R. J., "Trainer orientation and group composition in laboratory training." Doctoral dissertation, Case Institute of Technology, 1965.

Psathas, G., and R. Hardert. "Trainer interventions and normative patterns in the T-group." *Journal of Applied Behavioral Science,* 2:149-169, 1966.

Rubin, I. "Increased self-acceptance: a means of reducing prejudice." *Journal of Abnormal and Social Psychology,* 5:233-238, 1967.

——, "The reduction of prejudice through laboratory training." *Journal of Applied Behavioral Science,* 3:29-50, 1967.

Sarason, Seymour B. *The School Culture and Processes of Change.* College Park: College of Agriculture, University of Maryland, 1966.

Schein, E. H., and W. G. Bennis. *Personal and Organizational Growth through Group Methods.* New York: Wiley, 1965.

Schmuck, R. A. "Helping teachers improve classroom group processes." *Journal of Applied Behavioral Science,* 4:401-435, 1968.

Schutz, W. C. *An Approach to the Development of Human Potential.* Washington: National Training Laboratories, Subscription Service Report No. 6, 1964.

——,*Joy.* New York: Grove, 1967.

Schutz, W. C., and V. Allen. "The effects of a T-group laboratory on interpersonal behavior." *Journal of Applied Behavioral Science,* 2:265-286, 1966.

Shepard, H. A. "Changing relationships in organizations." In James G. March (ed.), *Handbook of Organizations*:1115-1143. Chicago: Rand McNally, 1965.

Sikes, W. "A Study of Some Effects of a Human Relations Training Laboratory." Doctoral dissertation, Purdue University, 1964.

Smith, P. B. "Attitude changes associated with training in human relations." *British Journal of Social and Clinical Psychology,* 3:104-112, 1964.

———, "T-group Climate, Trainer Style, and Some Tests of Learning." Working paper, University of Sussex, England, 1966.

Tannenbaum, R., and James Bugental. "Dyads, clans, and tribe: a new design for sensitivity training." *NTL Training News,* 7:1-3, 1963.

Wilson, J. E., D. P. Mullen, and R. B. Morton. "Sensitivity training for individual growth—team training for organization development." *Training and Development Journal,* 22:1-7, 1968.

Winn, A. "Social change in industry: from insight to implementation." *Journal of Applied Behavioral Science,* 2:170-185, 1966.

An Organic
Problem-Solving Method
of Organizational Change

In the opinion of the author of this essay, behavioral science literature does not give proper emphasis to the principle of confrontation as it relates to the improvement and development of organizations. Furthermore, sensitivity training is not effectively put into a larger context as a means to an end. This paper describes an extensive organizational development effort within TRW Systems which places a heavy emphasis on confrontation and the use of sensitivity training as part of an effort to improve the culture of the organization. The focus is on improving the quality of working relationships between interdependent individuals and groups. The paper examines the elements of this organic approach to organizational change and presents a generalized time-phased model.

AN ORGANIC PROBLEM-SOLVING METHOD
OF ORGANIZATIONAL CHANGE

Sheldon A. Davis

Industrial Relations, TRW Systems
Redondo Beach, California

A few months ago, I learned from a vice-president of a large national corporation that two of the three top executives in his company had recently participated
in a President's Conference on Human Behavior conducted by the National Training Laboratories. I learned further that, both before and after attending the
conference, these two persons were highly committed to Theory Y notions, as
described by Douglas McGregor in *The Human Side of Enterprise.* My acquaintance expressed concern, however, with the form this commitment was taking.
He mentioned that one of these two men had chaired a meeting during which he
expressed his commitment to those assumptions stated by McGregor. As a
concrete example of this commitment, he said that a few days earlier a key
subordinate presented some work for approval. The "boss" did not like the
quality of the work and said so. The subordinate pointed out that his people had
worked very hard in producing the work and were highly committed to it. The
top executive said, "OK. In that case, let's go ahead."

To me, this is *not* an example of what McGregor meant. It is an example of
very soft human relationships that are not task-oriented and therefore, in my
opinion, are irrational. It does represent, however, a problem presented in
laboratory training. How can we eliminate some of the soft, mushy, "sweetness
and light" impressions that some people feel are implicit in sensitivity training?

An example of a different approach recently took place within TRW Systems.

A section head, the lowest managerial level in the organization, discovered that a certain Quality Control procedure for Manufacturing hampered his effectiveness. He sought to get the procedure modified, only to be told that this was impossible because it covered all of the divisions and therefore could not be modified. He was further told that a change would raise the ire of at least one general manager of another division. The section head refused to accept the explanation and personally called a meeting of the general manager identified, the manager of Manufacturing—both vice-presidents of the company, and four levels above the section head—and the director of Product Assurance. Within an hour the procedure was modified in the direction desired by the section head.

The foregoing vignettes dramatize the differences which can occur because of markedly different applications of behavioral science theories within an organization. In both instances, the individuals involved were convinced that they were using the best of behavioral science techniques. The consequence of their interpretation and application had decidedly different payoffs.

Confrontation: The Missing Element in Behavioral Science Literature

The values that Douglas McGregor stood for and articulated regarding organizational development have within them a very real toughness: In dealing with one another, we will be open, direct, explicit. Our feelings will be available to one another, and we will try to problem-solve rather than be defensive. These values have within them a very tough way of living—not a soft way. But, unfortunately, in much of the behavioral science literature, the messages come out sounding soft and easy, as if what we are trying to do is to build happy teams of employees who feel "good" about things, rather than saying we are trying to build effective organizations with groups who function well and can zero in quickly on their problems and deal with them rationally, in the very real sense of the word. As an example of this kind of softness, I do not remember reading in any book in the field that one of the alternatives in dealing with a problem person is the possibility of discharging him.

There is no real growth—there is no real development—in the organization or in the individuals within it if they do not confront and deal directly with their problems. They can get together and share feelings, but if that is all they do, it is merely a catharsis. While this is useful, it has relatively minimal usefulness compared with what can happen if they start to relate differently within the organizational setting around task issues.

Laboratories Are Not Enough

I think one important theme of the nearly four-year organizational change effort at TRW Systems is that of using laboratory training (sensitivity training, T Grouping) clearly as a means to an end—that of putting most of our energy into on-the-job situations, real-life intergroup problems, real-life job-family situations, and dealing with them in the here-and-now. This effort has reached a point where sensitivity training, per se, represents only 10 to 15 per cent of the effort in our own program. The rest of the effort, 85 to 90 per cent, is in on-the-job situations, working real problems with the people who are really involved in them. This has led to some very important, profound, and positive changes in the organization and the way it does many things, including decision making, problem solving, and supervisory coaching of subordinates.

One generalization I would draw from this and other similar experiences is that laboratory training in and of itself is not enough to really make the kind of difference that might be made in an organization forcefully trying to become more rational in its processes of freeing up the untapped potential of its people and of dealing more sensibly with its own realities. Attending a strangers' laboratory or, in our case, a cousins' laboratory (that is, being in a T Group with people who are not necessarily from the same job family but are from the same company) is a very useful, important experience. Most people learn much in laboratory training, as has been well documented and discussed. However, this is not enough.

We have felt that the laboratory experience (the sensitivity training experience itself) should not be just three days or a week or whatever is spent in the off-site laboratory. As a result, we have undertaken important laboratory prework as well as postwork. The prework typically consists of an orientation session where the staff very briefly presents some of the theoretical aspects of the program and an explanation of why we do laboratories. During this time, participants in the coming laboratory can ask any kind of question, such as: Is this therapy? Is the company going to evaluate my performance? and so on.

Also, we typically hand out a questionnaire to the participants for their own use (they are not asked to turn it in). It presents questions such as: "What are the three most pressing problems you feel you pose for those who have to work with you?" It is an attempt to get the person to become introspective about his own particular work situation, to begin his articulation process within himself.

Then there is the laboratory itself. This is followed up by on-site sessions several weeks apart, perhaps one evening every other week for three or four sessions. At this time a variety of actions are taken in an attempt to help people phase into their work situation. There is continued working in the small training groups; there can be exercises such as intergroup competition.

The laboratory is a highly intensive experience. Attitudes toward it can be extremely euphoric, and people can experience tremendous letdowns when they return to the ongoing culture—even a highly supportive one. Therefore, there is major emphasis on working in the ongoing situation in real-life job families as well as in intergroup situations and mergers, for example.

Recently, we have added to the follow-on work an opportunity for the wives of the participants to experience a micro-laboratory. This might be a 1:00 to 5:00 p.m. session on a Saturday for the wives, with a staff available to give some feel for the laboratory experience.

One of the problems many people have as a result of laboratory training is returning to their continuing organizational culture and finding it quite hostile to the values learned and to the approaches they would like to try. The notion very early in the TRW Systems effort was to focus on changes in the ongoing culture itself: the norms, values, rewards, systems, and processes. If all we did was to have a lot of people attend sensitivity training, this might indeed be useful to them as individuals, but its usefulness would be quite limited with respect to the total organization.

We have had other kinds of concerns with laboratory training. We have tried hard not to *send* people to a laboratory but to make it as voluntary as possible. People who are *sent* usually spend much of their time wondering why they were sent instead of working on relevant issues.

If we look at the processes of change itself, it is quite clear that it is not enough for an individual to gain enormous insight into his own situation, his own dynamics, and his own functioning. Granted, this will help him develop a better understanding of how groups work and of the complexity of communication processes. However, if he cannot take this understanding and turn it into action in the on-the-job situation, if he cannot find other people who are interested in trying some of the same ideas, if he cannot bring about a difference in his real life, the value of the laboratory is very severely minimized. In real life, what do we find? We find organizations, typically, with highly traditional methods of management and with very unrealistic assumptions about people (the kind of Theory X assumptions that Douglas McGregor stated). There has to be an emphasis on changing the ongoing organization. The direction has to be toward working in the organization on a day-to-day basis.

Organizational Setting and Development of Program

I should like to describe the program under way at TRW Systems as an example of this kind of effort—of a nonmechanical, organic approach to career development—the development of the careers of the individuals in the organization and the career of the organization itself, both inextricably tied.

TRW Systems currently employs about 13,300 persons. About one third are professional engineers, and half of these have advanced degrees. It is an organization with products of tremendous innovation and change. It is an organization that is highly interdependent. We have a matrix organization: there are project offices and functional areas of technical capabilities such as structures, dynamics, guidance, and control. A project office, to perform its task, must call upon capabilities and people throughout the organization. This is a highly complicated matrix of interdependencies. No one can really get his job done in this kind of system without working with others. As a result, problems of relationships, of communication, of people being effectively able to problem-solve with one another are extremely critical.

The program started at a time when the company was going through a significant change in its role—from an organization with essentially one Air Force contract for systems engineering on ballistic missile programs (Thor, Atlas,

Titan, and Minuteman) to a company that would be fully competitive in the aerospace market. This has indeed happened over the past six years. We now have many contracts, many customers. Most of our work is done under fixed-price and incentive contracts; we produce hardware such as unmanned scientific satellites, propulsion engines for the Apollo mission, as well as other types of hardware. The company has become exceedingly more complex in its product lines and its mix of business.

All through this growth and diversification there has been a concern about the careers of the people in the organization, about trying to maintain certain qualities within the organization. Appendix A is a list of these qualities which was prepared in September of 1965 and is an attempt to list qualities which seem to have a direct bearing on the kind of success we have been having over the past six years. That success has been quite striking: a tremendous increase in sales, in the number of contracts, a good record in competitions for programs in our industry, and a large increase in the number of employees.

In the middle of 1961, TRW Systems, then called Space Technology Laboratories, began to think about organizational development. At that time, Herbert Shepard, then on the faculty at Case Institute of Technology, spent a portion of the summer at TRW, including some time with key executives. The following summer he spent a month with the organization. Just prior to this visit, the director of Industrial Relations and his associate attended a laboratory conducted by the University of California at Los Angeles.

Shepard's visit and discussions centering around it led to a growing articulation of what we might want to do with respect to career development. A number of things happened in the next several months.

One was the preparation of a white paper on career development—a statement of how we might approach the subject. The paper discussed why a program was needed, assumptions to be made about employees (a paraphrase of McGregor's Theory Y), the type of organizational climate and training needed, as well as some general indications of how we might proceed.

An assumption we made was that most of the people in the organization were highly competent, very intelligent, and certainly experimental. If they could be freed up enough to look at some of their behavior, to question some of their assumptions, to look at assumptions other people were making, to try new approaches, this group could, within limits, develop their own specific management theory.

The white paper was circulated to a number of key persons. Interviews were then conducted to determine possible next steps. A series of events led from this point.

One event was the first of many team development laboratories. (By team development laboratory, I mean an activity which might, for example, be a three-day off-site meeting involving a supervisor and the people who immediately report to him. The agenda for the meeting would be "How can we improve our own effectiveness?") The first team meeting involved one of the program offices in the company. It turned out to be quite successful. With this experience under our belts, we had further discussions to formulate what we wanted to do as an organization with respect to the careers of the people comprising it.

Employees within the Personnel organization began attending sensitivity training laboratories such as the Arden House Management Work Conferences, conducted by National Training Laboratories.

A very significant event in the total development of this change effort occurred in May of 1963 when a group of 12 key executives attended a laboratory. Their co-trainers were Herbert Shepard (an outside consultant) and myself (a member of the TRW Systems organization).[1]

The participants in this first laboratory were quite positive in their feedback to the director of Industrial Relations and to the president of the company, who himself was very much interested in how people were reacting to the training. The president had given support for us to be experimental: "Let's try things. If they work, continue them. If they don't, modify them, improve them, or drop them."

A consulting team evolved over time. The consultants were not used in any one-shot way but were asked to make a significant commitment of time over a long-term period. They have become involved with us. They have learned our culture and our problems. While our consultants are all qualified T-Group trainers, most of their time is spent in on-the-job situations. There is a need to function as a team, since we are all dealing with one organization, one culture, one social system. The kind of cohesiveness that takes place during consulting team meetings has been a critical part of the program here at TRW Systems.

In one sense we started at the top of the organization, and in another we did not. In the beginning, there was a shared general understanding between the president and the key people in Industrial Relations about the type of program we wanted. There were some shared values about the organization we had and wanted to maintain, build, and develop. So, in McGregor's term, this was not Theory X management and Theory Y training effort. Both had a Theory Y quality.

In another sense we did not start at the top: the president and others of the top management team were relatively late in becoming involved in laboratory training and in applying this training to their own job families. The president of the company attended an NTL Presidents' Conference on Human Behavior early in 1965. Directly after that experience, his top team had an off-site team development meeting in March of 1965. In April 1966, they had a follow-up meeting.

Prior to this top team activity many other things had happened with a

---

[1] This has been one of the important notions in the approach at TRW Systems. We use, at this point, about nine consultants who are members of the NTL Network—people like Richard Beckhard, Michael Blansfield, James Clark, Charles Ferguson, Jack Gibb, George Lehner, Herbert Shepard, Robert Tannenbaum, and others. These people are *always* coupled in their work, either in T-Group training or on-the-job consulting, with someone inside the organization, typically a personnel manager in one of the line operating units.

number of other people in other job families. In fact, this other activity helped us get to the point where the top management team became interested in trying to apply some of these techniques.

Since the program started, more than 500 key persons in the organization have attended sensitivity training laboratories, primarily laboratories conducted by the company. The staff of these laboratories is drawn from our consultants, the Personnel organization, and, more recently, from skilled and interested employees in line management positions.

We have also conducted more than 85 team development efforts. These vary in format, but a typical one involves interviews with each of the members of the team (a job family consisting of a supervisor and his immediate subordinates) and then perhaps a three-day off-site meeting where the interview data are fed back for the groups to work with. The team ends the meeting with explicit action items. Follow-on to the off-site meeting involves implementing the many action items.

We have been devoting much effort to intergroup problems: relationships between Manufacturing and Engineering, between Product Assurance and other parts of the organization, between various interfacing elements in the engineering organizations. We have found that these efforts have a great deal of leverage. We have done some work on facilitating mergers and with key people on approaching satellite launches. The latter become very tense, tight operations where people can become extremely competitive and behave in ways which clearly get in the way of having an effective launch.

Characteristics of the Process

We "wound up" with a number of notions. We did not want to have a program that was canned but one that was experimental. We wanted participation to be voluntary rather than something that the company forced upon employees. We did not want it to be a crash program (in our industry there are many crash programs). We wanted the training to be highly task oriented. (If it were not relevant to making a difference on today's problems, it would not be a successful program.) We wanted to have the emphasis on experience-based learning, which implies, in a very general sense, the use of laboratory methods, of people really looking at how they are doing, examining the assumptions behind their management style, identifying alternate ways of problem solving, and making choices based on a wider range of possibilities. We wanted to be concerned with the careers of all employees, not those of key people only. We wanted to be concerned about company goals and the actual, on-the-job work environment, since this has a profound effect on the careers of people. We wanted to place the emphasis on measuring ourselves against our potential, on being quite introspective on how we were doing. So, for example, if there were an either/or situation (and there usually is not), we would rather not have someone come in and lecture on how to conduct staff meetings, but would have ourselves look introspectively at the conduct of our own staff meetings. And we wanted to do continuous research on how we were faring so that it could be fed back into the program for further development.

I should like to describe what I think we have come to mean by an organic approach to organizational change within TRW Systems. There are a number of points which, at least for me, tend to describe what is meant by organic methods.

1. There is the notion that if you are interested in improving a particular culture—a particular social system—you must be able to step out of it in the sense of being very analytical about it, of understanding what is going on, by not being trapped within the culture and its own particular values. If you look at a culture from the viewpoint of its own values, you are not going to come up with anything very startling and different for it to do. You have got to be able to step out of it and say, "What really would make sense here?" This ability to step out of the culture and yet not leave it, not become alienated from it, is a very important one.

2. A bias toward optimism regarding the chances for meaningful organizational development to take place increases the psychological freedom for those trying to introduce the change. There is certainly a tremendous amount of evidence at this point that significant, even profound, changes can occur in the behavior of individuals and organizations.

3. Taking a systems engineering approach to the effort (i.e., looking at the totality of the system, dealing with fundamentals within it, considering how a change in one part affects parts elsewhere) provides an analytical approach which increases the conceptual freedom.

4. The extensive use of third-party facilitation is made with respect to interpersonal and organizational problems. A consultant who is not directly involved in an emotional sense in a situation can be useful just by that fact.

5. Direct confrontation of relevant situations in an organization is essential. If we do not confront one another, we keep the trouble within ourselves and we stay in trouble. With respect to confrontation, the whole notion of feedback is crucial. Giving persons feedback on how they are doing gives them a choice to do better. Caring plays an important part. Confronting without caring can be a rather destructive process. (See Albee's *Who's Afraid of Virginia Woolf?*) It does turn out that people in general can be very caring of one another.

6. Becoming the "other" is an important part of the organic method. This is the empathic notion that Carl Rogers and others have developed. To have a really meaningful exchange, one somehow has to look at the situation as the other sees it. For a consultant to work effectively with an organization, he has to be perceptive and under-

standing about the organization and its people from *their* point of view.

7. Dealing with the here-and-now and increasing the ability of people within the organization to do the same have a great deal of leverage. It is important in an organizational development effort to start with what is going on now within the organization and to deal with those things effectively. One of our objectives is to help the organization build its own capability, to deal with its problems as they emerge. Problems are constantly emerging in any live organization, and so our objective is *not* to end up with an organization that has no problems: that would be a very fat, dumb, and happy kind of place.

8. Multiplier planning is rather crucial in the early stages of introducing organizational change. What can we next do that will have the largest effect? There is always a wide range of alternatives and possibilities; there is never enough time, money, or energy to do all the things we might do, so we are constantly picking and choosing.

9. Fanning out is coupled with the multiplier planning aspect. It is important in an effort of this kind—if it is not to be subversive, sub rosa, hidden, squashed out—to be something that does fan out: someone does something that leads to others doing something that leads to still others doing something.

10. A person can act, then act again and then act again; or he can act, critique what he just did, then act, then critique, then act. And that is the whole notion of going back and forth between content and process, between doing the job and then looking at how we are doing it. Building that into the day-to-day culture is a major objective.

11. Finally, there is the notion of testing of choices. One always has choices within any particular situation. However, it is typically true that we do not test the choices we have. So someone might say, "Well, I really can't do that because these fellows won't let me," or "Yes, I would very much like to do the following, but I can't because of so and so." Given these limits, some choices do not get tested. One of the efforts is to get people to be aware of the various possibilities they have and to test them—not to accept the stereotypes in the situation, the sacred cows, that exist in any kind of organization, but to say, "OK, this is what makes sense to me in working that problem. This is what I want to try to do."

Underpinnings to the Effort

The principles of confrontation—that laboratory training must be seen as a means to an end, that most of the effort has to be done after people have attended the laboratory, and not in the laboratory itself—have been central to this effort. This has affected the way we budget time, the way we spend money, the assumptions we make about what we are doing.

Another significant development in this large-scale effort has been a deliberate, successful attempt to build up the internal resources to carry out the program. Two years ago, in a sensitivity training laboratory put on by the company, there would have been a staff of six, four or five of whom were outside consultants. This situation has completely reversed itself. Today, when a T Group cousins' laboratory is conducted, four or five of the persons are from inside the organization, and only one or two are external consultants.

Furthermore, in the on-the-job aspects of the program, the effort is carried on by people within the organization, primarily individuals in Personnel and, increasingly, managers from the line organization.

A very interesting aspect of the program has focused on the question of risk taking. In my opinion, those of us engaged in this kind of work are quite often too cautious, too constrained, and not experimental enough in trying out things within the organization. We do not behave as though we fully believe the implications of McGregor's Theory Y formulation: that people are creative, that they are strong, that they are motivated, that they want to make a difference. We tend sometimes to approach them gingerly and tentatively. These are constraints more within ourselves than within others or within the situation.

Many times our consultants have reported that their experience at TRW Systems has been a very "stretching" one: they have been fully challenged; people at TRW Systems are experimental, want to try things, are saying, "OK, that was useful, what should we do next?" Much of the effort in the consulting team meetings has been to push ourselves to be more developmental, more experimental in the approaches that we take within the effort.

For example, until quite recently, many people in the field felt that laboratory training was not something one could do within a job family. It seems to me that the whole objective of sensitivity training is to develop an on-the-job culture within which we can relate to one another interpersonally just the way we do in a T Group. We at TRW want to make that transfer; we do not want the T Group to be a separate, special kind of experience. We prefer to say: "All right, let's sit down and really level with one another. Let's do this on the job, and from day to day." That is the objective. It leads to a more effective, efficient, problem-solving organization.

Working with teams in real-life situations is exactly what we are after. Otherwise, the program can be ethereal—not particularly related to the company's real-life situations. It cannot be "gutty" if it does not come to grips with some of the tougher issues, pinpoint and deal with them, and cause people to become involved and to work actively to solve problems.

In September 1963, I put together a short paper which conceptualized several plateaus that we might be moving through as an organization in this change effort.

The first one is characterized as problem awareness—that point in time during which there is general recognition and awareness on the part of some people within the organization that there are crucial interdependencies which exist in order for us to function and that there are problems due to inappropriate means of dealing with these interdependencies.

The second plateau, the identification and freeing of key people within the organization, is seen as consisting of two parts. The first part is an effort to identify key people in the organization who seem to be perceptive about the problems the company is experiencing and have a desire to work on them. They are key people in the sense that their efforts to deal with organizational problems could produce a multiplier effect that would lead others to similar action.

The second part of this particular phase of the program is characterized by an effort to provide a situation that would initiate the process of freeing up these potential multipliers from the organizational and personal constraints which, in the past, kept them from responding effectively to their awareness of the problems. Here, the strangers' laboratories, the cousins' laboratories conducted by the company, and the team development laboratories are seen as being especially relevant.

The third phase, or plateau, involves action steps to follow-up—experimental steps stimulated by a participation in the various kinds of laboratories that are taking place. These action steps have taken many forms: a supervisor holding a team development laboratory within his own job family; a family group diagnosing the kinds of interaction problems it has with other parts of the organization and beginning to resolve these problems in an open, direct manner in a search for a creative solution rather than an avoidance compromise; two persons at odds moving in on the problem of relating and communicating with each other; new ways of looking at functions in the organization.

The fourth plateau occurs when the effort itself gains an independent status and becomes a self-supporting system. At this plateau there are norms within the organization that support open, direct confrontation of conflict, resolution of conflict without resorting to the power structure unless there is somehow a failure in the process, and a shared commitment to objectives as a consequence of being interdependent. These organizational norms would support the giving and receiving of feedback, openness, experimentation, and day-to-day problem solving.

In this fourth phase we are trying to build procedures into the day-to-day situation which, hopefully, put into concrete terms some of the things we have learned in the earlier phases. For example, when a new project office is started it is probably useful to program some team building early in its life. When there is a new merger within the organization, particular attention can be paid to the merger process. One of the things we have learned is that specific attention should continuously be paid to the processes within the organization: how we make decisions, how we fill key spots, how we communicate with one another, how we decide to reorganize, how we make other important decisions. There is a heavy people involvement in these processes, and, typically, they do not get enough legitimate attention. If I am concerned about the quality of staff meetings I attend, I tend to talk about them in the hallways or go home and kick the dog and tell my wife about them. I do not exert effort during the staff meetings to try to change their quality and improve them, because somehow that is not legitimate. "Let's keep personalities out of it. Don't get emotional." These are the kinds of expressions that inhibit me from dealing with the problem.

Development through the four plateaus requires considerable invention because the state of the art of organizational change, in my opinion, is such that one cannot program in advance everything he is going to do within the organization. There are some people who approach organizational change this way. I believe their efforts tend to be mechanical and relatively superficial.

Another important aspect of this effort which I think is particularly consistent with Theory Y formulation is that the direction and pace that the effort takes should be meaningful to the members who are participating in it. The consultant in any particular situation has to get in touch with the needs and concerns of the people involved from *their* point of view, not from *his*.

I have tried to suggest that in many situations in which behavioral scientists are trying to apply their principles the really serious limitations are not within the people or the organizations they are working with, but within themselves— their own skills and ability and courage to act. Theory Y has deeply ingrained in it a profound belief in the abilities, strengths, and motivations of people in general and specifically. Many times we do not act as if we fully believe or understand that set of formulations.

Next Steps

In TRW Systems, we are now moving in a number of directions, some of which I should like to describe. We are moving more toward day-to-day coaching—on-the-job feedback, if you will—with or without consultants and without calling special meetings, but just as we work together. We are paying continuing attention to process as a way of doing business. We are moving more and more toward using third-party facilitation as a standard operating procedure.

So far there has not been a heavy involvement of the rank and file. The first several years in the effort were specifically biased toward working with key people. These are the ones who have a large effect upon the culture, upon the processes of the organization, upon the tone of the climate. But we are now at a point where we want to get more and more involvement of all the employees within the organization.

I think that the experience of the past several years within TRW Systems has rather clearly demonstrated the potential high leverage of applying some of the behavioral science formulations of people like McGregor, Lewin, and Likert. I think it has also demonstrated that there needs to be much more organizational theory development based upon experience, not upon someone's sitting in a room by himself and thinking about the topic. Some of the statements written about organizational development are to me naïve, impractical, unrealistic, and unrelated to organizational problems as they actually exist. Through experiences gained at TRW Systems and many other places, we should be able to develop a more sophisticated understanding of organizational development.

In my opinion, there is great potential in the development of this theory and in its application within organizations. That seems to me to be one of the leading edges within the field of behavioral science.

Appendix A

Qualities of TRW Systems Which Have a Direct Bearing
on Its Success

In thinking about the problems associated with the very dramatic growth of
TRW Systems, I attempted to identify those qualities which have had a great
deal to do with our success in the past and ought therefore to be maintained in
the future.

1. The individual employee is important, and focus is on providing him
   the tools and other things that he needs to carry out his assignments.
2. The systems within the organization (policies, procedures, practices)
   have been designed to be a platform *from which* the individual
   operates rather than a set of ground rules *within which* he must
   confine himself.
3. One objective of the organization has been this: The work we do
   ought to be fun (personally rewarding, meaningful, enjoyable), and
   this has had a direct effect on assignments, among other things.
4. There is a great deal of trust displayed in the individual person: a
   minimum of rules, controls, and forces outside the individual telling
   him what to do and how to do it.
5. "Technical democracy": a society of peers rather than a rigid hierarchy. There is a relative lack of social distance between employees
   and managers and among the various echelons of management. There
   have been a spontaneous willingness and an interest in keeping social
   distance at a minimum; and while managers enjoy the accouterments
   of rank, they are not used as barriers between themselves and others
   at lower levels of the organization.
6. A heavy emphasis on quality: Attract best people, give them excellent
   working conditions, provide them with challenging assignments,
   demonstrate that paramount importance is placed on the professional
   and technical excellence of work assignments.
7. Although within TRW Systems there has been continuous and rapid
   change, the organization as a whole has been relatively stable,
   providing long-term career opportunities for a high percentage of our
   key people who are positive about the emphasis on internal, upward
   mobility and individual chance for many diversified job assignments.
   This is career development in a very literal sense.
8. In giving responsibility to individuals, we have had a bias toward
   giving "too much responsibility too soon" rather than being conservative. This has "stretched" the individual and, for those who are
   capable, it has led to rapid growth and outstanding performance.
9. There is, in a relative sense, less organization "politics" (e.g., people

ruthlessly working at getting ahead, back-stabbing) and more focus on task. Part of the language is "working the problem."

10. On task issues there is a great deal of direct confrontation rather than "passing the buck," maneuvering, and so on.

11. There is a great deal of delegation downward within the organization, so that a relatively large number of persons find themselves assigned to tasks with relatively high responsibility.

12. The management group has been quite experimental in its approach to its task rather than generally traditional.

13. The individual employee enjoys relative freedom to be personally responsible for himself and his job. The job is generally seen as an important one and as making a significant contribution to the noteworthy technological advances in our society.

14. People who will be markedly affected by decisions feel that they will have the opportunity, to a greater degree than is customary elsewhere, to participate in the decision-making process.

Changing Behavior as a
Means to Increased Efficiency

A firm in a highly competitive industry found itself operating below toler-able levels. Sensing "problems," it hired a new general manager who sought help from a change agent. An in-house laboratory was created where subjects, under the guise of skill training in communications, "simulated" giving and receiving descriptive, nonevaluative feedback in role play of cases. The assumption behind this approach to change was that it is easier to change behavior than attitudes. Environment was gradually transformed from Theory X toward Y as subjects became more open and risk-taking and grew in interpersonal competence. Subjects remedied the company's faltering production, poor quality, and high cost "significantly" within three months of the program's initiation. Application of behavioral science theories to allow people to help organizational per-formance does pay off.

234

CHANGING BEHAVIOR AS A MEANS TO INCREASED EFFICIENCY

Alton C. Bartlett
University of South Florida

Can a company change its style of leadership from McGregor's (1960) Theory X to Theory Y? Can it create a climate of trust, characterized by a concern for the individual's right to be himself, to take independent action, and to admit mistakes without fear of retribution?

This article reports the "action research" phase of such a long-term program of change. It tells how the Epsilon Corporation[1] employed behavioral science concepts to create such a climate and the resultant (a) increased efficiency and quality (monthly shipping dollars went up by 128 per cent); (b) decreased absenteeism and turnover (by 72 per cent and 50 per cent, respectively); and (c) reduced costs (by 10 per cent).

Background

Epsilon had begun manufacturing electronic component parts for both commercial and military markets with three employees on the upper floor of a

Reprinted from Alton C. Bartlett, "Changing Behavior as a Means to Increased Efficiency," *The Journal of Applied Behavioral Science,* III, No. 3 (July-September, 1967), 381-411, by permission of the NTL Institute of Applied Behavioral Science and the author. Copyright © by NTL Institute of Applied Behavioral Science, associated with the NEA.

[1] All proper names are pseudonyms to protect the anonymity of the company and its personnel.

two-story building in 1953.[2] By 1963, about 360 persons were at work in a beautiful new facility. But in July of that year, almost all of the small organizations in the industry were fiercely fighting for the available sales dollar, and thus, survival. As a result, Epsilon incurred losses from July 1963 through March 1964 and had to curtail much managerial and overhead personnel. In total, 17 were laid off, 9 discharged, and 25 quit. Those who survived had to double up and cover two or three different functions. Although the months of April through September were in the black, they were not far from the break-even point. Moreover, it was known that profits would increase at an accelerating rate if sales increased up to three times the present volume. Consequently, a higher volume of sales was obviously a top-priority problem; but it was not the major problem since it was clear Manufacturing could not even make, or ship, the current volume on time!

As a result, on October 1, 1964, the former Methods/Personnel Director, who had a long career in Production Management, was moved up to a newly created position of General Manager (GM). The sole Vice President (VP), formerly number-two man, now reported to the GM, as did all other "functional heads," except Finance and Marketing.

The structure of the organization he inherited could be characterized as "tall": over 300 "direct labor" employees reported through an eight-level hierarchy below the President! These included (a) one GM; (b) one Finance Manager and one Marketing Manager; (c) one Director for Purchasing, Production/Material Control, and Maintenance; (d) one Director for Quality, Testing, and Personnel and one Director for each of two Manufacturing/Engineering divisions; (e) 11 top-operating level "A" supervisors, plus 14 middle-operating level "B" supervisors; (f) 23 first-line "C" foremen, plus 30 various subforeman titles such as lead man, set-up man, and technician; and (g) an ever-varying number of "crew chiefs." There was one case where a Secretary was actually used instead of a supervisor, and another where the plant Nurse was considered a foreman.

The President, and founder of the company, had always been paternalistic: he gave the employees turkeys at Thanksgiving and Christmas, and he used "free coffee days" as bait for beating preset production goals. Everyone called him "Father" behind his back.[3]

The GM was overwhelmingly desirous of shifting managerial styles and wanted a company where everyone would feel free to grow as far as he wanted in whatever way he chose. He did not want any individual to be hurt as a result of the change, and he realized that some supervisors were going to take longer than others to adapt to a new style. Finally, in the event they did not adapt at all he did not want any man to lose his job as a result of this change. In short, he

[2]Taken from the General Manager's unpublished manuscript (not to be otherwise identified), State University of New York at Buffalo.

[3]Long-service employees always went over the head of everyone else and complained directly to him. He and the seven top managers once sponsored a cookout where *they* served hot dogs plus all the other trimmings for a picnic during the lunch hour on all three shifts, and once hired a jazz combo to play in the plant all day after especially good production weeks.

had a general idea of where he wanted to end up, but he did not know how to get there. In exchange for an ongoing laboratory in which to study the process of changing behavior, he asked for help from a change agent (CA). A list of problems was created.

Problem Areas

As Epsilon grew, the Vice President (VP), a fine line supervisor, had gradually been drawn in on managerial problems and policies so far over his head that he began to avoid decisions. As a result, the formal process of decision making had broken down except on a "management-by-crisis" basis. This left each department head to operate like a feudal baron: equal in power, independent, and in direct competition with all others.

1. Purchasing allowed virtually all material to be overdue. One major vendor supplied unusable, inferior quality, and overly costly material; no alternate vendor or substitute material was sought. In order to be safe, Production Control (a subpart of Purchasing) did not start making a schedule until they had physical control of material. Material Control (also a subpart of Purchasing) kept inventory records that varied by as much as (+ or -) $20 thousand from what was actually in the stockroom.

2. Manufacturing, even with the schedule and material on time, usually commenced the initial operation too late. Scrap was often 25 per cent; customer returns for rework were often higher than 10 per cent.

3. Engineering changes were so far behind that two and three revisions of the same drawing were in use at once, and "quotes" were months behind.

4. Quality constantly introduced and enforced *new standards—after the fact* that were *far tougher* than the customer wanted or was willing to pay for—only *more costly* to Epsilon.

5. Reliance upon formal rules had reached dysfunctional proportions. Communication between (and within) levels was often nonexistent. Where it did exist it was extremely defensive. Everyone was cautious and secretive. Morale was negative. At least 60 per cent were known to be earnestly seeking other employment.

6. Directors felt supervisors and foremen did not have any sense of urgency or responsibility. The latter two groups were begging (silently) for the authority needed to carry out their responsibilities. Almost everyone had chosen sides—to support either the GM or VP—in what was seen as a power struggle. There was also an old-men-versus-new-men dichotomy. It resulted from the President's gradually removing sections of the VP's domain each time the latter procrastinated. New men were brought in; it seemed easier to give his former responsibilities to them

than to divide them among his former subordinates. Old-timers, not realizing the situation, went farther than merely resisting any controls, standards, reports, and procedures the new men introduced: they sabotaged raw data and falsified their reports. As a result, despite a plethora of records—often in duplicate and mainly used to prove some other department was really to blame—most large orders were late and small ones were overlooked and often lost.

7. Production went through the shop in surges. Only stockroom and early operations were busy at the beginning of each week and month. Inspection and shipping were inundated on Fridays and at the end of the month. Typical proportion of shipping dollars sent out each day in a five-day week would be $(X = 1\% + 2\% + 3\% + 4\% + 90\%)$ where $X =$ shipping dollars. Typical proportion of shipping dollars sent out each week in a four-week month would be $(X = 8\% + 17\% + 25\% + 50\%)$ where $X =$ shipping dollars. Needless to say, this caused a "funds flow" problem of frightening proportions.

To summarize, the climate was one of antagonism and mistrust. In a futile attempt at escaping blame for the failure of Epsilon to manufacture and ship a sufficient quantity of its products according to a schedule, each individual was too busy to accomplish anything constructive. Blame fixing was the only vehicle being used to improve the situation. Everyone was in a win/lose framework. It obviously was not working!

Objectives

The principal objective was to obtain a shift from Theory X to Theory Y without any man's losing his job as a result and yet to provide rewards for those who "grew" into their new, broader roles. Ancillary to the main goal was the need to increase delegation of authority. At the same time, it would be necessary to flatten the "tall" organization structure. Certain fundamentals were seen as necessary besides providing supervisors an opportunity to prepare for a new (considerably changed) role. They would have to upgrade their problem-solving skills. This would require them to become facile in formal communications so they could increase their ability to work effectively with their subordinates, peers, and superiors.

The second main objective, growing out of the first, was to strive for a "climate" where each individual would feel free to grow as much as he wanted, and in whatever way. This meant setting the stage where the more open, empathic, creative supervisor could flourish.

Conceptual Framework

Foremost among my "action principles" as CA was that my entire approach would be based on the assumption that *it is easier to change behavior and then attitudes than to try to change attitudes first.*

238

The next principle was to work from the top down on the assumption that *change would be more easily accepted if it were to have the total, wholehearted, open support of the very top management,* especially as they were in the process of changing also.

The third principle assumed that *it would be imperative to break through their "attitudinal sound barrier,"* and to do this I had to shock them enough to jar them out of their proverbial rut in thinking about behavior.

Fourth, it was assumed that *the best way to get simulated behavior changes would be to provide a "climate" and a specially designated "laboratory" where trainees could learn about and experiment with new behavior under a cloak of* (not only impunity but in fact) *encouragement.* While recognizing the value of the so-called "cultural island," it simply was not feasible for this situation to remove them from their standard environment as prescribed by Lippitt, Watson, and Westley (1958, p. 111). What was attempted instead was to set up a form of "cultural island" in the plant. While not a country club, motel by the seashore, or even a university campus, there was a conference room which was our private sanctuary in the sense that McGregor (1960, p. 223) spoke of a cultural island as one which is "psychologically if not geographically remote from everyday life." One way in which the importance of this room was demonstrated was that no man was ever pulled out of it to attend to any matter of company business.

The Training Design

The basic training design (Bartlett, 1967) was built upon a foundation of "skill training" to improve formal communications. By doing this it was intended that the initial step, improving each man's formal communications ability, would be assured early.

An additional reason for selecting this method was that communications is a "neutral," noncontent subject focusing mainly on process (plus conceptual tools) rather than on content relating to Epsilon or its procedures and policies. This meant much of the structure would evolve in response to the needs of the participants. In other terms, since so much frustration, uncertainty, and bitterness were in evidence just below the surface, early sessions would be conducted specifically to provide ways for them to unload all these feelings and achieve catharsis. One could almost conceive of early sessions as a *nondirective group interview,* intended to move through three successive steps: *feelings, facts,* and *solutions* (Strauss & Sayles, 1960).

In the first meeting, an attempt was made to shock the *Ss* out of their complacency, and they were also introduced to concepts like "perception" and "frame of reference," plus many facets of "self" and "congruence." Next, brief "caselets" were used to let them work with the concepts. Outside readings (Asch, 1955; Gibb, 1961; McMurry, 1953; Rogers & Farson, 1966, Rogers & Roethlisberger, 1952; Tannenbaum, 1957; Tarnopol, 1959) were assigned. In the second meeting, the "feelings buildup" continued and considerable time and effort were spent allowing trainees to "own" concepts like "active listening," "feedback," "empathy," "defensive communication," "masterminding," "probe," "premature judgment," plus many others.

For the next five meetings the design called for working with case problems, including role playing, interspersed with spot lectures and special exercises. A short-run result of this would be to markedly upgrade problem-solving skills and enhance their ability to work much more effectively with others. Part of session seven would be devoted to "conference leadership" training. The last one would be conducted by some of the trainees in each group, as an actual conference—my role being primarily that of "process observer."

Two Tape Recorders

An important part of the design was the use of two recorders—one to play only during problem solving or a role play, the other to play all the time. Thus action could be stopped and played back on the spot so a speech could be analyzed for an actor, action diagnosed for the audience, or alternative courses of action suggested and tried. In this way both original action and subsequent discussion were preserved for later use and study. If anyone were to hear the tapes, anonymity would be preserved because each man was assigned the name of a fish, bird, or animal and because original tapes were re-recorded in a manner that made voices unrecognizable though clearly understood.[4] The CA owned the tapes. Everyone in the company knew he would never be allowed to hear another group's tapes. However, drawing upon the language laboratory concept, any member of a class could get any of the tapes of his class from the CA to replay privately. Over 60 per cent reheard at least one. Consensus was that a second listen-through heightened recall.

When combined, the design provided each S with three opportunities: (1) As *interviewers,* in this safe environment, they would have the time and place to test a variety of new approaches to real-life job problems using cases similar to those which they were facing every day and to receive feedback from peers concerning these new behaviors. (2) As *interviewees* they would have a chance for face-to-face exposure to any number of types of bosses (autocratic, unsure, demanding, empathic) which would provide a basis for comparison. (3) As *audience members* they would see and analyze actual interactions between people in a work-oriented situation and have a chance not only to speculate about what they would do in a like circumstance but to experiment with different approaches. From previous change experiences, the CA knew this design would allow maximum exposure and impact for Ss. There are six reasons: (a) none of them would be attacked, humiliated, or forced to defend the status quo; yet (b) their ideas and behaviors were under constant scrutiny from peers, which would make it hard to escape owning up to their inadequacies; thus (c)

---

[4]Excerpts could then be played to provide feedback at appropriate times. This provides a tremendous assistance to the learning process. Ss could hear the sentiments, attitudes, respect (or disrespect) for the symbols and norms of Ss in other groups and compare them with their own.

causing them to rethink their behavior which had suddenly been exposed in the limelight as being less than effective in coping even with classroom situations; so that (d) they modified or abandoned old behaviors, experimented with and adopted new ones; and (e) this, in turn, made behavior and attitude noncongruent, which (f) caused a gradual attitudinal change in the direction of congruence. This took place on the job as well as in the classroom because rewards for growth were plentiful, generous, and given in both places by everyone of high status, for the same kind of behavior.

Grouping of Participants

Two-hour classes were to be conducted twice a week during the workday for four weeks. Except for the President, who was persuaded to get his training alone in the privacy of his own office, all supervisors were included in three groups: (1) the GM, two Managers, and four Directors; (2) all A and B supervisors; and (3) level C plus the plant nurse and personnel secretary. Since no B reported to an A, there were no mixed superior/subordinate classes except the GM's, and in this case it was believed highly desirable. He was already "open," an advocate of Theory Y, and quite comfortable using management by objectives, delegation, and general supervision; yet he did not feel that he "knew it all." He too wanted to improve (change). The assumption was that he would *prove* how committed he was to the program by his enthusiasm, cooperation, and behavior during training and afterwards, when he would begin to practice immediately with his immediate subordinates what they had been exposed to that day.[5] This *did* happen. He also decided to have the CA watch his actions continually and "correct" him concerning process at any time, even in front of subordinates.[6] This had a strong favorable impact on all supervision. Over time, several others, at all levels, asked for similar monitoring and feedback.

Implementation

The President introduced the CA to the GM's group on a Monday at 10:00 a.m., when he briefly reviewed the firm's previous educational ventures, spoke positively about how much he "believed in the CA and what he was going to do," explained that the CA "threw me out of the classes before they started," wished them well, and left the room. This, plus a short speech of commitment by the GM, was repeated at 1:00 and 3:00 p.m. for the other two groups. Meetings took place semiweekly for four weeks.

As the President had been coached to do it, there was no need for a long warmup. Thus, the CA's opening remarks were confined to the careful explana-

---

[5]To keep the facts clear, he does have an M.B.A. degree, just recently earned, and was conversant with some behavioral science ideas.

[6]For example, "Mr. GM, let me hold a 'mirror' up so that you can hear what I heard you saying."

tion about the presence of the two recorders, a reiteration that he was a university professor doing action research (not a member of the firm), plus the following statement often to be repeated in ensuing weeks, "Remember, you can help me most when I'm around by just being yourself *as you really are.* Say whatever you believe! You will soon discover I have no desire to judge your actions as 'right' or 'wrong.' To judge is not my function. I do not care *what* you think, but *how* you think. Nothing you say to me will ever be carried back to your boss as coming from you. The aggregate consensus, carefully disguised, will be conveyed to help you."

Feelings, Facts, and Solutions

The hypothesis was that although this would begin as a basically noncontent communications course it would soon be shifted by *Ss* to a wide-open gripe session. The design was meant to "open them up" in a way conceptually similar to Lewin's (1947) "unfreezing." It was assumed that attitude change would be made easier as the group itself removed (indirectly) support for those attitudes currently in vogue. This would result partly from the encouraged open dialogue which would lead to much sharper agreement as to the group's real attitudes. Now, as each *S* begins to "unfreeze" all previously held norms and sentiments, he usually purges himself of his entire former behavior pattern. Many former *Ss* say it is when they suddenly discover nothing is left that the panic sets in: what may look like a relapse is really themselves trying to grasp at the past to fill the vacuum. This would seem to be the moment where the CA must let *Ss* experience a success at using "new" behavior. Argyris (1962) said: "If one is experimenting with new behavior, then one may predict that he will tend to defend himself from experiencing failure. One relatively safe defense is to 'try out the educator's behavior.' It is at this point that the individual is mimicking." The design in this program had developed from the concept called "simulation": let them mimic, in the short run, what had been said and done by the CA (the readings reinforced the same tools and concepts he was applying). This was to be done in the role playing and problem solving of cases. Thus this change process is meant to start by the mechanism of what Schein (1961) called "identification," but it is continued by what he labeled "internalization."

The Explosion

In the third session, the hypothesis became fact when the lowest (C) group suddenly shifted from a discussion of the implications to be drawn from the case being role-played to a heated exchange of thoughts or feelings about their real-world situation at Epsilon. They were scheduled to quit at 5:00 p.m., but they continued, oblivious of the CA and recorders, until 7:00 p.m., when they were reluctantly broken up because a blizzard raging outside threatened their getting home. After receiving their unanimous consent, the CA edited the tapes to pull off the "juicy" parts, making the voices sound different too, and then played excerpts to the GM's group at their fourth class. This, in turn, "blew the lid off" the GM's group. At first they were shocked, incredulous, and defensive: "My God! Is that *our* organization they're talking about? Are you *sure* you have *our* supervisor's tapes? It can't be, I *know all of my* people are happy! That's *me* they are describing, isn't it?" But as they grasped the degree of emotion and conviction implicit in the comments they began to accept the stark reality. As they listened to the tapes over again, it became clear they were viewing the criticism as constructive. They began to indicate a desire to deal with it. What they felt now can perhaps be best indicated by two comments, said with much resignation, on the tape: "I have always heard 'if the shoe fits, put it on.' Well, it hurts, but I'm wearing it," and "You're an ugly little monster (ha! ha! ha! ha!), but you're all mine." They requested the CA to tell the level C group to start to challenge them in this way, openly, face to face from now on. They wanted to be pushed and promised that they would grow to meet the occasion. They requested that A's and B's hear both the C's' tapes and their own responses. It appeared that a major breakthrough had taken place.

When the excerpts were played for A's and B's there was no immediate impact except silence. It seemed clear that they were hurt and stunned by all the charges from below. They too had gripes to get off their chests, but, unlike C's, they were extremely cautious of this new behavior from above. The promises of improvement and change were perceived variously as just a "passing fad," "temporary thaw," and a "good sign, but there is no hurry." Only gradually did they begin to awaken to the fact that a new climate did exist. Then, in the middle of the fifth session, they too unloaded. Their edited tapes were played for the other two groups and they were allowed to hear replays of how the others responded. By this time there was calm acceptance of the facts, empathy for their feelings, plus both encouragement and support.

All three groups were now pouring out their true emotions to one another (about work) both in and out of class. The *feelings* stage soon dissipated. Thoughts turned to searching for the reasons for the problems: the *facts* stage. From there they would shift unconsciously toward *solutions* they, themselves, were developing in and out of class.

Individual Solutions

Group changes were obviously due to individuals who were changing within them. Just as one example, consider the VP, now acting as Director of one of the two combined Manufacturing/Engineering functions. He had done the worst job possible on a role play where his only assignment was to get an employee (played by the GM) to do about five hours' work which had to be done at all costs, sometime between Friday at 4:30 p.m. and Monday at 8:00 a.m. No time was ruled out during the coaching. This was the only man trained to do it. Using perfectly normal (for him) Theory X, nonempathic, nonlistening techniques, he failed miserably. Losing control of his temper, standing red-faced, screaming, and pounding on the table, he fired the employee.

That day he asked the GM and CA to join him for lunch. He drove and as soon as they were started he expressed thanks for trying to soften the blow to his pride. He confided that he realized how poor he was in such matters and said he wanted to improve, adding, "Please work with me. I'll pay you—gladly—anything." The CA agreed to help but would take no pay. Within days he began to change. Everyone began to ask what had come over him. One day, with eyes sparkling and voice breaking with emotion, he told the GM and CA of an encounter with an employee the day before that was almost identical to the case he had role-played so poorly before: "Suddenly it came to me that this was really all we were doing in class, and I thought, 'Now there is nothing to be afraid of, how have I been doing it in practice?' and, by golly, it worked out perfectly! I actually did hear what the employee said—*me,* an old mastermind like me! Her request was legitimate from her frame of reference and we worked it out to our mutual satisfaction. You know, it was easy. Is it always so satisfying? Thank you for helping!" He had learned, and owned, the concepts and was actually applying them in his day-to-day situation. He began to be open in meetings, even saying (when appropriate), "I don't know." Perhaps most significant was the series of meetings *he initiated* with the GM, where he began to talk openly about his innermost feelings. After all, this GM was the same man who had been moved over him in authority, taken his big office (leaving him to move to the smallest occupied by any of the other Directors), reduced his areas of control, and who had the power (if not sufficient reasons) to fire him at a moment's notice.

The recapitulation of the behavior changes in this one individual is meant to stand merely as a symbol of the many other equally dynamic changes others experienced: it can be read as "he" or "they" by including or excluding the words in parentheses. Relieved of all his (administrative burdens) inhibitions, S (the VP) felt free to concentrate (on production) where he was highly competent; confronted with superiors', peers', and subordinates' feelings about his past dealings with them, but provided a "climate" in which to learn, try out, and get encouragement for, new and different behavior patterns, he looked and acted satisfied for the first time in years. More important to this case study, his (division's) performance began to improve significantly. So did his subordinates'.

Transition

The GM and CA sat before a tape recorder and reviewed for several hours what had been going on. They then planned where to go next, taking all ideas and decisions to the President for an additional point of view.

Part of the seventh class had been devoted to developing Ss' skills in conference leadership. A case problem was assigned to be taken home and prepared: They were to come to the final session and participate in a conference about that case as if it were a real problem confronting the company. (As a matter of fact, it was!) Various Ss were asked to lead it for a set length of time. The group was solely responsible for content while the CA would prompt them on process.

Although all three groups reached quite different conclusions, they were all really functioning as problem solvers by now. The atmosphere throughout was open, relaxed, and conducive to free inquiry. Most of the feedback was *descriptive nonevaluative* (Argyris, 1962). All their solutions were usable: one was used.

Process Observer

Time was left at the conclusion for a careful summary of the eight sessions. The difference between process and content (Strauss & Sayles, 1960) was given special attention: the role the CA had played in the last case was used to illustrate what a process observer did or did not do. Notice that "he *did not* care about *content;* he *did not care what* you decided; his *sole interest* was in the *process* by which you made your decisions." Then the CA thanked them for their cooperation, indicated he believed they had increased their interpersonal competence immeasurably, and went over to the side of the room and sat down. The GM, at the same time, took a position at the front of the class. He made a short statement which included his thanks to the CA for the "training phase" just completed, then unveiled a "process observer" phase which he strongly supported and desired at once: "From now on content will be decided by you, with consultation with me and/or other supervisors at the regular day-to-day meetings that will go on at and between all levels, on the shop floor, and at these semiweekly two-hour sessions which will continue as they did before except that it will be I who will conduct the discussion rather than Dr. Bartlett, and the problems will be the ones we are currently facing at Epsilon. Whenever he is present, however, there will always be tape recorders operating so that the tapes can be taken back to his office and analyzed for process: Just how well did we learn to communicate?" The reaction was unanimous and favorable to "get going and put into practice what we have learned." In fact, many supervisors asked afterwards to have a recorder at the meetings even if the CA were not present.[7]

Repeat Performance for the Lower Levels

During the process observer phase, the training program was started again for all indirect labor personnel. Included were secretarial, quality, accounting, marketing, technical, other assorted clericals, plus the lead men, set-up, and crew chiefs (both first and second shifts). It was the same program (with minor

[7]Obviously my university schedule limited the days when I could attend a meeting, and yet it was valuable to get as wide a collection of interpersonal behavior from meetings as possible. It was decided that at any meeting where *only* those favoring the idea were present, a tape recorder would be run during the meeting. My graduate research assistants (independently from me) and I determined that the tapes were comparable on specific preselected variables, whether I had attended the meeting or not.

modifications to take account of their lesser authority in the decision-making process), but it was spread over a 16-week period, one hour per week, with three similarly sized groups. Care was taken in arranging the groups to get a cross section of each of Epsilon's various functional areas in each one.

The program was well received by these *Ss* who had also been frustrated in the paternalistic Theory X environment. They knew supervisors were "going to school," were conscious of the changing climate, and quite curious as to what was going on. That they were important enough to get similar training most certainly had an impact on how well they grew.

A New Behavior Pattern

For several months the supervisors' groups continued to meet twice a week in the same spirit of "openness" under the chairmanship of the GM. The role of the CA became more and more pure process. A cursory perusal of the tapes would indicate how well they mastered both process and content roles: they were communicating! No longer did meetings drag on for hours and get nowhere, as before. No longer were the advisability of giving turkeys for Thanksgiving and whether female employees should be allowed to wear hair curlers or shorts in the shop, the *major* topics! Discussion now focused on the real Epsilon problems: the need to expand capacity, improve efficiency and productivity, and raise quality. The GM's report to the President for this period includes the following: "The 'general supervision' type of relationship between (top) management and supervision and the continued freedom of speaking out led persistently into the area of demands for more feedback of information. Accounting, Sales, Methods, Quality, and especially Production Control problems which continued unresolved and unexplained were brought out for discussion. The act of probing these problem areas telegraphed throughout the organization that change was imminent . . . ; the majority of the employees faced the prospects of impending change with a fair degree of stability and openness. The exercises in communication had prepared these employees for just this sort of real-life experience." This new behavior pattern extended all the way from the President through everyone in the organization, including all nonsupervisory "overhead" personnel. The next step would be to include the factory "direct labor" operators. This was to be done by Epsilon's own supervisors. After this they felt everything would be ready for a big change (Bartlett, 1967).

Success or Failure

Perhaps the most important part of this report concerns questions such as: What, if anything, did this change program accomplish? Was it worth the time, energy, and funds expended? How do we know? What substantive indicators are there by which improvement can be quantified? The evidence will be broken down into six categories.

Cost Reduction

Epsilon had a cost reduction program best described as a modification of the "Lincoln Electric" plan (Lincoln, 1951) combined with certain "Scanlon" plan (Lesieur, 1958) features. There was a labor base which was the amount of money they were willing to pay to obtain a given sales volume. The difference between this and actual costs, less material used in excess of norm, was stated as a per cent award. Half of this was paid quarterly. The balance was cumulated to be paid at the end of the year. Before the change program the award was minus 4.3%; at the end of one quarter following the program it was a plus 4%; at the six-month mark it reached 4.9%.

Planned Efficiency

The first three months of 1964 had been a loss operation. The next six months, although slightly in the black, were characterized by spasmodic performance. Shipments were made at the end of the week and at the end of the month, and only by herculean efforts above and beyond the call of duty. Chaos reigned supreme in the finishing departments at these times, while all activity and attention during the early part of the week and month were focused on the stockroom and starting operations.

The improvement in dollars shipped for the first three months of 1965 after the program was plus 26.6%. Over a period of eight months after the program, and after correcting for the addition of 150 new direct labor employees, the improvement was still plus 128%. But this is not the significant part. Even more important is that management now had both the confidence and ability to predict, at the beginning of each month, how many dollars would be shipped each day, and they posted a giant chart showing this target on the factory wall for all employees to see. They hit the monthly goal eight out of the next nine months, and 83.9% of the time they hit the daily goal.

Absenteeism

Level C supervisors discovered, during a meeting to find ways to step up production, that absenteeism was 8.5% of payroll hours. This, even for a predominantly female work force, is extremely high. They reviewed company policy, and had the Nurse interview all chronic absentees. She found that employees believed the firm wanted them to take *at least two* days per month off. Satisfied that it was a misunderstood norm which was at fault, the supervisors developed and sponsored a new policy and circulated it to everyone in the organization for discussion, modification, and testing before adoption. A reduction target was selected for the coming month: absenteeism fell to 4.9% in 30 days; it was halved again in 30 more.

Turnover

Levels A and B became interested in turnover. Study convinced them that not only was this costing money directly, but it reduced efficiency as a new employee took at least 60 days to learn the combination of speed and high quality. When a study indicated that the Personnel Secretary was more efficient than the supervisors in recruiting, screening, testing, and selecting of new hires, she was given the total responsibility for it. The entire responsibility for the decision as to whether a person passed the probationary period was placed on the (first line) C supervisors. Thus they had intimate knowledge about which person was not retained after probation, who quit, and why. They had to get to know all new employees as well as their performance. Turnover was reduced by 40% in the first three-month period. It fell another 10% over the next eight months.

Operator Training

During the research on turnover, the need for an operator training program became obvious. Clearly it would reduce learning time for new operators, and it would also lead to a more uniform understanding of what to do, how to do it, and why. It should lead to a higher quality of work from a speedier operator. Such a program was recommended and controlled by Manufacturing but prepared and offered by the Chief Engineer for "T."

Higher Quality

In the never-ending quest for higher quality, the Chief Engineer for "P" was invited to present his written and oral comments to all levels of supervision. Having been with another company until just before the program, his report thoroughly compared and contrasted this firm with Epsilon. His recommendations were collated with other knowledge concerning competitors and widely discussed. Lists were developed by categories, in meetings composed of a cross section of all levels and functions. All projects were then ranked, task forces were established, and action was begun on the basis of priority.

Improvements included (a) average scrap reduction 25%; (b) rework decrease 36%; (c) delay time for inspection cut 50% by updating processes and procedures; (d) returns from customers (faulty products) diminished 77%; (e) material usage decline to 80% (from 139%) of "standard"; and (f) usable ideas for improving manufacturing grew to 90% from 2.5%.

A Theoretical Epilogue

How to explain the changes that took place—Are they not all predictable within the existing concepts and theories of Behavioral Science? If so, all that seems necessary to understand them is the proper frame of reference. That will be established first, followed by an explanation.

Frame of Reference

1. There was no doubt as to the validity of the thesis that McGregor (1960), among others (Argyris, 1957; Blake & Mouton, 1964; Bennis, 1966), held. Most men do not need (or want) to be directed and controlled at work. They do not have to be passive, indolent, furtive, irresponsible, capricious, or idea-less. The literature is full of empirical evidence showing the obverse (Golembiewski, 1962; Lawrence & Seiler, 1961; Likert, 1961; Whyte, 1948, 1955). Man does represent an infinite, yet virtually untapped, potential source of help to any organization who seeks it. If his actions belie this latter idea and lend credibility to the one above, it is mainly because the organization tends to mould and shape man via the "technology" and "environment" (Argyris, 1965; Sayles, 1958) to epitomize what might be called the "organization man."

2. Incessant effort is expended to make work tasks ever more routinized and repetitive, despite the fact that doing the same thing, day in, day out, rapidly becomes first boring, then frustrating, finally fatiguing. Anyone not yet "aculturalized" is noticed because he is still trying to be himself and is seeking variety through innovation. Many may even be seen suggesting improvements in "the system," attempting to modify the "rules," plus a variety of other risk-taking behavior. Since "making waves" does not befit most organizations' ideas of a team player, however, plenty of "punishment-centered" rules (Gouldner, 1954) are continually introduced and relied on to remove his areas of freedom.

   For some, constant doses of Theory X merely leave them uninspired, discouraged, or demotivated: "I will put up with *anything* eight hours a day if the *bribe* is high enough to let the rest of life be enjoyable." But work *has* become a punishment! "Putting in eight hours" is the price to be paid for the wherewithal to satisfy needs *off the job* (waiting early at the time clock and rushing out of the plant are not signs of laziness so much as needs crying to be fulfilled). And for most in the throes of Theory X, needs that are satisfied at all get taken care of off the job with paid holidays, vacations, sick leave, pension, plus salary.

To the rest, each time the "screw is tightened" the (dysfunctional) challenge is issued to try to (a) get out of work (Whyte, 1961); (b) hoodwink authority figures (Roy, 1952); (c) short-circuit the system (Roy, 1954); or (d) out-bureaucratize the bureaucracy with needless ritual, petty red tape, and other time-consuming nonsense (Strauss, 1962, 1964).

Regardless of which path they follow, very few escape unscathed. Both "management-by-crisis" and a "win/lose" atmosphere take their toll: you learn the struggle is hopeless and join the cautious, frightened crowd. Avoid the boss or "yes" him, and tell him only what is favorable or cannot be concealed. This might seem to be a caricaturization, but it actually represents a summary of supervisory attitudes at Epsilon when this change program commenced. (Undoubtedly, it fits many other companies, too.)

3. An hypothesis was held that the most important task in changing or improving behavior is to ascertain that the environment and technology are conducive for growth and the satisfaction of personal needs. In real-world terms this meant a prime objective was to create opportunities, encourage growth, remove obstacles, and provide guidance which would release the potential of Epsilon's supervisors as it moved from management by control to management by results. Another hypothesis was that given half a chance, man will seek what Clark (1960-61) calls "interaction opportunity," "influence opportunity," "contribution opportunity," as well as "status congruence"; or what Strauss and Sayles (1960) call "egoistic" and "social" on-the-job needs satisfaction. A last hypothesis was that in maximizing the above, man can (and will) render positive contributions toward helping the organization satisfy its needs, and thus both will grow.

4. This means that the problem was not defined as being whether Epsilon's managers could (or wanted to) solve its problems. Rather, it was how best to remove the cultural restraints preventing them from making their own greatest contributions. How to create an atmosphere where everyone from sweeper to president wants to (and may) make a significant contribution—that was the aim.

5. An organization is not just things—it is people. The two are interdependent. In order to make things run, people must interact. The more effective their interpersonal competence, the more efficiently things go. A win/lose environment is inhibiting. It makes a man defensive. He must spend his time on accumulating detail, blame fixing, and short-run payoff. An open environment is exhilarating. It makes a man excited by the task, confident of his own ability, cooperative with subordinates, peers, and superiors, and anxious to give and receive descriptive nonevaluative feedback. He listens, trades ideas, plans, and solves long-run problems.

The simple explanation as to why the changes took place at Epsilon is this: (a) the supervisors already had sufficient ideas to vastly improve production and quality as well as to reduce costs; (b) they also had both the ability and the desire (which has been true for most supervisors whom the CA has known).

The duties of the CA (as is so often the case) were: (a) to oversee the establishment of a climate in which Ss could realize their desire to communicate their ideas for improvement, and (b) to provide information in the form of the tools and concepts from the behavioral sciences which could make the road to change easier to travel, as well as quicker.

A new climate for change was slowly created in which: (a) a laboratory was set up; (b) a feelings buildup was caused to break through an "attitudinal sound barrier"; (c) Ss unfroze, discarded old methods, and temporarily copied what the CA did and said in "simulation" exercises; (d) experiments were tried to find a successful way to cope with role plays and cases; (e) behavior changed and Ss became comfortable in using it in dealing with the real-life problems of the shop; (f) Ss began to describe the parameters of Epsilon's problems and to work out their own solutions; and (g) Ss completed the change and refroze.

Conclusion

A company can change its style of leadership from Theory X to Theory Y. It can create a climate of trust, characterized by a concern for the individual's right to be himself, to take independent action, and to admit mistakes without fear of retribution. It can do this and get an improvement in efficiency and quality at the same time. This change occurred at the Epsilon Corporation when a change agent applied the conceptual tools of behavioral scientists.

References

Argyris, C. *Personality and Organization.* New York: Harper, 1957.

Argyris, C. *Interpersonal Competence and Organizational Effectiveness.* Homewood, Ill.: Irwin-Dorsey, 1962.

Argyris, C. *Organization and Innovation.* Homewood, Ill.: Irwin & Son, 1965.

Asch, S. "Opinions and Social Pressure." *Scientific American,* 1955, 31-34.

Bartlett, A. A Theory Y Company Introduces Change. Unpublished manuscript, State University of New York at Buffalo, 1967.

Bartlett, A. "Changing Behavior Through Simulation: An Alternate Design to T-Group Training," *Training Development Journal* XXI, No. 8 (August, 1967) 38-52.

Bennis, W. *Changing Organizations.* New York: McGraw-Hill, 1966.

Blake, R. R., & Mouton, Jane S. *The Managerial Grid.* Houston: Gulf, 1964.

Clark, J. "Motivation in Work Groups: A Tentative View." *Human Organization,* 1960-61, 19 (4), 199-208.

Gibb, J. Defensive Communication. *Journal of Communications,* 1961, 11 (3), 141-148.

Golembiewski, R. *Behavior and Organization.* Chicago: Rand McNally, 1962.

Gouldner, A. *Patterns of Industrial Bureaucracy.* New York: Free Press, 1954.

Lawrence, P., & Seiler, J. *Organizational Behavior and Administration: Cases, Concepts and Research Findings.* Homewood, Ill.: Irwin-Dorsey, 1961, American Radiatronics Corporation (A), 266-302.

Lesieur, F. (Ed.) *The Scanlon Plan.* Cambridge, Mass.: Wiley, 1958.

Lewin, K. "Frontiers in Group Dynamics: Concept, Method, and Reality in Social Science." *Human Relations,* 1947, I, 5-42.

Likert, R. *New Patterns of Management.* New York: McGraw-Hill, 1961.

Lincoln, J. *Incentive Management.* Cleveland, Ohio: Lincoln Elec., 1951.

Lippitt, R., Watson, Jeanne, & Westley, B. *The Dynamics of Planned Change.* New York: Harcourt, Brace & World, 1958.

McGregor, D. *The Human Side of Enterprise.* New York: McGraw-Hill, 1960.

McMurry, R. "Empathy: Management's Greatest Need." *Advanc. Management,* 1953, 18 (7), 6-11, 34.

Rogers, C., & Farson, R. "Active Listening." in G. Bergen & W. Haney (Eds.), *Organizational Relations and Management Action.* New York: McGraw-Hill, 1966, Pp. 61-76.

Rogers, C., & Roethlisberger, F. "Barriers and Gateways to Communication." *Harvard Business Review,* July 1952, 46-52.

Roy, D. "Quota Restriction and Goldbricking in a Machine Shop." *American Journal of Sociology,* 1952, 57 (5), 427-442.

Roy, D. "Efficiency and 'The Fix': Informal Intergroup Relations in a Piecework Machine Shop." *American Journal of Sociology,* 1954, 60 (3), 255-266.

Sayles, L. *Behavior of Industrial Work Groups.* New York: Wiley, 1958.

Schein, E. "Management Development as a Process of Influence." *Industrial Management Reviews,* 1961, 2, 59-77.

Strauss, G. "Tactics of Lateral Relationship: The Purchasing Agent." *Administrative Science Quarterly,* 1962, 7 (2), 161-186.

Strauss, G. "Work-flow , Interfunctional Rivalry, and Professionalism." *Human Organization,* 1964, 23 (2), 137-149.

Strauss, G., & Sayles, L. *Personnel.* Englewood Cliffs, N.J.: Prentice-Hall, 1960.

Tannenbaum, R. "Dealing with Ourselves before Dealing with Others." *Office Executive,* 1957, 32 (8), 29-30, 35.

Tarnopol, L. "Attitudes Block Communications." *Personnel Journal,* 1959, 37 (9), 325-328.

Whyte, W. F. *Human Relations in the Restaurant Industry.* New York: McGraw-Hill, 1948.

Whyte, W. F. *Money and Motivation.* New York: Harper, 1955.

Whyte, W. F. *Men at Work.* Homewood, Ill.: Irwin-Dorsey, 1961.

Breakthrough in
Organization Development

The account which follows deals with organizational development as a means of changing behavior using the managerial grid. One concise definition of organizational development is: ". . . an effort (1) planned, (2) organization-wide, and (3) managed from the top, to (4) increase organization effectiveness and health through (5) planned interventions in the organization's 'processes,' using behavioral-science knowledge." [1]

In this selection, the authors outline the concepts and phases which constitute a Grid Organization Development (Grid OD) Program. Next, a detailed description of the Grid OD Program in action is presented as it was applied to the managers and technical staff at one plant within a large multiplant corporation. Finally, the results are examined. The authors conclude that ". . . even allowing for the non-program effects, the results of the Grid Program were impressive."

This study shows quite clearly that the behavioral sciences can be transferred quite effectively into an organization in such a way as to change behavior in a positive direction. [2]

[1] Richard Beckhard, *Organization Development: Strategies and Models,* (Reading, Mass.: Addison-Wesley Publishing Company, 1969), p. 9.

[2] For a subsequent program aimed at operative employees which also had favorable results, see Robert R. Blake, Jane S. Mouton, Richard L. Sloma, and Barbara Peek Loftin, "A Second Breakthrough in Organization Development," *California Management Review,* XI, No. 2 (1968), 73-78.

BREAKTHROUGH IN
ORGANIZATION DEVELOPMENT

Robert R. Blake
Jane S. Mouton
Scientific Methods, Inc.

Louis B. Barnes
Larry E. Greiner
Harvard University

This article describes how behavioral science concepts of team learning form a link between individual learning and total organization development. The link is important because it suggests some answers to a long-standing problem in industry: how to test and demonstrate the large-scale usefulness of human relations research and teaching. In the process, the article also describes a rather new approach to management development and, more broadly, to organization development.

AUTHORS' NOTE: Acknowledgement is due to the Piedmont and Sigma management for their support of and involvement in this project. Partial support for Dr. Barnes's time was furnished by the Division of Research, Harvard Business School.

AUTHORS' SPLIT ROLES IN GRID STUDY. Dr. Blake's and Dr. Mouton's work went into the earlier design stages of the Managerial Grid concepts, and teaching materials, and in Part 1 of the article (following the introduction, which represents the combined thinking of all four authors) they describe briefly the six phases of a Grid program in organization development. Then an actual program, carried out by the Sigma plant's line management with minimal help from Blake and Mouton, was independently evaluated by Dr. Barnes and Mr. Greiner, as set forth in Part II of the article. Because of this description-evaluation split, the two pairs of authors have deliberately restricted their roles in the article, just as they sought to avoid influencing each other's interpretations of company developments as they were taking place. In this sense, Barnes and Greiner are the independent auditors of a program originally designed by Blake and Mouton. For a far more complete development of the theory and phases, see Robert R. Blake and Jane S. Mouton, *The Managerial Grid* (Houston, Gulf Publishing Company, 1964).

*a successful
change program*

Barriers to Success

Strangely enough, large-scale organization development is rare, and the measurement of results is even rarer. Even though management has sought for years to grasp and implement the important findings of behavioral science research, the task has proved more difficult than it first seemed. Many findings are subtle and complex. Other findings relate to individual insights or knowledge which is hard to build into the organization's life stream. In addition, most behavioral scientists do a better job of communicating technical findings to each other than they do of communicating the relevance of their research to practicing managers.

There have been many earnest attempts to make the behavioral sciences useful to business, government, and service institutions. But, because of the complexities, success has been elusive. Consider:

> Within many organizations, pockets of human relations enthusiasts form. They typically find themselves bucking a complacent or skeptical management. The enthusiasts retaliate by overselling their beliefs (which simply generates more skepticism) or by withdrawing from accusations of being "soft" on workers, profits, and tough-minded traditions of management.

> Selected executives are sent to management development programs which feature human relations concepts. Quite often, companies send "those who need it most." Particularly in "sensitivity training"–type programs, these men are placed under considerable strain. Through pyschiatric problems rarely occur, they are a source of concern for staffs and faculties of such programs. Companies sometimes inadvertently send men with histories of previous mental illness. Under these conditions, psychiatric problems can occur and program effectiveness decrease for all concerned.[1]

> Other executives return from human relations programs highly enthusiastic. In at least some of these cases, there does seem to be real evidence of increased insight and individual learning. The problem for these men is one of implementation. Unless they have considerable organizational influence and/or a new, supportive climate, they will probably be forced back into old behavioral patterns and relationships.

> Occasionally, a total working group or department will be given human relations training within a company. At best, these efforts generate high morale and productivity within the group. At worst, the "chosen" group becomes the target or scapegoat of others in the organization, and the intergroup difficulties increase.[2]

[1]See Chris Argyris, "T-Groups for Organizational Effectiveness," HBR March-April 1964, p. 60.

[2]See Alex Bavelas and George Strauss, "Group Dynamics and Intergroup Relations," in W. F. Whyte, Melville Dalton, et al., *Money and Motivation* (New York, Harper & Brothers, 1955), pp. 90-96.

Most typically, in-company human relations training programs are established for foremen or other lower level managers. The almost universal response of participants in these programs is, "I wish my boss could learn what I've been learning." Then, as in the famous study of the International Harvester training program, most trainees go back to the job and apparently conform to their bosses' expectations, often at the expense of human relations concepts set forth in the program.[3]

In short, the over-all results of human relations and behavioral science training are questionable, at best, for on-the-job practitioners. Individual benefits are thought to be great, and personal testimonials are abundantly favorable.[4] However, the question of mobilizing these insights into collective organizational efforts has remained a serious issue.

Step Forward

The large-scale program in organization development described in this article may be a major step forward. It was regarded as highly successful both by the businessmen involved and by outside observers; the results *were* measured.

New to most executives in concept and design, the program makes use of a "Managerial Grid" approach to more effective work relationships. The Grid helps to give businessmen a language system for describing their current managerial preferences. It also involves classroom materials and an educational program for designing more productive problem-solving relationships. Even more important, the program is meant to be taught and applied by line managers over a time span involving six overlapping phases. These phases will be described briefly in Part I of this article; here you can see how a Managerial Grid program *should* work.

Then, in Part II you can see how such a program *did* work. The evaluation took place in a large plant (about 4,000 employees), which was part of a very large multiplant company. The parent company will be called "Piedmont" and the relevant plant unit "Sigma," for purposes of disguise. The Sigma plant had a reputation within Piedmont of being technically competent and had consistently been able to meet production goals over the past years. Among Sigma's 4,000 employees were some 800 managers and technical staff personnel. These managers and staff personnel were all exposed to a Managerial Grid training program beginning late in 1962. At the request of the research manager in Piedmont's employee relations department, an evaluation study was designed shortly thereafter to follow up the effects of that program. The study included

[3] E. A. Fleishman, E. F. Harris, and E. H. Burtt, *Leadership and Supervision in Industry* (Columbus, Personnel Research Board, Ohio State University, 1955).

[4] Instances of individual learning are documented in a series of HBR articles by Kenneth R. Andrews: see "Is Management Training Effective? I. Evaluation by Managers and Instructors," January-February 1957, p. 85; "Is Management Training Effective? II. Measurement, Objectives, and Policy," March-April 1957, p. 63; and "Reaction to University Development Programs," May-June 1961, p. 116.

questionnaires, interviews, observations, and a combing of company records in order to separate program effects from nonprogram effects. The findings suggest that, even allowing for the nonprogram effects, the results of the Grid program were impressive. In brief:

> There is some evidence that Sigma's organization development program was responsible for at least several million dollars of controllable cost savings and profit increase. In addition, the program seems to have been responsible for a sizable increase in employee productivity during its first year.
>
> Sigma's managers began follow-up projects having total organization implications to a degree never experienced prior to the organization development program.
>
> The relationships between Sigma and Piedmont were considerably improved, partly as a result of the program. In addition, both union and community relationships were better than they had been in the past.
>
> There is some evidence that major shifts occurred in the behavioral patterns, dominant values, and attitudes found among managers at Sigma. These shifts were in line with the goals of the Managerial Grid program. Improved boss-subordinate, group, and intergroup relations were reported by Sigma managers.
>
> Colleague support seemed to be more important than boss support as a factor in managerial improvement, according to subordinate managers.

Part I: How the Grid Program Should Work[5]

The Managerial Grid identifies five theories of managerial behavior, based on two key variables found in organizations. One variable reflects concern for production or output; the other variable, concern for people. In this instance the term "concern for" refers to the degree of concern, not the actual results. That is, it does *not* represent real production or the extent to which human relationship needs are actually met. It *does* indicate managerial concern for production and/or people and for how these influence each other.

Managerial Grid

These two variables and some of their possible combinations are shown in Fig. 1. The horizontal axis indicates concern for production, and the vertical axis indicates concern for people. Each is expressed on a scale ranging from 1, which represents minimal concern, to 9, which represents maximal concern.

Briefly, the lower left corner of the Grid diagram in Fig. 1 shows a 1,1 style. This represents minimal concern for production and minimal concern for people. The 1,9 style in the upper left corner depicts maximal concern for people but

[5]The authors of Part I are Robert R. Blake and Jane S. Mouton.

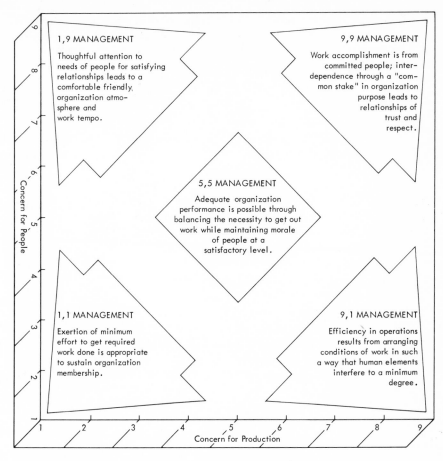

FIGURE 1. The Managerial Grid

minimal concern for production. The 9,1 style in the lower right corner portrays maximal concern for production and minimal concern for human relationships. The 9,9 style in the upper right-hand corner represents maximal concern for both human relationships and production. The 5,5 style in the center of the diagram is "middle of the road" in both areas of concern.

Once managers have studied the classroom material accompanying the Grid, it is possible for them to revise practices and procedures so as to work toward a 9,9 organizational climate. These efforts use an educational program as the core, in contrast to more conventional ways of getting better organizational results (e.g., changing organizational structure, leadership replacement, tightened accounting controls, or simple pressuring for more output).

Educational Steps

The educational steps are simple in concept, though complex in execution. They include the following:

An investigation by each man of his own managerial style, using certain Managerial Grid forms of analysis. These include self-evaluation instruments, self-administered learning quizzes, in-basket procedures, and organizational simulations.

A detailed and repeated evaluation of team effectiveness by groups which work with each other.

Diagnosis of major organization problem areas; e.g., long-range planning, profitability of operation, union-management relations, promotion policies, incentive awards, new-product development, absenteeism, utilities conservation, and safety.

We should emphasize that this entire approach to organization development is self-administered by management except for occasional consultation regarding major issues. As of now, the Managerial Grid approach has been used in both industry and government. Changes in the near future will be in degree rather than in basic approach.

Six-Phase Program

At the present time, we describe these organization development programs in terms of six overlapping phases. Taken sequentially, these phases can cover from three to five years, but they can also be compressed into a shorter period of time within a company.

Manager Development

The six phases can be divided realistically into two major parts. The first two phases involve *management* development so that the other four phases can help managers work toward the 9,9 goals of *organization* development. Here are the two management development phases:

1. Laboratory-Seminar Training. This is a one-week conference designed to introduce the manager to Grid concepts and material. From 12 to 48 individuals are assigned as members of problem-solving teams during each Laboratory-Seminar. These Seminars are conducted by line managers who already have been through the Seminar and thus know its material and schedules.

The Seminar begins with the study and review of one's own Managerial Grid style of behavior as outlined in a series of questionnaire booklets completed by each manager. It continues with 50 hours of intensive problem solving, evaluation of individual and team results, and critiques of team performance. The problems typically simulate organizational situations in which interpersonal behavior affects task performance. Each team regularly evaluates its own behavior and problem-solving capabilities. A team which performs poorly on one problem exercise is able to assess and adjust its problem-solving style in time for the next exercise. In addition, one exercise involves an attempted 9,9 "feedback" from team members to each individual concerning *team* impressions of his managerial styles.

Though Grid Seminars are sometimes compared with "T-Group" or "Sensitivity" training, the two training experiences are quite different. The strongest similarity comes in the face-to-face feedback experience of Phase # 1. Even here, however, the Managerial Grid Seminars take a more structured approach by focusing on managerial styles rather than on personal behavior characteristics which may or may not be related to management.

Phase #1 is not intended to produce immediate organization improvement. It serves more as the trigger which creates a readiness to really work on human problems of production. Participation in a Grid Seminar is set up so as to include a "diagonal slice" of the organization chart. No man is in the same group as his boss or immediate work colleagues. At the same time, this diagonal slice arrangement permits many organizational levels and departments to be represented in each session.

2. Team Development. This represents an on-the-job extension of Phase #1. The general 9,9 concepts and personal learning of the Grid Seminars are transferred to the job situation after each work group or department decides on its own 9,9 ground rules and relationships. Team development usually starts with the boss and his immediate subordinates exploring their managerial styles and operating practices as a work team. The ground rules of openness and candor which were established in Phase #1 can now become the daily operating style of Phase #2.[6]

Taken together, Phases #1 and #2 provide management development conditions which are designed to—

. . . enable managers to learn Managerial Grid concepts as an organizing framework for thinking about management practices;

. . . increase the self-examination of personal performance characteristics;

. . . increase a manager's willingness to listen, to face and appreciate work-related conflict, to reduce and work out interpersonal frictions, and to reject compromise as a basis for organizational decision making;

. . . build improved relationships between groups, among colleagues at the same level, and between superiors and subordinates;

. . . make managers more critical of outworn practices and precedents while extending their problem-solving capacities in interdependent situations. Words like "involvement" and "commitment" become real in terms of day-to-day tasks.

[6]See R. R. Blake, J. S. Mouton, and M. G. Blansfield, "How Executive Team Training Can Help You and Your Organization," *Journal of the American Society of Training Directors* (now called *Training Directors Journal*), January 1962, p. 3.

The last four phases build on this management development and help managers work toward the more complex goals of organization development.

3. Intergroup Development. This involves group-to-group working relationships and focuses on building 9,9 ground rules and norms beyond the single work group. Situations are established whereby operating tensions that happen to exist between groups are identified and explored by group members and/or their representatives.

The goal is to move from the appallingly common "win-lose" pattern to a joint problem-solving activity. This seems to be possible when competing groups work their problems through to resolution using intergroup procedures developed in behavioral science studies.

A second type of intergroup development helps to link managers who are at the same level but belong to different work units (e.g., foremen, district sales managers, department managers, and so forth). Their competitiveness may increase organizational productiveness, but it may also result in departmental goals being placed ahead of more important organizational goals. Here, the problem is again met using joint problem-solving efforts which confront interpersonal issues according to 9,9 ground rules and norms.

4. Organizational Goal Setting. This involves issues of major importance to all managers. Organization development moves beyond team areas into problems that require commitment at all levels. Such broad problems include: cost control, union-management relations, safety, promotion policies, and over-all profit improvement. These problems are identified by special task groups which may again come from a "diagonal slice" of the organization chart. Departmental groups may also help to define goals and assign roles. The goals prove to be "practical" when managers who must implement them also establish responsibilities for implementation. Commitment gained from the goal-setting procedures of this phase also avoids those negative responses now grouped under "resistance to change."

5. Goal Attainment. This uses some of the same educational procedures used in Phase #1, but here the issues are major organizational concerns and the stakes are real.

For example, when problem areas are defined by the special task groups, other teams are set up throughout the organization. These teams are given a written "task paragraph" which describes the problem and the goal. Team members are also given packets of information on the issue under discussion. This information is usually studied overnight, after which individual managers check themselves on a true-false test designed by the special task group. Once individuals have studied the information and the test, the teams begin discussion on the same items, checking their agreed-on answers against an answer key. This way, agreement is reached on the nature of the problem and its key dimensions. From this point on, the team members work toward a better statement of the problem and toward corrective steps. They also begin to assign responsibility for these corrective action steps.

Phase #5 also relies on a manager serving as a coordinator during Phases #4 and #5. His primary goal is to help achieve the goals set during Phase #4. His secondary aim is to help identify previously unrecognized problems. He should have neither line nor staff responsibility in the conventional sense, but should hold a position similar to an industrial medical officer. He would be a specialist in organization development and intervene at those times when proposed steps seem inconsistent with 9,9 theory. He would seek action based on understanding and agreement, not because of any formal authority he holds. This approach, though more difficult than access through authority, reduces resistance. It also improves the quality of joint effort.

6. Stabilization This final phase is designed to support the changes brought about in the earlier phases. These changes are assessed and reinforced so as to withstand pressures toward "slip back" and regression. This also gives management an opportunity to evaluate its gains and mistakes under the organization development program.

Summary

In this section we have briefly outlined the concepts and phases that go into an organization development program using Managerial Grid material. In some respects, the program sounds simple, and yet any manager recognizes the difficulties involved in influencing a large organizational unit toward changes in values and performance. Such was the challenge facing the Sigma management in 1962.

The next part of this article describes how Sigma faced that challenge with the help of the Grid program described above.

Part II: How the Grid Program Did Work[7]

This part describes the early findings and conclusions of a research study which evaluated the Sigma plant's program in organization development. The evaluation was suggested by the research manager in Piedmont's employee relations department. Those responsible for the program at the Sigma plant gave the idea immediate support. A research design was presented to the Sigma management and accepted. On-site field work began in June 1963 and ended in November 1963.

[7]The authors of Part II are Louis B. Barnes and Larry E. Greiner.

Evaluation Goals

The evaluation of this large-scale organization development program seemed important for a number of reasons:

As noted at the start of this article, corporate managements have had trouble in transferring behavioral science concepts into organizational action. The Sigma program represented a deliberate effort to move these concepts from the classroom into the mainstream of organization life.

The Sigma program was run by *line* managers. Even Phase #1, which introduced Managerial Grid concepts, was directed by rotating pairs of line managers. Staff experts and outside consultants played peripheral roles only. Typically, programs of this kind and scope involve considerable outside guidance and/or teaching.

Any management development program which focuses on self-introspection and self-other relationships runs some risk of psychiatric disturbances. The question was whether the Managerial Grid program at Sigma was able to avoid such problems by using exercises involving managerial styles rather than depending on the deeper exploration of personal characteristics. Altogether about 800 managers and technical men experienced Phase #1 at Sigma. These men were of varying ages and educational backgrounds. They came from all areas and levels of the organization.

The program at Sigma sought collective group changes, not just individual changes in attitudes and behavior. Most management development programs treat the individual as the learning unit. The six phases of the Grid program were explicitly aimed at group and cross-group shifts in attitudes and behavior.

Consequently, a "successful" program at Sigma might have important implications for business and the behavioral sciences alike. Sigma's experience might help answer the following questions implied in the above reasons for an outside evaluation:

Can a program based on behavioral science concepts be translated into meaningful organization action?

Can management take primary responsibility for such a program?

Can important attitude and behavior changes be accomplished without their being psychologically threatening?

Can a change of focus from the individual to the group aid collective learning and behavior change?

Measurement Problems

Given the possibility of Sigma's running a "successful" program, how were we to determine whether it was *really* successful? How was organization development to be adequately identified and measured? Such questions involve major issues in behavioral science methodology, and the answers are complex.

Put bluntly, there is no really satisfactory way of identifying and measuring organizational change and development. Too many variables are beyond control and cannot be isolated. An investigator never knows when "extraneous" factors are just as responsible for an important finding as are the "key" factors identified in his research.

Yet this complexity provides no excuse for not attempting to evaluate such programs. The important thing is to approach the project with some qualms and to apply caution. On this basis, we hope to show how different "measures" of Sigma's program furnish enough evidence for readers to piece together what happened before and during the program. These measures include productivity and profit indexes, results of opinion and attitude surveys from members of management, and evidence of behavioral changes taken from interviews and conversations.

None of these indexes is satisfactory by itself, and even when used jointly, they require cautious application. Each finding can only be treated as a piece in the over-all puzzle. It is the consistency and direction of the many different findings which lead us to believe that something important was happening at the Sigma plant.

Decision on Program

Historically, a number of factors influenced the management of the Sigma plant in making its decision to undertake the organization development program.

New Policies

The first significant factor occurred early in 1960. At that time, Piedmont was merged with another company. This merger disrupted a long-standing relationship between the Sigma plant and its parent organization. Among other things, the merger ended a prior contract that for over 25 years had assured Sigma of a cost-plus profit. It also brought with it a new headquarters management that stressed plant autonomy. Henceforth important decisions, which previously had been made almost exclusively by headquarters management, were to be delegated to the plant level.

However, complications arose when headquarters adopted its new policy of "hands-off" management. Headquarters hoped that the Sigma management would use its autonomy to solve chronic problems which had carried over from the more directive previous management. The most serious problem involved the use of Sigma manpower on construction work of new units. One headquarters manager described the situation as follows:

> *"We had heard from higher level people that Sigma had too much manpower. Our reaction, I suppose, was that this should have been reduced before the merger. But we were faced with it. And the Sigma*

plant was telling us that they were in balance. We got long memos from them, and finally the issue began to center on using manpower for construction work. This practice was typical of several plants in our organization, but Sigma appeared to be defensive, implying that they could do all the construction work better than contractors. This was the summer of 1961. We weren't sure about the true answer either, although I guess we thought they had a lot of people. Also, the vice president in charge of our group isn't one to go out and directly tell someone to do something. He would rather let them find out for themselves and then seek help. I believe in this. So we'd prod Sigma and ask questions. But I guess we weren't always too subtle. They became defensive, and some of our latter sessions became emotional."

In-Plant Relationships

A second major factor which helped to set the stage for the Sigma program involved the strained relationships between different departments and levels within the plant. Major operating and engineering departments were on the defensive. Accusations of "empire building" were not uncommon. Lower level supervisors still felt somewhat alienated because upper level management had frequently overruled them on union grievance decisions in the past. In short, while Piedmont was concerned about Sigma's major decisions, Sigma management worried more about day-to-day operating problems.

This factor was all the more crucial because of the complex technology of Sigma's plant, a technology that required constant interdepartment cooperation. Mistakes were costly and even dangerous. As a result, Sigma's management felt considerable pressure to resolve departmental differences and improve coordination. Yet these differences persisted, much to the frustration of many people.

The Plant Manager

Another key factor in setting the stage for the development program was the attitude and reputation of the Sigma plant manager. Prior to assuming operating control of the plant in 1959, he had worked at Piedmont headquarters on a reorganization study committee, and before that he had been research director at Sigma. Because of many important technical contributions he had made to the company, he was held in high regard within the Sigma plant. In his newer role as plant manager, he had tried to identify and correct the problems facing the plant. But he had experienced some difficulty in gaining full acceptance and cooperation on these desired improvements. One of the plant manager's key subordinates described his reaction to the plant manager's methods as follows:

"The plant manager would go around and ask people, 'What would you think if I made such and such a decision?' Actually, he already had his mind made up, but he was just testing people to see if they would accept it. He always wanted people to agree with him."

And a first-level supervisor made this specific comment:

"The plant manager came down and gave us a lot of company philoso-

phy. We started out with his 'Black Book'—he wrote it. It was pretty positive. It told the men to make decisions. But a new union had just come in, and a lot of people were suspicious that he only wanted us to make tough decisions rather than fair decisions."

The plant manager reported a cautious and circumspect reaction to the 1960 merger. This attitude was shared by most of the Sigma management. When Piedmont representatives asked the plant manager what he considered to be prying questions, he reacted rather strongly—"like Horatio defending the bridge," as he later described it.

Prior Plant Experience

Still another factor encompassed past efforts by Sigma's management to meet the production requirements. The plant was noted for its management and worker training. Like all of Piedmont's plants, Sigma had sent managers to university training programs, as well as running in-plant training programs with and without outside assistance. These efforts were intended to supplement an already high educational level in the plant, where over 48% of 800 managers and supervisors at all levels hold college degrees, including 80 with graduate degrees. In addition, Sigma was frequently characterized as a "family" and "meeting" plant where cooperation was considered important.

However, like many organizations, Sigma lacked a consistent way of fitting these concerns for productivity and people together. Instead, Sigma seemed to have emphasized one or the other, depending on headquarters directives and the other pressures on it at various times.

Consultant's Entry

Finally, the consultant, Dr. Blake, must be considered as a key factor. Blake had an impressive reputation as an organization analyst with management in other parts of Piedmont. Headquarters management had asked him to visit the Sigma plant, provided the plant manager approved. The plant manager described the entry of Blake as follows:

"I guess we decided on some sort of trial marriage with Blake. . . . I said, 'Why don't you look us over and we'll look you over.' In this trial period he began to look into our headquarters relations and concluded there were real problems. Then he asked if we wanted to explore these problems in a joint session with headquarters. I was impressed by that meeting. It did some real good. I guess headquarters at the end of the first day was ready to call off the dogs. We had a lot of misconceptions on the manpower problem—a lot of people in headquarters thought we weren't coming to grips with it. I guess one of the most enlightening things—when we started to let our hair down on the second day of these sessions—was when the vice president of manufacturing said, 'How should I know what Sigma is doing about manpower when they haven't told me?' I would have asked the same thing if I had been in his situation. But it shocked us."

"I'm not too clear on what happened from here on. But I feel we began to establish a rapport that we didn't have before. We ironed out a lot of misunderstandings on both sides. There was no longer a feeling of a lack of trust between us. This session convinced me and the whole group that Blake's methods had helped us—at least on this problem. He got us to see that conflict is something you get out on the table. Then four of us went to an outside Grid Seminar. We invited one manager from the headquarters group to come with us—and he did. All of these decisions to go ahead were made here at Sigma—mainly by a group of sixteen. It was a group decision to send the four of us to the Grid Seminar. We came back and reported—then we had some more discussions—and finally we evolved the development program."

Significant Changes

Phase #1 of Sigma's organization development program began in November 1962 with 40 managers participating in a one-week Managerial Grid Seminar. This phase continued until the summer of 1963, by which time 800 managers and technical men had completed it. Meanwhile, the earlier participants began to embark on later phases of the organization development program.

Our data collecting began about the same time. These data, accumulated over the next four months in the field and by reports thereafter, show significant changes in Sigma's operations. Both plant operations and internal-external relationships were influenced. In this section we shall describe these changes and attempt to show how the organization development program affected them. The data include changes in:

Productivity and profits.

Practices and behavior.

Perceptions, attitudes, and values.

The analysis of these data moves from "hard," relative objective material involving profits to "softer," more subjective data such as attitudes. The important things for readers to ask are: Do the different findings seem consistent? Do they reinforce each other? And do they suggest that the development program played an important role in Sigma's own development?

A. Productivity & Profits

There were significant increases in productivity and profits during 1963, when the organization development program was in effect. Table 1 indicates that total production rose somewhat (with fewer employees), and profits more than doubled. At first glance, it would seem that Sigma had struck gold, that its worries were over, and that the development program had been highly effective. But this in itself would be a gross oversimplification.

To begin with, Sigma's business involves widely fluctuating market prices,

TABLE 1
Relevant Operating Figures, 1960–1963

	1960*	1961	1962	1963
Gross revenue	100	101.6	98.2	106.6
Raw material costs	100	98.8	97.2	103.2
Noncontrollable operating costs	100	97.5	101.8	104.6
Controllable operating costs	100	95.0	94.1	86.2
Net profits before taxes	100	229.0	118.0	266.0
Number of employees	100	95.5	94.1	79.5
Total production units	100	98.5	98.2	102.2

*1960 used as a base year, since it was the first year that Sigma's records could be compared with post-merger years.

raw-material costs, and other uncontrollable factors. Possibly higher revenues or lower materials costs would explain profit increases. In addition, new automatic machinery and new plant equipment investments might be sufficient cause for the reduced labor force and increased profit picture. Finally, an over-all manpower reduction had occurred (involving over 600 employees), and this in itself might account for the increased profit picture in 1963, particularly if the increased overtime costs (at time-and-a-half) had been spread over the remaining work force. These possibilities make it difficult to draw simple cause-effect conclusions about Sigma's development program and operating performance.

Controllable Factors

At the same time, some of these noncontrollable factors can be identified and assessed for their contributions to profit. For example, noncontrollable factors can be separated from controllable factors. At Sigma, changes in certain of the noncontrollable factors—revenues, depreciation, taxes, and raw materials—accounted for about 56% of the increase in profits, despite the fact that noncontrollable costs as a whole had increased.

The remaining 44% of the profit increase was due to reductions in controllable costs—i.e., wages, maintenance materials, utilities, and fixed overhead—over which plant management had decision-making control. These reductions in controllable costs led to a profit contribution amounting to millions of dollars. Meanwhile, net investment had *not* increased appreciably (1.5% during 1963), and overtime had increased only slightly (5% over a small base) during the same time.

Consequently, it appears that a sizable part of the 1963 increase in Sigma's productivity and profit came from controllable factors. Furthermore, the explanation for this increase was *not* due to the addition of more efficient machinery or longer work hours. The next question, therefore, is: How much of this increase in profits was due to the manpower reduction, and how much to increased productivity on the part of remaining employees?

Company records show that 69% of the controllable cost savings came from the manpower reduction. The remaining 31%, amounting to several million dollars, came from improved operating procedures and higher productivity per man-hour. Figure 2 shows how these productivity and controllable cost measures for 1963 compared with previous years. (Productivity, in this case, is represented by dividing the number of employees for each year into the number of total production units.) The only really comparable year in terms of profit

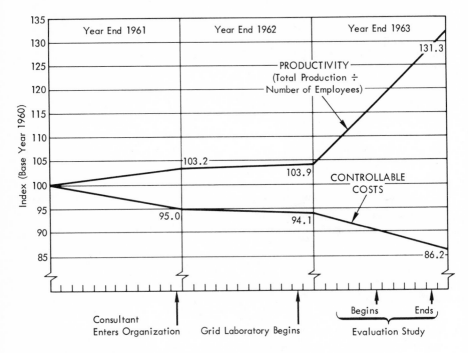

FIGURE 2. Productivity and Controllable Costs, 1960-1963

increase, according to Table 1, was 1961. However, the profit increase in 1961 was due more to factors outside of the Sigma management's control than in 1963. Figure 2 shows that the 1961 increase in productivity and decrease in controllable costs were very small compared with 1963. Most impressive, Fig. 2 shows that the productivity index per employee increased from a high in 1962 of 103.9 to a new high of 131.3 in 1963 without the aid of substantial investments in plant and equipment, as shown earlier.

Effects on Profits

The difficult problem now is to assess the role played by the organization development program in Sigma's improved productivity and profit picture. Concerning ourselves only with the controllable cost savings and productivity increases, how did the Sigma management account for these?

Manpower Savings. The largest saving was due to the manpower reduction. On this issue, consider the following comments from a talk given by the Sigma plant manager at a Piedmont conference:

> *"The group's decision-making process on the manpower question drew heavily on the approaches that had been developed in our development program. The approaches used stimulated a high degree of interplay of ideas and suggestions advanced by the various members of the group. It is believed that this permitted development of group answers that were better than the sum of the individual contributions. In the final analysis, it was evident that everyone involved was deeply committed to using methods and procedures that each had helped devise to accomplish or surpass goals that each had helped establish.*
>
> *"One of the key decisions made on a team basis involved the timing of the announcement. At the start of the discussions, most of the group favored the conventional approach, namely, that of deferring the announcement of the voluntary retirement program as long as possible and of delaying the announcement of the layoff until the completion of the voluntary program. However, a small minority took the reverse position and finally were able to convince the majority of the soundness of this position. We are convinced that this decision was a major factor contributing to the success of the manpower reduction. . . .*
>
> *"It was particularly gratifying that 520 of our employees accepted early retirement or termination voluntarily in comparison with an expected loss of only 196 employees by these measures. As a result, only 84 employees were laid off versus 260 that we had projected originally. The fact that the total reduction in forces was 160 employees greater than anticipated is particularly significant, since we foresee a continuing need to operate our plant with a fewer number of employees.*
>
> *"In addition to these numerical results, the program was successful in other important ways. Little bitterness or resentment toward the company has been evidenced by the relatively few employees involved in the forced layoff. Many employees expressed appreciation of the length of the advance notice and of the assistance given by the placement office. None of the unions took a stand against management's actions, nor did any union try to impede the implementation of the program. Community and press reactions were gratifying. There is some evidence of a trend that the community is moving in the direction of becoming more self-reliant and less dependent on Sigma.*
>
> *"The Sigma management feels very strongly that the quality of the decisions made in connection with setting manpower goals and the implementation of the reduction program was largely responsible for the success of the program. It feels equally as strongly that the quality of the decisions made was profoundly influenced by application of organization development principles."*

Comments by other Sigma managers indicate that they also give high credit to the program for the quality of the manpower reduction decision. At the same time, it appears that some such decision was inevitable under any circumstances. The plant manager had decided to reduce manpower before the organization development program began. However, he had not yet communicated this to headquarters (he did this during the joint headquarters-Sigma meeting suggested by Blake), nor had any official implementation plan been worked out. But here is one of those difficult points where observers will argue whether or not the quality and the implementation of this difficult decision were as important as the decision itself was. The Sigma management apparently believes that they were.

Work-Group Performance. Another measure of improved performance and profit consciousness is shown in Table 2. A voluntary response, anonymous questionnaire was sent to those men who had participated in Phase #1 of the Managerial Grid program. Each man was asked to compare several performance indexes of one year ago with those of the present time. The responses were marked on an eight-point scale and returned by 606 of these men. Table 2 shows perceived improvement on all of the performance-related items, including an increase of 30.5% in the profit-and-loss consciousness of the work group. The least improvement is reported in "Boss's work effort," which was the only one of the six items *not* explicitly addressed in the Phase #1 training. Apparently the Sigma respondents saw greater performance-productivity improvement in areas which had been stressed in Phase #1 than in areas not stressed.

TABLE 2

Perceived Changes in Group Performance, 1962–1963

	Per cent of managers rating dimensions of performance "high"*		
	In 1962	*In 1963*	*Increase or decrease*
"Boss's work effort"	67.1%	78.5%	+ 11.4%
"Leveling with other group members"	45.9	67.7	21.8
"Group's work effort"	50.2	74.2	24.0
"Problem liveliness in group discussions"	27.2	53.0	25.8
"Quality of decisions made in group"	38.8	64.6	25.8
"Profit-and-loss consciousness in group"	41.2	71.7	30.5
Average	45.1%	68.3%	+ 23.2%

*Refers to the per cent of 606 questionnaire respondents rating their managers either "7" or "8" on an eight-point scale.

Follow-up Projects. A final indicator of the program's contribution to the productivity-controllable cost picture is reflected in some part of the follow-up projects which were part of Phases #4 and #5 of the Managerial Grid program. These activities were intended to solve specific organizational problems using 9,9 concepts and methods, and in this sense they also represent changes in actual behavior (to be examined more closely in the next section). They include some projects which are directly related to productivity and cost improvement, as well as other projects less directly related. For example:

> During the period of contract negotiations with the union, a management team used problem-solving approaches learned in the Grid Seminar to keep all levels of management informed as to management's position.

An organization development coordinator was appointed to keep track of different follow-up projects.

A management team was established to work out a program for reducing utility costs. This team used Managerial Grid concepts to create awareness of the problem and to introduce the program to other managers.

Another. management team began work on reducing the costs of maintenance materials and supplies, again using Managerial Grid principles.

A new series of Grid programs was extended beyond lower level supervisors in the plant. These men included sliding supervisors who moved back and forth between worker and supervisor positions. In addition, an effort was made to extend Grid concepts to the labor force. Consequently, union officers were invited (and many accepted the invitation) to participate in these sessions.

A series of half-day sessions was held for second-level supervisors to discuss and determine guidelines which would help improve supervisor-subordinate relationships. These sessions were based on the Grid Seminar format, with both supervisors and subordinates participating in the discussions.

A safety-program, based on Grid methods, was designed to increase awareness of safety problems and to get new ideas for improvements. This program was to include all plant employees.

The plant manager initiated a plan whereby supervisors would encourage subordinates to set personal goals for the coming year. This was intended to replace previous performance appraisal methods wherein the supervisor set the goals and told the subordinate how he was measuring up to them.

An example of how one of these follow-up efforts, the utilities improvement program, was affecting profit consciousness is shown below in a conversation among two members of the program committee and the field researcher:

Researcher: How is the utilities improvement project coming along?

Manager A: Real well. This morning we attended a meeting of the project committee that has been created. They have a long way to go, but they're enthusiastic.

Manager B: They've set up a committee with a full-time project head, John J. They've put some real important people on the committee—all at the department head level.

Researcher: Management took Jim P. away from his line job on a full-time basis?

Manager A: Yes, he's off for at least a year. This shows the importance management is giving to utilities conservation.

Researcher: Have there been any noticeable P & L effects yet?

Manager A: Yes, just this morning I got the fuel bill for last month, and it dropped to such an extent that, if it keeps up, we could save over a million dollars for the year.

Manager B: And the best we can figure is that this was due to motivational reasons, as little else could account for the drop.

B. Practices & Behavior

Because the research was begun after the beginning of Sigma's organization development program, we have only a few accurate indexes of changes in practices and behavior. However, the ones available are important indicators of the changes taking place in the plant. They include:

Increased frequency of meetings.

Changing criteria for management appraisals.

Increased transfers within the plant and to other parts of the organization.

More Meetings

Table 3 shows the increase in meeting schedules from a representative sample of 30 Sigma managers. The calendars of these men showed a 31% increase in formal meetings scheduled during a summer week in 1963 as compared with a year before. Questionnaire data also showed managers reporting an average of 12.4% more time in "team problem-solving" meetings.

TABLE 3
Meeting Attendance by Managers

Number and Category		Average Number of Formally Scheduled Meetings Attended per Mgr/per Week		
		1962	*1963*	*Per cent Change*
21	Administrative Managers	5.5	7.5	+36%
9	Technical Managers	2.7	3.2	+19%
	Average	4.6	6.1	+31%

The fact that the character as well as the frequency of these meetings was changing is shown by the following statement made by a Piedmont headquarters representative, formerly quite negative toward Sigma's management:

> *"I think the recent change in the way that Sigma is being managed is the most drastic thing. You just go to a meeting now and you see it. I sat in on a recent meeting. People talk as though they are making decisions, and they are. This didn't happen before. A meeting would usually con-*

clude with the plant manager's reaction. You knew damn well that he made the final decision. There wasn't a meeting he wasn't in. You could never get hold of him. Now he is the most available guy in the place."

Table 3 also shows a discrepancy between the findings for administrative managers and those for technical managers. (Administrative managers are line and staff people whose work is concerned mainly with daily operating matters; technical managers are staff people dealing primarily with long-range technical problems. It should be pointed out, however, that almost all administrative managers at Sigma had technical backgrounds.) Administrative managers showed more frequent meetings and a greater increase over the year than technical managers did. Similar tendencies persist throughout these findings. Administrative managers consistently report behavior that is "in line" with Sigma's change trends and more positively oriented toward the organization development program.

Promotion Criteria

One reason for this difference appears in Table 4, which shows a second indicator of actual behavior change. This suggests that promotion criteria are changing at Sigma, as shown by the profile of the 50 most highly evaluated managers. Youth and a line position (largely held by administrative managers) now seem to be better predictors of success than higher age, company seniority, and position in the staff organization (largely populated by technical personnel).

These figures suggest shifting qualifications for promotion in a changing organization. They also suggest a shift in the power structure of the plant, with administrative-line managers becoming more highly rewarded than technical-staff

TABLE 4
Attributes of 50 Most Highly Rated Managers

Attribute	1962	1963
Average age (years)	42.2	39.4
Average length of service (years)	18.4	15.6
Per cent in line jobs	42%	64%
Per cent in staff jobs	58%	36%
Per cent in high-level jobs	64%	50%
Per cent in middle-level jobs	34%	36%
Per cent in low-level jobs	2%	14%

managers. We therefore begin to understand one possible reason for the greater acceptance of organization development by the administrative managers. For them, the reward potential was relatively high.

Manager Mobility

Table 5 shows the third indicator of actual change. Manager transfers, while not increasing sharply in total numbers, rose 52% over 1962 transfers within and outside of the plant. The number of transfers in 1962 tended to be typical of previous years. The increase in internal movement suggests greater flexibility within the plant, and the increase in transfers to outside units suggests stronger ties with headquarters and the other operating plants. Company records also show that managers typically spent (and wanted to spend) their careers within the plant. More recently, however, managers have been promoted out of Sigma.

TABLE 5
Change in Mobility of Management Personnel

Transfers	1962	1963	Per cent Change
Within plant	21	39	+86%
Out of plant	33	43	+31%
Total movement	54	82	+52%

In support of the conclusion that the plant has developed stronger outside ties, we find that in 1962 only 18% of the men transferred out were rated among the top 50 managers at Sigma. In 1963, 38% of those transferred out were rated among the top 50.

Effects on Behavior

In the previous section on productivity and profits, we saw evidence that follow-up project savings were credited largely to the organization development program. The same was true of the new emphasis on teamwork and problem solving. Again and again, specific behavioral changes were ascribed to effects of the program by Sigma personnel. For example, one higher level manager noted:

> "We had a pretty good example of group action here last Friday evening. We had a personnel problem; and if that problem had come up a couple of years ago, they would have used a 9,1 on it—told the complainer to go back to work—and that would have been the end of it. I was involved myself and still am. My two supervisors brought me and the other man together and used the Grid ideas. They gave us an opportunity to talk. Anybody could say what he wanted to. We got a little personal, but it works. It works because each of us got some things off his chest. I made a

mistake a long time ago in not reporting the trouble I was having. When they cut the other man in, he was able to tell us what he thought was wrong."

A lower level supervisor described the effects of Phase #1 in this fashion:

"The way I see it, we had an old philosophy that we had to get away from . . . this being a country club atmosphere, of doing nothing and just having a good time. Well, there are two ways you can change: One is that you can do it by attrition, but this takes too long. The other is that you can do it like the Chinese do it—by brainwashing. Now this may sound critical and I don't mean it this way, but this is how the Grid training program was done. You were under conditions of pressure and you kept getting those theories repeated to you over and over, and it has worked.

"I don't think it's so much that individuals have changed, but the philosophy has definitely changed. Why, there is one department where it used to be dog eat dog with them. But since March we have been able to work together much better. And I attribute this change to the program because the change is so uniform in that department. It couldn't have been done by one man in the department because then the difference would be more inconsistent."

Finally, a first-level supervisor and former union member commented:

"It's just here in the last year or so that company officials have branched out and let lower level people have a say in things. I guess I'd say, and all us working foremen do things differently, that I make 90% more decisions now compared to ten years ago. Routinely, we have a lot more responsibility now. It used to be that decisions came down from the top—it was all cut and dried—and you did it. In the last year particularly, the supervisors are giving us a lot more authority and getting better cooperation. They give a man a chance to do a job. It seems like they keep bringing things out and getting us to do more."

With regard to the increase in meetings, managers tended to have mixed feelings. Their time was precious, and some of their new problem-solving meetings failed to provide the answers. Furthermore, they, like so many managers today, felt sensitive to "committeeitis" and "group think" criticism. At the same time, there was wide support for the "team" and "problem solving" approaches stressed in the Managerial Grid Seminar, because they provided opportunities to confront problems that had been avoided or unrecognized earlier.

C. Attitudes & Values

The anonymous survey questionnaires asked each manager to report on his views of organizational relationships during the fall of 1963 as compared with a year earlier. Table 6 shows that improvements had occurred in boss-subordinate relationships, within departments, and between work groups.

TABLE 6
Changes in Working Relationships, 1962-1963

Per cent of Manager Respondents Reporting Improvement in:

	The Way They Work Together With Their Boss	The Way Their Work Groups Work Together	The Way Their Work Group Works With Other Groups
A. Over-all improvement (N=598)	49%	55%	61%
B. Departmental improvement			
Most improvement			
Administrative Services (N=67)	59%	68%	65%
Plastics (N=106)	55%	60%	68%
Least Improvement			
Research and development (N=43)	36%	41%	59%
Engineering (N=90)	37%	35%	55%

Note: Based on a questionnaire that asked each respondnet to compare in three separate questions: (a) the way he works together with his boss, (b) the way his work group works together, and (c) the way his work group works with other groups.

Perceived improvement was highest in intergroup and interdepartmental relationships, although impressively high in the other areas too. Improvement was again seen as higher in administrative-line than in technical-staff areas, as shown in Table 6-B.

Changing Ground Rules

These perceived improvements, theoretically, came from more basic changes in values and attitudes among managers and the technical people.

In order to test this, we devised a game whereby each member of a top-management committee (N=19) chose from a deck of 132 cards those statements which best described managerial ground rules and values as they were "five years ago," "today," and "preferred for future" in the Sigma plant. The 19 managers' choices indicated a 26% shift from "either-or" and "compromise" card statements to statements representing an integrative synthesis (as shown in Fig. 3). They hoped to see an even greater shift (17%) toward integrative values and ground rules in the future.

To the extent that "either-or" values still existed (as shown in the smaller circles), they had reversed direction from where they were five years ago. Current polarized values tended to emphasize stronger management. Five-year-ago values tended to emphasize weaker management direction. This weakness was apparently due to headquarters management's strong hand and the

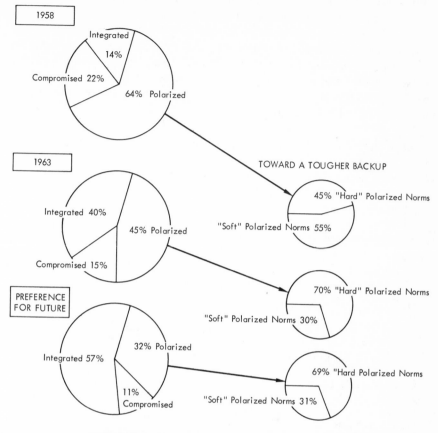

FIGURE 3. Perceived Changes in Management Values

lack of incentive provided by the cost-plus contract. After the 1960 merger, a "tougher" line was followed by the plant manager, although this was not enthusiastically received by suspicious lower level managers, as we saw earlier. By 1963, however, there had emerged an integrative value system that was backed up by "tougher" task-oriented values.

This figure suggests that the changes in management ground rules were both rapid and extreme. "Soft" practices were condemned in the 1963 value system by Sigma's top management. Integrative values were preferred; but where these were not currently practiced, management saw "hard" values as being preferable to the "soft" ones of five years ago.

Effects on Attitudes

How were these perceived changes influenced by the organization development program? The evidence from the survey builds up some impressive links.

To begin with, the changes were directly in line with the 9,9 concepts introduced in Phase #1 of the Sigma program. "Integrative" values were disguised but consistent examples of 9,9 ground rules and norms. The "polarized" examples were analogous to 9,1 and 1,9 procedures and beliefs. The "compromise" statements, of course, were akin to 5,5 practices and values. The Phase #1 Grid sessions had tended to reward 9,9 and 9,1 behavior over and above the other styles of management. These same two patterns seem to have been most widely practiced in 1963, according to the management group that sorted the 132 cards in the game described earlier.

Boss Behavior. Still further evidence of change directly in line with Phase #1 concepts is shown in Tables 7 and 8.

Table 7 is tabulated from the reports of 606 participants on 17 specific changes in their boss's and work group's behavior in 1962 as compared with more recent behavior in 1963. The questionnaire used for this purpose included

TABLE 7

Perceived Changes in Boss Behavior, 1962–1963

	Per cent of sub-ordinates rating manager "high"*		
	In 1962	In 1963	Increase or decrease
Dimensions stressed *in positive direction* in Grid Seminar			
"Keeps me informed"	45.3%	62.6%	+ 17.3%
"Aware of others"	42.9	55.3	12.4
"Plans ahead with me"	45.5	57.6	12.1
"Encourages suggestions"	53.1	64.7	11.6
"Sets goals with me"	48.1	59.5	11.4
"Helps me to learn"	44.7	56.1	11.4
"Gets me to have high goals"	54.4	65.8	11.4
"Follows up with me on action"	53.8	64.5	10.7
"Listens carefully to me"	60.6	71.3	10.7
"Aware of himself"	63.9	72.8	8.9
Average	51.2%	63.0%	+ 11.8%
Dimensions not stressed *either positively or negatively in Grid Seminar*			
"States his views clearly"	58.2%	69.3%	+ 11.1%
"Rewards me for good job"	48.5	56.6	8.1
"Stands behind me"	65.9	72.8	6.9
"Has management's backing"	62.3	68.4	6.1
"Controls his emotions"	76.0	82.0	6.0
"Acts self-confident"	72.8	78.7	5.9
"Acts at ease"	78.6	83.4	4.8
Average	66.0%	73.0%	+ 7.0%

*Refers to the per cent of 606 questionnaire respondents rating their managers either "7" or "8" on an eight-point scale.

some items which were consistent with and important to Phase #1 training and others which were "equally good" but not emphasized in the Grid sessions. Table 7 shows that 10 out of the 11 items depicting greatest boss improvement reflected ideas taken up explicitly in the Phase #1 training. Only one high-scoring item ("States his views clearly") had not been emphasized at that time. As for the other six items not stressed in the training, all show only moderate increases. Bosses had improved somewhat on these items, according to sub-ordinates, but not as much as on the items addressed during the Phase #1 training.

Table 8 also suggests a cause-effect relationship between the Sigma program and changes in work-group behavior over the year. This time, negative rejection

TABLE 8
Perceived Changes in Work-Group Norms, 1962–1963

	Per cent of managers rating dimensions of group behavior "relatively negative"*		
	In 1962	*In 1963*	*Increase or decrease*
Dimensions stressed *negatively in Grid Seminar*			
"Group's attitude toward a member who gives more importance to maintaining friendly relations than to solving work problems."	40.1%	65.2%	– 25.1%
"Group's attitude toward a member who prefers to keep his own opinions to himself rather than to lay his cards on the table."	44.5	66.8	– 22.3
"Group's attitude toward a member who prefers to do a job by himself rather than with other members of the group."	29.0	50.3	– 21.3
"Group's attitude toward a member who often compromises when disagreement arises."	25.3	42.0	– 16.7
Average	34.7%	56.1%	– 21.4%
Dimensions not stressed *either positively or negatively in Grid Seminar*			
"Group's attitude toward a member who doesn't make up his mind until others have expressed their opinions."	40.4%	51.3%	– 10.9%
"Group's attitude toward a member who prefers to spend his career at the plant rather than go elsewhere in the organization."	10.3	16.2	– 5.9
"Group's attitude toward a member who maintains a close friendly relationship with his boss."	59.1	51.2	+ 7.9
"Group's attitude toward a member who greatly outproduces other members of the group."	35.9	23.9	+ 12.0
Average	36.4%	35.7%	+ 0.8%

*Refers to the per cent of 606 questionnaire respondents rating dimensions of group behavior toward the negative end of an eight-point scale.

of some items (rather than positive reaction) was examined. We asked which items describing work-group practices were least accepted by managers in 1963, compared with those least accepted in 1962. Some of the items included were highly at odds with Phase #1 9,9 concepts, though not identified as such. Others were simply less relevant to the Phase #1 training. Table 8 shows that the most strongly rejected practices in 1963 were those at odds with 9,9 beliefs. The "irrelevant" practices were less strongly rejected or were positively accepted.

Positive Responses. Favorable attitudes toward Phase #1 also appear in Table 9. Participants were asked to evaluate their experience in the Grid Seminar. The results were generally favorable. The most positive responses came from the members of two administrative departments. The least enthusiastic responses (and even these were generally positive) came from the members of two technical departments.

These differences might reflect the fact that administrative men were currently receiving a larger share of evaluation and promotion rewards than before. They might also reflect the classic value differences associated with business, on the one hand, and science, on the other. Some interview data suggested that members of technical departments valued individualism over the team strategies of the organization development program. Although many of Sigma's managers (including the plant manager) were engineers or scientists by training and early work, our evidence suggests that they adopted managerial values when they left the technical departments. At any rate, administrative department managers were somewhat more enthusiastic about Sigma's program than were men from the technical departments.

TABLE 9

Rating of Managerial Grid Seminar

	Per cent Rating Grid Laboratory as:			
	Very High	*Somewhat High*	*Somewhat Low*	*Very Low*
A. Total respondents (N=580)	37%	47%	10%	6%
B. Highest and lowest departments				
Highest rating				
Administrative services (N=67)	51%	39%	8%	2%
Plastics (N=106)	46%	35%	12%	7%
Lowest rating				
Engineering (N=90)	33%	51%	9%	7%
Research and development (N=43)	26%	51%	14%	9%

Note: Based on data from questionnaire asking respondents to evaluate the Grid Seminar for its job-related usefulness. An eight-point scale was provided. The results were later combined into four categories, 7 to 8 for "very high," 5 to 6 for "somewhat high," 3 to 4 for "somewhat low," and 1 to 2 for "very low."

Generally speaking, the changes reported in the behavior of bosses and work groups, as well as the changes in work practices (shown in Table 2), are right in line with the 9,9 values and ground rules designed into the Phase #1 training. Taken together with the enthusiasm for the Grid as a training experience, it is clear that most Sigma participants valued the on-the-job results of their organization development program.

Some Underlying Factors

The material discussed so far suggests that Sigma's program made an important contribution to: (a) productivity and profits, (b) changes in practices and behavior, and (c) at least some changes in attitudes and values among managers.

Although the underlying motivation may have existed long before this program, Sigma's program seemed to provide the specific vehicles for mobilizing and directing managerial energy. Perhaps other programs or methods would have worked just as well, though, as already stated, Sigma and other Piedmont plants had earnestly engaged in a number of them without comparable results in the past. In addition, the "hands-off" policy of the new headquarters group had not gained widespread improvement at Sigma any more than the more directive line taken by the previous headquarters group had. Furthermore, the plant manager's early managerial toughness had gained resistance as well as slow results.

Therefore, what were the causal factors in and around the organization development program that permitted it to make a contribution to Sigma's improved position? To examine these (and to gain even further understanding of the program's influence), we turn our attention next to a review of evidence and opinion that describes the underlying factors which seem crucial to Sigma's program and its contributions.

Headquarters Role

Earlier, we described the events which led Piedmont to exert pressures on the Sigma plant management for improved performance. In some respects, the pressures may have been overly subtle. Sigma's management did not fully appreciate just how important certain issues were to headquarters until these issues emerged in open discussion. This occurred for the first time during the three-day meeting suggested by Blake. As a result of this meeting, headquarters personnel became the source of help they sought to be, rather than the ambiguous threat they had been. At the same time, headquarters left implementation, including the organization development program, in the hands of the Sigma plant management.

The results of this new relationship seemed to satisfy headquarters management. The verdict late in 1963 was that Sigma had made considerable progress and that headquarters-plant relationships had improved. After the first year of

Sigma's program, Piedmont's management expressed strong pleasure and partial surprise at Sigma's improved position.

Consultants' Contribution

At this point the work and reputation of Blake and Mouton provided the specific departure point for an organization development effort. Their prior design of the Grid Seminar and their six-phase concept of organization development represented a significant contribution, even though they themselves spent little time at the plant.

Plant Manager's Support

An early and especially important factor was the support and subsequent involvement of the plant manager. His enthusiasm became a strong stimulus and model for the rest of the plant. He remained in the middle of the program rather than on the outside where he might have guided the effort with impersonal mechanisms. More important, he made some significant modifications in his own behavior.

These changes in the plant manager's behavior could not be called major personality changes. Instead, they seemed to reflect changes in his concept of working with others on management problems. Most of the changes were consistent with behavior he had long practiced within the organization. He had a reputation for being a creator and advocate of new projects. He had always disliked being second to others. He had a profound respect for science and extended some of this respect to the behavioral sciences. Finally, he had always explained and shown his ideas to others before implementing them. During the program, the plant manager found that although the ground rules of management relationships had changed, none of them violated his basic beliefs. One of his top subordinates made the following comments:

> "He has certainly taken a hard look at the way he runs his business and is trying to change. I think he is trying to involve more people and is more considerate of others. It is not so much a change, though, as it is a recognition that others misunderstood him. I think he found that others saw him as intolerant because of his enthusiasm. I've always seen him as a pretty strong '9,9,' but no one else seemed to recognize it. He has a real strong '9,1' backup theory though. I think his experience in the Managerial Grid session made him stop and think; being a real intelligent man, he's made a change. He has learned to listen and to be more patient. Also, we have learned to talk better and insist on having a say. It's a two-way street."

Top-Management Involvement

The Sigma top-management group became involved at an early date in discussions of the program. More important, they chose to become involved not only as students in the Phase #1 training but as rotating instructors for two-week periods. Our material shows this group to be among the key supporters of the program and instrumental in the follow-up projects.

Moreover, the teaching-learning role provided further evidence of the program's impact. Using questionnaire data, we derived "most improved" and "least improved" categories from weighted scores taken from subordinates' ratings of superiors' improvement. As many as 16 of the 22 "instructors" were among the 87 "most improved" bosses as evaluated by their own managerial subordinates. Only one "instructor" was included in the 35 "least improved" superiors.

This finding suggests that being an instructor in Phase #1 served to reinforce a man's understanding of 9,9 principles as well as to aid his on-the-job practice.

The 9,9 commitment of this group had apparently been strengthened by their early success in reducing manpower under delicate community and union conditions. When 9,9 problem-solving methods helped them to accomplish the difficult manpower reduction task, the top-management group became strong supporters of the organization development program.

Considering their involvement and support, what did this group look like in action? Were they now a collection of 9,9 supermen? Had each made significant changes in his behavior? These questions are important, and the answers are "no." Instead, the top-management group had agreed collectively (and continued to reinforce) a set of 9,9 ground rules among themselves. The balance was precarious, however. Two or three key individuals seemed to be most highly respected as 9,9 interpreters and proponents. Several others were "take-charge" and "task-oriented" members who still demonstrated respect for the 9,9 ground rules. Still others helped to formulate issues in nonthreatening ways. The tie that bound the group together was its shared commitment to 9,9 concepts and practices. As long as this tie held, the members seemed to feel that they could continue their pacesetting role within the organization.

Learning Readiness

The factors identified above did seem to influence men at or near the top of Sigma's organization. But these factors were not sufficient to explain the diverse attitudes found among the managers. There were less-evident forces which affected each manager in the plant. One of these was the attitude of some managers which made them more ready than others to learn in the Phase #1 training and thereafter. Tables 3, 6-B and 9-B have already shown that technical-staff men were generally less involved and enthusiastic than administrative-line managers. Figure 4 shows that the technical managers were seen as less improved by their subordinates also. In general, technical managers from R & D, engineering, and production planning received fewer "improvement" ratings from subordinates than other managers.

Figure 4 also shows how these on-the-job "improvement" ratings correspond with a boss's self-evaluation *before* Phase #1 training, and his team's evaluation

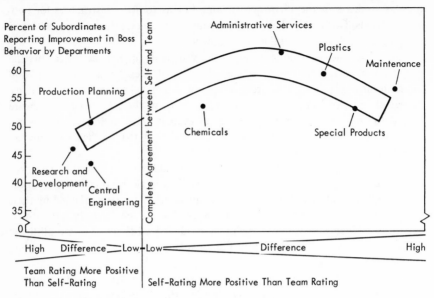

FIGURE 4.   Boss's Self-Evaluation versus Grid Team Rating

of him *during* Phase #1 training. (These two evaluations were done with the assistance of Grid teaching material made available to us.)

An analysis of this material shows that:

> Technical managers and staff tended to rate themselves as less 9,9 *before* Phase #1 than their colleagues did *during* Phase #1 training. In other words, technical men tended to be "overrewarded" by their colleagues.
>
> Administrative managers tended to rate themselves as more 9,9 *before* Phase #1 than their colleagues did *during* Phase #1 training. In other words, administrative men were "underrewarded" by their colleagues.

According to Fig. 4, it is the administrative managers, "underrewarded" by their teams, who showed more improvement than technical managers, who were "overrewarded." Why? One explanation is that administrative managers, rating themselves as 9,9 to begin with, were given an incentive to improve by the sobering comments of their Seminar teammates. Technical managers, who tended not to see themselves as 9,9 to begin with, were given little incentive to improve because their teams told them they were "better" than they thought they were. However, there is apparently such a thing as too much "underrewarding" (note the downturn of the curve to the right in Fig. 4). If the administrative manager's 9,9 self-rating was too much higher than the evaluation given him by his Seminar team, his subordinates would tend to find him less improved than those managers (at the peak of the curve) who were slightly "underrewarded" in the Seminar.

In other words, some Phase #1 participants seem to have been more ready and receptive to Managerial Grid learning than others (although even these were seen as improved by subordinates, according to Fig. 4). The higher-readiness learners described themselves as 9,9 managers before training and received team impetus toward further steps in that direction. The lower-readiness learners, with little team impetus toward improvement, tended to be technically (not managerially) oriented. In a later interview, one of these technical men talked as follows:

> "I see no point in having scientific personnel take this training course. We believe the results of reproducible experiments and can be informed and convinced without [personal] experience. The data from other experiments will do the job. . . . The program gives a much better understanding of people who can discuss Shakespeare endlessly, or who can enjoy baseball without paying attention to any other sport. One can get into the habit of enjoying a single activity to the exclusion of all else. Give the program enough time on the present tack, and we can become so interested in interpretation of management action that we can play happily at this for years and forget all about the realities of management."

Reinforced Efforts

The final factor underlying the plant changes at Sigma occurred after Phase #1 training. This involved the extent to which boss and colleagues reinforced a manager's efforts to change his behavior. To show the importance of this reinforcement, we can examine its presence among the "most improved" and the "least improved" managers (according to their subordinates' weighted ratings).

Table 10 shows that 77% of the 87 "most improved" managers had bosses who were also "most improved." This suggests that a man's superior is a major force in his learning and improvement, until we note that 55% of the 35 "least improved" managers *also* had bosses who were "most improved." Apparently the boss's improvement wasn't the most important reinforcing agent, although it does seem to have exerted some influence.

TABLE 10
Relationship Between Manager Improvement and
Superior-Colleague Support

(Evaluations by Subordinates)

	Superior also rated among "most improved"	*Setting where "most improved" colleagues outnumbered "least improved" colleagues*
Managers rated as "most improved" (N=87)	77%	92%
Managers rated as "least improved" (N=35)	55%	26%

Table 10 also shows that colleague reinforcement may have been a more important key than boss reinforcement. Of the "most improved" managers, 92% worked in settings where "most improved" colleagues outnumbered "least improved," while only 26% of the "least improved" managers worked in similar settings.

A closer analysis of these 26% "least improved" managers in "most improved" groups shows they were outnumbered by "most improved" colleagues by only a 2.55 to 1 ratio. In contrast, the 92% "most improved" managers worked in settings where "most" outnumbered "least" by a ratio of 3.41 to .33. This suggests that the chances for manager improvement in the eyes of subordinates were greatest when a manager worked with larger numbers of others who also sought improvement. Or put another way, possibly one "least improved" cynic was enough to dampen his fellows' enthusiams and therefore their chances of being among the "most improved." This possibility is supported by the fact that 60% of the "most improved" managers worked in settings where there were *no* "least improved" colleagues to disillusion the 9,9 atmosphere being built.

These data suggest that Phase #1, the plant manager, and a man's boss all played secondary roles when it came to making the lessons of Phase #1 "stick." The most important reinforcers were a manager's own colleagues who either encouraged and supported, or discouraged, his improvement efforts.

Conclusion

We can return now to the reasons for studying the Sigma program which were given at the start of Part II. To begin with, we wished to know whether the program had been successful in transferring behavioral science concepts into organizational action. Now, after reviewing the program and its consequences, even a conservative answer to this question would seem to be "yes." The program had become a part of day-to-day managerial activities at Sigma. Both in opinion and behavior, most managers endorsed the work patterns presented in the Phase #1 Grid Seminar.

A second reason for studying the Sigma program was the unusual teaching-learning role adopted by line management. The evidence shows that not only did senior line managers take the key "instructor" roles during Phase #1, but they later stood out as among the "most improved" managers in the eyes of their subordinates. It seems likely that the "instructor" roles helped to reinforce their attempted 9,9 behavior back on the job.

With regard to psychiatric difficulties, which was another concern in studying the Sigma program, there was, to the best of our knowledge, no evidence of any such issue among the 800 men who participated in the program. This suggests that the Phase #1 Grid training was relatively "safe" in this company setting because of its emphasis on managerial styles rather than on personal intro-spection.

The final reason given for studying the Sigma program involved the question of groups as units of learning versus individuals. As we have seen, learning (improvement in the eyes of subordinates) was greatest when supported strongly by colleague values and norms. Where this reinforcement was weak or not present, managers were far more likely to be evaluated as among the "least improved" by their own subordinates. Consequently, colleague groups apparently were crucial in helping individual learning become organization development.

The chances are fairly strong that this crucial factor has been missing in countless would-be organization development programs—including previous efforts within Sigma and Piedmont. In all of these cases, the supporting groundwork of shared values was most likely neglected or made too abstract to be implemented.

Management Implications

The lessons from this study also involve a number of implications for businessmen. Initially, it *does* appear that behavioral science and human relations education can assist with large-scale organization development under certain conditions. These conditions, as suggested by our data, include:

Demanding but tolerant headquarters.

An enthusiastic and involved top-manager and senior management group.

Educational strategy that effectively and continuously builds team problem solving and mutual support into work-related issues.

An organization whose work requires some interdependent effort and common values.

This study suggests that managerial and team effectiveness *can* be taught by managers with outside assistance. Furthermore, it appears that this type of educational strategy can help to make significant contributions to organizational effectiveness. This in itself seems to be an important lesson for management to recognize and use in its future efforts to build stronger organizations.

The Design of Jobs

In this essay Louis E. Davis argues that many of the management practices which are now in vogue—worker communications programs, participation techniques directed at providing workers with "feelings of importance," and human relations programs dealing with personal relationships and super-vision—are impotent for the purpose of improving organization performance. He believes that in reality they are nothing more than devices for concealing the gravity of essentially inappropriate organization and job structures. Real organizational improvement transpires when a systems approach he calls "job design" is used to take into account both the social and personal requirements of the job holder and the technological and organizational requirements of the system.

A large part of the paper is devoted to detailing a series of six change programs which demonstrate the power of job redesign as a means to positively improve organizational performance as well as the attitudes, perceptions, and satisfactions of the employees affected.

THE DESIGN OF JOBS

Louis E. Davis
University of California, Los Angeles

Job design means specification of the contents, methods, and relationships of jobs in order to satisfy technological and organizational requirements as well as the social and personal requirements of the jobholder.

For the purposes of discussion only, specification of job contents can be divided into two categories: (1) physical-environment and physiological requirements, and (2) organization, social, and personal requirements. An extensive body of knowledge exists on the first category and is assiduously applied in designing plant environment, work methods, equipment, and tools, and in fitting the physical work demand to the capabilities of workers. No conflict exists over the application of this physiological and ergonomic knowledge for it does not require any models of human behavior in complex organizations. Man's responses to the physical environments and work tasks are studied at the microscopic level with man taken as a machine element, albeit a human one, in the system. The objectives are either adjustment of man, as by training, or adjustment of environment or technology, as by design of tools, equipment, and dials and machine controls for rapid and error-free operation or to suit particular human capabilities, such as those of older workers.

On the side of organizational, social, and personal requirements, what is the

Professor of Business Administration, Graduate School of Business Administration, University of California, Los Angeles.

Reprinted from Louis E. Davis, "The Design of Jobs," *Industrial Relations,* VI, No. 1 (October 1966), 21-45, by permission of *Industrial Relations* and the author.

state of job design today? There is a large discrepancy between available knowledge and practice, although—paradoxically, perhaps—there is much evidence that management faithfully keeps abreast of developments in job and organization design research. The thinking of many a management today appears to be not unlike that of an old farmer who went to a lecture delivered by a county agent to a group of small farmers in a remote rural area about a new development in farming that would increase crop yield. When asked by the county agent whether he would use the new development, the old-timer said, "I won't—I already know how to farm better than I am doing."

Managements are well aware that there now exists a considerable body of evidence which challenges accepted organizational and job design practices. Experimental and empirical findings, for instance, indicate that imposed pacing of work is detrimental to output and to quality, yet paced work is common and is considered to be desirable.[1] There is extensive evidence concerning the positive effects of group reward systems in achieving an organization's primary objectives. There is also considerable evidence of the effects of variety of job content and of task assignments that permit social relationships and communication patterns to develop, all of which enhance performance and personal satisfaction on the job.[2] Yet in a very few instances do we find application of such findings to job designs.

The incentive to apply job design knowledge must be presumed to be strong, for the very simple reason that there are gains to be made all round—for the organization in productivity, quality, and costs of performance, and for workers in personal satisfactions. On the other hand, inhibitions against application are formidable. The status quo bristles with institutional barriers in the form of established personnel policies, job evaluation plans, union relationships and contracts, supervisory practices at all levels, and, not least, managerial practices. All of these barriers are perpetually present, prompting the manager to choose the path of least resistance and to do as little as the situation compels, that is, to satisfy the obvious needs of technology. At a deeper level, the status quo is reinforced by more basic and pervasive inhibitions which again and again lead the manager to fall back on time-honored, but inappropriate and unrealistic models which are based on unsupported dogma or on popular cliches regarding human behavior in productive organizations.

The practical consequences are inconsistent and incompatible job designs, as well as ad hoc use of piecemeal research results. With minor modifications, there is still a strong commitment to the proposition that meeting the requirements of

[1] R. Conrad, "Comparison of Paced and Unpaced Performance at a Packing Task," *Occupational Psychology*, XXIX (1955), 15-28; and L. E. Davis, "Pacing Effects on Manned Assembly Lines," *International Journal of Production Research*, IV (1966), 171.

[2] L. E. Davis and R. Werling, "Job Design Factors," *Occupational Psychology*, XXXIV (1960), 109; L. E. Davis, "Toward a Theory of Job Design," *Journal of Industrial Engineering*, VIII (1957), 305; L. E. Davis, R. R. Canter, and J. F. Hoffman, "Current Job Design Criteria," *Journal of Industrial Engineering*, VI (1955), 5; and F. L. W. Richardson and C. R. Walker, *Human Relations in an Expanding Company* (New Haven: Labor and Management Center, Yale University, 1948).

the technology (process, equipment) will yield superior job performance, measured by organizationally relevant criteria, and a deep-seated conviction that the same performance will *not* be achieved if technological requirements are not given exclusive consideration. Requirements such as communication, group formation, personality development, decision-making, and control are seen as marginal at best, and at worst as opposed to the satisfaction of technological requirements. This fictitious conflict reveals the poverty of present conceptualization of human behavior in productive organizations and helps to maintain the dominance of technological requirements as exclusive determinants of job contents and relationships.

Models of Human Behavior

Models and concepts of individual-organization relationships and of human behavior in productive organizations have a history almost as long as that of Western civilization. However, only two have been historically influential in their contribution to purposeful job design. Both were handed down to us by late eighteenth century economists—the ubiquitous model of man as an economic animal and the concept of the division of labor. The former has provided the rationale for our present reward systems, as well as for our concentration on monetary rewards as the only ones suitable for consideration. The division-of-labor concept provided the basis for specialization and, as a result, for our existing job and organization structures. Based on these approaches, organizations were able to make immediate use of an untutored and unskilled work force. To the extent that lack of education and skill are still the main characteristics of a work force, the concept has utility, even if there are secondary costs in the form of reduced contribution on the part of individuals and the need for a coordination apparatus.

During the late nineteenth century, a series of models were developed; all of them derived from the mechanistic model of human behavior in which man's role was conceived to be that of an element or cog in a complex production system dominated by costly equipment. In mechanical systems, elements must be completely designed if they are to function. When transposed to human effort, this requirement states that initiative and self-organization are not acceptable, for they may increase system variability and the risk of failure. (Incidentally, the question raised today of whether workers are responsible or irresponsible appears not to have entered into consideration.) The result was rigidly specified task assignments and complete job descriptions indicating the specific behaviors desired and their organizational and temporal bounds. The drive to achieve reduced sources of variability encouraged the development of the concept of minimum skill requirements for task performance. Given highly specialized or fractionated jobs consisting of few minimally skilled tasks, skills could be rapidly acquired with short training. That man might engage in behavior other than that specifically required by the system was never part of the conceptual framework of the mechanistic model. To insure successful outcomes, reward systems were designed that provided reinforcement only for the precisely specified behaviors desired. To be sure, many of these principles were applied without conscious design and in the euphoric atmosphere of applying science to complex organizations.

The more recent models of individual-organization relationships which have undergirded the evolution of job design can be classified into four groups. The oldest of these is the minimum interaction model, under which there is a minimal connection between the individual and the organization in terms of skill, training, involvement, and complexity of his contribution, in return for maximum flexibility and independence on the part of the organization in using its manpower. In other words, the organization strives for maximum interchangeability of personnel (with minimum training) to reduce its dependence on availability, ability, or motivation of individuals. This model has been the basis for the development of twentieth century industrial relations practices and for modern personnel management. In application, it frequently takes the form of the work-flow or process-flow model of job design. In this model the material or information processes are in themselves the job content, or determine it.

Evolving from and tied to the minimum interaction model is the welfare model, which gives nodding recognition to the inadequacy of the "economic man" theory. Without disturbing job and organization structures, it attempts to build extra-role and extra-job associations and, hopefully, loyalties to the organization. It places great faith in the prospect that meaningful social relationships can be built with fellow workers and supervisors outside the immediate production framework, which continues to operate on the basis of the restricted role of the individual and of minimum organizational interaction. In applying the model, organizations bubble with programs that provide fun and games for workers after hours, company newspapers that jolly workers along to make them feel part of the organization, extra-job rewards, profit shares, etc.

The third group of models grew out of the shock of the Hawthorne studies and is characterized by emphasis on leadership and personal relations. Growth of awareness that there are informal leaders and groups, and that groups have social standards and norms, led to the development of the human relations movement. If informal leaders and groups exist, no matter what the formal organization description indicates, then management had better get busy, either to capture these or provide leadership patterns and personal relations that go some way toward reconciling the informal and formal structures. Having been built on these objectives, the human relations movement is now seriously hampered by restricting itself to them. Its narrow approach, which completely overlooks job content and the interaction between social, organizational, and technological requirements, was bound to produce the limited success it has achieved thus far.

The last and most recent group of models grew directly out of the impact of social and behavioral science research. Results of various studies provide information on self-selected aspects of the whole man at work in an organization. In most instances, the studies are piecemeal approaches which nibble at the edges of the central problems of job design, the role of the individual in a productive organization, and his control over the functions performed. Most of these approaches unfortunately assume that job content is not a significant variable or is so fixed by the needs of technology that it is not worth examining, since it cannot be altered in any event. Only ignorance of technology can lead to such a conclusion. Within this group are such approaches as sensitivity development; group-member participation, and status and personality development; communication; and even job enlargement, whatever that may be. The unfortunate consequence is a series of competing fads, one continually replacing the other as offering the true answer.

Recent Job Design Studies

Job design research is relatively new, having originated only in the last decade. More recently, a few industrial firms have begun to manipulate some job contents and configurations. The first such experiment that was reported took place in the late forties in a large U.S. electronics firm which undertook a series of job changes in the form of job enlargement.[3] The changes were instituted as part of management industrial relations policy.

What characterizes the difference between job design research and personnel, industrial psychological, and sociological studies? Job design studies take technology as an operant variable and, as a consequence, are concerned with the interaction between personal, social, and organization needs and technology as manifested in jobs. The other studies take technology as given and therefore do not consider it as a variable to be examined. Job design studies can be classified into two groups, both based on field experiments: those carried out in the United States under the name of job design and those carried out in England, where they are known as socio-technical systems studies. The former studies have sought to manipulate the configuration of technology, as interpreted in task designs and assignments making up jobs, and to determine what variations are possible and what the effects of these are on personal, social, and organization variables. The latter studies have approached jobs and organization configurations from the direction of social psychology, modifying technological configurations of tasks to permit the development of social structure in support of functions and objectives of work groups. Both types of studies are concerned with jobs and organizations as socio-technical systems.

In presenting a brief review of results available, numerous informal reports known to the author, based on experiences of firms with various job configurations, will not be used. Published reports only will be examined. This may make the number of formal and informal job design studies appear to be smaller than it is in fact. Reports have appeared about operator jobs consisting of repetitive manual tasks and maintenance jobs organized around traditional crafts. Four studies of operator jobs taken from different technologies are presented: two studies of assembly-line jobs from the pharmaceutical and home appliance industries, a study of machine-tender jobs in the textile industry, and a study of pit-face jobs in coal mining. One study of maintenance craft jobs in the chemical

---

[3]Richardson and Walker, *op. cit.*

industry will be discussed. The first experimental field study of supervisory job design was recently reported, and the results are presented here to permit comparison with worker-level jobs. The studies presented are intended to indicate the multidimensionality of the job design problem and the pervasiveness of its influence on quantity and quality of output, costs, and job satisfactions.

Operator, Assembly Line:
Pharmaceutical Appliance Manufacture[4]

This study was the first controlled experiment on the shop floor to manipulate the configuration of technology as interpreted in task design and assignment as jobs. It followed a national survey of the methods used and decisions reached in designing jobs by specifying their contents and structure.[5] The study revealed that neither clearly developed theories of job specification nor design principles were available and that job design decisions were based on the very narrow criterion of minimizing immediate costs of an operation as interpreted through minimum unit operation time. It was also found that the job design process took place after the basic production process had been planned and separate operations in the production sequence were being developed. No methods for evaluating the effectiveness of job designs were found to exist.

Designers of jobs satisfied the criterion of minimum cost (or immediate cost) of operations by application of the following precepts or guides:

1. Specification of the content of individual tasks comprising a job to—
   a. achieve specialization of skills
   b. minimize skill requirements
   c. minimize learning time or worker training time
   d. equalize and permit the assignment of a full workload
   e. provide for worker satisfaction (no specific criteria for job satisfaction were in use)
   f. conform to the requirements of equipment or facilities layout and, where they exist, of union restrictions on work assignment
2. Combining individual tasks into specific jobs to achieve—
   a. maximum specialization by limiting both the number of tasks in a job and variations in tasks
   b. maximum repetitiveness
   c. minimum training time

The specific purpose of the assembly-line worker study was to explore the conditions under which improvement in productivity could be expected from

[4]L. E. Davis and R. R. Canter, "Job Design Research," *Journal of Industrial Engineering,* VII (1956), 275.

[5]Davis, Canter, and Hoffman, *op. cit.*

changes in job content. The major criteria used to evaluate the effectiveness of the modifications were quantity and quality of output. Worker attitudes and satisfaction were also measured.

A manufacturing department producing a line of similar small plastic appliances in a unionized West Coast firm was the setting of the study. Over the years the department's activities and organization had been subjected to careful and detailed study, reflecting the latest in manufacturing engineering practices. The product had been made on an assembly line, where the operations, at which 29 of the department's 35 women worked, were carefully specified and minutely divided. The workers' average experience on these jobs was four and a half years. The rest of the people were engaged in material preparation and removal, inspection, and supply. A similar department in the company was used as a control group to permit monitoring of the presence of plantwide changes which might affect employee attitudes, practices, and performance. The investigation centered around the jobs on the assembly line, and modifications were introduced through the department manager.

In the pre-existing Line Job Design each worker performed one of the nine operations, spaced at stations along the conveyor line required to assemble the appliance. Defective parts were rejected when necessary as part of each operation. Job rotation from hard to easy stations and vice versa took place every two hours. The operations were similar in skill requirements and technological content. Pacing eliminated responsibility for productivity, and job rotation, with the grouping of work stations for identical operations, practically eliminated individual responsibility for quality of work performed.

Two experimental job designs were compared with the pre-existing design:

1. Group Job Design: Here the conveyor (and pacing) was eliminated and workers rotated among nine individual stations using a batch method of assembly. Other conditions were the same as for the pre-existing design.
2. Individual Job Design: All nine operations, final inspection, and securing of materials were combined into one job and performed by workers at individual work stations.

The results supported the hypothesis that greater variety of tasks and responsibility for methods, quality, pacing, and product completion leads to higher productivity, quality, and satisfaction. The average hourly output over a period of consecutive days on the original or Line Job Design was taken as a productivity index of 100, and the quality over the period was taken as reported in per cent of defects per lot. Under the Group Job Design (no pacing by conveyor) the productivity index fell to an average of 89, while quality improved, with defects falling from an average of 0.72 per cent to 0.49 per cent per lot. After only six days on the Individual Job Design, the average productivity index rose slightly above the original Line average. Quality improved fourfold with defects per lot falling to 0.18 per cent.

In summary, the Individual Job Design—

1. Provided a slight improvement in output.
2. Brought about a large improvement in quality, although quality levels were very high originally.
3. Increased the flexibility of the production process.
4. Permitted identification of individuals having deficiences in productivity and quality.
5. Reduced external service and control functions in the department, e.g., material delivery, inspection.
6. Developed a more favorable attitude toward individual responsibility, individual work rate, effort expenditure, distribution of work load, and making whole units. After experience with the Individual Job Design, workers disliked the lack of personal responsibility characteristic of the Line Job Design.

Operator, Assembly Line:
Home Appliance Manufacture[6]

Enlargement of assembly-line jobs was undertaken recently by a midwestern home laundry manufacturing firm which sought to improve workers' attitudes toward work and to increase output and quality. The company felt it might have gone beyond the "optimum" division of labor on its assembly lines, so that increased costs of nonproductive work and line-balance delay might have exceeded the savings of fractionation. To the company job enlargement meant providing jobs that involved an increased number and variety of tasks, self-determination of pacing, increased responsibility for quality, increased discretion for work methods, and completion of a part- or sub-assembly. For a number of years the company had been pursuing a deliberate program of transferring work from progressive assembly lines to single-operator work stations; this transfer permitted study of the effects of enlarged jobs on workers' performance and attitudes.

Over a five-year period, 14 bench assembly jobs had been established. Thirteen of these were from elements previously performed on assembly lines. One of the jobs was pump assembly, in which six operators each doing six work elements on an assembly line had required 1.77 minutes to complete a unit. This was transformed into one job having 35 elements requiring 1.49 minutes per assembly, including inspection. Costs for pump assembly were reduced $2,000 annually. The other 13 jobs were similarly enlarged, with their average allowed time changed from 0.78 to 3.15 minutes and average number of work elements from 9 to 33. They showed an average decrease in rejects from 2.9 to 1.4 per cent and a slight average decrease in output efficiency from 138 to 126 per cent.

[6]E. H. Conant and M. D. Kilbridge, "An Interdisciplinary Analysis of Job Enlargement: Technology, Costs and Behavioral Implications," *Industrial and Labor Relations Review*, XVIII (October, 1965), 377.

Social interaction opportunities and actual work interaction showed sharp reductions in bench work. This may have resulted largely from the creation of independent jobs. The indications were that conditions were not very favorable for developing stable informal groups among the workers on enlarged jobs.

The attitudes and preferences of workers having experience on both line and bench work were examined by questionnaire. Enlarged bench jobs were preferred 2 to 1 over assembly-line jobs. There were no preferences associated with personal characteristics. All of the attributes of the enlarged jobs were liked; except for social interaction and short learning time, all of the attributes of the line jobs were disliked. Preference for self-pacing was the reason given in half of the cases for liking bench jobs. Where line work was preferred, no single reason was given; rather it was less disliked than bench work.

This study demonstrates that there may be an "optimum" division of labor on assembly lines. The authors make a case for job enlargement based on reduction of costs of nonproductive work and line-balance delays. It is unfortunate that these reductions were permitted to mask worker contributions to output flowing from enlarged job design. The results indicate strong contributions in the form of greatly improved quality of output and increased worker satisfaction with their jobs. These are gains for the company, perhaps otherwise unobtainable, along with savings in labor costs and greater production flexibility.

Operator, Machine Tender:
Textile Weaving[7]

The third operator study indicates the impact of the organizational component of job design on the productivity of work groups. A socio-technical systems study in an Indian textile mill revealed the poor consequences of job designs which center only about worker-machine allocations and lead to inhibition of interaction of workers. The field study took place in a mill which had recently been intensively studied by engineers for the purpose of laying out equipment and assigning work loads based on careful time measurements of all of the job components. After installation of the layout and work assignments, the mill still failed to produce at satisfactory productivity and quality levels. The job designs required 12 specialist activities to operate the equipment assigned to a weaving room containing 240 looms.

1. A weaver tended approximately 30 looms.
2. A battery filler served about 50 looms.
3. A smash-hand tended about 70 looms.
4. A gater, cloth carrier, jobber, and assistant jobber were each assigned to 112 looms.
5. A bobbin carrier, feller-motion fitter, oiler, sweeper, and humidification-fitter were each assigned to 224 looms.

[7]A. K. Rice, "Productivity and Social Organization in an Indian Weaving Shed," *Human Relations*, VI (November, 1953), 297.

The occupational tasks were all highly interdependent, and the utmost coordination was required to maintain continuity of production. However, the worker-machine assignments and consequent organizational grouping produced an interaction pattern which militated against continuity of production. The interaction resulting from work assignment brought each weaver into contact with five-eighths of a battery filler, three-eighths of a smash-hand, one-quarter of a gater, and one-eighth of a bobbin carrier.

After study of travel and communication patterns, the jobs were redesigned so that all of the workers who were interdependent were made part of the same work group. Work groups were organized so that a single group was responsible for the operation and maintenance of a specific bank of looms. Geographic division rather than functional division of the weaving room produced inter-action patterns which made for regularity of relationships among individuals whose jobs were interrelated, and they could be held responsible for their production. As a result of these changes efficiency rose from an average of 80 per cent to 95 per cent, and damage dropped from a mean of 32 per cent to 20 per cent after 60 working days. In the adjacent part of the weaving shed, where job design changes were not made, efficiency dropped to 70 per cent and finally rose to 80 per cent, while damage continued at an average of 31 per cent.

Operator, Miner: Coal Mining[8]

This is one of the earliest long-term socio-technical systems studies of a complex organization. Its uniqueness lies in the fact that mining technology and its physical environment sharply displayed the effect of organization design on socio-psychological relations, an effect which in other technologies is frequently masked by compensatory management action. Quite aside from mechanical devices, individual skill, or wage payment systems, the design of the organiza-tion, in its effect on all participants, is found to be a major factor contributing to system performance and personal satisfaction. During the study, coal mining was first carried out under an older nonmechanized technology with a tradi-tionally developed organization structure and then under a newer technology which operated under one and subsequently under another organizational design.

The premechanization, or single-place coal mining, technology was based on a pair of miners (with occasional reinforcements) making up a simple small-group organization structure. Work was done with hand tools and required great energy expenditure; performance depended on intimate knowledge of the mine and working conditions. Members of a group were self-selected and were multi-skilled, all-round workers performing the entire cycle of extraction as a joint undertaking. The group performed without supervision in dispersed, self-

[8]E. L. Trist, G. W. Higgin, H. Murray, and A. B. Pollack, *Organizational Choice* (London: Tavistock Publications, 1963); and E. L. Trist and K. W. Bamforth, "Some Social and Psychological Consequences of the Longwall Method of Coal Getting," *Human Relations,* IV (February, 1951), 3-38.

contained locations, was paid as a group, and developed high adaptability to local working conditions. Management was represented in the work area by a minor official who performed various services, including safety inspection and setting wage incentive payments. This system was effective because each work group had developed responsible autonomy and because the entire production system was slow, requiring little coordination at the coal face.

The successor to the single-place system was a partially mechanized technology, the maximum mechanization level possible at the time for low seam conditions in British mines. The first organization design introduced, known as the conventional longwall system, reflected in its organizational design and occupational roles the prevailing outlook of mass production engineering. Mine output depended on completion of a working cycle, which consisted of preparing an area for coal extraction, using machinery to dig the coal out of the face, and removing the coal with the aid of conveyors. Cycle activities were divided into seven specialized tasks, each carried out by a different task group. Each of the tasks had to be completed in sequence and on schedule over three working shifts. On each of the shifts, one or more task groups performed their work, provided that the preceding tasks had been completed. The filling tasks, for coal removal, were the most onerous, and incompletion frequently impeded the work cycle, reducing output. Having been assigned a specialized task and an ostensibly equal work load, each worker was paid an incentive to perform his task without reference to the other tasks of workers in his or other groups.

The outgrowth of this organization design was the development of isolated task groups, each with its own customs, agreements with management, and payment arrangements related to its own interests. Coordination between men and groups on different shifts and control of work had to be provided entirely from outside, by the management. To be effective, control had to be coercive, which was both unsuitable for, and impracticable in, the high-risk coal-face environment. Management lacked the means to weld the individual task groups into an integrated team for performance of the cycle as a whole, and intergroup self-coordination could not develop. The inability to develop work-team relationships resulted in hostility and conflict among workers, and between them and management. Each worker and task group viewed the assigned task in isolation, which indeed is how it existed. When mine conditions were bad or prior work was not completed, the individual could not cope and resorted to waiting for management to take corrective action and to absenting himself in frustration and self-protection. The lowest level of management in the mine spent most of its time in emergency action over technical breakdowns, systems disfunctioning, and bargaining with workers over special payment for abnormal tasks.

The second organizational design, known as the composite longwall method, was introduced to overcome the deficiencies of the conventional design. Composite design was aimed at providing an organization structure suitable for maintaining continuity and for achieving early conclusion of a work cycle requiring more than one shift for completion. Although the same activity groups were maintained, the overall group, comprised of the successive task groups of the three-shift cycle, developed into a corporate whole. This was aided by setting goals for the performance of the entire cycle and making inclusive payments to the group as a whole for the completion of all the tasks in the cycle, plus an incentive for output. Such payment placed responsibility on the entire group for all operations, generating the need for individuals performing different tasks over interdependent phases of the cycle to interrelate. Equal earnings required equal contributions from the cycle group's members, which led to the spontaneous development of interchangeability of workers according to need. Interchangeability required development of multiskilled face workers and permitted sharing the common fund of underground skill and identity.

The method of work employed in each shift was directed at maintaining task continuity. Each shift picked up where the previous shift had left off and, when an activity group's main task was done, redeployed itself to carry on with the next task even if this meant starting a new cycle. All of the required roles were internally allocated to members by the work group as it developed responsible autonomous behavior. Opportunity for equalizing good and bad work times was thus afforded. Teams as a whole also worked out their own systems for rotating tasks and shifts, thereby taking over regulation of deployment. Each team was of sufficient size to make enough men available to fill the roles that arose on each shift.

The autonomous cycle group thus integrated the differentiated activities of longwall mining by internal control through self-regulating mechanisms. By contrast, the integration practices used in conventional longwall mining were those of indirect external control through specialization of tasks with fixed assignments, wage incentive bargaining for each task, and skimpy attempts at direct supervision. Although the study was performed in British coal mines, the differences in concept between the two approaches characterize the present ambivalence on the part of U.S. management over the application of managerial authority. The attempts, so widely recommended, to apply "human relations— participative supervisorial methods" are likely to be ineffective, for they are inappropriate when used for external control purposes. Task and organization designs, compatible with technology, that permit the development of autonomous group functioning are very likely to be determinants for delineating the appropriate boundaries between authoritarian managerial action and internal control by participative self-regulatory mechanisms.

Some objective indicators of the appropriateness of composite organization for longwall mining were changes in absence rates, cycle progress, and productivity. Face work places many stresses on miners, particularly when difficulties arise. Changing tasks, shifts, or work places helps reduce stress. Table 1 shows the variety of work experiences possible under each organization. Where changing or sharing of difficult tasks was not possible, there was increased withdrawal or absence from work. Table 2 shows the difference in absence rates. It may be inferred that absence rates had an effect on cycle progress and productivity which are shown in Tables 3 and 4.

TABLE 1
Variety of Work Experience

	Averages for whole team	
	Conventional longwall	Composite longwall
Aspect of work experience		
Main tasks	1.0	3.6
Different shifts	2.0	2.9
Different activity groups	1.0	5.5

Source: E. L. Trist, G. W. Higgin, H. Murray, and A. B. Pollack, *Organizational Choice* (London: Tavistock Publications, 1963), p. 122.

TABLE 2
Absence Rates

	Percentage of possible shifts	
	Conventional longwall	Composite longwall
Reason for absence		
No reason given	4.3	0.4
Sickness and other	8.9	4.6
Accident	6.8	3.2
Total	20.0	8.2

Source: See source reference to Table 1, p. 123.

TABLE 3
State of Cycle Progress at End of Filling Shift

	Percentage of cycles	
	Conventional longwall	Composite longwall
State of cycle progress		
In advance	0	22
Normal	31	73
Lagging	69	5
All cycles	100	100

Source: See source reference to table 1, p. 124.

TABLE 4
Productivity as Percentage of Estimated Face Potential

	Conventional longwall	Composite longwall
Without allowance for haulage system efficiency	67	95
With allowance	78	95

Source: See source reference to Table 1, p. 125.

Modification of job content and organization units of general maintenance craftsmen was undertaken by a West Coast branch plant of a national industrial chemical manufacturing company. Local management was seeking to improve productivity, to respond to worker demands for more creative activities and for opportunities for closer identification with the job, and to eliminate jurisdictional disagreements among the various crafts. After the program was under way for about two and a half years, a study of the effects was undertaken to identify job content and job perception factors correlated with quantitative criteria of effective performance, i.e., that which minimizes total costs of production.

Prior to the change, each operating department had had its own maintenance crew that looked after 60 to 75 per cent of its needs. The remainder was supplied by central crafts shops. When a centralized maintenance department was organized—introducing planning, scheduling, and work under control—skill and function enlargement for general maintenance and repair workers was decided upon. The jobs of workers in the maintenance shops remained unchanged, being specialized to a single craft. The jobs of the newly designated maintenance repairmen were enlarged to include general welding, layout and fabrication, pipe fitting, boilermaking, equipment installation, and dynamic machine repair. The additional skills were acquired by means of a formal on- and off-the-job training program. Jobs were reclassified and wages increased accordingly. To support the broad-spectrum repairmen, two specialist classifications were introduced to perform special welding and machine repair. Two classes of specialist instructors were created to increase skills and develop new methods. Perhaps crucial to the entire undertaking was the presence of a strong industrial union and a long history of mutual trust and respect in union-management relations.

The changes in organization and enlargement of jobs produced positive results shown in a number of criteria of operational effectiveness, namely, quantity and quality of output, costs, and personal relationships and reactions. Prior to the changes, the company's total maintenance labor costs had moved upward, paralleling the national index. After reorganization and job enlargement, they fell from an index of 130 to 110 in two years (1954=100), while the national index continued to rise from 110 to 120. The labor costs of the enlarged maintenance repairmen, considered separately, fell from an index of 90 to 65 over the same period. When the index of performance (output/direct labor costs) was examined, the production departments showed no change over the period, while the maintenance repairmen showed an increase from 150 to 230. Total employment in the firm was reduced from an index of 100 to 95. The ratio of complaints about product quality and packaging to orders shipped, which is an indirect measure of quality, fell from an index of 100 to 55 over the same period.

To identify job content and job perception factors correlated with perfor-

[9]Davis and Werling, *op. cit.*

mance criteria, a questionnaire was administered based on hypotheses concerning the effect on worker performance of job content and relationships.[10] Questions reflected such variables as sequential relation of job duties and size of technological process segment included in jobs; inclusion in job of supply and inspection tasks and of final and completion activities; control over work content, rate, and quality; communication with related work stations; extent of decision-making and participation in improvement activities; perception of value of contribution and of role in work group and organization; identification with produce and process; feedback on quality and quantity of performance; measures of performance and incentives or rewards. The questionnaires were anonymously answered during working hours by 223 workers in 7 departments. The remaining 11 employees, in the eighth department, were unavailable and did not participate.

Two analyses were made. The first identified job factors associated with criterion variables and the second examined the questionnaire responses which distinguished the enlarged jobs from the others in the plant. The criteria used reflected the total cost of performance concept previously proposed as the inclusive criterion for measuring effectiveness, which includes quantity and quality of output, departmental operating costs, and absences. Because grievances and employee turnover were almost nonexistent and transfers took place by union-management agreement, neither was used as a criterion. A summary of job factors associated (correlated at the 5 per cent level or better) with performance criteria is given below. The criterion variables "Improvement in quantity of output" and "Reduction in operating costs" correlated .759 (p=.05), and both correlated .964 (p=.01) and .777 (p=.05) respectively with "absence rate." No suitable explanation of intercorrelation with absence rate was available. The average absence rate was approximately 2 per cent.

Workers with enlarged higher skill jobs were concerned with the importance of their jobs, control over job content and work methods, high variety of assignments, special training, responsibility for quality, and performance of preparatory activities. The responses of this group indicate that they were concerned with matters to which management attaches great importance, which may foreshadow the development of identity in objectives between workers on enlarged jobs and management. They indicated that they wished to make contributions to improvements of operations, related company success to their own, related their own advancement to better skills and performance, identified learning of new skills as a positive value of the job, and indicated readiness to accept additional duties to help improve their own and group performance. The negative responses of this group dealt with lack of variety of assignments and lack of control over work in process, and indicated that company, supervision, and management ranked low on what was liked about jobs. Attitudes of enlarged jobholders toward performance were positive and so was their responsiveness to management goals, which seemed to have developed in spite of negative attitudes toward company, management, and supervision.

[10] Davis, "Toward a Theory of Job Design."

TABLE 5

Summary of Job Factors Associated With Performance Criteria

Criterion variable (performance indicator)	Job factors
1. Improvement in quality of output	Fully specified work assignment and work rate
2. Reduction in operating costs	Full work assignment
3. Mean quality of output	1. Perception of job as being important 2. Identification of high quality needs; independence as to control of quality; identification of high performance with success in company 3. Self control of organization of work, including rate; high evaluation of fellow workers 4. Peer communication
4. Improvement in quality of output	1. Full work assignment and some independence as to variety and rate of work; wide job knowledge 2. Specified work assignment and independence as to preparatory activities 3. Relates success to management fairness; minimal standards of performance; specified work rate
5. Absence rate	1. Wide job knowledge 2. Full work assignment consisting of production activities 3. Full work assignment

Supervisor: Aircraft Instruments Repair and Manufacture[11]

The design of supervisory jobs is also plagued by poor models of individual-organization relationships and of human behavior in productive organizations. It is further complicated by the supervisor's conflicting objectives vis-à-vis workers and management, by the conflict between the supervisor's management objectives and his superior's, by his uncertainty over behavior required for effective leadership, by the implied threat to his status and effectiveness inherent in the authoritarian-participation conflict, and by the ambiguity that exists over the discharge of his responsibility. For purposes of design of supervisory jobs there is a general lack of information and data apart from some generalities concerning leadership behavior.

The management of the industrial facility of a large West Coast military installation introduced modifications in organization and in duties, responsi-

[11]L. E. Davis and E. S. Valfer, "Supervisor Job Design," *Proceedings of the Second International Congress on Ergonomics, Ergonomics,* VIII (1965), 1; and "Intervening Responses to Changes in Supervisor Job Designs," *Occupational Psychology,* XXXIX (1965), 171.

bilities, and authority of some first-line supervisors, as part of a planned experimental field study directed by a University of California research team. The primary function of the facility was to overhaul, repair, and test military aircraft and their components. With the exception of the senior executives, all of its 5,900 employees were civilians, of whom 3,800 were in line functions. The study was confined to 11 shops, the basic (first level) organization units, in which the sensing, power, and control accessories of aircraft systems were overhauled, repaired, and tested. The shops, each under a supervisor, employed from 12 to 30 craftsmen and processed many subtypes of relatively homogeneous types of equipment, such as flight instruments.

The study was intended to test the primary hypothesis that higher economic productivity (lower total cost) and greater need satisfaction for all members of a work group will result when the supervisor's authority and responsibility is increased by giving him direct control over all operational and inspection functions required to complete and determine final acceptance of the products or services assigned to his work group. A response mechanism model was developed which postulated that changes in a supervisor's performance result from intervening sequential changes in his perceptions, attitudes, motivations, and consequent behavior toward tasks and toward other members of the organization. Intervening criteria reflecting perceptions, attitudes, and behavior toward others were developed; questionnaires and interviews were used as measuring instruments. Changes in supervisors' task behaviors were assessed by random activity sampling and job content inventory.

Two modifications in supervisors' jobs were introduced separately into a number of experimental shops. Control shops matched to these as to type of work, style of supervision, worker skills, and past performance were used.

The treatments were as follows:

1. Product Responsibility treatment provided supervision of all functions required to complete the products processed in a shop. It was introduced into two experimental shops with two control shops.
2. Quality Responsibility treatment added inspection to the functions required to complete a product, including authority for final quality acceptance of products. It was introduced into four experimental shops with three control shops.

The Product Responsibility treatment moved two experimental shops from their initial or functional organizational state to the second or product organizational state. In the initial state, the functions of overhaul and repair, calibrate and test, and quality acceptance were each performed by different groups. In the second state, all functions required to complete its products, with external quality acceptance, were performed by one work group. The differences in functions between the first and second states were technically complex, requiring the acquisition of additional knowledge and skills by supervisors and workers.

The Quality Responsibility treatment moved four experimental shops from the second to the third organizational state of full responsibility for product completion, including quality acceptance. The tasks added in the third state were largely replicative and only trivially different from those performed by the shops in their initial (second) state. The major differences were in the explicit delegation of responsibility for quality and authority to perform quality acceptance. For this purpose quality control inspectors were withdrawn from the experimental shops and their authority for product acceptance was transferred to the shop supervisors, who, not long afterward, transferred the authority to key workers.

Proper evaluation of the treatment responses required that the pre-existing organizational environment be completely delineated, particularly since the expected effects were generated through supervisors of units which tended to become more autonomous as a result of the treatments. This environment was one of known overall demand for products and services, varying in the short run and requiring a highly skilled work force. Such skilled workers were in limited supply in the area, making it difficult, if not impossible, to rely on hiring as a means of adding workers to a unit to suit immediate needs. This situation generated manpower-maintenance goals directed at conserving manpower in preparation for meeting overall known demand requirements under "emergency" (short-run) conditions. Goal conflicts could and did arise between this real goal of supervisors and such usual and stated goals of top management as efficiency and cost reduction. In implementing its goals, management reviewed each supervisor's performance every three months by comparing the productivity, quality, and costs of his shop against a standard. Based on this review and planned quarterly work load, a supervisor would expect to have workers added or removed from his shop for the next calendar quarter. When unplanned increases in work load occurred, a supervisor could request, and receive, additional workers transferred from other shops. Whether these were the workers he wanted, or may even previously have lost, can be left to conjecture.

If supervisors responded positively to the treatments, they were expected to achieve changes in the objective criteria of cost reduction and quality improvement, satisfying management's stated goals without violating their own real goal of manpower-maintenance. Achievement of improvement in productivity was not expected since this might have resulted in a loss of manpower, constituting a negative incentive to the supervisor in maintaining the capability of his shop to meet anticipated fluctuating work load.

The study lasted for 24 months. During the first 9 months data were collected on all of the criterion variables for operation of the 11 shops in their initial states. After the experimental treatments were introduced into 6 shops, data on objective criteria were collected for 6 months and data on intervening criteria were collected for 15 months. The results of the study can be summarized as follows.

Personnel costs in the form of absenteeism, grievances, transfers, injuries, etc., were not significantly affected by the treatments. It is difficult to evaluate whether the nonsensitivity was specific to the treatments or to the short duration of the study. Historically personnel costs were markedly low and unchanging in the organization and this pattern continued into the postchange period.

The treatment which enlarged the responsibility and authority of the supervisors and the operational functions of their organizational units resulted in the following changes in objective criteria:

Criteria	Product Responsibility (Technically complex change)	Quality Responsibility (Technically trivial change)
1. Compatible with supervisors' goal:		
a. Quality	Significant improvement	No significant change, but indications of improvement
b. Costs	No change	Significant improvement
2. Incompatible with supervisors' goal:		
a. Productivity	No change	No change

As can be seen, those objective performances improved that were compatible with the supervisors' goal of manpower maintenance.

Supervisor behavior became more autonomous and more oriented to the technical problems of producing the product and to worker training. The treatments shortened the quality and process information feedback loops to workers and concentrated dispersed functional authority. In moving toward technological aspects of management, giving more time to planning, inspection, control, etc., supervisors did so at the expense of management of men. This change in management style appeared to be salutary as judged by positive worker attitudes.

Positive attitudes of workers and supervisors were enhanced, indicating satisfaction of personal needs in the direction of developing individuals who were contributing to the organization's viability or health. The major response perceptions and attitudes were:

Treatment	Favorable	Unfavorable
Product Responsibility (Technically complex change: new tasks and skills required)	1. Greater autonomy	1. Loss of man-orientation
	2. Less limiting internal structure	2. Loss of concern for worker
	3. Greater skill for workers in long run	3. Low rate of transfer of treatment tasks and responsibilities
	4. Greater product control	4. Low delegation
	5. Increased information flow to workers	

continued

Treatment	Favorable	Unfavorable
Quality Responsibility (Technically trivial change: addition of inspection and authority for product acceptance)	1. Greater authority	1. Loss of man-orientation
	2. Greater autonomy	2. Greater internal structure
	3. Greater concern for worker	3. Low delegation
	4. Higher rate of transfer of treatment tasks and responsibilities to workers	
	5. Reduced conflict with staff group	
	6. Increased information flow to workers	

Conclusions

The studies reviewed here lend support to the general model of responsible autonomous job behavior as a key facet of individual-organizational-technological relationships in productive organizations. Responsible behavior as defined here implies (1) acceptance of responsibility by the individual or group for the cycle of activities required to complete the product or service, (2) acceptance of responsibility for rate, quantity, and quality of output, and (3) recognition of interdependence of the individual or group on others for effective progress of a cycle of activities. Similarly, autonomous behavior encompasses (1) self-regulation of work content and structure within the job, where the job is an assignment having inputs, facilities, and outputs, (2) self-evaluation of performance, (3) self-adjustment to changes required by technological variability, and (4) participation in setting up of goals or objectives for job outputs.

Furthermore, the studies provide a partial demonstration of the positive effects on total performance of job and organization designs which lead to responsible autonomous job behavior, i.e., positive effects on objective organization performance, as well as on the attitudes, perceptions, and satisfactions of members of the organization. Such designs also tend to maintain a production system in an on-going state of relative equilibrium. For example, in many of the studies total performance was found to have been enhanced substantially by job designs which provided compatibility among technological, organizational, and personal requirements. This suggests that here, as elsewhere, the system approach leads to more effective designs of organizations and jobs. The component or piecemeal approach (so prevalent at present), which concentrates on job designs exclusively tailored to one component of the system, namely technology, tends to result in less than optimal total performance. While failing to achieve the output and quality levels possible, it imposes higher direct costs on management and workers alike, reflected in increased inspection, supervision, and absenteeism, coupled with reduced satisfactions, negative attitudes, and hostility.

That some processes or activities may be automated does not alter the fact that for the organization as a whole people are the prime agents for the utilization of technology in the interests of achievement of an organization's objectives. The model of responsible autonomous job behavior makes it both permissible and imperative to view personal requirements in the focus of job design activity. But if the model is to be used as a basis for job (and organization) design, then these nonmodifiable personal requirements and the characteristics of their interactions with technology and the organization will have to be specified as design criteria aimed at achieving compatibility. Variations in design may result from interpretations of nonmodifiable criteria and from the introduction of others.

Some of the job characteristics of importance to job and organization design have asserted their dominance in the studies reviewed. They can be classified into two types: (1) job content and structure characteristics, which reflect the interaction between personal and technological requirements, and (2) job environment characteristics, which reflect the interaction between personal and organizational requirements. Job content characteristics are concerned with the number and kinds of tasks and their interrelationships. Many of these are specific illustrations of the need for the development of a work role which provides comprehensiveness, i.e., the opportunity to perform all tasks required for product or process completion and at the same time imposes the responsibility and confers the authority for self-direction and self-regulation.

Improvement in total performance was thus frequently obtained when the scope of jobs included all tasks required to complete a part, product, or service; when the job content included all four types of tasks inherent in productive work: auxiliary or service (supply, tooling), preparatory (set-up), processing or transformation, and control (inspection); when the tasks included in the job content permitted closure of the activity, if not product completion, permitting development of identity with product or process. Tangible gains in performance were also obtained by the introduction of task variety in the form of larger numbers and kinds of tasks and skills as well as more complex tasks. The characteristics of processing tasks which led to improved performance were self-regulation of speed of work and self-determination of work methods and sequence. Total performance also improved when control tasks were included in jobs, permitting outputs to be evaluated by self-inspection, and when product quality acceptance was within the authority of the jobholder.

The job environment characteristics that contributed to improvement in total performance were again those that supported the development of responsible autonomous job behavior. They indicate a job structure that permits social interaction among jobholders and communication with peers and supervisors, particularly when the maintenance of continuity of operation is required. A reward system that supports responsible autonomy was shown to provide gains beyond those of simple increases in task output.

Appropriate management behavior is, of course, required for jobs having these characteristics. The behaviors called for are supportive in providing service, general planning of activities, and evaluation of results on the basis of organizationally meaningful objectives. They stand in contrast to present overly specific task planning and work measurement, obtrusive supervision, coercive external control, imposed external integration of specialized tasks, and external coordination of fractionated activities.

Certain important aspects of organizational design were also brought to light by the studies. Where small organizational units, or work groups, are required, group structures having the following features appeared to lead to improved performance: (1) group composition that permits self-regulation of the·group's functioning, (2) group composition that deliberately provides for the full range of skills required to carry out all the tasks in an activity cycle, (3) delegation of authority, formal or informal, to the group for self-assignment of tasks and roles to group members, (4) group structure that permits internal communication, and (5) a group reward system for joint output. As regards the design requirements for larger organizational units with more complex interactions, it would be hazardous to draw any conclusions from the studies reviewed. Whether or not present extensive research will make a contribution to our understanding of the design requirements of large organizations is not yet clear.

Overall it is obvious that we are only beginning to identify relationships among technology, organization, and the individual which are capable of being translated into organization and job design recommendations. Nevertheless, it requires no very great powers of foresight to suggest that we are rapidly approaching the time when re-evaluation of management precepts and practices will have to take place. Many currently fashionable management programs are mere palliatives, addressed to patching up essentially inappropriate organization and job structures. Among these, the so-called worker communications programs, participation techniques directed at providing workers with "feelings of importance," and human relations programs dealing with personal relationships and supervision (often in the abstract, outside the industrial or business context) do not stand up under objective scrutiny. Almost without exception their achievements fall short even of their own stated objectives.

In summary, changes in organization and job design similar to those reviewed are indicated, as are associated changes in management behavior. Whether and when they will take place cannot be forecast. Industrial and business history is replete with examples of the continuation of superannuated institutions and procedures.

Work Flow as the
Basis for Organization Design

Using three change programs as their basis, Chapple and Sayles demonstrate their social engineering approach which holds that the actual work flow linkage *should be the criterion of organizational design and change. They point out that, regardless of the business, there is some type of technology which separates out a series of jobs that must be accomplished if the product or service is to materialize. In other words, getting favorable results from a change action means locking in on the various stress points along the work flow sequence and introducing changes in task and structure to eliminate them.*

However, the authors note that this is only the first step. Other structural factors to be considered as means of creating better organizations include: combining unit work flows into a larger work flow system with a span of second-level supervision, establishing controls to indicate when the flows are not meshing properly, and defining staff-line relationships.

WORK FLOW AS THE
BASIS FOR ORGANIZATION DESIGN

Eliot D. Chapple
President
E. D. Chapple Co., Inc.

Leonard R. Sayles
Graduate School of Business
Columbia University

In a business of any size, decisions that affect its organizational design are made almost daily. Constant changes in technology, markets, and financial conditions impel management to make decisions to keep the company on its course. The personalities of top management also shape the design; as its members come and go, changes are made to suit their private philosophies and their attitudes toward "proper" organization, although such changes are usually rationalized as fitting the demands of internal conflict or external forces.

For guides to decisions on organizational design, a manager has available the writing of experts in the "management movement" or he can call on a present-day consultant. Taken as generalizations from experience, the rules, doctrines, and principles of organization are thought-provoking. They represent the accumulated experience and wisdom of clinicians. Interpreted in the light of a specific problem, they often can help find the way to a solution. Yet, as in the comparable case of clinical medicine, they do not, in fact cannot, provide the precise criteria for diagnosis and therapy.

The medical axiom "Nature is the great healer" applies to organizations as well as to human beings. Far too many triumphs of clinicians stem from the persistence or inertia of the system. Thus, organizations often show extraordi-

Reprinted from Eliot D. Chapple and Leonard R. Sayles, *The Measure of Management* (N.Y.: The Macmillan Company, 1961), with permission of The Macmillan Company. Copyright©1961 The Macmillan Company.

nary resistance to poorly considered attempts to change them. Surveys are made, often costing many hundreds of thousands of dollars; new charts and new manuals of procedure are prepared; and orders are issued to put the recommendations into action. Then, frequently within a few months, the enterprise sloughs off its new organizational skin, and only a few of the new titles remain. The expensive reports and manuals are put in an unused file, and the rest is abandoned.

Many organizations, both private and governmental, are reorganized almost yearly and usually by a different set of experts, each with their personal remedies for presumed organizational illness. The human damage is often great. People are fired, resign, or are moved from one end of the country to the other and back again. Yet, the organization holds together. The old habits are soon reestablished if they were ever put aside even temporarily. Employees with such ill-starred companies, which are often in a financially successful market position, soon develop the uneasy caution of the inhabitants of the Great Plains in the tornado season. At the barest tremor of the barometer or the first trace of blackness in the sky, they dive headfirst into the inactive safety of whatever organizational storm cellar they can find.

Toward a Science of Organization

Certainly there is no lack of clinical experience, but what is needed is a science of organization. To do the job, the criteria for decision on which the practitioner can call, as the physician relies on the laboratory to substantiate or overrule his clinical judgment, must be developed. Fortunately, most of the essentials are already at hand, the tools of measurement and accurate observation.

In the approach to be taken into organizational structure, two elements will appear. The technology or flow of work is the major criterion for designing the structure. This contrasts sharply with a well-established tradition of planning the organization from the top down. Secondly, any tendency to group people and activities together simply because they have or involve similar or purportedly similar functional responsibilities is avoided.

Traditionally, the scientific approach in studying any human group considers the environment and the technology developed to adapt to the environment. Each individual operation involves an implement or machine using some sort of power, a sequence of actions to accomplish the task, and possibly the interaction of several people in some kind of team activity. In this sense, the term "implement" can be applied to any object, a sheet of paper, a loom, an accounting machine, or a bulldozer. The products of business, or of any organization for that matter, result from interrelated techniques, some of which are essential and others secondary.

If an entire technique or series of techniques can be performed by a single individual, such as a silver craftsman who sells his wares himself, no organization results. But, if a division of labor occurs, some interaction between technicians must take place, and organization on the work level results. On the production level, a relatively large number of techniques may be linked together to make up the work flow through the plant, with a single owner-manager providing the entire management. If there is only a small number of employees and few demands on his time for other activities (for example, if he subcontracts for a larger corporation on a regular basis), the owner may have a foreman in the shop even though the operation does not require one. The ensuing growth of such enterprises usually comes about rather simply with the owner taking a partner who is often a relative. Then, the management begins to specialize, typically with one man selling and the other overseeing production.

Design the Structure from the Bottom Up

Regardless of the type of business organization—a small retail shop, the trader or merchant acting as intermediary between buyers and sellers, or a bank—a similar elaboration of organization takes place. The division of labor on the work level may involve sales people, clerks recording transactions, or cashiers; as the division of labor proliferates, so does management. The development of specialized managers or of a management division of labor is clearly secondary in the evolution of business to the growth of specialization on the work-flow level. This sequence is of critical importance in designing the organization.

Yet, in many writings about modern business organizations, the prime and determining influence of technological process is lost sight of. In their writings, the designers of the organization, who are perhaps under the spell of a two-dimensional chart, start at the top. Beginning with the directors and the president, they work down, level by level, discussing the functions of the various divisions, considering the relationships of "staff" or "service" departments to the "line," weighing the importance of the "span of control," and defining their graphic representations by referring to the nature of executive authority and responsibility. They may casually mention the first-line supervisor, but what he supervises is usually incidental to their recommendations.

The Tradition of Functional Concentration

Most decisions on "proper" organizational structure are based primarily on similarities of activities or functions. Traditionally, organizations are divided into such major functions as sales, production, finance, and personnel. Each may have subsidiary functions such as engineering, training, market research, inventory control, etc., that, in many companies, compete for equal standing with the others. It is usually recognized, of course, that a common location, product, customer, or specialization may vary the design, but within each divisional setup functional considerations predominate.

If a new function or activity is identified or grows in importance, the question always is, "Who will take it over?" For instance, should sales engineering be assigned to the sales division or engineering? It is an important adjunct in making the sale and helping the sales force bring in business. On the other hand, is it wise to divorce the sales engineers from first-hand involvement in engineering activities? What about sales training, another constant source of conflict? The sales division is sure personnel does not understand what it takes to make a salesman, but the personnel division does have a training department with broad responsibility for the entire corporation. Personnel has the specialized skills and specialists to do the training that salesmen are supposed to be incapable of doing well.

The endless arguments about proper placement of organizational activities are usually only temporarily settled. Because only verbal criteria exist, no one can define a function accurately, and no one wins a conclusive victory. In the meantime, the organization may acquire a cover of charts which, like a turtle's shell, conceal what goes on inside the animal.

Organization Based on Actual Work Flow

Clearly, a different approach to the problem of organizational design is needed. The structure built for members of management can be ignored for the moment to go back to the bottom where the work is done.

This requires looking at the way the technology separates out a series of jobs that must be accomplished if the product is to result. We may manufacture something, buy it for resale, or hire it, as in the case of money, but whatever the business—manufacturing, retailing, banking, or service—we follow certain techniques. There is a beginning; when the process starts, something is done, and the process ends. Put another way, something comes in the door, something is done to it, and it moves on its way out another door to the customer.

In the cases to follow, which are drawn from the authors' field studies, the problems created when the work-flow sequence is not used as a criterion of organizational design, as well as the techniques of analyzing the work process and identifying the work-flow sequences will be examined. By using a comparative point of view, we shall describe a method to isolate some general principles of organization.

Case 1—The Sales-Credit Controversy

In this case, the general sales manager of a manufacturing company was engaged in a major battle with both the credit manager and the treasurer, who was the credit manager's boss. Such conflicts are not rare. Salesmen usually believe the credit department tries to prevent them from making sales, and credit personnel often think the salesmen will sell to anyone, no matter how bad the risk, to get their commissions. This case illustrates the nature of the problem and why management structure and work flow are too often incongruous.

Although interpreted by management as a clash of personalities, the argument between the sales manager and the credit manager stemmed from much more mundane sources. To understand it, it is necessary to look at the actual work flow through their departments and observe the way the work was organizationally split up. The key implement was the salesman's order, which he mailed in to the home office after filling out what the customer required and extending the dollar figures. Figure 1 illustrates what happened to the order and how the people who handled it were divided between the various functional divisions.

When the office opened in the morning, the mail was sorted in the mail room. Orders were separated and taken immediately by a mail boy to the sales office which occupied one section of the large, open general office of the company, a one-floor layout. There, the clerks checked over the orders to see if there were any special problems of handling shipments or questions raised by the salesmen that might require correspondence. Any order presenting a problem was given to a sales correspondent who wrote to the customer or the salesman, if necessary.

When the sales department completed its work, the order was sent to what was called an order-editing department. This was under the jurisdiction of the factory manager because he superintended warehousing. The orders were checked to see that they were correct, the prices up-to-date, the arithmetic accurate, and the goods in stock at the warehouse nearest to the customer. A copy of the order was sent to another warehouse if the closest one did not have the stock. If inventory records showed no stock available, the order editor made out a back-order form to be mailed to the customer.

Then one of the editors would take a batch of orders to the credit department, where credit analysts (clerks) checked the credit ratings to be sure each customer's credit was within the limits set by management. They ascertained whether it was permissible to sell on any other terms than C.O.D. and whether the volume of the order was within the limits of his credit rating. If there was a credit problem, i.e., a deviation, the order was given to a credit correspondent who wrote the customer, with a copy for the salesman, telling him his order could not be accepted and stating the terms, if any, on which he could still buy from the company. If the customer was a big-volume account whose credit rating had dropped, the credit manager would make a final decision before the correspondent wrote a letter. It should be mentioned that each salesman had a reference book of the credit ratings for all accounts in his territory and was not supposed to call on any account whose line of credit was below a specified level.

After this processing, the orders were assembled, one copy of each order was sent to the warehouses to be filled and another to be tabulated for accounting purposes. The IBM accounting processing was supervised by the treasurer, and the warehouses were, as mentioned above, under the manager of the factory. Work was organized so that, in theory at least, all of the orders were processed through this office work flow in one day. Thereafter, there was a definite break in timing because accounting did not receive the orders until a batch was completed at the end of each day. The same was true for the warehouses where goods were pulled for shipment and billed.

There was tension between the credit manager and the general sales manager because the credit department, following its procedure faithfully, occasionally canceled an order that a salesman had made, sometimes a large one. Because credit ratings fluctuate, this had happened recently to two large accounts, and

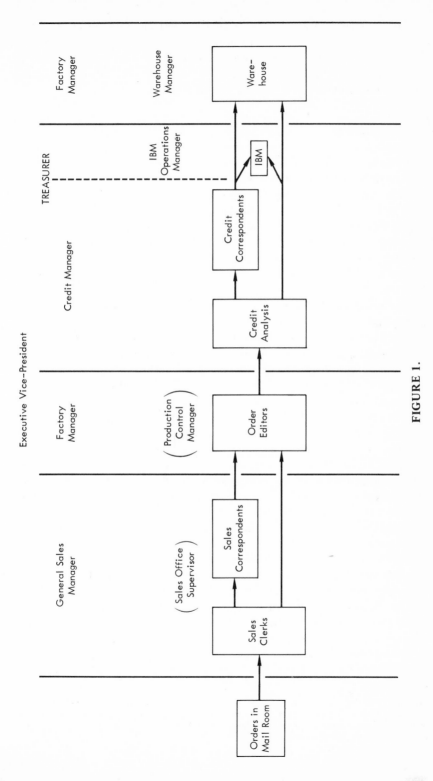

FIGURE 1.

319

the general sales manager was understandably furious. Both customers threatened not to buy from the company again. The situation was more embarrassing because the general sales manager had written each customer a personal letter to thank him for his confidence in their product after the sales correspondent handling the accounts called the orders to his attention.

Reorganization

Now let us look at a series of improvements in the organization. The first and most obvious change in the work flow of handling orders was to reverse the position of the sales and the credit departments. If credit could not be extended, there was no point in checking the accuracy of an order or carrying out the "sales" functions involved. Moreover, this change would prevent recurrences of the kind of embarrassment the general sales manager had undergone. The rearrangement was also more efficient because it eliminated the processing of orders that ultimately would be thrown out. However, it did not deal with more basic issues.[1]

As the organization chart (Fig. 1) indicates, three separate divisional heads, reporting to the executive vice-president, were involved in the movement of a piece of paper and its carbons from one clerical position to another in the general office. Not only were three separate divisions writing to the customer (sales, credit, and the order editor if he issued a back order) but also there was no assurance that there would be any coordination in what each said. Credit correspondents were accused by sales of being too brusque with customers and they, in turn, accused sales of promising too much.

Many other practical problems of management arose. The policy of the company was to clear the orders in a single day. Tight scheduling was sometimes necessary to get the work completed because volume fluctuates. Absenteeism, inadequate performance, or the assignment of other work to the people in a department would upset the even flow of work. If there was disagreement because one department was holding up another, the only recourse when the immediate supervisors could not agree was to settle the dispute on the level of the executive vice-president. Thus, in heated disagreements between the general sales manager and the credit manager, the executive vice-president had to listen not only to complaints about customer relations, but also to all the petty grievances each had about the performance or management of the other.

The difficulty was created when the work flow was divided into separate pieces on the basis of functional similarities. The solution was to put it back

[1] The reader may consider the illogical arrangement of having the credit checked after sales correspondents and order-editors worked on an order as an obvious mistake that anyone should have recognized. However, because it was not recognized for many years in a relatively alert company, it reflects the strong attraction of organizing by functional specialty. All the sales activities were put together and handled first, with salesmen contacting their own departments. Then, and only then, was it time for the next function to begin, in this case, that of the credit department. Unfortunately, the logic of functional organization is rarely challenged in practice.

together as a single flow under a single supervisor. He would control the entire flow of an order from the time the paper arrived in the mail room until it left the general office to go to the tabulating department or the warehouse as well as credits, payments, and invoices after the billing was completed. He was responsible for individual performance and could move people around to fit the needs of fluctuating volume. He did not have to argue with other divisions on the management of the process. See Fig. 2.

There was still the problem of functional responsibilities. Sales wanted and deserved some voice in the quality of letters sent to customers. Credit, too, had some legitimate concerns, primarily that company policies regarding credit be followed and any cases not under these policies be referred to higher authority. Both departments outlined standards and procedures that could be carried out by the new department. In this way, representatives of sales or credit would only come into the picture when an exceptional situation required higher-level attention. These procedures also included a periodic auditing program so the sales department could satisfy itself that the correspondents' letters to customers were not antagonistic. The credit department checked that this new work unit only made routine credit decisions and all exceptions needing the credit manager's decision actually got to him. As a result, only one correspondent, a credit-sales-order editing specialist, wrote to each customer although several did identical work. In turn, the correspondent was supervised, together with the clericals handling the proceduralized work flow of the order, by one individual. Credit, sales, and factory set the standards of action for which this single supervisor was responsible.

Case 2—Integrating Inspection, Material Handling, and Machine Maintenance

The case just described has many counterparts in manufacturing organizations. Because work flow is more easily associated with traditional production processes, a typical assembly operation has been chosen. Some of the parts are produced directly from raw materials purchased by the company, and others are purchased from subcontractors. Both types of components are combined into subassemblies and final assemblies. Figure 3 illustrates the flow of work and the organizational segmentation. The existence of material-handling units between each production unit is typical. They report to the production planning department whose manager reports to the vice-president in charge of manufacturing, rather than to the general superintendent. The inspection units, again reporting through a separate channel of authority to the same vice-president, are less typical. Mechanical maintenance, which also had its own chain of command, was the third specialization organizationally separated from production.

Inspection may appear to be the greatest justification for a separate structure because production people might ignore, or at least slight, the quality problem. On closer examination, however, it could be observed that two types of in-

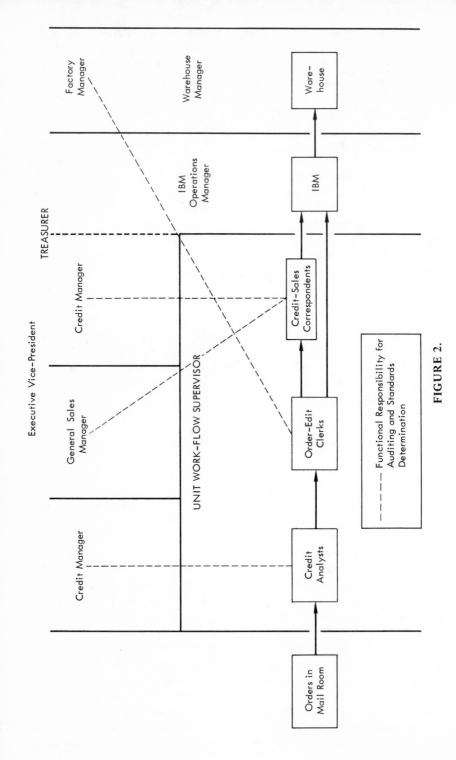

Executive Vice-President

Credit Manager

General Sales Manager

Credit Manager

TREASURER

IBM Operations Manager

Factory Manager

Warehouse Manager

UNIT WORK-FLOW SUPERVISOR

Orders in Mail Room

Credit Analysts

Order-Edit Clerks

Credit-Sales Correspondents

IBM

Ware-house

- - - - - - Functional Responsibility for Auditing and Standards Determination

FIGURE 2.

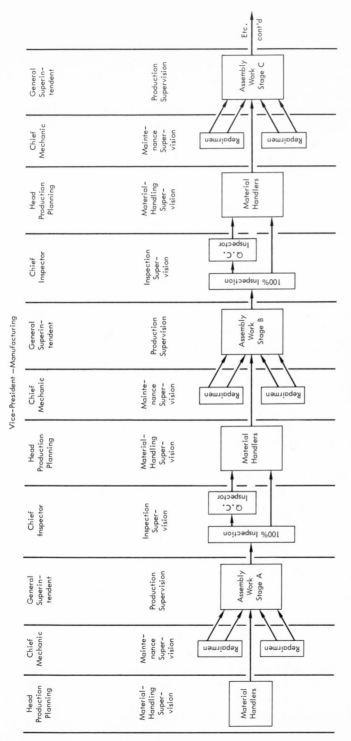

FIGURE 3.

spection were really being carried on. As a regular part of the finishing operation, a cursory visual check was given to all products by one group of inspectors. This check was paced identically with the production process itself as another step after finishing. There was also a quality-control procedure handled by other inspectors who followed routine sampling methods, quite distinct from the 100 per cent inspection process.

The first group of inspectors was the source of frequent holdups that seriously aggravated the relationship of production and inspection personnel. In retrospect, the obvious basis for the friction over the complete inspection stage can be noted. The source of intramanagement feuds is usually not hard to discover. The 100 per cent inspection stage was clearly an integral part of the finishing work flow. Materials passed through all of the stages, including inspection, at the same rate, or at least were supposed to if production schedules were to be maintained. This meant that the "balancing" problem within this work process was always shuttled back and forth between two separate jurisdictions. Quality-control inspection, on the other hand, involved a different sequence of product movement and had no effect on the flow of work.

The remedial steps were obvious. First, 100 per cent inspection was recognized as a necessary part of the production process and transferred to the general foreman so inspection became merely an audit or visual checking within the production framework. Quality-control inspection, which did not interfere with the flow of work since it was done on a sampling basis, remained where it was. This and other organization changes are illustrated in Fig. 4.

Matters were made worse by the material-handling department, which supplied the lines with parts on the basis of a schedule set up by production planning to whom the supervisor of material handling reported. The master schedule for the month's production was broken down by weeks and operations planned around it. However, day-to-day and even hour-to-hour upsets would interfere. A key machine went down. The production rate of a given unit was greater, or slower, than expected. The crucial parts needed to keep production moving were not available, and foremen, general foremen, and superintendents were constantly calling each other, and the material-handling supervisors and the production planning department to straighten things out. The constant arguments could only be settled by the vice-president in charge of manufacturing.

The source of the difficulty was twofold: the scope of production planning, that is, the inherent conflict between a master schedule and the day-to-day variation that every factory experiences, was not adequately analyzed, and, more important, the inevitable lack of coordination between the several units making up a single continuous work-flow system.

In a reorganization, the material-handling units were transferred to production. Units that tied together work groups of two foremen were to report to the general foremen. If departments under the supervision of general foremen were involved, the material-handling reported to the superintendents who bridged the general foremen. Production planning was also re-examined to differentiate between day-to-day and long-range scheduling operations.

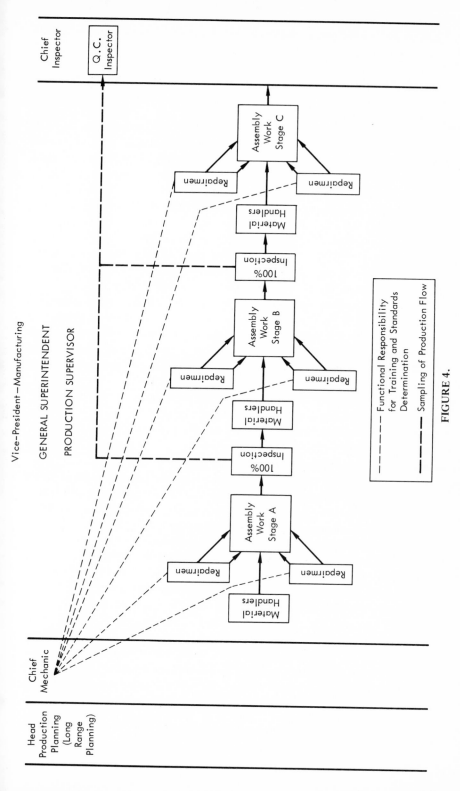

FIGURE 4.

The factory manager acquired two planners whose sole responsibility was to control the daily variations and relate them to the long-range schedule, which involved purchasing of parts and raw materials. Thus, control of raw materials, processes, and finished inventories remained unchanged in the organizational structure.

The company was also plagued by a slightly different problem. As the chart in Figure 3 indicates, the chief mechanic reports to the vice-president in charge of manufacturing, which is traditional functional specialization. The assumption is that placing all the people concerned with mechanical service together in one department leads to more efficient operation and thereby saves money.

But what happened in this case? The floor mechanics, who repaired the machines, worked under their own foremen. The production foreman used a call light to signal for a mechanic when a machine went down. If the mechanic was already working on a machine in another department, the production foreman had to ask the mechanical foreman to take the mechanic off the job he was doing and send him over to the new machine. The mechanics and their foremen usually objected to this even though the whole line might otherwise be held up. The mechanics complained that most of the breakdowns resulted from bad maintenance by the operators and there would be no trouble if the production foremen would make sure their people kept the machines oiled and adjusted. The production foremen countered by saying the mechanics always fixed the wrong machines, had no understanding of production problems, and usually were just stubborn when they insisted on fixing an unimportant machine, i.e., unimportant to the production foreman at the moment. Moreover, the production foremen were constantly arguing among themselves. If all the mechanics were busy in one department and another department needed one, the first-come, first-served principle was not . . . satisfactory to the man with a rush order to get out.[2]

As in the other cases, the heated arguments were complicated by personalities and also had to be settled on the top-management level. No matter how carefully the vice-president tried to get the foremen to agree on a procedure to determine the importance of any machine breakdown and to emphasize preventive maintenance, the foremen usually ended up in his office.

He finally decided the only way to elimiante the stress was to assign mechanics to the general foremen in production and in some instances superintendents. The mechanical department continued to train the mechanics in its shops, and set up repair performance standards to make sure each mechanic's work met specifications. Most importantly, however, the assignment of mechanics was controlled by production. As a result, the conflicts ended, and the vice-president was able to devote time to more constructive activities than settling intramanagement rows. In terms of cost, the company was better off than before. Although the original centralization of facilities appeared efficient, no additional mechanics were needed for the reorganization, and it reduced

[2]Cf. George Strauss, "The Set-Up Man: A Case Study of Organizational Change," *Human Organization*, vol. XIII, no. 2, 1954, pp. 17-25.

delays in the work flow because of mechanical failure, actually saving money for the company.

So far, the examples of work flow have dealt with the processing of paper or materials through a production line. The final case illustrates how work flow also involves people.

Case 3—Handling the Training Function

The conflict between employment and training is a common problem in many personnel departments. At the simplest level, it is often a matter of scheduling because it is difficult to synchronize recruiting and hiring with the training necessary after the employee is hired. Training activities include both the initial training and indoctrination programs the individual receives before he is sent to a specific department and also on-the-job training that may include a wide range of activities from counseling to sales promotion or educational programs.

Here, the same pattern of functional specialization repeats itself. In this company all training was concentrated organizationally in a single department although the component parts were very different. The initial training program was actually a part of the employment process (Fig. 5).

Large numbers of applicants applied in person at the employment department where they were given an application form by the receptionist. Those who passed a preliminary interview with a screening interviewer were sent to a systematic employment interview and a clerical stage where all the record forms were filled out. If several departments requisitioned personnel, the newly hired employees were sent to a training class that met the next day. Coordination was necessary if employees were to complete this stage and get on the payroll. When there were delays, some of the newly hired people did not come back because they became discouraged waiting for a class which would qualify them for the job. Furthermore, operating departments became impatient when requisitioned personnel had not been "processed" and were not ready when they were needed.

Within the training department, many pressures competed for the time available. Top management was constantly trying out new programs, some of them on a crash basis, although sometimes an existing program simply needed bolstering. Furthermore, there was never an even flow of ready-to-be-trained applicants. Sometimes there were too few for a class and at others a group too large for a single class was hired at once. Many times when classes were scheduled to tie in with requisitions for personnel, not enough qualified people applied. At other times, people were hired simply because they made themselves available even though there were no pressing needs for new personnel. As a result, it was impossible to schedule classes on a regular basis. The training department complained they could not plan their work efficiently because they had no advance notice, and when they did plan, employment let them down. On the other hand, the employment people thought the training group was uncooperative and unwilling to be flexible in view of the difficulties inherent in the hiring

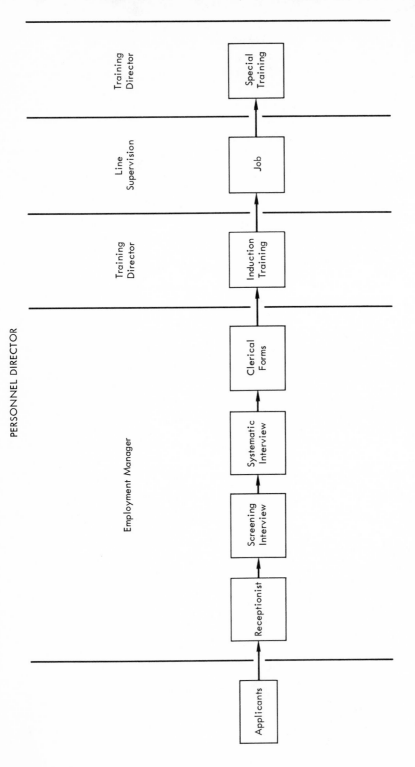

PERSONNEL DIRECTOR

Employment Manager   Training Director   Line Supervision   Training Director

Applicants → Receptionist → Screening Interview → Systematic Interview → Clerical Forms → Induction Training → Job → Special Training

FIGURE 5.

operation. This pattern is typical of functional specialization that divides single work processes into organizational compartments.

The solution was to separate the initial induction training from the other training functions and combine it with the other employment operations described above. See Fig. 6. As a result, a single supervisor now controlled the entire process by which an applicant at the "gate" was moved from the initial inquiry through all of the stages of the hiring procedure, largely eliminating the bickering between employment and training.

Identification of Unit Work Flow

Any organization that has more than one supervisor must decide which employees and, therefore, which processes should be under the jurisdiction or span of control of a given manager. This is the old question of who reports to whom. The preceding text was directed to finding some criterion upon which to base this crucial decision. The case studies were presented to illustrate the significance of technology as the critical determinant of this aspect of organizational structure.

But, this concept of technology needs a more careful explanation than the implications of the cases. It should be clear at the outset that the technology or work method of the organization does not refer primarily to the equipment or to the mechanical, electrical, or chemical processes utilized. Every organization has a method of performing work that involves some sequence of operations. These work flows, so crucial in the cases cited, can be identified wherever there is a sequence of techniques that must be performed in a regular or predetermined order by separate individuals. Thus the technology of the organization is the "who does what with whom, when, where, and how often."

These kinds of work flows are not the same as the work-flow analyses of the industrial engineer, which chart each operation in the production process chronologically. In constructing an organizational structure, the interest is in the person-to-person flow. Thus, one individual may perform what the engineer would identify as several separate operations before the work or paper goes to the next person in the production sequence.[3]

The next step is to separate the elements of the work flow that should be considered as a single supervisory unit, which will be called "unit work flows." The concern here is with the quantitative characteristics of the work flow regardless of whether that which "flows" is a person, paper, or material. These characteristics are necessary to set up criteria to identify the unitary work flows and to understand their implications behaviorally in organization design.

In broad terms, the flow of materials, in a manufacturing company for

[3]It is necessary, of course, to know the total time required by each person to complete his activities to determine the duration of that particular stage in the production sequence. This helps establish the rate at which the paper, material, or a person moves through the line. This rate is set by the time required to complete the slowest or longest step in the sequence.

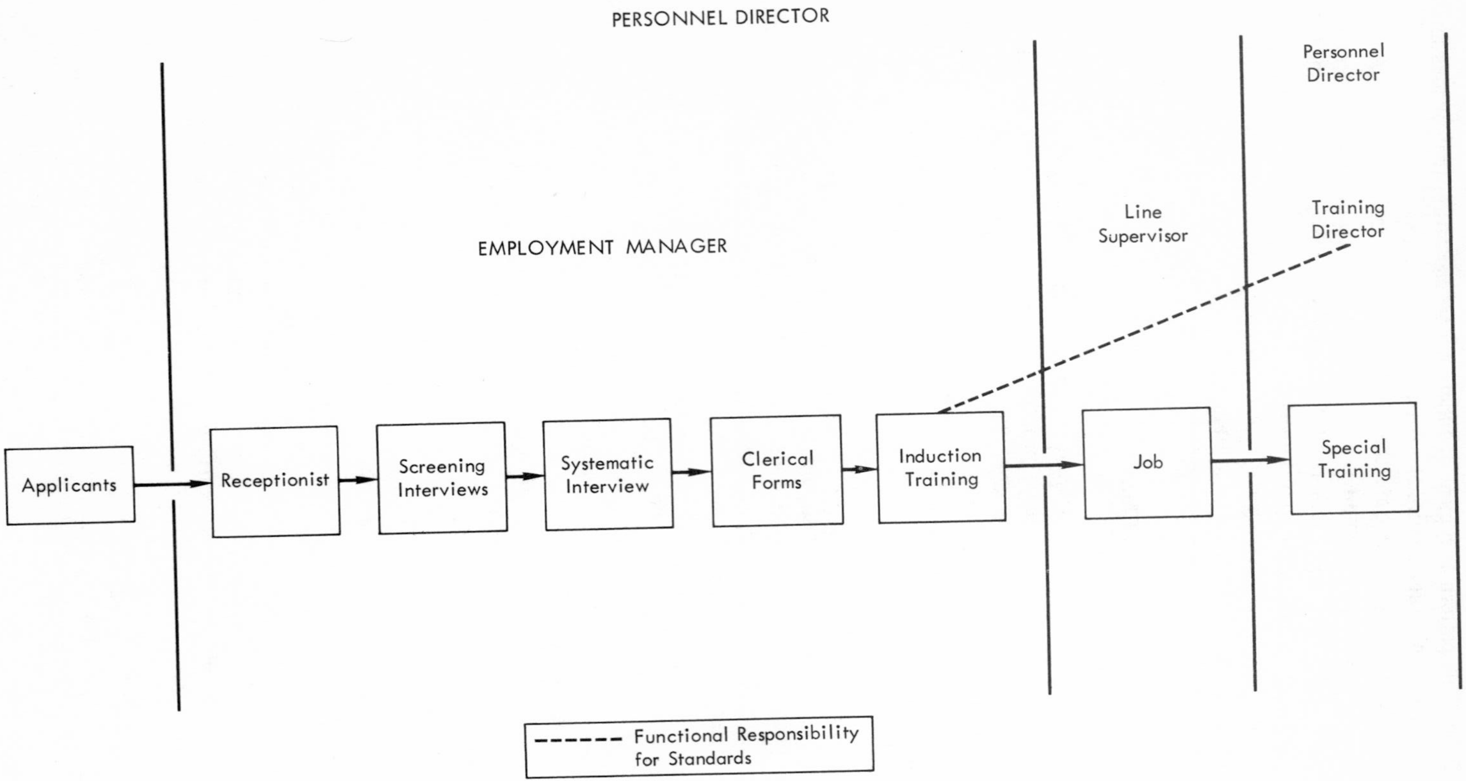

PERSONNEL DIRECTOR

EMPLOYMENT MANAGER

Personnel Director

Training Director

Line Supervisor

Applicants → Receptionist → Screening Interviews → Systematic Interview → Clerical Forms → Induction Training → Job → Special Training

- - - - - Functional Responsibility for Standards

FIGURE 6.

example, that begins at the receiving dock and finally appears at the shipping door as finished product ready for the customer could be considered a single work flow. However, the time coordinates of the complete process are generally too wide; sometimes a matter of weeks or months are needed to complete the manufacturing cycle. Besides the question of physical contiguity is relevant. Physical location or layout is an important factor in identifying the unit flows that make up an organizational design.

In the example of processing the salesman's order, a controlling factor in the separation of warehousing work flow from the office work flow was location. Although they are physically separate out of necessity, the warehouses could be contiguous. In this case they were located in various parts of the country. Consequently, there was a time lapse between the processing of the orders by the clerical groups and their receipt at the appropriate warehouses.

Yet, even if this time was reduced to a minimum and the location of the warehouse was, so to speak, at the end of the order processing line, the order-filling work flow would still differ quantitatively from the order-processing work flow in its time characteristics. When the day's orders were received in the warehouse, they were sorted according to customer location and given to each order filler in groups having a common shipping route. He then assembled the order from bins or bulk locations and placed it with the order copy (with the amounts checked off) on a conveyor that moved the orders through a checking station, a manifest clerk, a packer, etc. The order-filling work flow did not begin until after the orders for an entire day were processed; the office work flow essentially was done one order at a time. Hence, this procedural difference caused a break in continuous flow similar to the one in geographical location.

If the existing procedural and locational discontinuities can be determined by time criteria, a total work flow can be divided into its unitary parts.[4] Obviously, by changing the technological system, the constituent techniques in a single unit flow can be varied and combined into more inclusive units, through the introduction of a conveyer, for example. Such changes are continually being made in business and require concurrent organizational changes to avoid creating management problems.

Sources of Stress in Organization

A unit work flow becomes segmented and its parts placed under different chains of command largely, although not necessarily entirely, as a result of the emphasis on functional specialization in organizational design. Sales and credit managers were both responsible for the order-processing flow in one company, and chaos resulted. In the second case, material handlers, maintenance employees, and the inspectors all had separate chains of command that conflicted with the management responsible for maintaining production. In the

[4]With the use of statistical techniques, it is possible to determine the homogeneity of the measurements within any unitary flow and to develop accurate criteria to test for discontinuities.

third illustration, the employment and training departments failed to coordinate the induction training procedure with the employment office functions. The true interrelationships among the processes, eventually merged under a single supervisor, had been disguised by artificial functional designations.

However, in one instance the problem was procedural not structural: the sequence within one group had not been thought through in terms of work flow. As a result, orders reached the credit checking clerks after they passed through earlier stages rather than at the beginning of the process which is more efficient.

Let us look more closely at the resulting organizational disturbances. In a situation requiring cooperative endeavors, whether it is a work group, employees and managers, or staff and line officials, each tries to develop a stable pattern of work, of interaction. When these stable patterns are disturbed, individuals experience stress or an uncomfortable feeling of pressure and dissatisfaction. A breakdown in the flow creates opposition as the individuals struggle to restore it. The expected responses from the individuals in the sequence prove inadequate, and new coordination problems arise. . . .

The regularities of actions and interactions disappear when this stress occurs, and erratic variation takes over. The difference is obvious between a smoothly running operation and one with a problem. Under stress, people react emotionally, and, because more than one individual is involved, the reactions usually conflict with each other. . . .

Thus, a vicious circle is established. Something happens in the work situation that causes the relationship of individuals to change or to depart from the normal pattern. This creates a stress, either of opposition or nonresponse, that is further complicated by higher levels of supervision and staff specialists whose unexpected interactions, i.e., outside the usual organization pattern, irritate the disturbed work-flow relations. People get upset; they become angry with each other and, depending on their individual characteristics, react temperamentally. These personality conflicts have direct ramifications in the work process because the emotional reactions change the pattern of contact and interaction. Joe is angry with Bill, so he does not check with him before starting a new experimental run. Consequently, a special test that should have been included in the run is left out, and the whole thing has to be done over. To complete the circle, these emotional disturbances damage the work-flow sequence, which causes additional personality stresses.

Robert Guest of the Yale Technology Project described this accurately when he said:

> *Foremen are always getting caught in this familiar vicious circle. Material inspection, say, has failed to spot some faulty pieces. Something goes wrong at a welding operation. The general foreman is on the foreman's neck to "get it straightened out, or else!" The foreman drops everything to spend time on this one item. He cannot pay attention to the man he was breaking in on a new job. He cannot check on the stock bin which the stock man forgot to replenish. He meant to warn an operator about a safety condition. He knew another man was down in the dumps about a personal problem. By the time he has cleared up the original trouble and*

satisfied the boss, something else has blown up and the general foreman is roaring down the aisle again. [5]

What produced these stresses and where do these changes come from? They are not directly interactional on the worker level. With rare exceptions, the work flow does not require a direct interactional contact between two contiguous persons as team operations do. That is, the upsets and bickerings are not caused by people who occupy adjacent positions in the flow process and place pressures on one another. In fact, orders could be put on the next desk or on a conveyer without any real contact. Material or parts in an assembly operation usually move from one operator to the next on a conveyer. But, they may also be brought and taken away by service personnel, just as a mail boy may move orders from one group to the next in the office. In these examples, the flow of work does not cause any direct interpersonal problems, [6] except that the action of one person depends on the action of his predecessor, causing him not to act and thus breaking the sequence. As Guest indicates, however, the initiating sources of stress are primarily fluctuations in the rate at which work flows through the supervisory unit. The critical variable is time. Production schedules require tight coordination; holdups must be avoided. If they occur, production suffers and the relationships of the supervisor to his workers and of the workers among themselves change as a consequence.

The objective of any organizational structure is to minimize the incidence of deviations from the established interaction patterns of the work process. The realistic administrator knows complete stability is a never-to-be-achieved utopia. Equipment will always break down; employees will always be absent; and changes in procedures will be introduced continuously. Work will not always come through on time, or when it does, the quality may be so poor the normal process time must be increased significantly. Rush orders or a flood of work may press upon his unit. Whatever the type of fluctuation, his interaction patterns have to change. He may have to spend more time with individual workers, supervisors in other departments, engineers, mechanics, maintenance men, or various persons in control positions, such as production planners or factory cost controllers, who occupy a place in the paper-work flow of which the line supervisor also is a part. And, as a result, less time is available to maintain other vital contacts.

Even if his unit flow is not complicated by other supervisors who directly affect him, the supervisor will still have coordination and timing problems in his own unit and in his relations with those who give him work and to whom he

---

[5] Robert H. Guest, "Of Time and the Foreman," *Personnel,* May, 1956, pp. 478-486.

[6] This contrasts with the usual conception of work-flow stress. Among the best known studies in this area is William F. Whyte's work in the restaurant industry. Whyte found stress was caused by the direct pressure emanating from interworker contacts. "Lower-status" runners placed pressure and thus disturbed "higher-status" kitchen personnel, and demanding customers upset the waitress who could not tolerate a high frequency of demands. (William F. Whyte, *Human Relations in the Restaurant Industry,* McGraw-Hill Book Company, Inc., New York, 1948, pp. 49-59, 104-128).

transmits it. The possibility of stress is much greater if he does not have control over the key individuals who work directly with his segment of the flow and cannot get a response from them when he needs it, as in the case of the maintenance mechanics, or if he must constantly gear his segment to the next one, as in the examples of the material handling and inspection.

This is the major point of the discussion. Although the dynamic organization will always experience changes that cause variations in the work-flow system, most of these can be dealt with effectively by the supervisor affected. But, his job becomes almost impossibly difficult if there is no semblance of stability.[7] If the parts of a unit work flow are distributed among several supervisors, the individual manager cannot hope to maintain any stability in internal relationships because erratic changes are introduced by individuals whose behavior he cannot control. Because these other supervisors are meeting different organizational needs, they do not and cannot adjust to the requirements of any single manager. Significant irregularities in the rate of flow and significant changes in the interaction of the individuals concerned indicate the existence of a point of organization stress.

In companies where such problems are common, informal working arrangements usually develop over the course of time. Assuming the individual supervisors get along, i.e., the frequency or intensity of stress is not too great or their personalities are not obviously incompatible, they frequently get together to plan the work and discuss their mutual problems. The objective is for each supervisor to create the least upset to the next group in the line. Unfortunately, it is almost impossible because the segmentation of the work flow makes informal arrangements vulnerable to unexpected changes emanating from higher up.

Higher Level Management Problems

Because people, not lines on a chart, are the major concern, the elimination of points of stress within the work flow should be the first consideration of organization design. This means the traditional functional classification must be abandoned and each job analyzed as a part of one or perhaps, as in the case of an executive, many work flows. Merely recognizing that "informal" organization exists and hoping that management will grant it equal importance to the "formal" structure will not solve the problems.

Studies of the informal organization discuss how people actually relate themselves to each other in the process of getting the work done. Thus, the pattern of relationships that evolve in completing the job is what some observers consider the uncontrolled or spontaneous aspect of the organization. The

[7]The degree to which the use of functional organization introduces stress and instability is cogently analyzed by James Worthy, Sears Roebuck and Co., in his paper, "Some Aspects of Organization Structure in Relation to Pressures on Company Decision-Making," in *Proceedings of Fifth Annual Meeting of the Industrial Relations Research Association* (ed. L. Reed Tripp), IRRA Publ. 10, 1953, pp. 69-79.

authors believe this aspect must be the objective of the consciously contrived organizational structure. The organization must be designed for people not in the hope that people will somehow fit into it.

Accordingly, the first step is to identify the unit work flows and set their boundaries, placing each one under a single supervisor. As stated previously, these work flows consist not only of the people through whom the material, paper, or person flows, but also all the individuals who help maintain the flow, the mechanics, service people, etc. All the factors required to get the work done should be concentrated under a single person with responsibility centered at the lowest managerial point, not at the highest, as in the examples where top management officials were constantly arbitrating interdepartmental disputes.

Span of Second-level Supervision

So far, a series of unit flows, each with its own supervisor, has been constructed. However, each still depends upon the other. Although the stress points within the unit work flows are eliminated by effective organizational design, areas of interdependence between these units necessarily remain. As noted above, the pace of the work generally shifts between unit work flows, there are different rhythms and sequences, and, as a result, the coordination problems are not as great, but there is still an obvious need to coordinate relationships. In the example, the application of quantitative criteria revealed that orders went to the warehouse or tabulating or material from a fabricating unit to assembly with a definable discontinuity. This indicates the need for at least one further level of supervision, a manager over the unit work-flow managers whose responsibility is to see that they are coordinated into a larger system.

Controls

Combining unit work flows into a work-flow system does not depend upon arbitrary assumptions as to the number of individuals such a manager can supervise. These factors are determined by analysis of the controls the manager has available to maintain the system, not by abstract formulas. Worthy pointed out that in the Sears organization a store manager may have thirty to forty department heads reporting to him.[8] This works not merely because the company does not want a manager spending too much time with any single department head but, more fundamentally, because the department store manager receives daily and weekly reports which are sufficient to tell him whether significant deviations are occurring in the ratio of stock (inventory) to sales, in markdowns, markups, etc. Consequently, he spends time with subordinates only in cases where managers are in trouble or where the reports suggest difficulties. As the theory of administrative controls is developed, similar control procedures can be adopted for any business operation. . . .

[8]William F. Whyte, *Modern Methods in Social Research,* prepared for the Office of Naval Research under Contract Nonr-401(2), pp. 25-28.

Many companies find it difficult to organize for effective operation because their reporting systems do not adequately pinpoint responsibility. Most administrative controls are by-products of accounting controls. They were developed for financial record keeping, not management control. Consequently, they are issued by the controller as financial documents and, although completely accurate, they are usually so late as to be matters of ancient history and too general because costs are both prorated and arbitrarily assigned. As such, these reports have little use as operating tools.[9] Thus the number of unit work-flow supervisors reporting to the second management level is a function of the state of development of the organization's controls: the measures which assess how things are going in the production process. Primarily, controls signal troubles at the points where two unit work flows come into contact. These juncture points are the potential stress areas that the second level manager oversees. Improvements in management reporting technology, particularly by the computer, will substantially increase the span of control at this management level.

The use of controls is based on the same criterion utilized in defining each of the unit work flows, the time coordinates of the system. The controls should indicate when the individual unit flows are intermeshing with one another. If they show homogeneity, in the statistical sense, in the interrelationships of the component units, the system is operating as planned. If the sequential movement of goods, paper, or people between units is stabilized, as reported through appropriate controls, the manager can relax. He must go into action when his controls show stressful situations are developing that require attention and action to avoid complete breakdowns in the system.

Assuming some ingenuity is shown in the development of controls, the number of unit supervisors within the flow is of little significance, because each unit is self-sufficient.

Handling the Staff-Line Relationships

What is to be done with specialists such as the chief mechanic, the chief inspector, the production planning manager, the training director, and the credit manager? As pointed out previously, the specialists are responsible for developing standards, the procedures to implement these standards, and auditing results. Although this was mentioned explicitly only in the case of the credit manager, each specialist also plays a part in one or more work flows, . . . The significance of the specialists' development and auditing is that they have been removed from direct work-flow decision. The chief mechanic, for example, does not directly or through the foremen decide on what machine the mechanic is to work. He is

[9]There is an increasing concern with what is called "management accounting." However, present practice indicates it has by no means reached its declared goal of defining organizational responsibility within an accounting framework. Too many costs are still allocated and prorated. True managerial accounting cannot be achieved without loosening the bonds placed in the way of organizational change by poor accounting logic.

responsible for the standards of mechanical repair, the program of preventive maintenance, and the evaluation of the mechanic's performance.

Thus, the unit work-flow supervisor and the chief mechanic have a dual responsibility for performance: the first, for the mechanic's contribution in maintaining the production flow, and the latter for the quality of his work. Both factors must be considered in evaluation and control. Otherwise, it is easy to overemphasize short-term gains in production at the cost of the long-run impact on the mechanical equipment.

Moreover, this shift in responsibility gives the specialist time to develop programs and to carry out his auditing responsibility. Otherwise, he is too busy with the day-to-day operating decisions to determine the source of the problems. Under the pressure of the immediate situation, his only interest would be to put the fire out; he would have little time to see what caused the problem in the first place.

However, the specialists need to be fitted into the organizational system. Because they are concerned with developing programs to expedite the work flow and eliminate stresses both within and between unit work flows that affect the total work-flow system, the specialists inevitably become the specialized assistants of the work-flow system manager. Their responsibility then is to act for him in their respective areas to improve the operation on the unit work-flow level. It is important to note the word "responsibility." In the usual sense of the word, specialists do not have staff responsibility with advisory or consultative relations to the line, nor do they have the responsibility of line supervisors, one step removed. They are actually *of* the staff of the manager and accountable to him for developing, installing, and auditing the result of programs in terms of the major objective of removing stress.

Conclusion: Work Flow and Organization Design

The type of organization design just described, based on the actual work flow within a technological and procedural framework, requires the complete use of time measurements as its basis. Not only is the delimitation of unit work flows dependent on the possession of quantitative criteria, but improvements of the technological process, in its broadest sense, require the examination of how each individual, whether worker, specialist, or supervisor, spends his time. The effective use of the method by any company depends also upon layout and location, the techniques by which paper, materials, or people are handled, and the controls used to signal real or impending deviations.

For example, if the record system is not or cannot be tied to individual responsibility, it is that much more difficult to locate points of stress and, in the absurd but common case, the supervisor may have to spend his time continually "on the floor" looking and listening because he does not routinely receive adequate information about his operation. The exception principle, one of the oldest in management, is useful in organizational planning only if the systems and procedures make its use possible.

The work-flow theory requires the specification of what each person does, when, where, with whom, how long, and how often. Therefore a type of job analysis or job description, to use a somewhat discredited term, is needed to outline the flows for each individual and to specify in quantitative measurements the duration of the action and interaction required to carry them out. . . . Any contact, whether it is a mechanic repairing a machine, a service boy bringing parts, or a set-up man making adjustments for a new run, involves some interaction, and the time involved is not simply a matter of the actual physical action.

Variations introduced by personality must also be considered within the organization design that results from the application of work-flow theory to any particular technological system. The supervisor who fails to act when stress is indicated in his control reports, waiting until someone calls it to his attention, hinders the operation of his unit work flow if it is set up on close time tolerances. Similarly, the manager who cannot spend the time with his staff specialists to see that preventive programs are developed and installed always faces stress within his area. In contrast, a staff specialist may find his development and audit responsibilities uncongenial in terms of his personality and, unconsciously, try to build a segregated work unit for himself, isolated from the people with whose performance he is concerned. The results of all of these are damaging to the work-flow system.

Personality and the reactions of the individual to specific types of stress limit both the construction of an organization to a given design and also its operation under the specifications. Fortunately, the same methods used to assess organization design also apply to the evaluation of individual personality and temperament. . . . Through measurements of interaction, it can be determined precisely how an individual adjusts to a given type of organizational position and its potentialities for stress. In this way, it is possible to offset shortcomings either by modifications on the job or by selecting assistants who complement the individual's abilities.

The purpose here has been to suggest criteria upon which to base the design of an organization: the structure must be built from the bottom up and it must be superimposed upon a known technology. In fact, technology, as defined earlier, should be the basis for the distribution and assignment of supervision. Supervisory jobs are largely products of the time coordinates of the production process, regardless of the kind of work the organization does.

Improving Patient Care through Organizational Changes in the Mental Hospital

This paper reports substantial changes made in the organizational structure of a 2,000-bed, state-supported mental hospital, mainly through the application of principles developed and tested in the industrial-sociological field. Although the larger goal of the program was the rehabilitation of chronic patients and the treatment of new patients so as to avoid chronicity, the authors found that their most important single operational approach was to improve the morale and change the basically custodial attitudes of the nursing staff. In a hospital such as the one sutdied here, where the ratio of patients to doctors is high, almost all contact of the hospital staff with patients takes place through the nursing staff. Thus, although the whole social structure of the hospital was in some measure changed, this paper is concerned specifically with the mechanics of changing the policy, the structure, and the function of the nursing hierarchy.

IMPROVING PATIENT CARE
THROUGH ORGANIZATIONAL CHANGES
IN THE MENTAL HOSPITAL

Elaine Cumming
Cornell University

I. L. W. Clancey
Saskatchewan Hospital

John Cumming
Cornell University

The authors of this paper, working as a team, undertook, with the support of the Hospital Superintendent,[1] the general task of designing and carrying out changes which would lead to improved patient care. One member of the team was a sociologist whose role included research and consultation. Another was Clinical Director of the hospital and thus had an executive role, and the third was a senior psychiatrist who had administrative, clinical, and research duties, and whose role on the team was a linking one.

At the beginning of our study, the hospital described in this paper, like many other large, state-supported mental hospitals, constituted a reasonably permanent social system. Its location in a geographically remote place, far from cities, gave it a striking "total community" quality. The social structure of its staff was granulated—that is, crosscut horizontally by caste lines, and vertically by the functional autonomy of its parts. The medical staff turnover was high, a

Reprinted by special permission of The William Alanson White Psychiatric Foundation, Inc., from E. Cumming, I. Clancey and J. Cumming, "Improving Patient Care through Organizational Changes in the Mental Hospital," *Psychiatry* (1956) 19:249-261. Copyright © 1956 by The William Alanson White Psychiatric Foundation, Inc.

Elaine Cumming, Department of Sociology and Anthropology, Cornell University, Ithaca, New York. I. L. W. Clancey, Saskatchewan Hospital, Weyburn, Saskatchewan. John Cummings, Department of Sociology and Anthropology, Cornell University, Ithaca, New York.

[1] Dr. Humphry Osmond.

few patients were treated with insulin and electric shock, and the patients on the "back wards" were "deteriorated."

On paper, the formal structure of the hospital staff was that of a modern bureaucracy; promotion was based upon specified standards of qualification and performance, jobs were described in terms of specific functions, and authority lines were clear-cut. But much of this was on paper only; informally, the hospital had many of the features of a paternalistic, traditional society, rather than a democratic, rational one. There were cliques of elite who exercised power which went far beyond their legitimate authority; this they could do because some members abrogated their authority through ignorance, error, or a desire to be relieved of it. As traditional ways of doing things were emphasized, once such authority was abrogated, it was difficult to return it to its legitimate holders. Since one group of legitimate authority holders, the doctors, were often not the people with the longest tenure in the hospital, tradition tended to support ways of doing things which resulted in the withholding of power from them. In consequence, informal groupings were very important, a fact expressed in phrases such as, "So-and-so *really* runs the place." No one knew how this had come to be; it was vaguely attributed to "political influence," or nepotism.

With this pattern of traditional ways of doing things, there was a devaluation of new ways, and a compensating ideology that "this is the best hospital in this part of the country." Obviously, innovations were not needed in a society which was already so satisfactory! In the higher reaches of the hierarchy, few regulations were committed to paper; rules, guiding principles, and even the personal records of the nurses[2] and attendants were filed in the memories of the senior staff members. This lore was passed from role-holder to role-holder by word of mouth. Rumors were the lifeblood of the institution because they were often the only way of receiving vital information.

In this hospital, like most institutions of its kind, there was seldom more than one doctor for every two hundred patients. This meant that although the doctor might influence the condition of the patients, he must do it through the nurses. But the doctor was often much less acquainted with the hospital and its lore than were the nurses. Furthermore, there was little interaction across the caste lines.[3] Because of this, and because of traditionalism, it became important to "know the ropes," seniority was valuable, and having "been through the mill" was a virtue. Young doctors attempting to make changes were discouraged by the repeated, "When you've been here as long as I have, Doctor . . . ," which they heard from senior ward staff. Traditional and static, such a mental hospital is hard to change, and especially hard for the doctor to change because he is always outnumbered and usually outmaneuvered.

These were not the only reasons why this mental hospital was hard to change; just as important was the low level of integration at which it operated. There was,

---

[2] The word *nurse* in this paper refers to psychiatric nurses trained in mental hospitals, not to registered nurses.

[3] See in this connection: Edwin M. Lemert, *Social Pathology;* New York. McGraw-Hill, 1951; p. 417. Howard Roland, "Friendship Patterns in the State Mental Hospital," Psychiatry (1939) 2:363-373.

in other words, a high level of functional autonomy in the various hospital departments regarding both goals and methods of reaching them. For example, the farm had its traditional patterns of using patient labor in order to reach its goal of food production, while the wards had different goals and patterns of reaching them. The members of these two systems seldom interacted except in the ritualistic handing over of patients in the morning and evening. Thus the policies and procedures throughout the hospital were not closely integrated, and there was little chance of effecting change by reorganizing one part of the greater social system and waiting for the other parts to fall in line, through a necessary adaptive process. If, for example, the occupational therapy department changed its daily routine, all that would happen would be that a few patients affected by the change would stop attending O.T. sessions, and slowly a few would replace them. There would be no corresponding shift in the routines of other departments, no planned adaptive process.

Autonomy was strikingly evident between the "male side" and the "female side." For instance, during the early part of our reorganization, when some fifty female patients from a chronic ward were allowed to go out unaccompanied for the first time, the resulting incidents caused rather dramatic reactions on the part of the townfolk; but the staff on the male side did not know until these incidents had been reported in the press that the female side had even contemplated such a program.

The level of communication between departments was low because there was little need of much communication as long as the hospital functioned mainly custodially. The resulting type of integration was the "mechanical solidarity" of Durkheim;[4] that is, the hospital organization hung together because all were concerned ultimately in the custody of the patients; it was a common task, undertaken for a common goal to earn a living. There was, on the other hand, a low level of the interdependence, or "organic solidarity," which arises from a greater division of labor. Because each person or unit did a more or less complete task—either ran a ward, or administered a portion of the hospital—people were not forced to communicate and to integrate their activities. In our hospital we lacked that specialization which, as Durkheim says, "creates among men an entire system of rights and duties which link them together in a durable way ... and gives rise to rules which assure pacific and regular concourse of divided functions." Such integration as existed in the hospital was brought about high in the hierarchy; at the ward level no decisions were made which might affect general policy; thus a minimum was done, for nothing could be done without decisions.[5] Therefore changing the hospital entailed raising the level of integration of the system.

In general, our hospital was neither better nor worse than most. Many

[4] Emile Durkheim, *The Division of Labor in Society;* Glencoe, The Free Press, 1947; see especially pp. 396-409.

[5] See, in this connection, C. I. Barnard, *The Functions of the Executive;* Cambridge, Harvard Univ. Press, 1938.

hospitals such as ours have wrestled with the problem of improving the condition of their chronic wards, lifting the level of their treatment programs, and changing staff attitudes. We propose here to describe some of the techniques which we employed, we believe successfully, in our attempt.

Our goal was to integrate the system so that a new "therapeutic" policy could be introduced to displace the older "custodial" one. The meaning we assigned to these terms is a little different from that used by other workers. Briefly, we designated those attitudes as custodial which centered in the conviction that most mental illness, particularly schizophrenia, is incurable. We called those attitudes therapeutic which centered in the assumption that *most mental illness, and particularly schizophrenia, are, like rheumatoid arthritis, chronic, recurrent disorders for which there is no known cure, but which can be so treated as to allow the patients long periods of remission.* Two secondary assumptions we felt necessary for a therapeutic attitude were, first, that mentally ill patients require a high level of interaction with other patients and with staff members in order to improve; and, second, that in almost every case, life in the community is preferable to life in a state mental hospital. The small number of doctors made a goal of personality transformation untenable; our last assumption implied that in our hospital a "social recovery" would be the goal choice for most patients.

Two Earlier Attempts at Change

As with most "reforms," we stood upon the shoulders of others. Our first step was to examine past attempts at change in the hospital under study. Of these, two were outstanding, although neither had been entirely successful.

The Nurses' Training Program

The first of these attempts at change had been a new nursing training program, which had been introduced seven years before our study. This program was designed to introduce more modern and humane attitudes, and to raise the prestige of the psychiatric nurse. It has been fully described by McKerracher,[6] and, as is evident from his description, it was an excellent program. However, by the time of our study the new training staff had in fact failed to gain access to the wards for teaching purposes, and the most frequent complaint we heard from the training staff was, "We train the new nurses, but after a while the ward culture gets them; the old-line staff ridicule them if they use our ideas, and they are gradually broken down." Thus the training program was, in its effect, encapsulated and academic, and did not seem to have much impact upon the

---

[6]D. G. McKerracher, "A New Program in the Training and Employment of Ward Personnel," *American Journal of Psychiatry* (1949), 106:259-264.

custodial quality of the hospital. It was said, on the other hand, to have raised the standard of physical nursing care, and through its affiliation with the Provincial University, it did raise the prestige of the nursing group.

We tried to find the answer to the vital questions, Why did the program fail to change the ward culture? Why did not the old-line staff learn at least as much from the new trainees as they taught them? We found three main answers. First, the failure to change the ward culture could be attributed to the failure to introduce structural changes in the social system so as to raise the level of integration of the hospital. We know from many sources[7] that values, beliefs, and attitudes—that is, norms—are changed, as they are made, in interaction. This is as true for the work group as for the friendship group or the family group. As Brown says, "The primary group is the instrument of society through which in large measure the individual acquires his attitudes, opinions, goals, and ideals; it is also one of the fundamental sources of discipline and social controls.[8]

If this is true, in a granulated system where the rate of interaction is low, one must either raise the level of integration and hence of interaction of the total system, or else arrange for persistent interaction between members at all parts of the system, thus changing each semiautonomous part separately. Clearly, the latter approach would require a tremendous number of training staff members. The training staff, in fact, interacted only with student nurses, who not only were at the bottom of the nursing hierarchy, but were also unable to support one another on the wards because they were spread out over the hospital. This failure to integrate the granulated social structure acted against the new training course.

The second reason for the failure of the program lay with the failure of its designers to recognize the importance of seniority in the static hospital society.[9] They had by-passed numerous senior ward supervisors by promoting two capable but junior staff members to high-ranking training positions, on the basis of their attitudes and orientation. At the same time they made the training staff independent of the nursing hierarchy and responsible, under a director trained in pedagogy rather than nursing, directly to the Medical Superintendent.

As we have said before, little is written down in a large mental hospital; what is actually expected of a ward supervisor, beyond a minimal list of duties, is never recorded. If the principle of seniority is violated in making promotions, it throws great doubt into the minds of the old-line staff as to their own status. They have no way of knowing whether or not they are performing well enough to be promoted.

---

[7] See, J. A. C. Brown, *The Social Psychology of Industry;* Harmondsworth, Middlesex, Penguin Books. 1954. See also: Kurt Lewin, "Group Decision and Social Change"; in *Readings in Social Psychology,* edited by Guy E. Swanson, Theodore M. Newcomb, and Eugene L. Hartley: New York, Henry Holt, 1952. George Homans, *The Human Group;* New York, Harcourt, Brace, 1948.

[8] Reference footnote 7.

[9] Questioning revealed that no old-line supervisor could remember a doctor or training staff member ever asking his opinion on the grounds that the *long tenure alone* made his a valuable opinion.

Moreover, just as the designers of the training program had not reckoned with the meaning of seniority, so they overlooked the earlier and somewhat less adequate training program, unrecognized by the University, in which the old-line staff had been trained. There was a tendency to refer to "before the training course," and to think of the old-line staff as "untrained." In fact, most employees who had been in the hospital only two or three years were unaware that there had been an "old training course." While the old-line employees were given honorary membership in the new nursing organization, their traditional training was not incorporated into the new program. It was to be new, and it failed by being too new.

A third error lay in the violation of the principle that the most highly chosen people are most likely to be the norm-bearers.[10] The two men chosen from the nursing ranks to join the training staff were both *deviant by definition,* for they were selected as being the *least custodial* people in a custodial institution. The old-line supervisors had reason to be adamant in the face of this innovation; one of the problems which faces all mental hospitals is the performance of the function of "protection of the public" without slipping into custodialism.[11] Medical men do not like being charged with the duty of "protecting the public," for it runs counter to their perception of themselves as therapists. Yet this function must be performed and the doctor must, by giving certain orders about the patients' daily routines, take his part in performing it. But he is in conflict, and one of his resolutions of this conflict is to exaggerate the "custodialism" of the nursing hierarchy. Many times we have heard a physician complain of "nursing office" attitudes and how they cripple his attempts to give the patients maximum freedom. We believe that our senior nursing staff members had been assigned the mantle of custodialism, and that they had no way of refusing it. Furthermore, the old-line nurse had certain compensations. *In effect* he had made an even trade with the doctors; he had tacitly agreed to wear the mantle of custodialism in return for the power to run the custodial wards himself, in his own way, and with a minimum of interference. In spite of this, when we interviewed senior ward supervisors we found that their reference point for advice and guidance in the care of patients tended to be the medical staff and not the custodially oriented head nursing offices, as had been generally supposed. They had, in short, latent therapeutic attitudes, never called into play.

When all of the foregoing factors are considered, it is not surprising that the efforts of the recently promoted training staff members to teach on the wards were blocked by the old-line people over whose heads they had been promoted. On the other hand, the training program undoubtedly did a good deal of useful work, both in teaching nursing techniques, especially of the concrete, physical sort, and in constantly reminding the students of a more ideal sort of psychiatric nursing care than they were seeing on the wards.

[10]For a discussion of this point, see, for instance, William Foote Whyte, "Corner Boys: A Study of Clique Behavior," *Amer. J. Sociol.* (1941) 46:647-664.

[11]This problem is discussed by Alfred H. Stanton and Morris S. Schwartz in *The Mental Hospital;* New York, Basic Books, 1954.

A second and quite different attempt at change had been undertaken four years before by an enterprising and energetic team of two doctors.[12] They had demonstrated on a treatment ward that deteriorated and incontinent schizophrenic patients would show social improvement if they were placed in an improved social environment, *no matter whether they had physical treatment or not.* This demonstration, though strikingly successful, was not followed by any sustained attempt to improve the status of deteriorated patients in the hospital; and indeed it had been intended only as a demonstration. Our assumption is that one cannot create *permanent* changes in attitudes, values, and behavior by such an example, no matter how good, because there seems little doubt that values and beliefs are changed *in interaction,* and only a small proportion of the staff members had a chance to interact in the improved situation. Further, the structure of the organization which had been serving the purposes of the old values was literally unchanged. As soon as the tremendous energy of the two doctors was removed, the old situation reappeared. Thus, some of the staff said cynically, "What is the use of improving the patients' condition, if it is inevitable that they revert to a deteriorated state?" Yet there was an important residue of change in the personal outlook of a few staff members, who hoped that this sort of improvement could some day be made permanent throughout the hospital. This small group of nurses represented a strain in the nursing ranks, for they had a constant latent role conflict. They knew that as nurses they could be doing better, but they did not know how, and their membership in the staff group kept them from voicing this belief very often. But had it not been for them, our task would have been much more difficult. Our predecessors had demonstrated that change was possible, and although they were unable to interact with sufficient people to change the culture of the total group, they had overcome an immense hurdle by convincing a certain number of the old-line staff that something could be done.

Recapitulating, we found that we had before us the task of raising the level of integration of the formal structure, and of providing a high level of interaction with staff members so as to succeed in motivating them to adopt more therapeutic attitudes.

The Structural Change

So far, while we have tried to describe the general characteristics of the hospital, we have touched only peripherally on its structure. At this point, a brief but more specific description of the old structure will help evaluate the new one. Our hospital, like many others, had two separate nursing hierarchies,

[12]This program has been described by Derek H. Miller and John Clancey in "An Approach to the Social Rehabilitation of Chronic Psychotic Patients," *Psychiatry* (1952) 15:435-443.

one for the male side and one for the female side, each headed by a chief nursing officer.[13] One of the main characteristics of the nursing structure was a lack of coordination between these two services. In theory, both were responsbile to a Superintendent of Nursing, but in practice this post was often empty. Even when it was filled—always by a woman, since the post required general hospital training as well as psychiatric nursing training—there was never an effective coordination of the two nursing services; in actual fact, the role-holder tended to do the job of the chief nursing officer on the female side, while the holder of this role did the job of her deputy.

The two chief nursing officers were responsible directly to the Medical Superintendent, and a system of daily reporting kept a routine communication going between them. Actually the nursing services had been run by their chief offices almost without interference through the years. Since promotion to positions in these offices was based almost exclusively on seniority, the role-holders, on the male side of the hospital especially, were people who had been trained in those custodial principles of mental hospital care which existed when they had first joined the hospital staff.

While the two chief nursing offices were the fulcrum of the medical side of the hospital, beyond this very little was laid down regarding proper lines of communication. Therefore, entrenched informal groupings tended to control the flow of information. These offices often received information directly when it should have come through ward supervisors, and they often withheld information which should have been distributed to the ward staffs. This, of course, greatly enhanced the power of the chief nursing offices, as the control over communication must always do.[14]

Another major characteristic of the old structure was the limited authority of the doctors. The doctors on both sides were responsible to the Clinical Director and hence to the Medical Superintendent, but no one was responsible directly to the doctors. Ward staff had, of course, to obey medical orders from the doctors, but in all other matters their final authority was their chief nursing office. Differences of opinion between doctors and one or the other of these chief nursing offices were resolved by the Medical Superintendent usually in favor of the nursing hierarchy, for doctors were, by and large, expendable, but the good will of the nursing hierarchy was not. The doctors, themselves, furthermore, did not wish the responsibility for running the wards which authority over the staff would entail.[15]

One of the outstanding aspects of the structure of the nursing service was the small size of the executive echelon, which consisted of the two chief nursing officers, a deputy for each, and three administrative asssitants on the male side, and two on the female side. Considering that there are nearly 2,000 patients and

[13]The chief nursing officer on the male side was called the Chief Attendant, and on the female side the Head Nurse, titles which were dispensed with in our reorganization.

[14]Reference footnote 11.

[15]This will be discussed further in a forthcoming article in *Psychiatry*.

a nursing staff of about 350, the nursing executive echelon was large enough for only the most routine daily administrative duties. This, together with an almost total absence of meetings with staff, and the lack of formal job specifications, practically guaranteed that the minimum would be done, and that integration would be low.[16]

All socio-structural change in our hospital were timed to take place on one day. Just prior to this, meetings were held with various staff groups, and formal announcements were made of the new social structure within which they had to work. We did this not because we felt that they would absorb the information particularly well, but to put the formal intention of the highest hospital authorities before the total staff. This move had a latent purpose, preventing rumors about the change. In a sense it was a rite of passage: the formal announcement of a new status for the hospital.

The New Executive Echelon

Our first move was to expand the executive echelon by creating ten new "coordinating" roles in the nursing hierarchy. Two of these were at the Deputy Nursing Officer level, and the remainder at the Assistant Nursing Officer level. The general purpose was a double one—to increase the efficiency and improve the quality of the nursing service and to integrate ward activities. The number selected was small enough for intensive interaction with the medical doctors in discussions and meetings, yet large enough to meet with the ward staffs sufficiently often to have an appreciable effect upon their attitudes and beliefs—that is, to change their norms. In this way, the new therapeutic approach could be spread out fan-wise through the hospital.

Amont their specific duties, these new officers were charged with the job of total hospital planning for the ancillary services, such as recreational and occupational therapies, and of securing the cooperation of the people engaged in these services. Since the development of the special therapeutic departments had been slight, there were no entrenched positions to consider in placing the new Nursing Officers in a coordinating role with respect to them.

Furthermore, the simple matter of getting things and getting things done fell within the scope of these new roles—the kinds of activity necessary in a large bureaucracy for procuring needed equipment and material. Hitherto the nursing hierarchy had been too weakly staffed at the executive level to spend any time on such matters, especially if anything the least bit out of the ordinary was required. For instance, the doctors who had run the total-push ward had experienced great difficulty in getting wood for carpentry activities; since

[16]The relationship of the nursing service to the business hierarchy will be discussed in a forthcoming article in *Psychiatry*. We should like to mention here only that the tradesmen who attended to the maintenance of the hospital were on strained terms with the ward staffs. Without going into detail, we can say that this was another evidence of the low level of integration of the hospital structure. The tradesmen thought the nursing staff irrationally demanding; the latter considered the tradesmen to be arbitrary and withholding in their approach to ward needs.

carpentry had not been done on the ward before, obtaining the materials was a major operation.

The new roles, then, in their acting out, were to provide a more efficient, integrated, and therapeutic nursing service, and the medical staff could use the nursing structure to introduce their own attitudes right down to the ward level.

The New Formal Lines of Authority Communication

As a second step, we laid down firm lines of communication and announced that for the time being protocol would in all cases be observed. We did not want people to fall back into their old patterns of informal communication, which would be bound to short-circuit some of the new role-holders, especially as most of these people had only recently been subordinate to the chief nursing offices. Furthermore, although we were prepared to allow some informal channels to develop, we were determined that this should not happen until the proper channels were institutionalized enough so that every time any person used an informal channel he would be perfectly well aware he was doing it. If vital information was withheld or misdirected, formal sanctions could be employed against the act. Sanctions had, in fact, to be used in this regard on several occasions.

The Training Office

A drastic change was made in the authority position of the Training Office. It had stood outside the nursing hierarchy, and the old-line nurses in the chief nursing offices had had no power to discipline the training staff, who in turn had no power to force their program upon the nursing hierarchy. The result was an almost inevitable stalemate, and encapsulation. Nursing training was restored to the Nursing Service under a well-qualified Nursing Officer. The creation of a Personnel Department to perform a previous function of the training staff informally allowed some members of the training staff to remain outside the nursing hierarchy, but the training staff—itself long insulated from the nursing service—once again became an integral part of it.

This step not only greatly facilitated the use of ward staff for practical training purposes, but also was designed to break up the granulation of the structure and to bring the training staff, with its therapeutic orientation, into close contact with the ward staffs. At the time of writing, the process of institutionalization is incomplete, and the training staff and personnel staff informally appear to consider themselves unitary.

Authority of the Medical Staff

A final change in lines of authority gave the doctors authority over the new Nursing Officers in charge of coordinating therapeutic activities. In administrative matters these Nursing Officers were still responsible to the Superintendent of Nursing, and therefore formal regulations regarding communication with the Nursing Office were introduced. It was important not to have over-lapping areas in the divided authority;[17] moreover, until the responsibilities of the new officers to the Nursing Office were institutionalized, we felt that they might be tempted to communicate solely with the medical staff, who were, after all, in charge of the more interesting of the activities required by their roles.

Integration of the Two Sides

Getting the hospital to operate as one institution was the biggest single under-taking. After all, it had run along fairly comfortably for years without much contact between the two sides. It is true that some female nurses had been nursing on the male side, but only because of the inability of the hospital to recruit male staff in sufficient numbers, and not because anyone had planned it as a desirable thing.

The first step we took in this direction was to place the two chief nursing officers together with all the new appointees and the Training Office staff, in new common quarters.[18] Previously, they had been separately housed on their own sides, but now they were in the administration wing of the building together, on neutral ground.

Since the choice of people to fill the new coordinating positions was very important to hospital integration, we will digress here to discuss the selection process. The new appointees had to be able to work with both male and female patients if necessary—not an easy task for some; they must be amenable to the therapeutic approach, although we did not feel that they had to be already enthusiastic about it; and finally, they had to be acceptable to the nurses with whom they would have to work.

With these considerations in mind, we took advantage of the waiting period, while the new posts were being formally approved through bureaucratic channels, to conduct a campaign of anticipation. The following examples of the preliminary work are taken from the male side, because, while that term is fast becoming less meaningful in our hospital, two of us[19] were working closely with the male staff at the time of the reorganization.

A meeting of all the ward supervisors was called; the new jobs, of which six were to be filled by men, were described to them and they were asked to fill out sociometric ballots indicating which male staff members they thought should be promoted to these new positions, as well as to two administrative nursing posts which happened to be vacant. Although the voting did not follow rigid seniority lines, all of the eight men who received *almost all* of the votes were among the

[17]This problem has been discussed by Jules Henry in "The Formal Social Structure of a Psychiatric Hospital," *Psychiatry* (1954) 17:139-151.

[18]This move was suggested to us by Dr. Robert Hyde, Assistant Superintendent, Boston Psychopathic Hospital.

[19]John Cumming and Elaine Cumming.

fifteen most senior male staff members in the hospital. (Five of the remaining seven men were within a year or two of retirement and had expressed their disinclination for promotion to the new jobs.) Thus only two of the most senior old-line men were considered inappropriate for the new therapeutic positions by their peers.

When we examined this list of highly chosen men, we found it to coincide exactly with our own list of the senior men most able to do a good job. Although we knew that there were some exceptionally good young men of less seniority, we had decided that the following three principles were too important to violate:

(1) Norm-bearers—those who most clearly express the attitudes and beliefs of a group—are highly chosen. New programs, to be accepted, should be introduced by norm-bearers rather than by deviants.

(2) In a stable system, when all else is equal, seniority is the fairest criterion for promotion.

(3) Very few roles in any society should be structured so that only exceptional people can hold them, since most people are unexceptional.[20]

The next step in anticipatory socialization was to assign special tasks to these highly chosen men in order to orient them to the type of problem with which they would be dealing when they were formally appointed. From among the chosen men, several small committees were set up to study ward procedures such as the condemning of old clothing and the requisitioning of new, in order to recommend how these procedures could be changed so as to maximize patient welfare. A committee drafted a plan for the reorganization of a geriatrics ward, and a key man was assigned the task of preparing a weekly bulletin to keep all branches of the hospital informed of any news which might otherwise circulate only by rumor.

These activities proceeded while the men still held their old roles. Although they were never asked to work overtime, they put in many evening hours.[21] Although we asked our staff to work hard at specific jobs for specific purposes during this period, and although we expected them to orient themselves to the welfare of the patient, it was through activity, not through formal teaching of any special attitude, that we hoped that a common sentiment of involvement in therapeutic goals would emerge. These planning committees reported to us, and in these reports we were able to discern a good deal of the "ward culture." In this way we knew which of our planned changes would be immediately acceptable, which might be acceptable eventually, and which would be intolerable to this group of men.

[20]This point is discussed by Ralph Linton in *The Study of Man;* New York, Appleton-Century, 1936; see Chapter 8, "Status and Role."

[21]We tried to avoid the pitfall of assuming that nursing is an avocation and that we were justified in asking more than a day's work for a day's pay.

During this anticipatory period we made a great many informal contacts among the staff. A lot of our effort was spent in persuading the "old guard" that things *could* be done. A great deal of their skepticism about improving the hospital was founded upon their own experience in attempting minor enterprises of their own. The low level of integration of the structure had convinced them, for example, that it was impossible to get the cooperation of the tinsmith to repair the lockers. Unless they could be fixed, how could the men be expected to care for their clothes? There was a tendency to some defeatist grumbling about past frustrations, even among the new appointees. A certain amount of "charisma" was needed at this stage, as well as demonstrations that the re-organizing team meant business.

All of the above-mentioned activity took place before the new appointments were made. By the time we made them, we had a fairly good idea of the kind of people we were dealing with and the kind of job we could expect them to do. The restructuring of the nursing hierarchy followed.

Besides the establishment of the new executive positions, two main changes were made in the interests of a closer integration of the two sides. The three top nursing roles, the Superintendent of Nursing—long unfilled, at this time—and the two chief nursing officers were consolidated into two posts, the Superintendent of Nursing, and her Deputy. It was stipulated that if the Superintendent were a woman, the Deputy would be a man, and vice versa, and that one of them must have a general nursing training. These two role-holders were made jointly responsible for nursing services, and charged with the duty of unifying these services across the two sides of the hospital.

At the same time, it was announced that applicants for the Ward Supervisors' posts, made vacant by promotion to the new positions, would be received from both male and female nurses for both sides of the hospital. This broke cleanly with tradition. Men went for the first time into supervisors' posts on the female side of the hospital, because many male staff members had a great deal more seniority than any female members.[22]

Neither the sick rate nor the resignation rate among the women changed in the months following the introduction of this practice. There were undoubtedly certain advantages to the women nurses in working on teams which also included men, for certain work on the wards is more easily done by men because they are stronger, and certain work is more appropriately done by men because of the difference in male and female roles in this society. We predicted that the women would appreciate a division of labor along these male and female role lines, and we have informal evidence that they did; for instance, nurses have commented that they are less exhausted, are less afraid on certain wards, and so on. These compensations appear to offset the dissatisfaction resulting from the women's reduced chances of promotion.

---

[22]This had resulted from the higher turnover among the female staff; approximately three years seniority had been needed before promotion to the supervisor post on the female side, and fifteen years on the male. However, the trend is toward a greater proportion of women, and while the supervisors' posts will be overweighted with men in the near future, almost all senior posts will eventually belong to women, if this trend continues.

Division of Labor by Function

As we have said before, the lack of integration in the hospital was partly a result of the low level of functional specialization. As an example of the increased division of labor at the executive level, we consolidated the booking procedures—that is, the assignment of nurses to wards and shifts—into the hands of one staff member. Previously each side had done its own booking and each had operated on the basis of a different set of principles. Now one person, in consultation with the Deputy Nursing Officer in charge of training and the Superintendent of Nursing, was assigned this task for the whole hospital.

On the same principle, two large male wards were consolidated for the purpose of administration. One supervisor was put in charge of administration and two shared the responsibility for the therapeutic program. This division of labor forced communication and coordination across these two wards, with a rise in efficiency. Such administrative roles seemed an important safety valve for certain senior staff members, whose old, military-like indoctrination into mental hospital procedures made them uncomfortable in the new "therapeutic" situation.

The Changes in Attitudes

Interaction and Communication

The importance of changing norms and values through interaction, and of appointing norm-bearers to key positions, which we have mentioned in describing the structural changes, cannot be emphasized too strongly. The impossibility of changing norms in a didactic fashion is aptly illustrated by an unsolicited comment from a Training Office staff member, now attached to the Personnel Office: "All my stereotypes of the old, custodial ward supervisors have gone down the drain." He went on to say, "I see people going around doing all sorts of things that we've been trying to talk them into for years."

An important element in our program was the committee work we have described, which is now being continued in other committees all over the hospital. When a change was considered we tried to ask a committee to find the most therapeutic way of doing it. We did not ask our staff to have good attitudes toward the patients; we assigned them the job of finding out which of several alternatives would most favorably influence the patients. A by-product of this technique was the delegation of the decision-making function to the executive nursing echelon. These people had never in the past had to assume the responsibility for making decisions about changes, and a feeling of increased status and involvement resulted. They became identified through this program of action with the goals of the medical staff, and with the remembered goals of the two doctors who had engineered the total-push ward.

A second by-product of our technique was a high level of communication of vital information where it was needed. Not only did the nursing executive echelon meet together and establish therapeutic norms in interaction, but they also started meeting with groups of ward nurses. Their discussions were focused on the relationship of the new jobs to the starting of therapeutic activities. Thus for the first time, the problems generated on the ward were discussed on the ward, and were passed on for discussion, coordination, and action at the top of the nursing hierarchy.

To coordinate these nursing activities with medical and clinical activities, policy-making committees were formed, composed of the Clinical Director, two Senior Psychiatrists, the Superintendent of Nursing, her Deputy, and, when applicable, the Deputy Nursing Officer in charge of training.

The Didactic Program

Since many of our older nurses were unfamiliar with the content of modern psychological theory, a series of evening lectures was offered, and morning meetings were held to review papers, discuss problems, and evaluate changes. Didactic material included principles of psycho-dynamic psychiatry, but the emphasis was on social dynamics and interaction patterns. The social process on the wards was the focus.

In the meantime, one of us[23] started a group therapy training seminar with the new Nursing Officers, and each of these in turn started one group therapy program among the admission ward patients, and one among chronic ward patients. Thus, through the manipulation of the interaction pattern in our hospital, we were able to make the new nursing program very shortly reach the patients.

The Effects of the Changes

The success of the techniques we have described must be measured by the results, as indicated by better staff morale and improved patient care. For both of these there are accepted indices, but since the change is very recent these cannot yet be reported on.[24] Some immediate signs of success are discernible, however. We had expected that there might be a temporary recession in morale as a result of the dislocation of old patterns, but sickness and absenteeism rates,

[23]John Cumming.

[24]Since this paper was written, more specific information has become available. Against a steadily rising admissions rate, there has been a slow but steady decline in hospital population. For 1954, the total admissions were 533, while the hospital population on December 31 of that year was 1,880. For 1955, total admissions were 683, while the hospital population on December 31 was 1,809. By June 19, 1956, the population had further decreased to 1,790.

While there have also been dramatic decreases in the use of isolation, restraint, and electroconvulsive therapy to control behavior, clear-cut conclusions are complicated by the fact that the tranquilizing drugs have come into use during the period under study. The use of these drugs does not, however, appear to be a factor in the decrease of hospital population; the initial drop occurred well before the use of any of these drugs, and, so far as we are able to determine, the later discharges of patients have not been attributable to these drugs.

staff resignations, and the frequency of secluding and restraining patients have remained stable. This encourages us to believe that not only have we avoided arousing the antagonism of the old-line staff but have perhaps aroused in them latent therapeutic attitudes which have in turn provided them sufficient satisfaction to compensate for the dislocation of their accepted ways of doing things.

This impression is strengthened by spontaneous revolt among the male nursing staff against the entrenched practice of using them to relieve shortages in the cleaning and servicing departments. They actively demanded relief from the non-nursing chores which they had always done, such as carting mattresses to and from the upholsterer. They complained that they were being hampered in their rehabilitative and nursing efforts by routine jobs of cleaning, sanitation, and maintenance which could in no way be considered therapeutic.

Evidence of increased integration of goals has appeared in increased cooperation between departments. For example, the Maintenance Department, through a spokesman, has suggested that some of their patient-laborers should be placed under the supervision of the nursing staff in order that these patients might have planned therapeutic occupations.

Increased patient activity, both in occupations and in recreation, is evident. We estimate an increase to date of twenty-five percent in the number of chronic patients who are occupied rather than idle. All admission ward patients and many chronic ward patients are in group therapy. The significant point is that this raised level of activity comes from the initiative, planning, and action of the nursing staff. We believe that we have succeeded in some measure in creating a hospital less dependent for its therapeutic activities upon the initiative of the doctors, who are so few and so much less permanent in tenure than the nurses.

There have been some unexpected and negative consequences of the change which are at present being worked out. On the female wards three of the four new male supervisors were well accepted, but the fourth man was rejected in a curious way. He was cut off from ward activities by the female staff and forced into an inactive role of making out charts in the office. After complaining for some-time about it, he "went off sick" and remained so for a long period.

Another problem arose when a small group of men from the old chief nursing office suffered serious loss of status relative to the new members of the executive echelon. Their complaints were of "increased work," although there was no objective reason for this complaint. They had, however, inadvertently been put in the position of working more evening and night shifts than they had done before the reorganization; and not having to do shift work is an important sign of status in any organization which works around the clock.

In many ways, our task is far from completed; for instance, the training staff are only formally attached to the nursing program, and their functional attachment awaits the restatement of training goals and the changes in function which this will imply. There are, moreover, general signs of a tendency to slip back into old patterns; perhaps the most outstanding of these is the occasional automatic response of a nurse to a doctor: "I agree, Doctor, but the ward staff don't have time for that." This is the phrase which for years was used to maintain the *status quo* in the face of the attacks of interfering newcomers; it usually has little to do with time, and expresses mainly desire to resist. On the other hand, we have much evidence that most nurses are more involved in their work than they ever were before, and we have confidence that the hospital can never quite return, under the worst of circumstances, to where it was before.

In general, we worked with our nursing group as we would have with any other staff of workers, assuming that they would do a better job in the interests of our new therapeutic approach if they felt a sense of involvement in our goals and if their statuses were not called into question by the reorganization. Changing the attitudes and values of the staff was accomplished, as such changes are always accomplished, by interacting with norm-bearers in primary groups. We believe that our efforts have resulted in higher morale, in much improved patient care, and in a fundamental change in the basically pessimistic "custodialism" of the nursing staff.

The Experimental Change of a Major Organizational Variable

This now classic field experiment examines the effect of modifications in the organizational decision-making system upon job satisfaction and productivity. Both job satisfaction and productivity increased *for the work groups in the two divisions where the decision-making power was pushed down to the rank-and-file workers (the Autonomy program). Job satisfaction* decreased *and productivity* increased *for the work groups in the two divisions where the decision-making power was centralized in the hands of upper management (the Hierarchically controlled program).*

Although the reasons for the increase in productivity in both situations are rather complex, they are adequately explained by the authors. The most striking point in this study is the significant difference between the centralized and decentralized units relative to job satisfaction. Changing the formal authority structure of an organization in terms of the locus of decision making seems to be a potent device for altering the attitudes and behavior of its members.

THE EXPERIMENTAL CHANGE
OF A MAJOR
ORGANIZATIONAL VARIABLE[1]

Nancy C. Morse
The Merrill-Palmer School

Everett Reimer
Office of Personnel, Commonwealth of Puerto Rico

This experiment is one in a series of studies of social behavior in large-scale organizations undertaken by the Human Relations Program of the Survey Research Center. Its primary aim is to investigate the relationship between the allocation of decision-making processes in a large hierarchical organization and

[1] This is a short description of an experiment done while the authors were on staff of the Human Relations Program of the Survey Research Center, University of Michigan. Financial support for field work and analysis of the data came from the Rockefeller Foundation, the Office of Naval Research Contract No. N6 onr-232 Task Order II, and the company in which the research was done. In addition to the authors the field staff of the experiment included: Arnold Tannenbaum, Frances Fielder, Gilbert David, Arlene Kohn Gilbert, Barbara Snell Dohrenwend, Ann Seidman, Jean Kraus Davison, and Winifred Libbon. The analysis staff included: Nancy Morse, Arnold Tannenbaum, Arlene Kohn Gilbert, and Ruth Griggs. The experiment will be described fully in a book now in preparation. Floyd H. Allport provided extensive assistance on the theoretical problems of the study. The experiment was under the general direction of Daniel Katz, director of the Human Relations Program during the field phase of the experiment, and Robert Kahn, director of the Human Relations Program during the analysis phase. The authors wish to express their appreciation to the staff members on the experiment and to the people in the company who cooperated in the experiment. They also want to thank particularly Daniel Katz, Robert Kahn, Arnold Tannenbaum, Carol Kaye, and Jane Williams for their helpful comments and criticisms of this article.

(*a*) the individual satisfactions of the members of the organization, (*b*) the productivity of the organization.

The results of several previous studies suggested that the individual's role in decision-making might affect his satisfaction and productivity. The effectiveness of decision-making in small groups shown by Lewin, Lippitt, and others (4, 5) and the successful application of small-group decision-making to method changes in an industrial setting by Coch and French (1) both indicated the possibilities for enlarging the role of the rank and file in the ongoing decision-making of an organization. The practical experience of Sears, Roebuck and Co. with a "flat," administratively decentralized structure, described by Worthy (8), pointed in the same direction, as did the survey findings by Katz, Maccoby, and Morse (2) that supervisors delegating greater authority had more productive work groups. The logical next step seemed to be the controlled testing of hypotheses concerning the relationship between role in organizational decision-making and two aspects of organizational effectiveness: satisfaction and productivity. Two broad hypotheses were formulated:

Hypothesis I. An increased role in the decision-making processes for rank-and-file groups increases their satisfaction (while a decreased role in decision-making reduces satisfaction).

Hypothesis II. An increased role in decision-making for rank-and-file groups increases their productivity (while a decreased role in decision-making decreases productivity).

Both these hypotheses deal with the effects on the rank and file of different hierarchical allocations of the decision-making processes of the organization. The rationale for the satisfaction hypothesis (I) predicts different and more need-satisfying decisions when the rank and file has decision-making power than when the upper echelons of the hierarchy have that power. Furthermore, the process of decision-making itself is expected to be satisfying to the majority of people brought up in American traditions. Underlying the productivity hypothesis (II) was the consideration that local unit policy-making would increase motivation to produce and thus productivity. Motivation should rise when productivity becomes a path for greater need satisfaction. The productivity hypothesis predicts a higher degree of need satisfaction (as does Hypothesis I) *and* an increase in the degree of dependence of satisfactions upon productivity under conditions of greater rank-and-file decision-making. It is expected that when rank-and-file members work out and put into effect their own rules and regulations, their maintenance in the organization (and thus their satisfactions) will depend much more directly upon their performance.

Procedure

The experiment was conducted in one department of a nonunionized industrial organization which had four parallel divisions engaged in relatively routine clerical work. The design involved increasing rank-and-file decision-making in two of the divisions and increasing upper-level decision-making in the other two divisions. The time span was one and one-half years: a before measurement, one-half year of training of supervisors to create the experimental conditions, one year under the experimental conditions, and then remeasurement. The two pairs of two divisions each were comparable on relevant variables such as initial allocation of the decision-making processes, satisfaction and productivity, as well as on such background factors as type of work, type of personnel, and type of supervisory structure.

The rank-and-file employees were women, mostly young and unmarried, with high school education. The usual clerk's plans were for marriage and a family rather than a career. The population used in the analysis except where noted is a subgroup of the clerks, the "matched" population. These clerks were present throughout the one and one-half year period, and their before and after questionnaires were individually matched. While they comprise somewhat less than half of the clerks present in these divisions at any one time, they are comparable to the total group, except on such expected variables as length of time in the division, in the work section, and on the job.

One aspect of the work situation should be mentioned, as it bears on the adequacy of the setting for a test of the productivity hypothesis. The amount of work done by the divisions was completely dependent upon the flow of work to them, i.e., the total number of units to be done was not within the control of the divisions. With volume fixed, productivity depends upon the number of clerks needed to do the work, and increased productivity can be achieved only by out-placement of clerks or by foregoing replacement of clerks who leave for other reasons.

The Development of the Experimental Conditions

Creating the experimental programs included three steps: (a) planning by research staff and company officials; (b) introducing the programs to the division supervisory personnel and training of the supervisors for their new roles; and (c) introduction to the clerks and operation under the experimental conditions.

The experiment was carried out within the larger framework of company operations. The introduction, training, and operations were in the hands of company personnel. The experimental changes were not made through personnel shifts; the changes were in what people did in their jobs with respect to the decision-making processes of the organization.

Two main change processes were used in both the Autonomy program, designed to increase rank-and-file decision-making, and in the Hierarchically-controlled program, designed to increase the upper management role in the decision-making processes. First, there were formal structural changes to create a new organizational environment for the divisions in each program. In both programs the hierarchical legitimization of new roles preceded the taking of the new roles.[2] In the Autonomy program authority was delegated by upper management to lower levels in the

---

[2]Weber and others have used the word "legitimization" to refer to the acceptance by subordinates of the authority of superiors. We are using the word in quite a different sense. By hierarchical legitimization we mean the formal delegation of authority by superiors to subordinates. This delegation *legitimizes* the subordinates' utilization of this authority.

hierarchy with the understanding that they would redelegate it to the clerical work groups. In the Hierarchically-controlled program, authority was given to the higher line officials to increase their role in the running of the divisions and to the staff officials to increase their power to institute changes within the two divisions in that program. Second, there were training programs for the supervisors of the divisions to ensure that the formal changes would result in actual changes in relations between people. (For a longer description of the change programs see Reimer [6].)

Measurement

The results of the changes were gauged through before and after measurements and through continuing measurements during the experimental period. The major emphasis was on the attitudes and perceptions of the clerks as reflected in extensive questionnaires. In addition, the training programs and the operations phase of the experiment were observed. Before and after interviews were conducted with the supervisory personnel of the division. Data from company records such as productivity rates, turnover figures, etc., were also included.

The data reported here will be confined to material most pertinent to the testing of the two hypotheses. For other related aspects of the experiment, see Tannenbaum's study of the relationship of personality characteristics and adjustment to the two programs (7), Kaye's study of organizational goal achievement under the Autonomy program (3), as well as forthcoming publications.

Results[3]

Success of Experimental Manipulation

The first question was to discover whether or not the change programs were successful in creating the conditions under which the hypotheses could be tested. Two types of data are pertinent. The first is descriptive data concerning the actual operations of the two programs. The second is perceptual data from the clerical employees themselves indicating the degree to which they saw changes in their role in organizational decisions.

The operations of the divisions in fact changed in the direction expected. In the Autonomy program the clerical work groups came to make group decisions about many of the things which affected them and which were important to them. The range of the decisions was very great, including work methods and processes, and personnel matters, such as recess periods, the handling of tardiness, etc. Probably the most important area in which the clerks were not able to make decisions was the area of salary. Some of the work groups were more active in the decision-making process than others, but all made a very great

[3]For the statistical tests used in this section, we have assumed that the individuals were randomly chosen, while the selection of individuals by divisions undoubtedly results in some clustering effect. The levels of significance should, therefore, be considered as general guides rather than in any absolute sense.

variety of decisions in areas important to them. In the Hierarchically-controlled program the changes decreased the degree to which the employees could control and regulate their own activities. One of the main ways in which this greater limitation was manifested was through the individual work standards that staff officials developed for the various jobs. Also the greater role of upper line and staff officials in the operation of the divisions meant that the indirect influence which the clerks could have on decisions when they were made by division managers and section supervisors was reduced.

The clerks were operating under different conditions in the two programs as the result of the experimental changes, but did they perceive these changes? The method of measuring the perception of changes in decision-making was by asking clerks about their part and about the part of people above their rank in decisions with respect to a wide variety of areas of company operations, or company systems. The following questions were asked about each major area of company operations or system: "To what degree do company officers or any employees of a higher rank than yours decide how the——System is set up and decide the policies, rules, procedures or methods of the——System?" (followed by a line with the landmark statements: not at all, to a slight degree, to some degree, to a fairly high degree and to a very high degree) and, "To what degree do you and the girls in your section decide how the——System is set up and decide the policies, rules, procedures or methods of the——System?" (followed by a line with the same landmark statements as the first question).

The extreme degree of perceived hierarchical control of the decision-making processes would be shown by the clerks answering that employees of a higher rank than theirs made the decisions, "to a very high degree" and the clerks made them "not at all." Table 1 shows the number of systems where there are half or more of the clerks endorsing these two statements for the before situation and for the two experimental situations. (The Autonomy program is designated in Table 1 and thereafter as Program I and the Hierarchically-controlled program as Program II.) Questions were asked for 27 company systems in the before measurement and 24 systems in the after measurement.

Table 1 shows that the clerks perceived the decision-making processes for

TABLE 1
Number of Company Systems in Which Clerks Perceive Very
High Upper Level Control of Decision-Making Allocation

Response	Number of Systems in Which Half or More Clerks gave Specified Response		
	Before All Divs	After Program I Divs	After Program II Divs
Upper levels decided policies to a very high degree	20	7	24
Clerks did not decide policies at all	25	9	23
Total number of systems measured	27	24	24

362

most of the company operations measured as located at hierarchical levels above their own, prior to the introduction of the experimental changes. The experimental changes in the Autonomy program divisions resulted in their seeing decision-making activities as much less exclusively confined to levels above theirs. The changes in the Hierarchically-controlled program were less striking but they resulted in the clerks judging that all of the systems about which they were asked in the after situation had their policies molded to a very high degree by people above their level.

The relative role of the hierarchy compared to the rank and file as perceived by the clerks was measured by assigning scores from 1 to 9 for the landmark positions on the scales for the two questions and then dividing the score for upper-level decision-making by the score for rank-and-file decision-making. The theoretical range for the resulting index is from 9.0 to 0, with numbers less than 1 indicating greater local control than upper-level control. Table 2 includes the average index scores for the systems from the before and after measurements calculated by division.

Table 2 indicates the change in the divisions in the Autonomy program toward greater perceived rank-and-file role in decision making, but also shows that the upper levels are seen as still having the major role in the after situation. (The downward shift in perceived decision-making control in the Autonomy program is significant above the 1 per cent level by the Student's t test for paired data. A statistically significant, but slight, change toward greater upper-level control took place in the Hierarchically-controlled program.)

Both Tables 1 and 2 show that the clerks in the Autonomy program perceive as predicted a significant shift away from upper-level control when their before-after answers are compared, and that the clerks in the Hierarchically-controlled program see some increase in upper-level control over policy-making, even

TABLE 2

Effect of Change Programs on Percpetion of Decision-Making Allocation

Index of Perceived Decision-Making Allocation

Experimental Groups	Before Mean	After Mean	Diff	SE Diff.	N
Program I					
Div. A	5.69	4.39	−1.30**	.24	61
Div. B	6.49	4.08	−2.41**	.26	57
Average	6.08	4.24	−1.84**	.18	118
Program II					
Div. C	6.15	6.87	+ .72**	.22	44
Div. D	6.78	7.13	+ .35	.26	44
Average	6.41	7.00	+ .59**	.17	88

Note:—Higher values correspond to perception of predominance of upper levels of organization in decision-making.

**Significant at the 1% level.

though it was already perceived as highly controlled from above before the experiment.

These measures of successful experimental manipulation suggest that the conditions in the two programs are sufficiently different to permit tests of the experimental hypotheses.

Hypothesis I

This hypothesis states that an increase in the decision-making role of individuals results in increased satisfactions, while a decrease in opportunity for decision-making is followed by decreased satisfaction. The general hypothesis was tested for a variety of specific areas of satisfaction. The attitudinal areas to be reported include: (a) self-actualization and growth, (b) satisfaction with supervisors, (c) liking for working for the company, (d) job satisfaction, (e) liking for program. Students's one-tailed t test for paired data was used for tests of significance. Results reaching the 5 per cent level or above are considered significant.

Self-actualization. One of the hypotheses of the study was that greater opportunity for regulating and controlling their own activities within the company structure would increase the degree to which individuals could express their various and diverse needs and could move in the direction of fully exploiting their potentialities. An increase in upper-management control on the other hand was predicted to decrease the opportunities for employee self-actualization and growth.

Five questions were used to measure this area: 1, Is your job a real challenge to what you think you can do? 2, How much chance does your job give you to learn things you're interested in? 3, Are the things you're learning in your job helping to train you for a better job in the company? 4, How much chance do you have to try out your ideas on the job? 5, How much does your job give you a chance to do the things you're best at? These five items, which were answered by checking one position on a five-point scale, were intercorrelated and then combined to form an index.[4] Table 3 shows the means for the four divisions and two groups on the self-actualization and growth index.

While both groups of clerks indicated that their jobs throughout the course of the experiment did not give them a very high degree of self-actualization, the experimental programs produced significant changes. In the Autonomy program, self-actualization increased significantly from before to after, and a corresponding decrease was shown in the Hierarchically-controlled program. At the end of the experimental period, the Autonomy program is significantly higher on this variable than the Hierarchically-controlled program.

Satisfaction with Supervision. A variety of indices were developed in order to test the hypothesis that the Autonomy program would improve satisfactions

---

[4]The items were intercorrelated by the tetrachoric method. When these correlations were converted to z scores the average intercorrelation was .62, corrected for length of test, a reliability index of .89 was obtained.

TABLE 3
Effect of Change Programs on Feelings of Self-Actualization on Job

Index of Perceived Self-Actualization

Experimental Groups	Mean Before	Mean After	Diff	SE Diff.	N
Program I					
Div. A	2.67	2.74	+.07	.09	52
Div. B	2.18	2.39	+.21*	.11	47
Average	2.43	2.57	+.14*	.07	99
Program II					
Div. C	2.43	2.24	−.19	.14	43
Div. D	2.30	2.23	−.07	.10	38
Average	2.37	2.24	−.13*	.07	81

Note:—Scale runs from 1, low degree of self-actualization to 5, a high degree.
*Significant at the 5% level, one-tailed t test for paired data.

with supervisors and that the Hierarchically-controlled program would reduce such satisfactions. Two general types of attitudes were separately measured: (*a*) satisfaction with relations with supervisors and (*b*) satisfaction with supervisors as a representative. These two types of attitudes were studied before and after the experimental period with respect to three levels of supervision: the first-line supervisor, the assistant manager of the division, and the manager of the division. The following three questions were asked for each of these levels in order to tap the clerks' degree of satisfaction with relations with supervisors:

1. How good is your supervisor (assistant manager, manager) at handling people?
2. Can you count on having good relations with your supervisor (assistant manager, manager) under all circumstances?
3. In general, how well do you like your supervisor (assistant manager, manager) as a person to work with?

These three questions were combined to form indices of satisfaction with relations with supervisors, assistant manager, and manager. (The items were intercorrelated for the satisfaction with relations with supervisor index. Through converting to z scores, the average intercorrelation of items is found to be .78. Correcting for length of test, i.e., using three items to form the index rather than one, the reliability index is .91 with an N of 360.)

Table 4 shows that in general there was a shift toward greater satisfaction with supervisors in the Autonomy program and toward less satisfaction with supervisors in the Hierarchically-controlled program. The divisions, however, show certain characteristic differences in satisfaction at the outset and shift in the expected direction to different degrees.

Both divisions in the Hierarchically-controlled program show a decrease in satisfaction with the first-line supervisor, although the changes are not statistical-

TABLE 4

Effect of Change Programs on Satisfaction with Relations
with Three Levels of Supervision

Experiemental Groups		Index of Satisfaction				
		Mean Before	Mean After	Diff.	SE Diff.	N
Relations with Supervisor						
Program I	Div. A	4.18	4.15	−.03	.09	62
	Div. B	3.19	3.50	+.31*	.14	54
	Average	3.71	3.80	+.09	.08	116
Program II	Div. C	3.80	3.67	−.13	.11	46
	Div. D.	3.43	3.29	−.14	.16	45
	Average	3.64	3.48	−.16	.10	91
Relations with Assistant Manager						
Program I	Div. A	3.49	3.61	+.12	.12	59
	Div. B	3.97	4.11	+.14	.11	53
	Average	3.71	3.86	+.15*	.08	112
Program II	Div. C	3.80	3.34	−.46**	.12	43
	Div. D	3.57	3.22	−.35**	.11	43
	Average	3.64	3.28	−.36**	.08	86
Relations with Manager						
Program I	Div. A	3.84	4.11	+.27**	.08	62
	Div. B	4.04	4.20	+.16*	.09	52
	Average	3.93	4.15	+.22**	.06	114
Program II	Div. C	3.23	2.59	−.64**	.15	43
	Div. D	3.87	3.37	−.50**	.13	40
	Average	3.50	3.01	−.49**	.10	83

Note:—Degree of Satisfaction with Relations with Supervision: five point scale ranging from 1, low degree of satisfaction to 5, high degree of satisfaction.

*Significant at the 5% level one-tailed t test for paired data.

**Significant at the 1% level.

ly significant. The after differences between the Autonomy and the Hierarchical-ly-controlled programs are, however, significant.

Satisfaction with relations with both the assistant manager and the manager increased significantly in the Autonomy program and decreased significantly in the Hierarchically-controlled program. Each of the divisions within the groups likewise shifted in the hypothesized directions for the two managerial indices. In the Autonomy program the assistant manager index shifted in the right direction for both divisions, but the changes were not statistically significant when each division was tested separately.

Thus while the employees were generally quite satisfied with their relations with their different supervisors, the experimental programs did have the expected effects of increasing the satisfactions of those in the Autonomy pro-gram and decreasing the satisfaction of those in the Hierarchically-controlled program. The effects of the programs appear to be most evident in attitudes toward the managerial level and least marked in attitudes toward the first-line supervisors, probably because the managers occupy the key or pivotal positions in the structure (see Kaye,[3]).

The second type of attitude toward supervisors measured was satisfaction with the supervisors as representatives of the employees. Three questions were asked employees as a measure of this type of satisfaction:

1. How much does your supervisor (assistant manager, manager) go out of her (his) way to help get things for the girls in the section?
2. How effective is she (he) in helping you and the other girls get what you want in your jobs?
3. How much does your supervisor (assistant manager, manager) try to help people in your section get ahead in the company?

These three items were intercorrelated for the attitudes toward the supervisor as a representative index and the average intercorrelation was .83 with a corrected reliability of .94 (N of 340).

The findings for the three levels of supervision on the satisfaction with supervisors as representatives index are shown in Table 5.

The employees' attitudes toward their supervisors as effective representatives of their interests show significant changes in the predicted directions in the two programs. Those in the Autonomy program became more satisfied than they had been previously, while those in the Hierarchically-controlled program became less satisfied. On satisfaction with the first-line supervisor as a representative both Division B in the Autonomy program and Division D in the Hierarchically-controlled program shifted significantly in the hypothesized directions, although the other two divisions did not shift significantly. The two program groups were not matched on degree of satisfaction with manager and assistant manager as a representative at the beginning of the experiment, as there was significantly more satisfaction in the Autonomy program divisions than there was in Program II. However, the changes for both groups of divisions were statistically significant and in the predicted direction. For attitude toward manager all of the division differences are in the predicted direction and all except Division D are statistically significant.

Satisfaction with the Company. One general question was used to measure company satisfaction: "Taking things as a whole, how do you like working for _____ (the name of the company)?"

The answers for this question presented in Table 6 indicate an increase in favorableness toward the company under the Autonomy program and a decrease under the Hierarchically-controlled program.

All of the changes are significant in the predicted direction, except for the before-after difference in Division B which is only at the 10 per cent level of significance.

TABLE 5

The Effect of Change Programs on Satisfaction with Three Levels of
Supervision as Representatives of Employees

Index of Satisfaction

Experimental Groups		Mean Before	Mean After	Diff.	SE Diff.	N
Supervisor as Representative of Employees						
Program I	Div. A	3.98	4.06	+.08	.12	59
	Div. B	2.91	3.43	+.52**	.14	49
	Average	3.48	3.74	+.26**	.09	103
Program II	Div. C	3.73	3.67	−.06	.13	45
	Div. D	3.52	3.16	−.36*	.18	41
	Average	3.59	3.43	−.16	.11	86
Assistant Manager as Representative of Employees						
Program I	Div. A	3.32	3.75	+.43**	.14	51
	Div. B	3.54	3.76	+.22*	.13	53
	Average	3.43	3.75	+.32**	.09	104
Program II	Div. C	3.07	2.81	−.26*	.12	41
	Div. D	3.23	2.92	−.31*	.13	42
	Average	3.15	2.86	−.29**	.10	83
Manager as Representative of Employees						
Program I	Div. A	3.82	4.37	+.55**	.11	57
	Div. B	3.76	3.96	+.20*	.10	53
	Average	3.79	4.17	+.38**	.07	110
Program II	Div. C	2.70	2.19	−.51**	.13	41
	Div. D	3.14	2.92	−.22	.16	30
	Average	2.92	2.52	−.40**	.10	71

Note:—Five-Point scale ranging from 1, low degree of satisfaction to 5, high degree of satisfaction.

*Significant at the 5% level one-tailed t test for paired data.

**Significant at the 1% level.

Job Satisfaction. Three questions were used as an index of job satisfaction:

1. Does your job ever get monotonous?
2. How important do you feel your job is compared with other jobs at (the company)?
3. In general, how well do you like the sort of work you're doing in your job?

These three questions showed an average intercorrelation of .47 with a corrected reliability of .73 (N of 369). The results on this index are reported in Table 7.

TABLE 6
The Effect of Change Programs on Satisfaction with the Company

Index of Satisfaction with Company

Experimental Groups	Before Mean	After Mean	Diff	SE Diff.	N
Program I					
Div. A	4.16	4.32	+.16*	.09	62
Div. B	3.83	4.02	+.19	.13	53
Average	4.01	4.18	+.17*	.08	115
Program II					
Div. C	4.04	3.80	−.24*	.14	46
Div. D	4.26	3.95	−.31**	.12	43
Average	4.15	3.88	−.27**	.09	89

Note:—Five point scale, ranging from 1, low degree of satisfaction to 5, high degree of satisfaction.
*Significant at the 5% level one-tailed *t* test for paired data.
**Significant at the 1% level.

TABLE 7
The Effect of Change Programs on Job Satisfaction

Index of Job Satisfaction

Experimental Groups	Before Mean	After Mean	Diff	SE Diff.	N
Program I					
Div. A	3.29	3.29	0	.08	58
Div. B	3.03	3.09	+.06	.09	55
Average	3.16	3.19	+.03	.06	113
Program II					
Div. C	3.14	2.94	−.20*	.10	42
Div. D	3.12	3.07	−.05	.12	46
Average	3.13	3.00	−.13*	.07	88

Note:—A five-point scale ranging from 1, low degree of satisfaction to 5, a high degree of satisfaction.
*Significant at the 5% level one-tailed *t* test for paired data.

While the trend for the changes in job satisfaction are in the direction predicted, the differences are not sufficiently great to be statistically significant except for Division C. The lack of change in job satisfaction in the Autonomy program may be due to the fact that the job content remained about the same. It is also possible that the increases in complexity and variety of their total work were offset by a rise in their level of aspiration, so that they expected more interesting and varied work.

Satisfaction with the Program. In the after measurement additional questions were asked concerning attitudes toward the programs. Most of these questions were open-ended and required the employee to write her response in her own words. Although less than half of the clerks taking the after measurement filled them out, the results on questions relevant to the satisfaction hypothesis deserve brief mention. The clerks in the Autonomy program typically: wanted their program to last indefinitely, did not like the other program, felt that the clerks were one of the groups gaining the most from the program and described both positive and negative changes in interpersonal relations among the girls. The clerks in the Hierarchically-controlled program, on the other hand, most frequently: wanted their program to end immediately, liked the other program and felt that the company gained the most from their program. Not one single person in the Hierarchically-controlled program mentioned an improvement in interpersonal relations as a result of this program. All of the noted changes were for the worse, with increases in friction and tension being most frequently mentioned.

Taking all of these results on the attitudinal questions together, the first hypothesis would appear to be verified. Increasing local decision-making increased satisfaction, while decreasing the role of rank-and-file members of the organization in the decision-making decreased it.

Hypothesis II

This hypothesis predicts a direct relationship between degree of rank-and-file decision-making and productivity. Thus, in order for the hypothesis to be verified, productivity should increase significantly in the Autonomy program, and should decrease significantly in the Hierarchically-controlled program.

We have previously described the problems of assuming a direct relationship between motivation to produce and productivity in a situation in which volume is not controllable by employees and level of productivity depends upon the number of people doing a fixed amount of work. The Autonomy program was handicapped by both the fact that increasing productivity required reducing the size of their own work group and the fact that the upper management staff and line costs were not included in the measure of costs per volume of work.

The measure of productivity, then, is a measure of clerical costs. These clerical costs are expressed in percentage figures, calculated by dividing the actual clerical costs by a constant standard of cost expected for that volume. Since this way of estimating productivity makes the higher figures indicate lower productivity, we have reversed the signs for purposes of presentation. The results for this measure are shown in Table 8.

The clerical costs have gone down in each division and thus productivity has increased. All these increases in productivity are statistically significant (by t tests). In addition, the productivity increase in the Hierarchically-controlled program is significantly greater than that in the Autonomy program. These increases in productivity do not seem to be accounted for by a general rise in productivity throughout the company, since the divisions outside the experi-

TABLE 8
Comparison of the Four Divisions on Clerical Productivity for Year Control
Period and Year Experimental Period

Index of Productivity

Experimental Groups	Mean Control Period	Mean Experimental period	Diff. %	SE Diff.	N
Program I					
Div. A	46.3%	55.2%	+ 8.9**	1.3%	12
Div. B	51.0	62.0	+11.0**	1.3	12*
Average	48.6	58.6	+10.0**	1.2	24
Program II					
Div. C	50.2	63.2	+13.0**	1.2	12
Div. D	46.8	62.0	+15.2**	1.1	12
Average	48.5	62.6	+14.1**	.9	24

Note:—Higher values correspond to greater productivity.
**Significant at the 1% level.

mental groups which were most comparable to them showed no significant gain in productivity during this period. The rise in productivity appears to be the result of the experimental treatments. The two divisions initially low in productivity showed the greatest differential change. Division D increased its productivity the most of the four while Division A increased the least.

A second measure of the organizational costs of the two programs is the degree of turnover which could be attributed to on-the-job factors. A method of control and regulation which reduces clerical costs, but which produces the hidden costs of training new employees is of greater cost to the organization than would at first appear evident. In this company turnover, however, is not high and much of the turnover that does occur is due to personal reasons (marriage, pregnancy, etc.) rather than on-the-job reasons. Out of the 54 employees who left the company from the four divisions during the time of the experiment, only nine resigned for other jobs or because of dissatisfaction. Out of these nine, however, all but one were in the Hierarchically-controlled program. In the exit interviews conducted by the company personnel department 23 of the girls leaving made unfavorable comments about pressure, work standards, etc. Nineteen of these girls were from the Hierarchically-controlled program.

These results indicate that the productivity hypothesis is clearly not verified in terms of direct clerical costs, since the Hierarchically-controlled program decreased these costs more than the Autonomy program, contrary to the prediction. The indirect costs for the Hierarchically-controlled program are probably somewhat greater. But even when this is considered the evidence does not support the hypothesis.

The results on productivity might suggest a "Hawthorne effect" if it were not for the satisfaction findings. The increase in satisfaction under the Autonomy program and the decrease under the Hierarchically-controlled program make an explanation of productivity changes in terms of a common attention effect unlikely.[5]

The Hierarchically-controlled program reduced staff costs by ordering reductions in the number of employees assigned to the tasks. Increases in productivity for Divisions C and D were brought about as simply as that. This temporary increase in one measure of productivity is not surprising and is traditional history in industry. In the Autonomy program, decrease in costs was more complex but can be simply stated as follows. The Autonomy program increased the motivation of the employees to produce and thus they did not feel the need for replacing the staff members who left the section. In addition, they were willing to make an effort to try to outplace some of their members in other jobs which they might like. The reductions in staff in the two programs came about in different ways. Those occurring by order in the Hierarchically-controlled program surpassed in number those occurring by group decision in the Autonomy program, but it is not clear how long the superiority of the Hierarchically-controlled program would have lasted.

The results of the experiment need to be placed in a larger theoretical framework in order to contribute to the understanding of the functioning of large-scale organizations. We shall first consider briefly the role and function of the social control processes, as it is these processes which were changed by the experimental manipulations.

The high degree of rationality which is characteristic of the institutional behavior of man is achieved through a complex system for controlling and regulating human behavior. Hierarchy is a requirement because human beings must be fitted to a rational model. There are essentially two functions which the usual hierarchy serves: a *binding-in* function and a *binding-between* function. By *binding-in* we mean insuring that there will be individuals present to fill the necessary roles. The role behavior required by the organization must be a path to individual goals. Money is the most important means used for binding-in, but all ways to motivate a person to enter and remain in the system are means of binding-in. By *binding-between* we mean the insurance of the rationality of action, that is, the setting up and continuation of institutional processes which will accomplish the ends for which the organization is designed. The role behavior of individuals must be integrated into a pattern to produce interrelated action directed toward the goals of the organization. The development of assignments, work charts, job specifications, etc., are but a few examples of the many means used by organizations for binding-between.

---

[5]It is unlikely that even in the Hawthorne experiment the results were due to attention. There were a number of changes in addition to an increase in attention, including relaxation of rules, better supervisors, no change in piece rates despite raises in productivity—to name a few.

Any means for controlling and regulating human behavior in a large organizational setting, then, needs to serve these two functions. The experiment shows that the allocation of decision-making processes to the upper hierarchy results in a greater emphasis on the binding-between function, while the function of binding-in is handled by an external reward system. Such a direct stress on the binding-between function was shown in the Hierarchically-controlled program and resulted in the increase in productivity (an indication of binding-between) and a decrease in employee satisfaction (an indication of degree of binding-in) and some increase in turnover (another indication of binding-in).

The greater allocation of the decision-making processes to the rank-and-file employees in the Autonomy program resulted in an emphasis on both the binding-between and the binding-in functions.Thus there was both an increase in productivity and an increase in satisfaction. While the program is addressed primarily to the binding-in function, in such a context the binding-between function is also served.

The problems of the Hierarchically-controlled system are maintaining the employee effectively "bound-in" to the organization and continuing favorable relations between the supervisory personnel who have involvement in the organization and the rank and file who must do the work. Indications of these problems are dissatisfaction, distortions in communications up the hierarchy, the tendency to "goof off" and cut corners in the work, and the greater turnover.

The Autonomy program is an integrated means of handling both the binding-between and the binding-in functions, but it requires in the long run that the organization be willing to grant employee decision-making in the key areas of binding-in such as pay and promotions. The granting of "safe" areas of decision-making and the withholding of "hot" ones is not likely to work for long. It is necessary for the rank and file to be sufficiently bound in to the organization for them to want to make decisions which are rational for the system. But the rationality of their decisions will also depend upon the orientation of the key supervisors whose values they will interiorize. (Thus the clerks in Division B were more organizationally oriented than those in Division A—see Kaye [3].)

Summary

A field experiment in an industrial setting was conducted in order to test hypotheses concerning the relationship between the means by which organizational decisions are made and (a) individual satisfaction, and (b) productivity.

Using four parallel divisions of the clerical operations of an organization, two programs of changes were introduced. One program, the Autonomy program involving two of the divisions, was designed to increase the role of the rank-and-file employees in the decision-making processes of the organization. The other two divisions received a program designed to increase the role of upper management in the decision-making processes (the Hierarchically-controlled program). The phases of the experiment included: (a) before measurement, (b) training programs for supervisory personnel lasting approximately 6 months, (c) an operations period of a year for the two experimental programs, and (d) after measurement. In addition, certain measurements were taken during the training and operational phases of the experiment. Findings are reported on the question of the experimental "take" and on the general hypotheses on individual satisfactions and productivity. Briefly, it was found that:

1. The experimental programs produced changes in decision-making allocations in the direction required for the testing of the hypotheses.
2. The individual satisfactions of the members of the work groups increased significantly in the Autonomous program and decreased significantly in the Hierarchically-controlled program.
3. Using one measure of productivity, both decision-making systems increased productivity, with the Hierarchically-controlled program resulting in a greater increase.

The relationship of the findings to the so-called "Hawthorne effect" is examined and the experimental programs and their results are considered in the light of a theoretical description of the role of the control and regulation processes of large organizations.

References

1. Coch, L., & French, J. R. P., Jr. "Overcoming Resistance to Change." *Human Relations,* 1948, 1, 512-532.
2. Katz, D., Maccoby, N., & Morse, Nancy. *Productivity, Supervision and Morale in an Office Situation.* Ann Arbor: Survey Research Center, University of Michigan, 1950.
3. Kaye, Carol. *The Effect on Organizational Goal Achievement of a Change in the Structure of Roles.* Ann Arbor: Survey Research Center, 1954 (mimeographed).
4. Lewin, K. "Group Decisions and Social Change." In G. E. Swanson, T. M. Newcomb, & E. L. Hartley (Eds.). *Readings in Social Psychology* (2nd Ed.). New York: Holt, 1952, 459-473.
5. Lippitt, R., & White, R. K. "An Experimental Study of Leadership and Group Life." In G. E. Swanson, T. M. Newcomb, & E. L. Hartley (Eds.). *Readings in Social Psychology* (2nd Ed.) New York: Holt, 1952, 340-354.
6. Reimer, E. *Creating Experimental Social Change in an Organization.* Ann Arbor: Survey Research Center, 1954 (mimeographed).
7. Tannenbaum, A. *The Relationship between Personality Variables and Adjustment to Contrasting Types of Social Structure.* Ann Arbor: Survey Research Center 1954 (mimeographed).
8. Worthy, J. C. "Factors Influencing Employee Morale." *Harvard Business Review,* 1950, 28, 61-73.

part IV

RESISTANCE TO CHANGE: COPING WITH A CRITICAL PROBLEM

Part IV treats an important dimension of change or changing—namely, resistance to change. It is a subject that any prospective change agent would do well to assimilate and internalize. Fortunately, this is one of the better defined areas in terms of both the quantity and quality of significant literature available for review. Our brief focus concentrates upon a combination of five readings: the first three pieces, "The Problem of Resistance to Change in Industry" by Robert N. McMurry, "How to Deal with Resistance to Change" by Paul R. Lawrence, and "Resistance to Change—Its Analysis and Prevention" by Alvin Zander, explore the various causes of resistance to change and methods by which it can be alleviated, if not prevented. The article by Robert Albanese, "Overcoming Resistance to Stability," points out that in particular situations resistance may be quite necessary and appropriate. Donald Klein's selection, "Some Notes on the Dynamics of Resistance to Change," concludes this unit and examines the role of the defender of the status quo.

One of the main themes running through the literature of resistance to change is the premise that people—alone or in groups—do not resist change per se. What they resist is the uncertainty conjured up by a change. The process begins when a new method, new program, new leader, or new policy, is announced as a *fait accompli* or, worse, is implemented without warning. Such an action either disrupts or is perceived as disrupting the social system. Note that it is usually the social system rather than the technical system that lies at the root of the matter, for it is the prospect of decimation of the social system that leads to uncertainty as to what new patterns, challenges, or problems may emerge. This uncertainty can cause fear—fear of the unknown. Confronted with this very real fear of the unknown, people or groups attempt to preserve the status quo and the behavioral patterns they manifest in doing so are collectively called "resistance to change."

These behavioral patterns are further complicated by other factors not easily ascertained. To begin with, the magnitude and severity of the effort to resist a change is not always directly correlated with the extent of the proposed change or the degree of real trauma it will cause. The reason for this phenomenon is that circumstances less obvious than the scope of the change also influence the resistance. Two brief illustrations from our own experience will demonstrate this.

Case number one concerns an organization which virtually underwent a total wall-to-wall overhaul, with rather serious negative effects upon a majority of the employees as well as the supervisors. Yet this major change program met very little resistance because this company was on the verge of bankruptcy and everyone realized that a drastic upheaval was needed to maintain solvency.

Case number two concerns an organization which tried—for the hot summer months only—to reduce the one-hour unpaid lunch hour to thirty minutes so that the employees could go home earlier. The furor that resulted defies description. This seemingly minor change, instituted with good intentions on the part of management, cut by fifty percent the free time for social interactions. The lunch period at this firm was looked upon by the employees more as a daily picnic than as a company lunch hour.

In order to truly understand resistance one should realize that there are times when change is contraindicated. Where this is the case, resistance should be welcomed. The problem is how to find out when resistance is legitimate and appropriate and when it is a reaction based upon fear of the unknown. When is the defender of the status quo a crackpot with a personal ax to grind and when is he the spokesman for a substantial majority of trusted, faithful employees who are trying to save you from yourself?

Perhaps the solution to this dilemma lies in constantly encouraging and rewarding, by word and deed, the existence of a "loyal opposition." Although it may sound strange to call for a model that builds in dissent and challenge, it is an interesting proposition full of potential.

This section on resistance to change, then, contains fundamental ideas for understanding and coping with a critical managerial problem. Every administrator or prospective administrator should be conversant with the how and why of this topic for two reasons. First, if he attempts to change his organization's technical system without the proper attention to its social system, he easily can precipitate a costly, dysfunctional resistance effort on the part of his employees. Second, if the manager works through and with the social system of his organization when he introduces the change, and if he explores any resistance for its legitimate aspects, he will increase his chances of improving employee creativity, motivation, and performance in making the changes work.[1]

[1]For some additional and valuable information about resistance to change, see Dorwin Cartwright, "Achieving Change in People: Some Applications of Group Dynamics Theory," *Human Relations,* IV, No. 4 (1951), 381-92; Joan Woodward, "Resistance to Change," *Management International Review,* VIII (1968), 137-43; L. W. Gruenfeld and F. F. Foltman, "Relationship among Supervisors' Integration, Satisfaction, and Acceptance of a Technological Change," *Journal of Applied Psychology,* LI (1967), 74-77; Paul C. Agnew and Francis L. K. Hsu, "Introducing Change in a Mental Hospital," *Human Organization,* XIX, No. 4 (Winter 1961), 195-98; Donald Roy, "Efficiency and 'The Fix': Informal Intergroup Relations in a Piecework Machine Shop," *American Journal of Sociology,* LX, No. 3 (1954), 255-66; Alvin W. Gouldner, *Patterns of Industrial Bureaucracy* (New York: The Free Press, 1954), especially pp. 70-85, Ch. IV, "Succession and the Problem of Bureaucracy"; but see also pp. 59-69 and 86-101.

The Problem of Resistance to Change in Industry

This paper explores an involute problem. The logic is compelling and astute, yet simple. It says that people do not resist change per se; they resist the uncertainties that change can cause. This is because uncertainty causes fear. If this is so, it follows that in order to reduce resistance to change, one need only reduce fear. This, in turn, is done by reducing uncertainty.

Steps that management might follow in order to reduce uncertainty include moving slowly with a change program, giving affected personnel maximum opportunity to participate in the planning of the proposed changes in advance of their introduction, and providing outlets for the expression of the hostilities that will almost surely arise.

One should not be deluded into thinking that these ideas are as easy to implement as McMurry makes them seem. Proper execution requires not only skill, but also unusual care.

THE PROBLEM OF
RESISTANCE TO CHANGE
IN INDUSTRY

Robert N. McMurry
President, The McMurry Company

A medium-sized Middle Western manufacturing company recently installed a new and greatly improved wage incentive plan at a cost in excess of $20,000. The work was done entirely by outside engineers. These engineers did an excellent job technically and management was satisfied; the only difficulty was that three weeks later the new plan had been completely abandoned and the investment of $20,000 had been totally lost. Why was this?

Industrial progress finds one of its greatest handicaps in the frequent resistance of both management and workers to change of any sort. This is especially marked if the change is introduced without proper advance notice and explanation to those whom it will affect. Even innovations which are obviously advantageous are often objects of attack. Where the changes threaten either the status or job security of either workers or management, their reaction is certain to be quick and violently negative. In those organizations where employee and supervisory insecurity is present, even minor revisions of policies or procedures may evoke profoundly disturbing reactions among individuals and groups. An effort is made at once either to block the introduction of the new methods or to discredit them after their installation and force their removal.

Even ordinarily honest and loyal workers and executives will sometimes lie, misrepresent, and engage in outright sabotage of the new procedures, so bitter

Reprinted from Robert N. McMurry: "The Problem of Resistance to Change in Industry," *The Journal of Applied Psychology*, XXXI, No. 6 (December 1947), 589-93, by permission of the American Psychological Association and the author.

are the antagonisms aroused. Nor are these manifestations limited to individuals. Large groups of employees may react with equal violence when their security or status is at stake. An example of this is the frequent reaction of white employees to the introduction of Negroes into the work force. The latter are a threat both to their security (the Negroes are considered as competitors in the labor market) and to their status (the whites resent being grouped with the Negroes whom they regard as of lower status). Actually the Negroes may be highly desirable as employees and may contribute to the welfare of the organization as a whole. Nevertheless, their introduction is violently resisted. While it is customary to attribute these resistances to the reluctance of people to change well-established habits, it is probable that the chief causes lie far deeper.

The principal root of this hostility to anything which threatens security or status is *fear* (frequently reinforced and rationalized by accumulated resentments and rivalries). The hostility which this fear generates, in turn, leads to attacks upon the sources of the anxiety. The amazing feature of these attacks is that many of them come from employees who, because of their rank or long service, have no real ground to fear for either their status or security. Nevertheless, quite without adequate justification, many feel extremely insecure. This is because deep-seated fears exist within the individual himself. Everyone knows fear. Even the infant is prey to this emotion because it is innate, inborn. Furthermore, everyone is constantly faced by very real and tangible grounds for anxiety and insecurity. Nature is cruel. The law of the fang prevails to a greater extent than many recognize. The world at large is no place for the weakling. Even business is highly competitive. Rivalries and conflicts exist within nearly every business. Realistically regarded, life is far from a bed of roses for most people.

Hence, the real and justifiable fears which beset the average person are legion. There is always somewhere in the future the danger of economic disaster, of another depression with its threat to savings, to the home, to security. Everyone is faced with the problem of old age and its attendant likelihood of illness, suffering, and dependence. Even in youth and the prime of life, there is always the immediate possibility of illness, of accidents, and the inevitability of death. Nor are these real grounds for fear confined to the individual himself. There is also the fear of misfortune to loved ones; a fear, again, which the war years have greatly stimulated. Finally, there is almost always the more or less immediate danger to everyone of loss of his job or of being displaced or demoted, with its attendant loss of prestige, "status," and earnings.

It must be kept in mind that the average rank-and-file employee in industry today, unlike his counterpart of fifty years ago, does not even own his own tools. The only commodity he has to sell is his labor or some readily replaceable skill. He is, therefore, much more dependent economically upon his job tenure than was the case with the man who could, if necessary, set up in business for himself. In addition, the longer he has remained with a particular company, often the greater his difficulty in getting work elsewhere. This is because the bulk of the routine jobs in industry today do not require great skill; certainly not in the sense of the old-time master craftsman. Consequently, the employee who has spent ten to twenty-five years in a particular line of work has gained little that is saleable, but has lost his youth, his vigor, and his adaptability to new lines of endeavor. He has given the best years of his life and often has little of vocational value to show for it.

It is because of this that there is such a feeling of need for some sort of job security among most working people (whether it be seniority or some other form of property rights in the job). For the same reason, anything which threatens job security or hard-won status, such as it is, is desperately feared and resented.

Unfortunately, these real and understandable grounds for fear are not the only ones which contribute to employee insecurity. Nearly all persons also suffer to a greater or less degree from neurotic anxieties and fears which have no basis in reality whatever. Among these latter are the insecurities which grow out of the passive dependent tendencies of the emotionally immature. Others grow out of the repeated rejections to which the individual may have been subjected during childhood or youth. Still others have their origin in an over-strict conscience, resulting from too rigorous an upbringing. (Nearly everything such persons do makes them feel guilty.) Likewise, many neurotic anxieties have their basis in buried but powerful hostilities toward loved ones and others which produce a free-floating sense of guilt and anxiety and lead to constant worrying.

Many of these fears, regardless of their nature, are too painful to be faced; they cannot be lived with. Hence, they have been thrust out of the center of the individual's consciousness; they are vaguely present on the periphery. They are not entirely repressed; merely out of sharp focus. Nevertheless, they continue to exist in a latent state, their power to disturb quite undiminished. Their presence constantly disturbs the individual's emotional equilibrium and makes its balance a precarious one. When any new challenge to his status or security occurs, it accentuates his existing anxieties and feelings of insecurity. These added fears almost inevitably upset his emotional balance. His latent fears, having been reinforced, once more threaten to become painfully conscious. This must be avoided at any cost. Hence, he has powerful incentive to rid himself of the source of danger to his status and security.

Fears which even trivial changes arouse are often so powerful that they are overwhelming. The fear thus induced is so real and poignant that it may even induce a state of actual panic. At this point, the victim ceases to be entirely rational, in spite of the fact that he may appear outwardly calm and possessed. If it appears politically expedient, he may even indicate a high degree of favor for the very changes which have excited his anxiety. Nevertheless, he will stop at nothing to save himself. (This attitude of superficial acceptance of an innovation is sometimes barefaced hypocrisy; more often the individual's fears are so acute that he cannot take an open stand against anything.)

Because of the highly emotional character of these resistances to change, a direct, logical presentation of the merits of the change is often futile. The more they are discussed, the more violent the anxieties they are likely to arouse and the greater the individual's need to discredit and eliminate them. Even worse, however, is to attempt to explain to him the *sources in himself* of his antagonisms to the projected change. This only makes him react more violently because it mobilizes fresh anxieties within him and breaks down his defenses against them. It not only forces him to face his naked fears himself, but makes him aware that others know his weaknesses. This adds to his anxieties—and to his aggressiveness.

In view of the foregoing circumstances, great caution must be exercised in making any changes in organization or methods, even those which are obviously and badly needed. It will never be possible wholly to eliminate anxieties in workers and supervisors with consequent resistances to change for its own sake and as a threat to their status or security. Hence, it is essential that any modification of product, procedures, organization, or policies which may affect status or may be interpreted as an implied threat to job security should be considered carefully before it is made. It is particularly important that its implications be considered from the standpoint of the insecurities and possible anxieties of the employees affected. It must always be kept in mind that, regardless of the facts, those who will be affected may interpret it somehow as a threat to them and respond accordingly.

Sometimes it is better, in the long run, not to make moderately needed changes because the disturbance they will occasion may be more costly in the end than will a continuance of the *status quo*. In those cases, where there is some real threat to an employee's status and security in the change, it will prove wiser and cheaper to "kick him upstairs" to some "advisory" job (thus retaining his status and job security), rather than risk the organization-wide disturbance of morale which his demotion or other "face" destroying course of action might bring with it. It is entirely possible for *one* individual, if sufficiently aroused, to disrupt the morale and smooth functioning of an entire segment of a business by pointing out that what has happened to him *could* happen to many others.

If it is finally decided that a change must be made, it is wise to move very slowly. Only one innovation should be introduced at a time; ample warning must precede it, and a full statement must be given of the reasons for it and the benefits which are expected to result from it. If this is done, there is less likelihood that the emotional equilibrium of the individual or group will be upset. Informing the employee in advance will do much to allay the fears that a sudden change might otherwise arouse. There will always be some anxiety, but this will help to minimize it.

Further to allay the fears of those affected, they should be given maximum opportunity to participate in the discussion and planning of proposed changes in advance of their introduction. They should also have some voice in deciding how and when they will be made effective. This gives them a feeling of having had at least some part in the determination of their own destinies. This tends to minimize their feelings of helplessness and consequent anxiety in the face of the changes. At the same time, it will give them a better insight into, and understanding of, the conditions calling for the innovations and the way in which they will be of personal benefit to those affected. This, in turn, will allay their anxieties and discourage the development of resistances and hostilities.

Finally, if a program calling for other than minor changes is to gain acceptance and use, it is imperative that ready outlets be provided for the expression and relief of the hostilities which will almost inevitably arise. Under the best of conditions, some of those affected will be disturbed and unhappy. Therefore, it will be necessary to provide these employees with easily accessible facilities to "talk out" their anxieties and resentments from time to time. They will not be aware that it is largely *fear* which stimulates their aggressions and needs for reassurance; all they will know is that having talked about them, they will feel better. Periodic, informal meetings between small groups of the affected employees and a representative of top management are to be recommended for this purpose. He must be patient and sympathetic and give the employees' complaints about the changes, no matter how absurd or unreasonable, a fair hearing. This thus provides a release for their accumulated tensions. Such meetings, by bringing resistances out into the open, have the advantages both of relieving the rancor of the disgruntled worker or supervisor before he has had a chance seriously to disrupt departmental morale, and of reviewing the worthwhileness of the new procedures and methods. Sometimes it will be indicated that even further changes are necessary.

The resistance of workers, supervisors, and executives to change is irritating and often frustrating. This is especially true when the improvements are designed specifically to help them and the company as a whole. However, if it is recognized that it is their basic anxieties and insecurities which underlie and stimulate their lack of cooperation, not sheer stubbornness, selfishness, and stupidity, a more understanding and sympathetic view can be taken of the problem. These resistances will probably never be totally overcome, but through the awareness of the basic fears and the application of the principles outlined above, an informed and constructuve course of action can be undertaken to insure the acceptance and continued use of the new procedures and policies, even though they may incorporate a number of radical innovations.

How to Deal with Resistance to Change

Ever since the Coch and French studies at the Harwood Manufacturing Company, many academicians and businessmen have seemed to advocate participation as the tool for overcoming resistance to change in an organization.[1] In this classic, Paul R. Lawrence makes it extremely clear that although participation can be a most potent tool, it is not a panacea which conquers resistance regardless of when or how it is used. Rather, participation should be viewed as a way of life—a style of leadership—based upon a philosophy akin to McGregor's Theory Y.[2] It cannot be used effectively to manipulate people to follow like sheep.

Also critically examined in this paper are the roles of the technical system and the social system in a change program. The author suggests that what people are resisting when change is introduced in the technical system is not the technical change per se, but the accompanying changes in human relationships. Often the change program is resisted because of the way it was handled by the staff specialists. Lawrence presents several "blind spots" that staff specialists bring to their work which compound resistance, and notes that this problem can be diminished. He concludes with an exploration of various kinds of management action for reducing worker resistance to staff-initiated changes.

[1] Lester Coch and John R. P. French, Jr., "Overcoming Resistance to Change." *Human Relations*, I, No. 4 (1948), 512-32.

[2] See Douglas McGregor, *The Human Side of Enterprise* (New York: McGraw-Hill Book Company, 1960), pp. 45-57.

HOW TO DEAL WITH RESISTANCE TO CHANGE

Paul R. Lawrence
Harvard University

One of the most baffling and recalcitrant of the problems which business executives face is employee resistance to change. Such resistance may take a number of forms—persistent reduction in output, increase in the number of "quits" and requests for transfer, chronic quarrels, sullen hostility, wildcat or slowdown strikes, and, of course, the expression of a lot of pseudological reasons why the change will not work. Even the more petty forms of this resistance can be troublesome.

All too often when executives encounter resistance to change, they "explain" it by quoting the cliche that "people resist change" and never look further. Yet changes must continually occur in industry. This applies with particular force to the all-important "little" changes that constantly take place—changes in work methods, in routine office procedures, in the location of a machine or a desk, in personnel assignments and job titles.

Reprinted from Paul R. Lawrence, "How to Deal with Resistance to Change," *Harvard Business Review,* XLVII, No. 1 (January-February, 1969), 4-12, 166-76. Used by permission. Copyright © 1969 by the President and Fellows of Harvard College; all rights reserved.
Foreword: This "HBR Classic," the fourth in a series of articles from the past with retrospective commentary, was first published in the May-June 1954 issue of HBR. It has been used and reused by businessmen ever since; requests for reprints, for instance, have continued steadily to this day—evidence that the author's analysis of the problems and of how to deal with them continues to be valid. Mr. Lawrence is still associated with the Harvard Business School, where he is now Wallace Brett Donham Professor of Organizational Behavior. His (retrospective) commentary on the article appears on page 399.

No one of these changes makes the headlines, but in total they account for much of our increase in productivity. They are not the spectacular once-in-a-lifetime technological revolutions that involve mass layoffs or the obsolescence of traditional skills, but they are vital to business progress.

Does it follow, therefore, that business management is forever saddled with the onerous job of "forcing" change down the throats of resistant people? My answer is *no*. It is the thesis of this article that people do *not* resist technical change as such and that most of the resistance which does occur is unnecessary. I shall discuss these points, among others:

1. A solution which has become increasingly popular for dealing with resistance to change is to get the people involved to "participate" in making the change. But as a practical matter "participation" as a device is not a good way for management to think about the problem. In fact, it may lead to trouble.

2. The key to the problem is to understand the true nature of resistance. Actually, what employees resist is usually not technical change but social change—the change in their human relationships that generally accompanies technical change.

3. Resistance is usually created because of certain blind spots and attitudes which staff specialists have as a result of their preoccupation with the technical aspects of new ideas.

4. Management can take concrete steps to deal constructively with these staff attitudes. The steps include emphasizing new standards of performance for staff specialists and encouraging them to think in different ways, as well as making use of the fact that signs of resistance can serve as a practical warning signal in directing and timing technological changes.

5. Top executives can also make their own efforts more effective at meetings of staff and operating groups where change is being discussed. They can do this by shifting their attention from the facts of schedules, technical details, work assignments, and so forth, to what the discussion of these items indicates in regard to developing resistance and receptiveness to change.

Let us begin by taking a look at some research into the nature of resistance to change. There are two studies in particular that I should like to discuss. They highlight contrasting ways of interpreting resistance to change and of coping with it in day-to-day administration.

Is Participation Enough?

The first study was conducted by Lester Coch and John R. P. French, Jr. in a clothing factory.[1] It deserves special comment because, it seems to me, it is the

[1] See Lester Coch and John R. P. French, Jr., "Overcoming Resistance to Change," *Human Relations,* Vol. 1, No. 4, 1948, p. 512.

most systematic study of the phenomenon of resistance to change that has been made in a factory setting. To describe it briefly:

The two researchers worked with four different groups of factory operators who were being paid on a modified piece-rate basis. For each of these four groups a minor change in the work procedure was installed by a different method, and the results were carefully recorded to see what, if any, problems of resistance occurred. The four experimental groups were roughly matched with respect to efficiency ratings and degree of cohesiveness; in each group the proposed change modified the established work procedure to about the same degree.

The work change was introduced to the first group by what the researchers called a "no-participation" method. This small group of operators was called into a room where some staff people told the members that there was a need for a minor methods change in their work procedures. The staff people then explained the change to the operators in detail, and gave them the reasons for the change. The operators were then sent back to the job with instructions to work in accordance with the new method.

The second group of operators was introduced to the work change by a "participation-through-representation" method—a variation of the approach used with the third and fourth groups which turned out to be of little significance.

The third and fourth groups of operators were both introduced to the work change on a "total-participation" basis. All the operators in these groups met with the staff men concerned. The staff men dramatically demonstrated the need for cost reduction. A general agreement was reached that some savings could be effected. The groups then discussed how existing work methods could be improved and unnecessary operations eliminated. When the new work methods were agreed on, all the operators were trained in the new methods, and all were observed by the time-study men for purposes of establishing a new piece rate on the job.

Research Findings. The researchers reported a marked contrast between the results achieved by the different methods of introducing this change:

No-participation group—The most striking difference was between Group #1, the no-participation group, and Groups #3 and #4, the total-participation groups. The output of Group #1 dropped immediately to about two thirds of its previous output rate. The output rate stayed at about this level throughout the period of 30 days after the change was introduced. The researchers further reported:

> *Resistance developed almost immediately after the change occurred. Marked expressions of aggression against management occurred, such as conflict with the methods engineer, ... hostility toward the supervisor, deliberate restriction of production, and lack of cooperation with the supervisor. There were 17% quits in the first 40 days. Grievances were filed about piece rates; but when the rate was checked, it was found to be a little "loose."*

Total-participation groups—In contrast with this record, Groups #3 and #4 showed a smaller initial drop in output and a very rapid recovery not only to the previous production rate but to a rate that exceeded the previous rate. In these groups there were no signs of hostility toward the staff people or toward the supervisors, and there were no quits during the experimental period.

Appraisal of Results: Without going into all the researchers' decisions based on these experiments, it can be fairly stated that they concluded that resistance to methods changes could be overcome by *getting the people involved in the change to participate in making it.*

This was a very useful study, but the results are likely to leave the manager of a factory still bothered by the question, "Where do we go from here?" The trouble centers around that word "participation." It is not a new word. It is seen often in management journals, heard often in management discussions. In fact, the idea that it is a good thing to get employee participation in making changes has become almost axiomatic in management circles.

But participation is not something that can be conjured up or created artificially. You obviously cannot buy it as you would buy a typewriter. You cannot hire industrial engineers and accountants and other staff people who have the ability "to get participation" built into them. It is doubtful how helpful it would be to call in a group of supervisors and staff men and exhort them, "Get in there and start participation."

Participation is a feeling on the part of people, not just the mechanical act of being called in to take part in discussions. Common sense would suggest that people are more likely to respond to the way they are customarily treated—say, as people whose opinions are respected because they themselves are respected for their own worth—rather than by the stratagem of being called to a meeting or being asked some carefully calculated questions. In fact, many supervisors and staff men have had some unhappy experiences with executives who have read about participation and have picked it up as a new psychological gimmick for getting other people to think they "want" to do as they are told—as a sure way to put the sugar coating on a bitter pill.

So there is still the problem of how to get this thing called participation. And, as a matter of fact, the question remains whether participation was the determining factor in the Coch and French experiment or whether there was something of deeper significance underlying it.

Resistance to What?

Now let us take a look at a second series of research findings about resistance to change. . . . While making some research observations in a factory manufacturing electronic products, a colleague and I had an opportunity to observe a number of incidents that for us threw new light on this matter of resistance to change.[2] One incident was particularly illuminating:

[2]For a complete report of the study, see Harriet O. Ronken and Paul R. Lawrence, *Administering Changes: A Case Study of Human Relations in a Factory* (Boston, Division of Research, Harvard Business School, 1952).

We were observing the work of one of the industrial engineers and a production operator who had been assigned to work with the engineer on assembling and testing an experimental product that the engineer was developing. The engineer and the operator were in almost constant daily contact in their work. It was a common occurrence for the engineer to suggest an idea for some modification in a part of the new product; he would then discuss his idea with the operator and ask her to try out the change to see how it worked. It was also a common occurrence for the operator to get an idea as she assembled parts and to pass this idea on to the engineer, who would then consider it and, on occasion, ask the operator to try out the idea and see if it proved useful.

A typical exchange between these two people might run somewhat as follows:

> *Engineer:* "I got to thinking last night about that difficulty we've been having on assembling the x part in the last few days. It occurred to me that we might get around that trouble if we washed the part in a cleaning solution just prior to assembling it."
>
> *Operator:* "Well, that sounds to me like it's worth trying."
>
> *Engineer:* "I'll get you some of the right kind of cleaning solution, and why don't you try doing that with about 50 parts and keep track of what happens."
>
> *Operator:* "Sure, I'll keep track of it and let you know how it works."

With this episode in mind, let us take a look at a second episode involving the same production operator. One day we noticed another engineer approaching the production operator. We knew that this particular engineer had had no previous contact with the production operator. He had been asked to take a look at one specific problem on the new product because of his special technical qualifications. He had decided to make a change in one of the parts of the product to eliminate the problem, and he had prepared some of these parts using his new method. Here is what happened:

He walked up to the production operator with the new parts in his hand and indicated to her by a gesture that he wanted her to try assembling some units using his new part. The operator picked up one of the parts and proceeded to assemble it. We noticed that she did not handle the part with her usual care. After she had assembled the product, she tested it and it failed to pass inspection. She turned to the new engineer and, with a triumphant air, said, "It doesn't work."

The new engineer indicated that she should try another part. She did so, and again it did not work. She then proceeded to assemble units using all of the new parts that were available. She handled each of them in an unusually rough manner. None of them worked. Again she turned to the engineer and said that the new parts did not work.

The engineer left, and later the operator, with evident satisfaction, commented to the original industrial engineer that the new engineer's idea was just no good.

Social Change: What can we learn from these episodes? To begin, it will be useful for our purposes to think of change as having both a technical and a social aspect. The *technical* aspect of the change is the making of a measurable modification in the physical routines of the job. The *social* aspect of the change refers to the way those affected by it think it will alter their established relationships in the organization.

We can clarify this distinction by referring to the two foregoing episodes. In both of them, the technical aspects of the changes introduced were virtually identical: the operator was asked to use a slightly changed part in assembling the finished product. By contrast, the social aspects of the changes -were quite different.

In the first episode, the interaction between the industrial engineer and the operator tended to sustain the give-and-take kind of relationship that these two people were accustomed to. The operator was used to being treated as a person with some valuable skills and knowledge and some sense of responsibility about her work; when the engineer approached her with his idea, she felt she was being dealt with in the usual way. But, in the second episode, the new engineer was introducing not only a technical change but also a change in the operator's customary way of relating herself to others in the organization. By his brusque manner and by his lack of any explanation, he led the operator to fear that her usual work relationships were being changed. And she just did not like the new way she was being treated.

The results of these two episodes were quite different also. In the first episode there were no symptoms of resistance to change, a very good chance that the experimental change would determine fairly whether a cleaning solution would improve product quality, and a willingness on the part of the operator to accept future changes when the industrial engineer suggested them. In the second episode, however, there were signs of resistance to change (the operator's careless handling of parts and her satisfaction in their failure to work), failure to prove whether the modified part was an improvement or not, and indications that the operator would resist any further changes by the engineer. We might summarize the two contrasting patterns of human behavior in the two episodes in graphic form; see Table 1.

It is apparent from these two patterns that the variable which determines the result is the *social* aspect of the change. In other words, the operator did not resist the technical change as such but rather the accompanying change in her human relationships.

Confirmation: This conclusion is based on more than one case. Many other cases in our research project substantiate it. Furthermore, we can find confirmation in the research experience of Coch and French, even though they came out with a different interpretation.

Coch and French tell us in their report that the procedure used with Group # 1, i.e., the no-participation group, was the usual one in the factory for introducing work changes. And yet they also tell us something about the

TABLE 1

Two Contrasting Patterns of Human Behavior

	Change		
	Technical aspect	*Social aspect*	*Results*
Episode 1	Clean part prior to assembly	Sustaining the customary work relationship of operator	1. No resistance 2. Useful technical result 3. Readiness for more change
Episode 2	Use new part in assembly	Threatening the customary work relationship of operator	1. Signs of resistance 2. No useful technical result 3. Lack of readiness for more change

customary treatment of the operators in their work life. For example, the company's labor relations policies are progressive, the company and the supervisors place a high value on fair and open dealings with the employees, and the employees are encouraged to take up their problems and grievances with management. Also, the operators are accustomed to measuring the success and failure of themselves as operators against the company's standard output figures.

Now compare these *customary* work relationships with the way the Group # 1 operators were treated when they were introduced to this particular work change. There is quite a difference. When the management called them into the room for indoctrination, they were treated as if they had no useful knowledge of their own jobs. In effect, they were told that they were not the skilled and efficient operators they had thought they were, that they were doing the job inefficiently, and that some "outsider" (the staff expert) would now tell them how to do it right. How could they construe this experience *except* as a threatening change in their usual working relationship? It is the story of the second episode in our research case all over again. The results were also all the same, with signs of resistance, persistently low output, and so on.

Now consider experimental Groups #3 and #4, i.e., the total-participation groups. Coch and French referred to management's approach in their case as a "new" method of introducing change; but, from the point of view of the *operators* it must not have seemed new at all. It was simply a continuation of the way they were ordinarily dealt with in the course of their regular work. And what happened? The results—reception to change, technical improvement, better performance—were much like those reported in the first episode between the operator and the industrial engineer.

So the research data of Coch and French tend to confirm the conclusion that the nature and size of the technical aspect of the change does not determine the presence or absence of resistance nearly so much as does the social aspect of the change.

The significance of these research findings, from management's point of view, is that executives and staff experts need not expertness in using the devices of participation but a real understanding, in depth and detail, of the specific social arrangements that will be sustained or threatened by the change or by the way in which it is introduced.

These observations check with everyday management experience in industry. When we stop to think about it, we know that many changes occur in our factories without a bit of resistance. We know that people who are working closely with one another continually swap ideas about short cuts and minor changes in procedure that are adopted so easily and naturally that we seldom notice them or even think of them as change. The point is that because these people work so closely with one another, they intuitively understand and take account of the existing social arrangements for work and so feel no threat to themselves in such everyday changes.

By contrast, management actions leading to what we commonly label "change" are usually initiated outside the small work group by staff people. These are the changes that we notice and the ones that most frequently bring on symptoms of resistance. By the very nature of their work, most of our staff specialists in industry do not have the intimate contact with operating groups that allows them to acquire an intuitive understanding of the complex social arrangements which their ideas may affect. Neither do our staff specialists always have the day-to-day dealings with operating people that lead them to develop a natural respect for the knowledge and skill of these people. As a result, all too often the men behave in a way that threatens and disrupts the established social relationships. And the tragedy is that so many of these upsets are inadvertent and unnecessary.

Yet industry must have its specialists—not only many kinds of engineering specialists (product, process, maintenance, quality, and safety engineers) but also cost accountants, production schedulers, purchasing agents, and personnel men. Must top management therefore reconcile itself to continual resistance to change, or can it take constructive action to meet the problem?

I believe that our research in various factory situations indicates why resistance to change occurs and what management can do about it. Let us take the "why" factors first.

Self-preoccupation: All too frequently we see staff specialists who bring to their work certain blind spots that get them into trouble when they initiate change with operating people. One such blind spot is "self-preoccupation." The staff man gets so engrossed in the technology of the change he is interested in promoting that he becomes wholly oblivious to different kinds of things that may be bothering people. Here are two examples:

In one situation the staff people introduced, with the best of intentions, a technological change which inadvertently deprived a number of skilled operators of much of the satisfaction that they were finding in their work. Among other things, the change meant that, whereas formerly the output of each operator had been placed beside his work position where it could be viewed and appreciated by him and by others, it was now being carried away immediately from the work position. The workmen did not like this.

The sad part of it was that there was no compelling cost or technical reason why the output could not be placed beside the work position as it had been formerly. But the staff people who had introduced the change were so literal-minded about their ideas that when they heard complaints on the changes from the operators, they could not comprehend what the trouble was. Instead, they began repeating all the logical arguments why the change made sense from a cost standpoint. The final result here was a chronic restriction of output and persistent hostility on the part of the operators.

An industrial engineer undertook to introduce some methods changes in one department with the notion firmly in mind that this assignment presented him with an opportunity to "prove" to higher management the value of his function. He became so preoccupied with his personal desire to make a name for his particular techniques that he failed to pay any attention to some fairly obvious and practical considerations which the operating people were calling to his attention but which did not show up in his time-study techniques. As could be expected, resistance quickly developed to all his ideas, and the only "name" that he finally won for his techniques was a black one.

Obviously, in both of these situations the staff specialists involved did not take into account the social aspects of the change they were introducing. For different reasons they got so preoccupied with the technical aspects of the change that they literally could not see or understand what all the fuss was about.

We may sometimes wish that the validity of the technical aspect of the change were the sole determinant of its acceptability. But the fact remains that the social aspect is what determines the presence or absence of resistance. Just as ignoring this fact is the sure way to trouble, so taking advantage of it can lead to positive results. We must not forget that these same social arrangements which at times seem so bothersome are essential for the performance of work. Without a network of established social relationships a factory would be populated with a collection of people who had no idea of how to work with one another in an organized fashion. By working *with* this network instead of *against* it, management's staff representatives can give new technological ideas a better chance of acceptance.

Know-how of Operators Overlooked: Another blind spot of many staff specialists is to the strengths as well as to the weaknesses of firsthand production experience. They do not recognize that the production foreman and the production operator are in their own way specialists themselves—specialists in actual experience with production problems. This point should be obvious, but it is amazing how many staff specialists fail to appreciate the fact that even though they themselves may have a superior knowledge of the technology of the production process involved, the foreman or the operators may have a more practical understanding of how to get daily production out of a group of men and machines.

The experience of the operating people frequently equips them to be of real help to staff specialists on at least two counts: (1) The operating people are often able to spot practical production difficulties in the ideas of the specialists—and iron out those difficulties before it is too late; (2) the operating people are often able to take advantage of their intimate acquaintance with the existing social arrangements for getting work done. If given a chance, they can use this kind of knowledge to help detect those parts of the change that will have undesirable social consequences. The staff experts can then go to work on ways to avoid the trouble area without materially affecting the technical worth of the change.

Further, some staff specialists have yet to learn the truth that, even after the plans for a change have been carefully made, it takes *time* to put the change successfully into production use. Time is necessary even though there may be no resistance to the change itself. The operators must develop the skill needed to use new methods and new equipment efficiently; there are always bugs to be taken out of a new method or piece of equipment even with the best of engineering. When a staff man begins to lose his patience with the amount of time that these steps take, the people he is working with will begin to feel that he is pushing them; *this* amounts to a change in their customary work relationships and resistance will start building up where there was none before.

The situation is aggravated if the staff man mistakenly accuses the operators of resisting the idea of the change, for there are few things that irritate people more than to be blamed for resisting change when actually they are doing their best to learn a difficult new procedure.

Management Action

Many of the problems of resistance to change arise around certain kinds of *attitudes* that staff men are liable to develop about their jobs and their own ideas for introducing change. Fortunately, management can influence these attitudes and thus deal with the problems at their source.

Broadening Staff Interests: It is fairly common for a staff man to work so hard on one of his ideas for change that he comes to identify himself with it. This is fine for the organization when he is working on the idea by himself or with his immediate colleagues; the idea becomes "his baby," and the company benefits from his complete devotion to his work.

But when he goes to some group of operating people to introduce a change, his very identification with his ideas tends to make him unreceptive to any suggestions for modification. He just does not feel like letting anyone else tamper with his pet ideas. It is easy to see, of course, how this attitude is interpreted by the operating people as a lack of respect for their suggestions.

This problem of the staff man's extreme identification with his work is one which, to some extent, can only be cured by time. But here are four suggestions for speeding up the process:

1. The manager can often, with wise timing, encourage the staff man's interest in a different project that is just starting.

2. The manager can also, by his "coaching" as well as by example, prod the staff man to develop a healthier respect for the contributions he can receive from operating people; success in this area would, of course, virtually solve the problem.

3. It also helps if the staff man can be guided to recognize that the satisfaction he derives from being productive and creative is the same satisfaction he denies the operating poeple by his behavior toward them. Experience shows that staff people can sometimes be stimulated by the thought of finding satisfaction in sharing with others in the organization the pleasures of being creative.

4. Sometimes, too, the staff man can be led to see that winning acceptance of his ideas through better understanding and handling of human beings is just as challenging and rewarding as giving birth to an idea.

Using Understandable Terms: One of the problems that must be overcome arises from the fact that the typical staff man is likely to have the attitude that the reasons why he is recommending any given change may be so complicated and specialized that it is impossible to explain them to operating people. It may be true that the operating people would find it next to impossible to understand some of the staff man's analytical techniques, but this does not keep them from coming to the conclusion that the staff specialist is trying to razzle-dazzle them with tricky figures and formulas—insulting their intelligence—if he does not strive to his utmost to translate his ideas into terms understandable to them. The following case illustrates the importance of this point:

A staff specialist was temporarily successful in "selling" a change based on a complicated mathematical formula to a foreman who really did not understand it. The whole thing backfired, however, when the foreman tried to sell it to his operating people. They asked him a couple of sharp questions that he could not answer. His embarrassment about this led him to resent and resist the change so much that eventually the whole proposition fell through. This was unfortunate in terms not only of human relations but also of technological progress in the plant.

There are some very good reasons, both technical and social, why the staff man should be interested in working with the operating people until his recommendations make "sense." (This does not mean that the operating people need to understand the recommendations in quite the same way or in the same detail that the staff man does, but that they should be able to visualize the recommendations in terms of their job experiences.) Failure of the staff man to provide an adequate explanation is likely to mean that a job the operators had formerly performed with understanding and satisfaction will now be performed without understanding and with less satisfaction.

This loss of satisfaction not only concerns the individual involved but also is significant from the standpoint of the company which is trying to get maximum productivity from the operating people. A person who does not have a feeling of comprehension of what he is doing is denied the opportunity to exercise that uniquely human ability—the ability to use informed and intelligent judgment on what he does. If the staff man leaves the operating people with a sense of confusion, they will also be left unhappy and less productive.

Top line and staff executives responsible for the operation should make it a point, therefore, to know how the staff man goes about installing a change. They can do this by asking discerning questions when he reports to them, listening closely to reports of employee reaction, and, if they have the opportunity, actually watching the staff man at work. At times they may have to take such drastic action as insisting that the time of installation of a proposed change be postponed until the operators are ready for it. But, for the most part, straightforward discussions with the staff man in terms of what they think of his approach should help him, over a period of time, to learn what is expected of him in his relationships with operating personnel.

New Look at Resistance: Another attitude that gets staff men into trouble is the *expectation* that all the people involved will resist the change. It is curious but true that the staff man who goes into his job with the conviction that people are going to resist any idea he presents with blind stubbornness is likely to find them responding just the way he thinks they will. The process is clear: whenever he treats the people who are supposed to buy his ideas as if they were bullheaded, he changes the way they are used to being treated; and they *will* be bullheaded in resisting *that* change!

I think that the staff man—and management in general—will do better to look at it this way: When resistance *does* appear, it should not be thought of as something to be *overcome.* Instead, it can best be thought of as a useful red flag—a signal that something is going wrong. To use a rough analogy, signs of resistance in a social organization are useful in the same way that pain is useful to the body as a signal that some bodily functions are getting out of adjustment.

The resistance, like the pain, does not tell what is wrong but only that something *is* wrong. And it makes no more sense to try to overcome such resistance than it does to take a pain killer without diagnosing the bodily ailment. Therefore, when resistance appears, it is time to listen carefully to find out what the trouble is. What is needed is not a long harangue on the logics of the new recommendations but a careful exploration of the difficulty.

It may happen that the problem is some technical imperfection in the change that can be readily corrected. More than likely, it will turn out that the change is threatening and upsetting some of the established social arrangements for doing work. Whether the trouble is easy or difficult to correct, management will at least know what it is dealing with.

New Job Definition: Finally, some staff specialists get themselves in trouble because they assume they have the answer in the thought that people will accept a change when they have participated in making it. For example:

In one plant we visited, an engineer confided to us (obviously because we, as researchers on human relations, were interested in psychological gimmicks!) that he was going to put across a proposed production layout change of his by inserting in it a rather obvious error, which others could then suggest should be corrected. We attended the meeting where this stunt was performed, and superficially it worked. Somebody caught the error, proposed that it be corrected, and our engineer immediately "bought" the suggestion as a very worthwhile one and made the change. The group then seemed to "buy" his entire layout proposal.

It looked like an effective technique—oh, so easy—until later, when we became better acquainted with the people in the plant. Then we found out that many of the engineer's colleagues considered him a phony and did not trust him. The resistance they put up to his ideas was very subtle, yet even more real and difficult for management to deal with.

Participation will never work so long as it is treated as a device to get somebody else to do what you want him to. Real participation is based on respect. And respect is not acquired by just trying; it is acquired when the staff man faces the reality that he needs the contributions of the operating people.

If the staff man defines his job as not just generating ideas but also getting those ideas into practical operation, he will recognize his real dependence on the contributions of the operating people. He will ask them for ideas and suggestions, not in a backhanded way to get compliance, but in a straightforward way to get some good ideas and avoid some unnecessary mistakes. By this process he will be treating the operating people in such a way that his own behavior will not be perceived as a threat to their customary work relationships. It will be possible to discuss, and accept or reject, the ideas on their own merit.

The staff specialist who looks at the process of introducing change and at resistance to change in the manner outlined in the preceding pages may not be hailed as a genius, but he can be counted on in installing a steady flow of technical changes that will cut costs and improve quality without upsetting the organization.

Role of the Administrator

Now what about the way the top executive goes about his own job as it involves the introduction of change and problems of resistance?

One of the most important things he can do, of course, is to deal with staff people in much the same way that he wants them to deal with the operators. He must realize that staff people resist social change, too. (This means, among other things, that he should not prescribe particular rules to them on the basis of this article!)

But most important, I think, is the way the administrator conceives of his job in coordinating the work of the different staff and line groups involved in a change. Does he think of his duties *primarily* as checking up, delegating and following through, applying pressure when performance fails to measure up? Or does he think of them *primarily* as facilitating communication and understanding between people with different points of view—for example, between a staff engineering group and a production group who do not see eye to eye on a change they are both involved in. An analysis of management's actual experience—or, at least, that part of it which has been covered by our research—points to the latter as the more effective concept of administration.

I do not mean that the executive should spend his time with the different people concerned discussing the human problems of change as such. He *should* discuss schedules, technical details, work assignments, and so forth. But he should also be watching closely for the messages that are passing back and forth as people discuss these topics. He will find that people—himself as well as others—are always implicitly asking and making answers to questions like: "How will he accept criticism?" "How much can I afford to tell him?" "Does he really get my point?" "Is he playing games?" The answers to such questions determine the degree of candor and the amount of understanding between the people involved.

When the administrator concerns himself with these problems and acts to facilitate understanding, there will be less logrolling and more sense of common purpose, fewer words and better understanding, less anxiety and more acceptance of criticism, less griping and more attention to specific problems—in short, better performance in putting new ideas for technological change into effect.

Retrospective Commentary

In the 15 years since this article was published, we have seen a great deal of change in industry, but the human aspects of the topic do not seem very different. The human problems associated with change remain much the same even though our understanding of them and our methods for dealing with them have advanced.

The first of the two major themes of the article is that resistance to change does not arise because of technical factors per se but because of social and human considerations. This statement still seems to be true. There is, however, an implication in the article that the social and human costs of change, if recognized, can largely be avoided by thoughtful management effort. Today I am less sanguine about this.

It is true that these costs can be greatly reduced by conscious attention. Managements that have tried have made much progress during the past 15 years. Here are some examples of what has been done:

> Fewer people are now pushed out of the back doors of industry—embittered and "burned out" before their time.

Fewer major strikes are the result of head-on clashes over new technology and its effects on jobs.

Progress is being made in putting the needs of people into the design of new technological systems.

Relevant inputs of ideas and opinions of people from all ranks are being solicited and used *before* (not after) plans for change are frozen.

At the same time that well-established work groups are disrupted by technical imperatives, special efforts are made to help newly formed work groups evolve meaningful team relations quickly.

Time and care have been taken to counsel individuals whose careers have to some degree been disrupted by change.

All of these ways of reducing the human costs of change have worked for the companies that have seriously applied them. Still, I am more aware than in 1954 of the limits of such approaches. They do not always enable management to prevent situations from developing in which some individuals win while others lose. The values lost as skills become obsolete cannot always be replaced. The company's earnings may go up but the percentage payouts from even an enlarged "pie" have to be recalculated, and then the relative rewards shift. In these situations enlightened problem solving will not completely displace old-fashioned bargaining, and better communication will only clarify the hard-core realities.

The second theme of the article deals with ways of improving the relations between groups in an organization—particularly when a staff group is initiating change in the work of an operating or line group. The gap that exists in outlook and orientation between specialized groups in industry has increased in the past 15 years, even as the number of such groups has continued to escalate. These larger gaps have in turn created ever more difficult problems of securing effective communication and problem solving between groups. Coordinating the groups is probably the number one problem of our modern corporations. So this second theme is hardly out-of-date.

Today, however, there is both more knowledge available about the problem than there was in 1954 and more sophisticated skill and attention being given to it. And there is increasing understanding of and respect for the necessity for differences between groups. There is less striving for consistency for its own sake. More managerial effort is being applied, in person and through impersonal systems, to bridge the gaps in understanding. While the conflicts between specialized groups are probably as intense now as ever, they are more frequently seen as task-related—that is, natural outgrowths of different jobs, skills, and approaches—rather than as redundant and related only to personality differences.

The major criticism that has been brought to my attention about the article is that it has damaged the useful concept of participation. Perhaps this is true. But the view of participation as a technique for securing compliance with a predetermined change was a widespread and seductive one in 1954—and it is not dead yet. Subsequent research has not altered the general conclusion that participation, to be of value, must be based on a search for ideas that are seen as truly relevant to the change under consideration. The shallow notion of participation, therefore, still needs to be debunked.

As a final thought, I now realize that the article implied that workers resist change while managers foster and implement change. Many of the changes of the intervening period, such as the computer revolution, have exposed the inadequacy of this assumption. It is difficult to find any managers today who do not at times feel greatly distressed because of changes, with their own resistance level running fairly high. We are all, at times, resistors as well as instigators of change. We are all involved on both sides of the process of adjusting to change.

In light of this, let me reemphasize the point that resistance to change is by itself neither good nor bad. Resistance may be soundly based or not. It is always, however, an important signal calling for further inquiry by management.

Resistance to Change—
Its Analysis and Prevention

Alvin Zander's discussion first sets forth six major conditions conducive to resistance to change. He next suggests that "resistance will be prevented to the degree that the changer helps the changees to develop their own understanding of the need for the change, and an explicit awareness of how they feel about it, and what can be done about those feelings." He concludes by proposing four techniques that he believes are paramount in overcoming resistance to change.

RESISTANCE TO CHANGE—
ITS ANALYSIS AND PREVENTION

Alvin Zander

University of Michigan

In order to derive the benefit from research in industrial relations, someone must plan a program of action to apply them. When one begins implementing, he must change the social system in some way. The creation of this change can cause the development of resistance in those influenced by the change.

First, we shall look at what resistance is; second, the conditions that appear to be associated with its development; and third, some means whereby resistance may be prevented or decreased.

Nature of Resistance

Let us look at some examples of resistance growing out of administrative changes.

A large number of foremen in a company were given training in how to treat their men like human beings. They liked the course and were eager to apply their learnings on the job. The company found, however, that relatively few of the foremen are really behaving any different on the job. They know their stuff but do not use it.

Alvin Zander is affiliated with the Research Center for Group Dynamics, Institute for Social Research, University of Michigan.

Reprinted from Alvin Zander, "Resistance to Change—Its Analysis and Prevention," *Advanced Management,* XV, No. 1 (January, 1950) 9-11, by permission of Advanced Management Journal and the author.

In one of the paper-shuffling government agencies a new data form was developed which all admitted was briefer, more logical, and easier to use. Yet, this department found that the employees often omitted much of the data needed on this form, their speed of work decreased, and they objected to it on many insignificant grounds.

Our favorite example of resistance was furnished by a farmer in the TVA area. He assured us that he knew all about contour plowing, the rotation of crops, and the use of what he called "phosaphate" for improving the soil. He allowed as how these were good ideas, "But," he said, "I don't do it that way."

These examples have one common denominator which might serve here as a definition of resistance. They describe behavior which is intended to protect an individual from the effects of real or imagined change. This reaction might be to either real or imagined change since the resister might be reacting to things that were really not changed but he thinks were, or fears that they might be. If a person believes a change has been made, or fears potential change, it makes no difference whether or not it is true in fact. He will act as though there has been a change.

How can one recognize when resistance is working? Unfortunately, there is no list of typical behavior which can be described as the symptoms of resistance, which, if present, indicate that one is dealing with this phenomenon. It is the protective function which the behavior is providing which determines whether or not a person is resisting, rather than the kind of thing he does. By the same token, all behavior which opposes change is not necessarily resistance. Some opposition to change may be perfectly logical and grounded on well-supported reasons. The behavior must be attempting to protect the person against the consequences of the change in order for it to be resistance. This may be clearer if we look at the origin of the concept.

The Hostility Pattern

The term and the concept we are using here has been borrowed from psychotherapy. When a therapist is attempting to change the behavior of the patient, he expects resistance from him. The therapist takes the position that the pattern of behavior used by the patient (which makes him a "sick" person) is a means to some satisfaction for him even though it also may make him ineffective or unhappy. Resistance occurs in the patient when the process of change (therapy here) comes close to being successful. When faced with the unpleasant necessity of giving up the behavior he does not like, but somehow needs, he begins to balk. He becomes silent, blushes, changes the subject, tells fibs, comes late to appointments, becomes angry with the therapist, or any of a number of similar things. The therapist watches for the context in which these signs of resistance occur since these indicate the crucial problems in the way the patient sees and deals with his world.

For the administrator, resistance may occur under fairly similar conditions.

When he attempts to create a change the administrator may develop, unintentionally, many threats to the person or groups with whom he works. The behavior used by the resister may take many forms.

It may take the form of hostility either openly expressed or obliquely implied. The aggression may be directed against the change itself or against the administrator. What is done depends on how the person can safely resist without further endangering himself in that situation. Other symptoms of resistance may be sloppy effort after the change has been made, or fawning submissiveness which is a hybrid of applepolishing and apathy. It can occur by lowering the level of aspiration to an inefficient degree, discouragement, or the development of unhappy cliques and outspoken factions. It is important, however, to remind ourselves, that it is the function which such actions are performing for the person that makes them resistance rather than what they look like.

Where Resistance Starts

It will be helpful if we look at a few conditions conducive to resistance.

1. Resistance can be expected if the nature of the change is not made clear to the people who are going to be influenced by the change. In one of the largest government agencies, a change required one department which originally had the responsibility of processing papers involved in contacts with certain industries to share this task with another office. Announcement of the change was issued in a brief statement. The immediate reaction was violent objection, even though some of the workers privately admitted that it was a wise and necessary move. They were reacting to incomplete information. Many people fear incomplete information about changes which influence them. It is more comfortable to know exactly where one stands.

There is some evidence to support the hypothesis that those persons who dislike their jobs, will most dislike ambiguity in a proposed change. They want to know exactly what they must do in order to be sure to avoid the unpleasant aspects of their jobs. Some administrators may attach too much importance to the value of information itself. Apparently they reason that people "ought not" to resist the way they do because the administrator has told them everything he thinks is important for them to know about the impending change.

2. Different people will see different meanings in the proposed change. Some of the resistant reaction described above came about because some workers saw the change as an indication that they had been doing a poor job, others assumed it meant their office would soon be abolished, still others were troubled since they were losing some of the power they had formerly controlled. We tend to see in our world the things that we expect to see. Complete information can just as readily be distorted as incomplete information, especially so if the workers have found discomfort and threats in their past work situation.

3. Resistance can be expected when those influenced are caught in a jam

between strong forces pushing them to make the change and strong forces deterring them against making the change.

4. Resistance may be expected to the degree that the persons influenced by the change have pressure put upon them to make it, and will be decreased to the degree that these same persons are able to have some "say" in the nature or direction of the change. In a garment factory a change was required. The switch meant that workers would be asked to change their jobs and, in many cases, to develop working relationships with new people. An experiment was made in which three different styles of introducing this change were tried out. One group of workers were simply informed about the change and were allowed to ask questions. They developed the most resistance as measured by turnover, absenteeism, and slowness in learning the job. Resistance was *less* in those groups who sent representatives to a meeting in which the nature of the change was discussed and all persons present made plans to carry out the change.

Resistance was *least* in the groups in which those to be affected discussed the nature of the change, laid plans for making it, and as a total group made decisions which were satisfactory to the entire group. In this latter group everyone participated. They had an opportunity to develop their own motivation instead of making the change only on the basis of orders from the boss. The fact that they were able to develop their own understanding of the need for the change and their own decisions about how to do it, reduced resistance most effectively.

5. Resistance may be expected if the change is made on personal grounds rather than impersonal requirements or sanctions. A supervisor posted the following notice:

I have always felt that promptness is an important indicator of an employee's interest in his job. I will feel much better if you are at your desk at the proper time.

Employees responded to this notice by appointing a committee to get information which would justify their late arrival at the office. Many administrators can expect trouble in establishing a change if it is requested in terms of what "I think is necessary"; rather than making the request in the light of "our objectives," the rules, the present state of affairs, or some other impersonal requirement.

6. Resistance may be expected if the change ignores the already established institutions in the group. Every work situation develops certain customs in doing the work or in the relations among the workers. The administrator who ignores institutionalized patterns of work and abruptly attempts to create a new state of affairs which demands that these customs be abolished without further consideration will surely run into resistance.

These are a few of the conditions in which resistance might be expected to occur. There probably are many others.

Decreasing Resistance

Some procedures on the part of the administrator might be useful in pre-venting or decreasing the resistance which arises in a changed situation. Let us look at a major principle in preventing resistance and some of its basic implica-tions:

Resistance will be prevented to the degree that the changer helps the changees to develop their own understanding of the need for the change, and an explicit awareness of how they feel about it, and what can be done about those feelings.

This principle implies that the administrator can use resistance as an important symptom. Specifically, he can use the nature of the resistance as an indicator of the cause of resistance. It will be most helpful to him as a symptom, if he diagnoses the causes for it when it occurs rather than inhibiting it at once. The same resistant behavior, for example, may indicate that one person feels that he has lost prestige by the change, to another it may mean that he has lost power over an area of influence which he formerly controlled, and to still another it may mean that he fears that his friends will think less well of him. An administrator must know what the resistance means in order that he may effectively lessen it by working on the causes instead of the symptom.

There has been a good deal of experience in recent years in staff meetings and in work conferences like the National Training Laboratory for Group Develop-ment with the use of a group observer. This observer gives to the group, and the leaders, information about the group and the nature of any resistance. In these cases, the data about itself is made common group property for all members to discuss and to use in planning better work relations.

This communication must go in both directions. If two-way communication is not maintained, negative attitudes created during resistance will tend to persist.

Restoring Understanding

In a utility company a new office was formed with a new set of supervisors. The entire staff of supervisors called the workers together and scolded them for shortcomings in their performance. The tone used by the supervisors was so aggressive that the employees found it difficult thereafter to discuss anything with them except those topics directly related to the effectiveness of produc-tion. The workers kept themselves at a distance from the supervisors and the supervisors made no move to close the gap. The result was that distance between these two groups made it impossible for them to come to any new understanding of each other. This mounting hostility was lessened only when the personnel department advised a number of "gripe-sessions" with small groups of workers in which the two levels developed a new understanding of each other.

Another implication in the above principle is that there is value in blowing off steam. The psychologists call this a "catharsis." There is good evidence that new attitudes can be accepted by a person only if he has a chance to thoroughly air his original attitude. Resistance to accepting the rigid, and often apparently meaningless, rules of military life, showed itself in flagrant violation of the rules, often in a most aggressive manner. Punishment only increased the resistance. Relief was provided by group sessions in which men were able to thoroughly gripe. After this relief of tension, they were able to turn to a reasonable discussion about what they could do to learn to live in terms of these requirements. It is as though new air can be put in the tire only after the old air is released.

A third implication of the earlier expressed principal is that resistance may be less likely to occur if the group participates in making the decisions about how the change should be implemented, what the change should be like, how people might perform in the changed situation, or any other problems that are within their area of freedom to decide. The experiment in which three ways of introducing a change were tried out showed that the workers, who had a chance to make a group decision about the ways in which the change should be made, developed much less resistance than did those who were simply called together to be told about the change and have all of their questions answered. What is important here is that the workers feel that they have a chance to discuss the major factors involved in the change, a chance to understand the nature of the fears they have in facing this change, and a chance to plan what they will do to calm their fears.

Self-diagnosis Gets Action

Still another implication is that resistance will be less likely to develop if facts which point to the need for change are gathered by the persons who must make the change. A number of high level supervisors in a utility industry came to feel that the workers had many negative attitudes about their jobs which were due to poor supervisory practices. Each supervisor, quite naturally, felt that other supervisors were at fault. Top management set up a number of study groups in which the supervisors first learned how they could diagnose the causes of these negative attitudes. Each supervisor then returned to his own work place and gathered facts that would be necessary for him to analyse the causes of negative attitudes he could spot among his workers. Later the supervisors came together to report their findings. At this meeting their enthusiasm for change in their own practices was high because they had participated in gathering the facts which best described their problems. People will be more likely to act in terms of information they gather themselves than in terms of information gathered by others and delivered to them. If it is clear that a change is indicated in a given state of affairs, but the people who must abide by the change are resisting the shift, they can come to see it themselves by obtaining the facts which properly "case" the situation.

To summarize, we have said that resistance is a problem which any person who is responsible for social change must face. Even though it is strange and unexpected behavior, there are causes for the development of this phenomenon. These causes may be understood, and resistance may be prevented, if the administrator will help the changes develop their own understanding of the need for change and explicit awareness of how they feel about it, and what can be done about those feelings.

Overcoming Resistance to Stability
A Time to Move;
A Time to Pause

This exposition will serve well as the bridge between the first three selections, which focus upon overcoming resistance to change, and the final one, which concentrates upon the role of the defender of the status quo as not only legitimate, but essential. Robert Albanese postulates five reasons for the present emphasis on change, suggests how the mutually exclusive needs for change and stability or continuity can be balanced, and argues strongly for both (a) precautions to ensure that the right and the skill to resist change will be a valued part of the organization climate, and (b) an understanding (by change agents and managers alike) that the right to resist is an organizational liberty. We wholeheartedly agree, especially with the notions about the right to resist.

Clearly, an organization within a democratic culture should offer a democratic environment. One of the fundamental precepts of a democratic environment is the right to resist—as long as resistance is carried out within the rules established by the system. We reject the idea of destroying the system with the hope that a new one will emerge automatically from the ashes of the old. A wise old mentor, Jack Barbash, summed it succinctly when he said in another context:

> *My view is that democracy ... should be asserted to the point of inconvenience if necessary, but not to the point of critical impairment of*

vital functions. The problem in developing a theory of... democracy, then, as I see it, is to find the common ground between society and the ... going, effective, decision-making institution in modern industrial society.[1]

It is important to note that we do not see any disparity between these views about the right to resist and those of Schein's concept of "coercive persuasion" discussed in Part II.

Albanese also makes reference to the dual tendencies of human systems. One is toward growth, the other toward homeostasis. While most of the emphasis in the literature is on growth, Albanese stresses the maintenance aspects. He contrasts the exciting concepts of changing—dynamism and unprogrammed behavior—with the less exotic ingredients associated with maintenance—stability, control, and programmed behavior. He continues with a very insightful elaboration of Lewin's force-field model, presenting a variation on the main theme that carries us far beyond the level to which Schein or Lippitt, Watson, and Westley had carried it.[2] *Here it is being considered as a strategy not for achieving change but for resisting it! What comes out of this approach is, among other things, a viable model for intelligent resistance along with a recipe for stability and continuity.*

Another of the skillfully made points has to do with the unfreezing stage of the Lewin model and what Albanese calls nonsupport. In the process of the introduction of change, it is certain that the client system must receive some feedback to the effect that its present behavior and/or attitude is unacceptable. This nonsupport is the precipitator of the felt need to change behavior, even if the change is made grudgingly. This is precisely why Bartlett calls for a change design that has as its primary focus a change of behavior, not attitudes.[3]

A final note is the elaboration of a concept called "organizational slack," defined by Cyert and March as "the difference between the payments required to maintain an organization and the resources obtained from the environment. . . ."[4] *Organizational slack appears to have great functional value in explaining why American society continually ends up with a change in the form of faster automobiles but no change in the form of adequate roads to go with it. It also appears to represent a link between cost/benefit analysis and human asset accounting.*

[1] Jack Barbash, *Labor's Grass Roots* (New York: Harper & Row, Publishers, Inc., 1961), p. 217.

[2] Edgar H. Schein's "Management Development as a Process of Influence," is reprinted in this volume, pp. 135-52. Cf. also Ronald Lippitt *et al., The Dynamics of Planned Change* (New York: Harcourt, Brace, Jovanovich, Inc., 1958).

[3] Alton C. Bartlett, "Changing Behavior as a Means to Increased Efficiency" and "Changing Behavior through Simulation," both reprinted in this volume, pp. 234-53 and pp. 118-34 respectively.

[4] Richard M. Cyert and James G. March, *A Behavioral Theory of the Firm* (Englewood Cliffs, N.J.: Prentice-Hall, Inc., 1963), p. 278.

OVERCOMING RESISTANCE TO STABILITY
A Time to Move; A Time to Pause

Robert Albanese
University of Illinois

One of my children recently brought home a paper on which she had written the figure three backwards. I asked her why the three was that way, and she replied, "Just for a change." A good answer, I thought to myself. The world needs people willing to try new things; we should not be boxed in by accustomed ways of behaving and thinking; we need to be open to new experiences and willing to take the risks involved—even when the risks cannot be calculated. The "old ways" no longer seem to work. Change for the sake of change *is* desirable and even necessary sometimes, although the result is from bad to worse.

Increasingly, our stance must be to take the risk of experimenting with new ways of being and doing. Individuals are finding that their most prized possession is the capacity to cope with and adapt to changes while still maintaining a unique identity and personality. Groups need to acquire new skills and attitudes that will make them effective vehicles of growth and performance, and provide satisfaction to individual members. Organizations of all kinds not only have to experiment with applying new knowledge to problems of internal operations, but they must also learn to know their external environment and utilize decision

Mr. Albanese is a visiting associate professor of business administration at the University of Illinois.

Reprinted from Robert Albanese, "Overcoming Resistance to Stability," *Business Horizons,* XIII, No. 1 (April 1970), 35-42. Copyright ©1970 by the Foundation for the School of Business, at Indiana University. Reprinted by permission.

processes that recognize environment as an integral part of the organization. Communities, cities, and nations face new and enormous problems that, if solvable at all, require imaginative and untried approaches.

This general notion of being receptive to change and willing to experience new behaviors and attitudes is a common theme in today's business literature; it became popular after the appearance of two well-known articles on the subject.[1] The idea has assumed an identity of its own, separate from the reality it describes—one can be for or against change without reference to any particular subject. The main thrust of the writing is toward the idea of accepting and coping with changes, and becoming more open (less resistant) to those proposed and desired. Managers are called on to be "change seekers" and to recognize the management of change as their main function: "The future belongs to those leaders of organizations who can demonstrate the necessary managerial skill and imagination to cope with the enormous changes around them"; "Existing organizations will have to learn to reach out for change as an opportunity, will have to learn to reach out for change as an opportunity, will have to learn to resist continuity."[2] Change is necessary! Resistance is dysfunctional!

There is a tendency to want to be on the side of change and to participate in a continuous process directed toward progress and growth. However, continuity and stability are also necessary ingredients of progress and growth, and they require analysis. They are necessary because progressive change is almost always a process of blending innovations with prevailing behaviors, attitudes, and values. They require analysis if we are to better understand that mysterious process by which human systems grow and develop. What exists today is the origin of what will exist tomorrow.

The idea of resisting change does not receive adequate attention. Over fifteen years ago, and again in the article cited previously, Lawrence cautioned against viewing such resistance as either good or bad or as something to be overcome: "Resistance may be soundly based or not. It is always, however, an important signal calling for further inquiry by management." But the *absence* of resistance may also be an important signal calling for further inquiry. Even resistance considered natural and understandable is frequently considered as a problem to be dealt with and overcome. The implicit assumption in most discussions of change is that the proposals are desirable and worthy of adoption. Calling into question the efficacy of a change is interpreted as resistance:

> To some will come a time when change
> Itself is beauty, if not heaven.

[1] Lester Coch and John R. P. French, "Overcoming Resistance to Change," *Human Relations,* I (1948); Paul R. Lawrence, "How to Deal With Resistance to Change," *Harvard Business Review,* XLVII (January-February, 1969).

[2] First quotation from Alfred J. Marrow and others, *Management by Participation: Creating a Climate for Personal and Organizational Development* (New York: Harper & Row, Publishers, 1967), p. 247. Second from Peter F. Drucker, "Managements' New Role," *Harvard Business Review,* XLVII (November-December, 1969), p. 52.

[3] E. A. Robinson, "Lewellyn and the Tree."

This article explores some reasons for the present emphasis on change, argues for a need for more intelligent resistance, and suggests some ways to balance the needs for change, stability, and continuity. First, it is worth noting that words used in discussions of this topic do not have precise meanings. For example, what does it mean to speak of change? Most changes in organizations probably are not resisted. Even if two individuals could agree on the substance of a change they would differ in their interpretation of its meaning and significance. Similarly, what precisely does continuity mean? What actually happens when continuity and change are balanced? What is stability? The absence of precise definitions for such terms makes communication more difficult.

The Emphasis on Change

Why is change emphasized so heavily today? Five explanations are suggested: change is needed; businesses with organizational slack are more receptive and willing to experiment; the notion of novelty is appealing; basic theories of operations help business measure proposed changes: and changes are being called for by social scientists, who have often been involved in a program as consultants.

The Need for Change

The explanation that requires the least discussion is the most important: the great and urgent need for change. It is only a mild exaggeration to say that wherever one looks one can see an overdue need to reshape the priorities, values, structures, and behavior that characterize social systems. Indeed, we should be genuinely concerned if the literature dealing with change did not reflect this need and urgency.

Today this need is recognized on a broad scale and is felt in a personal way. In addition, change is viewed more as an ongoing process than as a discrete event, and the knowledge and understanding required for implementation have increased. All of these factors have helped the idea catch on that things can be changed and that they will be changed. Now!

Effect of Organizational Slack

The concept of organizational slack is useful in understanding some organizational innovations and change efforts. This condition is defined as "the difference between the payments required to maintain an organization and the resources obtained from the environment. . . ."[4] Not all business organizations are experiencing affluent times but most are experiencing slack, as defined.

[4]Richard M. Cyert and James G. March, *A Behavioral Theory of the Firm* (Englewood Cliffs, N.J.: Prentice-Hall, Inc., 1963), p. 278.

The following linkage exists between slack and innovation: organizational effectiveness and success tend to cause slack; slack tends to deemphasize the priority of problems of scarcity; this deemphasis results in a loosening of the review of budget requests by organizational subunits; as a result, more requests motivated primarily by concerns of status and subunit prestige are approved (as opposed to requests motivated primarily by concern for performance goals and problem solving). The innovations and changes that result from such requests may or may not be organizationally worthwhile. Slack is their source of funds, and such innovations are often organizationally non-rational, that is, the relationship between the innovation and some measure of total organizational effectiveness is problematical.

It is difficult, in practice, to distinguish innovations motivated primarily by performance goals from those motivated primarily by status and prestige goals of organizational subunits, but the distinction is real. Many business organizations are more open to change and willing to experiment with change today because they have "organizational slack." They are less concerned with evidence that a proposed change or innovation is going to solve an immediate problem and contribute to the fulfillment of organizational goals. There is less insistence on organizationally rational behavior.

The Appeal of Novelty

Change may be admired more for its novelty than for its utility. There is evidence that "striving for stimulation, information, knowledge, or understanding is a universal motive among the primates, and especially man." Berlyne suggests that "prolonged subjection to an inordinately monotonous or unstimulating environment is detrimental to a variety of psychological functions. How much excitement or challenge is optimal will fluctuate widely with personality, culture, psychophysiological state, and recent or remote experience."[5]

Was the seemingly unending search for novelty, excitement, and new experience that characterized the late 1960's in the United States a collective reaction to the "inordinately monotonous or unstimulating environment" of the 1950's? The label Fabulous Fifties notwithstanding, there is some agreement that the fifties were unexciting. Perhaps it is possible to add up all the dullness of the fifties and imagine some total social capacity for dullness that was exceeded. Was there a social cost to this decade of inadequate stimulation? Such stimulation may be required, even when there is no apparent extrinsic reward involved, simply to keep the social nervous system balanced.

The notion of novelty helps explain many organizational changes that are now taking place in business organizations. Although not without substantive merit, the extensive use of current practices such as management by objectives,

[5]First quotation from Bernard Berelson and Gary Steiner, *Human Behavior: an Inventory of Scientific Findings* (New York: Harcourt, Brace & World, Inc., 1964), p. 245. Second from D. E. Berlyne, "Curiosity and Exploration," *Science,* CXLIII (July, 1966), pp. 25-33.

PERT (Performance Evaluation and Review Technique), sensitivity training, and PPBS (Planning-Programming and Budgeting System) cannot be explained fully without recognizing the need in organizations for stimulation and for keeping up with the organizational Joneses. There is some novelty component in the current interest in participative management. Participative approaches to decision making, if adequately informed by an understanding of the assumptions and requirements involved, are frequently superior to unilateral approaches. Sometimes participative approaches are useful and sometimes they are not, but, when used, they are almost always different from previous practices. The novelty of this difference, rather than the substantive aspects of participation, may be the attraction to organizations.

Theory as a Measure

Despite the fact that many theories can find no reality to explain or predict, it is still true that nothing is more practical than a good theory. Among other benefits, an operational theory helps an organization respond to change in a rational manner. If an organization knows why it is doing what it is doing, it is in a better position to evaluate proposed changes. If there is no good reason for an organizational practice ("It's just policy"), it is no wonder that resistance frustrates those who seek to change the practice.

Barzun has noted that American universities until recently were governed by principles of influence, deference, rationality, civility, and reciprocity. Study was the sole aim and test of the university. He further observes that these principles were not broadly understood:

> *Most people, including some academic men, had, of course, no idea how American or any other universities were run and could discern no principles whatever in the day-to-day operations. So when the cry of tyranny and revolt was raised, they rushed to pull down the fabric, on the assumption that where there's a complaint there must be an evil. The questions of what evil and where it lay precisely were never thought of. Indignation in some, passivity in others conspired to establish as a universal truth that the American university was an engine of oppression, rotten to the core, a stinking anachronism. So down it came.*[6]

If American universities had an adequate, broadly understood and supported theory of operations they would be in a better (although always imperfect) position to assimilate crucial changes required by contemporary needs. As it is, many changes are made on the basis of short-run expediency with almost no consideration of the trade-offs involved. Such changes, sometimes harmful in themselves, bear the additional burden of making it more difficult to detect the principles that guide day-to-day operations.

American business organizations have a reasonably adequate and broadly

[6] Jacques Barzun, "Tomorrow's University—Back to the Middle Ages," *Saturday Review* (Nov. 15, 1969), p. 25.

understood basic theory of operations. Although the theory is incomplete as a theory of total organizational effectiveness, its emphasis on performance and productivity provides a focus for behavior and a criterion against which to measure proposed changes. Sometimes the very clarity of performance measurements and the insistence on short-run pay-offs in business organizations relative to other types of organizations present a barrier to change that hinders organizational growth and development. Nevertheless, the theory provides some modicum of assurance that proposed changes will be consistent with the focus. Its incompleteness, however, assures business organizations of their share of organizationally irrational changes.

Change and the Social Scientist

Social scientists are in the forefront of those calling for change in individuals, groups, organizations, and communities; their writings are frequently supported by empirical studies of change efforts. Often the writers have been involved in a program as consultants. Since they are not called in by a firm to facilitate the continuance of a stable situation, it is understandable that their writings focus on system features that need to be altered. They are in the change business; they are change agents.

Such agents enter organizations for the purpose of facilitating a process of change, and descriptions of their efforts appear in the literature as contributions to a greater understanding of organizational change. In addition, most social scientists are concerned about the world and the opportunities for growth and development open to individuals and organizations if certain basic attitude and behavior shifts were to occur. Thus, their emphasis on the need for change is understandable, even if not tempered by the obligation of implementing and being responsible for such efforts.

The Need to Resist Change

The preceding factors help to explain some of today's emphasis on change. Nevertheless, in particular situations, the need may be to resist and to emphasize the need for stability and continuity.

Maintenance and Growth

Human systems, including individuals, groups, organizations, communities, nations, and so on, tend to maintain themselves and to grow.[7] The maintenance

[7]For two brief but useful discussions, see Gene W. Dalton, "Criteria for Planning Organizational Change" in Paul R. Lawrence and John A. Seiler, *Organizational Behavior and Administration* (Homewood, Ill.: Richard D. Irwin, Inc., 1965), pp. 914-15; and Robert F. Bales, "Adaptive and Integrative Changes as Sources of Strain in Social Systems," in A. Paul Hare and others, eds., *Small Groups: Studies in Social Interaction* (New York: Alfred A. Knopf, 1962), pp. 127-31.

tendency refers to behavior aimed at keeping the human system in a steady state, and produces conditions that include predictability, stability, control, conformity, and programmed behavior. This tendency requires change and adaptation in order to remain useful in the human system. The growth tendency refers to behavior aimed at development of the human system in terms of its increased capacity to cope with its environment, and produces conditions that include unpredictability, dynamism, change, freedom, ambiguity, uncertainty, divergence, and unprogrammed behavior.

The growth and maintenance tendencies are widely recognized, but the major emphasis in the literature is on the former. It is important to remember that both are part of all human systems. An individual needs to grow and develop, but he also needs to maintain a steady state that is suitable for him—some minimum level of imbalance between himself and his environment. Therefore, resistance to proposals that human systems change their present state can indicate a fully functioning system. The absence of resistance can be a danger signal for an organization just as the presence of resistance can be. If a human system can be overly defensive, it can also fail to accept its necessary and natural tendencies to maintain its present system capacities.

At the individual level, there is a need for emphasis on owning and accepting our own experience. Although an individual may not be able to articulate to the satisfaction of others why he holds to a particular position or behavior, it is not accurate to conclude that the position or behavior is wrong and should be changed. Perhaps change is eventually called for, but perhaps the first need is for a clearer understanding of the behavior and an acceptance of it as appropriate for that person. The same general idea applies to groups and other social systems.

We, need to accept both maintenance and growth tendencies in human systems as part of the system. To the extent that either tendency is prevented from operating, the system is less capable of choosing its own direction. An interest in maximizing opportunities for individuals and other human systems to make their own choices requires also an interest in developing the capacities of the systems to respond to both maintenance and growth tendencies. Resistance to change *is* natural and understandable; care should be taken in dealing with and overcoming it.

Diagnosis and Prescription

Another reason for resisting change is the low state of the art of diagnosis and prescription of human system problems. Organizations, in particular, have difficulty in getting agreement on what the problem is and what causes it. The total systemic impact of the problem may not be seen or understood, and opinions will differ regarding the proper solution. Nevertheless, one solution must be selected. It is important that the changes benefit from intelligent resistance in order to ensure that the solution chosen is the best one.

Often a particular solution is known to be favored by management and consequently does not benefit from a thorough discussion. Under such conditions, acceptance is built in, and the organization's growth and change is limited to the diagnostic and prescriptive capacities of those who proposed the change. The absence of intelligent resistance may be attractive in the short run, but the long-run price paid for such built-in acceptance is the loss of the unique contributions of a larger cross section of the organization's members.

Even when an organizational problem has been correctly diagnosed and an adequate solution prescribed, resistance may be needed to the pace and manner of introducing the change. A general guide for introducing major organizational changes is that they must be introduced gradually in order to avoid anxiety and hostility. When this guide is violated, as it often is today, the organization should anticipate dysfunctional consequences. Such consequences may have a detrimental effect on the over-all long-range effectiveness of the organization.

Manipulation

It is often difficult to distinguish acceptance of change from manipulation. This seems particularly true today when so much of the discussion of change is in humanitarian terms. Manipulation and control are shunned; collaboration, consensus, and influence are valued.

Nevertheless, unless precautions are taken to ensure that the right and skill to resist change is an accepted organizational value, collaboration and consensus may be merely new labels for the manipulation and control of behavior. There may be, for example, more actual manipulation of employee behavior through a managerial style described as participative than through a style that is clearly autocratic. The conditions for genuine collaborative decision making are seldom realized in practice. However, the vocabulary of collaboration is enough in some cases to mesmerize participants into accepting predetermined behavioral changes.

Leavitt has commented on the presence of manipulation in the classic studies by Lewin and Coch and French dealing with resistance to change. More recently, Marrow's study of organizational change in the Weldon Manufacturing Company is an example of the potential danger hiding behind such words as collaboration and participation.[8] This unique study reports what happens when a group of consultants, applying general principles of social science research, diagnose, prescribe, and implement a change program in the Weldon Manufacturing Company. The study is essentially a report of the two contrasting managerial approaches of Weldon and Harwood Manufacturing Corporation and how the Harwood approach was used as a model for revising the Weldon approach.

Elements of manipulation and coercion were clearly present in the change program; required attendance at sensitivity training programs is only one

[8]Harold J. Leavitt, "Applied Organizational Change in Industry," in James G. March, ed., *Handbook of Organizations* (Chicago: Rand McNally & Co., 1965), pp. 1152-53. Also see *Management by Participation: Creating a Climate for Personal and Organizational Development.*

example. As one reads this study, the question of the freedom of Weldon employees to resist change frequently arises. It is only conjecture to suggest that the total organizational change described in this study might have been more effective had there existed a climate in which the employees felt free to resist the specific changes imposed on them. This observation is all the more significant because the study "makes clear the contribution which quantitative social science research can make to an enterprise: General principles and new specific insights emerging from such research were used to plan and guide all changes made in the Weldon plant."

Do such principles and insights include an adequate appreciation for the legitimacy of resistance to change? It is a serious undertaking to ask people to alter their behavior and attitudes. Such changes strike at the core of a person's identity and self-esteem. They simply may not be able to assimilate these changes into their present mode of behavior; they may not be able to articulate their opposition; and they may not feel free to express their opposing views. The presence of such conditions in an organizational setting can only be detrimental to the long-run effectiveness of the organization.

Balance Change and Stability

Are there any special tools that the manager can use in overcoming resistance to stability? Many defensive mechanisms and tactics of obstruction can be used by managers, groups, and organizations to stifle innovation.[9] Such devices are obstacles to essential renewal and create an atmosphere unsympathetic to change. There is an adequate amount of that kind of behavior and it is performed skillfully and effectively.

The question here concerns intelligent resistance. In particular situations, the most progressive, rational, modern, future-oriented stance may be to resist change. However, the organizational climate may be totally unfriendly to the idea of resistance. One who resists is considered defensive, old-fashioned, nonadaptable, over-the-hill, and not part of the managerial Mod Squad. It could be career suicide for a manager to resist the latest program that has attracted the fancy of the company president.

There are no special tools for intelligent resistance of change. What is needed is a way of looking at individual, group, and organizational proposals that is complete enough to recognize that, in some situations, a change should be resisted and even rejected. Lewin's force-field model for thinking about change and the expansion of this model by Lippitt, Watson, and Westley into several phases of planned alteration is at present the most complete way of looking at the problem.[10] This model is usually discussed as a strategy for achieving

[9]John W. Gardner, *Self-Renewal, the Individual and the Innovative Society* (New York: Harper & Row, Publishers, 1963), pp. 43-53.

[10]Kurt Lewin, "Frontiers in Group Dynamics," *Human Relations* (1947), pp. 5-41; Ronald Lippitt and others, *The Dynamics of Planned Change* (New York: Harcourt, Brace & World, Inc., 1958).

change—not as a strategy for resisting, a fault of discussions of the model and not of the model itself.

For example, in the Lewin model, the present level of behavior is seen as a dynamic balance of driving and restraining forces working in opposite directions. The balance between the two sets of forces represents behavior at a quasi-stationary equilibrium. In order to achieve a behavior change, an imbalance has to occur between the sum of the driving forces and the sum of the restraining forces. Therefore, using this model, intelligent resistance requires that the magnitude of the driving forces be decreased, that the magnitude of the restraining forces be increased, or that some combination of these occur in order to maintain behavior at its present level of balance or equilibrium.[11] Stability or continuity will prevail when no imbalance occurs between the sum of the restraining forces and the sum of the driving forces.

The phases of planned change as described by Lippitt are an expansion of Lewin's three-phase process of change. Lewin noted that a successful behavioral change had three aspects: an unfreezing or disruption of the initial steady behavioral state, a period of adapting and moving toward a new behavioral level, and finally a period of refreezing in a new steady state. One of the crucial elements in the unfreezing phase is nonsupport; the potential changee must receive some signals that present behavior patterns are inadequate. Such signals are unsupporting information; they tell the changee that something is wrong with present behavior or attitudes.

How does an organization know when it is receiving nonsupport? What precise behavior or attitude is the target? Intelligent resistance to change requires validation of such alleged information. The capacity to discern a temporary inability to cope with a situation arising from nonsupport requires skill and an accepting of one's own (individual, group, or organization) behavior.

The second phase of the change process involves moving to a new level of behavior. This phase suggests the need for a model representing the new behavior. Does such a model exist? If so, can it be understood and is it operational? Intelligent resistance to change insists on an understood and operative model of new behavior before discarding older behavior patterns. What is the objective function and the constraints of the new model versus the old?

Although the above factors are worth noting, they are secondary to the more general factor of climate. Precautions must be taken to assure that the right and skill to resist change is a valued part of the organizational climate. Such a right should be valued as much as the right and skill to innovate and to propose change. Given the tendencies of organizations to rigidify and to discourage innovation, it is understandable why so much attention in recent years has focused on organizational change. Nevertheless, the right to resist change is an organizational liberty.

If there is agreement on anything these days it is that we live in a period of radical and rapid change. Business managers live and work in the reality of reshaping markets, technology, environment, attitudes, and values. Adaptation is

---

[11]For another view, see "Adaptive and Integrative Changes as Sources of Strain in Social Systems."

necessary just to stand still. Often the choice open to the manager is not whether or what change, but how and when. Strong resistance, however, still prevents many essential changes from taking place in business organizations. Perhaps there is such a need for change that it is a disservice to caution against it, even when excesses can be seen.

However, there is no need to become "change happy." An individual will not perform well when there is an excessive imbalance between himself and his environment; he will not grow, or develop, or self-actualize. Individuals, groups, and organizations cannot enhance their sense of competence in a continuous state of flux. It is essential to recognize that stability and continuity are needed and that they are two parts of the growth process.

During the past decade, the business literature has served the manager well, not only because it has recognized the need for change, but also because it has communicated new knowledge and techniques for overcoming resistance to necessary change. However, it is also desirable to apply such knowledge and techniques to overcoming resistance to necessary stability and continuity. A healthy organizational climate recognizes such resistance as a legitimate tendency of human systems.

Some Notes on the Dynamics of Resistance to Change: The Defender Role

It seems appropriate to us to employ the concept of "defender role," and ancillary points made by Donald Klein as the concluding treatise of this volume. After all, what more fitting conclusion could one desire for a section on resistance to change than a study of the role of the chief resister(s). Who are they: troublemakers, crackpots, or well-respected members of the establishment? It depends, says Klein, on the environment being changed, the nature of the change, the traits of the change agent(s), and the methods used to implement the change design.

Even if people the change agent perceives as rabble-rousers or kooks surface as the defenders, the primary question is whether they are being backed by any sizable portion of the "public" in their activities. If they are not, obviously the resistance movement is not being perceived as legitimate and will soon atrophy. If, on the other hand, they are being supported, the resistance is being perceived as legitimate and the rhetoric and tactics employed are the responses of all or at least an important part of the system to be changed.

The change agent should realize that the defender's behavior, however bizarre, is an attempt to communicate vital information about the target system. Refusal to heed this information may result in either failure of the change program, or a zero-sum game where all efforts of both the change agent(s) and the *defender(s) are directed at winning, making compromises and tradeoffs impossible.*

In such a battle to the death, the benefits that were to have been realized by the change must be sacrificed to the need for survival. Production is subverted; while the energies formerly expended on it are wasted on the fight. Creativity and imagination are channeled into ideas for thwarting the system rather than facilitating it.

A better model is one in which the change agent, displaying empathy toward the symbols the defenders are seeking to protect, either involves them in the planning and implementation of the proposed change or at least modifies the plan so as to show respect for the things being protected. This could lead to a situation in which the energies of all parties are directed toward the success of the proposed change. To paraphrase Klein, before starting a change, a necessary prerequisite for success is the determination of who is likely to be against it, and why. Effort can then be made to "win them over" so that their energies will be mobilized toward implementation rather than resistance.

One other salient point of this fine discourse is that there is seldom a change of any magnitude in a social system that does not adversely affect some person or group. The exciting part of this piece for us is its broad applicability in explaining today's world, whether one talks of campus disturbances, war protest, black militancy, urban renewal, school integration, women's liberation movements, or planned change in any organization where work is the central focus.

SOME NOTES ON THE DYNAMICS OF RESISTANCE TO CHANGE: THE DEFENDER ROLE

Donald Klein
Antioch College

The literature on change recognizes the tendencies of individuals, groups, organizations, and entire societies to act so as to ward off change. Though it is generally acknowledged that human beings have a predilection both to seek change and to reject it, much of the literature has isolated the latter tendency for special emphasis. In fact studies of change appear to be taken from the perspective or bias of those who are the change agents seeking to bring about change rather than of the clients they are seeking to influence. It seems likely, therefore, that our notions of change dynamics are only partially descriptive. It is interesting that Freud used the term "resistance" to identify a phenomenon which from his point of view, had the effect of blocking the attainment of his therapeutic objectives. One wonders whether patients would use just this term to refer to the same sets of interactions between themselves and their therapists.

Freud, of course, emphasizes that resistances were a necessary and even desirable aspect of the therapy. He pointed out that without resistance patients might be overwhelmed by the interventions of the therapist, with the result that inadequate defenses against catastrophe would be overthrown before more adaptive ways of coping with inner and outer stimuli had been erected.

Reprinted from Goodwin Watson (ed.) *Concepts for Social Change,* Cooperative Project for Educational Development Series, Vol. I, National Training Laboratories, Washington, D.C., 1966. Reprinted by permission.

Desirability of Opposition

It is the objective of this paper to suggest that, as in patient-therapist dyads, opposition to change is also desirable in more complex social systems. It is further suggested that what is often considered to be irrational resistance to change is, in most instances, more likely to be either an attempt to maintain the integrity of the target system to real threat, or opposition to the agents of change themselves.

Opposition to Real Threat

Change of the kind we are considering consists not of an event, but of a process of series of events occurring over a period of time, usually involving a more or less orderly and somewhat predictable sequence of interactions. Though it involves the reactions of individuals, it also entails reorganization of group, organizational, or even community behavior patterns and requires some alteration of social values, be they explicit or only implicitly held.

Few social changes of any magnitude can be accomplished without impairing the life situations of some individuals or groups. Elderly homeowners gain little and sometimes must spend more than they can afford for new public school buildings or for the adoption of kindergartens by their communities. Some administrators may lose their chances for advancement when school districts are consolidated to achieve more efficient use of materials and resources. Other examples of real threat could be cited from public health, urban renewal and other fields. There is no doubt that some resistance to change will occur when individuals' livelihoods are affected adversely or their social standings threatened.

However, there are more fundamental threats posed by major innovations. Sometimes the threat is to the welfare of whole social systems. Often the threat is not clearly recognized by anybody at the time the change occurs; it emerges only as the future that the change itself helped shape is finally attained.

For example, the community which taxes property heavily in order to support kindergartens or costly educational facilities may very well be committing itself to further homogenization of its population as it attracts young families wealthy enough to afford the best in education and drives out working class groups, elderly people, and those whose cultural values do not place so high a priority on education. The community which loses a small, poorly financed local school in order to gain a better equipped and perhaps more competently staffed district facility may also be committed to a future of declining vigor as its most able young people are as a result more readily and systematically siphoned off into geographically distant professional, industrial and other work settings.

It is probably inevitable that any major change will be a mixed blessing to those undergoing it in those instances when the status quo or situation of gradual change has been acceptable to many or most people. The dynamic interplay of forces in social systems is such that any stable equilibrium must represent at least a partial accommodation to the varying needs and demands of those involved. Under such circumstances the major change must be desired by those affected if it is to be accepted.

Maintenance of Integrity

Integrity is being used here to encompass the sense of self-esteem, competence, and autonomy enjoyed by those individuals, groups, or communities who feel that their power and resources are adequate to meet the usual challenges of living. Unfortunately such integrity sometimes is based on a view of reality that is no longer tenable. When changes occur under such circumstances they force us to confront the fact that our old preconceptions do not fit present reality, at least not completely. Dissonance exists between the truths from the past and current observations. In some cases relinquishing the eternal verities would resolve the dissonance but would also entail a reduction of integrity. However irrational, the resistance to change which occurs in such cases may have as its fundamental objective the defense of self-esteem, competence and autonomy.

In our complex, changing world the assaults on individual, group, and community integrity are frequent and often severe. The field of public education is especially vulnerable to such assaults. So much so, in fact, that one sometimes wonders whether there are any truly respected educational spokesmen left who can maintain the self-esteem, sense of competence, and necessary autonomy of the schools against all the various changes which are being proposed and funded before they have been adequately tested.

Resistance to Agents of Change

The problem is further complicated by the growing capacity, indeed necessity, of our society to engage in massive programs of planned change and by the development of ever-growing cadres of expert planners capable of collecting and processing vast bodies of information, or organizing such information into designs for the future apparently grounded on the best available expertise, and of marshalling arguments capable of persuading great numbers of political, business, and other civic leaders that action should be taken. The difficulties which arise stem from the very magnitude of the changes being projected, from the rapidity with which such changes can occur, and from the troubling realization that these changes often are irreversible as well as far reaching, thus ensuring the prolongation of error as well as of accuracy.

Most important of all, however, as a generator of defense would appear to be the frequent alienation of the planners of change from the world of those for whom they are planning. The alienation is one of values as much as it is one of simple information. It exists in many fields but is perhaps most apparent in the field of urban renewal, where planners have yet to devise mechanisms whereby they can adequately involve their clients in the planning process. Many examples can be cited. Health professionals feel that matters of the public health should be left in the hands of the experts most qualified to assess the facts and to take the necessary action. They often decry the involvement of the public in decisions about such matters as flouridation through referenda or other means. Educators, too, are often loath to encourage the development of vigorous parent groups capable of moving into the arena of curriculum planning, building design, or other areas of decision making.

Few expert planners in any field are prepared to believe that their clients can be equipped to collaborate with them as equals. What can the lay person add to the knowledge and rationality of the technical expert? And is it not true that the process of involving the client would only serve to slow down if not derail the entire undertaking? The result is that each planning project proceeds without taking the time to involve those who will be affected by the planning until such a point when it is necessary to gain the client's consent. And if decisions can be made and implementation secured without involving his public, the planner's job is greatly simplified.

However, the failure of planners to work collaboratively with those for whom they plan contributes to the well known American mistrust of the highly trained, academically grounded expert. Under the most benign circumstances, the client may be skeptical of the planner's recommendations. Given any real threat to livelihood or position, or given any feared reduction in integrity, clients' skepticism may be replaced by mistrust of planners' motives and open hostility towards them.

The motives of innovators are especially apt to be suspect when the planning process has been kept secret up until the time of unveiling the plans and action recommendations. By this time the innovators usually have worked up a considerable investment in their plans, and are often far more committed to defending than to attempting to understand objections to them. They are not prepared to go through once again with newcomers the long process of planning which finally led them to their conclusions. And they are hardly in the most favorable position to entertain consideration of new social data or of alternative actions which might be recommended on the basis of such information. The result often is that opposition to the recommended change hardens and even grows as the ultimate clients sense that their reactions will not materially influence the outcome in any way short of defeating the plan in open conflict.

Defense as Part of the Process of Innovation

Studies in such fields as agriculture and medicine have helped clarify the sequence of processes involved in successful innovation of new practices. Even in such technical fields where results can be more or less objectively judged in terms of profit, recovery rates, and the like, successful innovation occurs only after initial resistances have been worked through.

Innovation in any area begins when one or more people perceive that a problem exists, that change is desirable and that it is possible. These people then must decide how best to go about enlisting others to get the information needed to assess the problem further and to develop the strategy leading to implementation of a plan of action. However, we know that those people who are prepared to initiate change within their own groups, organizations or communities are often in a very unfavorable position from which to do so. In stable groups especially it is the marginal or atypical person who is apt to be receptive to new ideas and practices or who is in a position where he can economically or socially afford to run the risk of failure.

Thus it has been found necessary to carry out sustained efforts at innovation in which experimentation with new ideas can be followed by efforts at adapting or modifying them to fit more smoothly into existing patterns until finally what was once an innovation is itself incorporated within an altered status quo.

The Importance of Defense in Social Change

Up to this point, this paper has touched on some of the factors contributing to the inevitability of resistance to change and has presented but not developed the major thesis, which is that a necessary pre-requisite of successful change involves the mobilization of forces against it. It has suggested that just as individuals have their defenses to ward off threat, maintain integrity, and protect themselves against the unwarranted intrusions of other's demands, so do social systems seek ways in which to defend themselves against ill-considered and overly precipitous innovations.

The existence of political opposition virtually ensures such defense within local, state and national government to the extent that the party out of power is sufficiently vigorous. The British system of the loyal opposition perhaps even more aptly epitomizes the application of the concept of necessary defense in the area of political life.

In more implicit ways, non-governmental aspects of community life have their defenders. These latter individuals and groups constitute the spokesmen for the inner core of tradition and values. They uphold established procedures and are quick to doubt the value of new ideas. Their importance stems from several considerations:

First, they are the ones most apt to perceive and point out the real threats, if such exist, to the well-being of the system which may be the unanticipated consequences of projected changes;

Second, they are especially apt to react against any change that might reduce the integrity of the system;

Third, they are sensitive to any indication that those seeking to produce change fail to understand or identify with the core value of the system they seek to influence.

The Defender Role

The defender role is played out in a variety of ways depending on such factors as the nature of the setting itself, the kind of change contemplated, the characteristics of the group or individual seeking to institute change, and the change strategy employed. In a process of orderly and gradual change, the defender role may be taken by a well established, respected member of the system whose at least tacit sanction must be gained for a new undertaking to succeed. In a situation of open conflict where mistrust runs high the defender role may be assumed by those able to become more openly and perhaps irrationally vitriolic in their opposition. These latter are often viewed by the proponents of change as impossibly intractable and are dismissed as "rabble rousers" or "crack pots." This was frequently the attitude on the part of pro-fluoridationists toward the anti's.

Though crack pots may emerge as defenders under certain circumstances, it is suggested here that so long as they are given support by a substantial segment of the population even though it may be a minority, they are expressing a reaction by all or part of the target system against real threat of some kind. In one community, I observed a well educated group of residents vote overwhelmingly against fluoridation at town meeting even though (as I viewed it) the small body of antifluoridationists expressed themselves in a highly emotional, irrational way. In later conversations it appeared that many who voted against actually favored fluoridation. They were influenced not by the logic of the defenders but by other dynamics in the situation which presumably the defenders also were reflecting. Some of those who voted "no" were unprepared to force fluorides on a minority; others pointed out that those presenting the case for fluorides had neglected to involve the voters in a consideration of the true nature and extent of the problem of tooth decay; and a third group wondered why the health officer and others fighting for the change were so insistent on pushing their plan through immediately rather than asking the town through the more usual committee procedure to consider the problem at a more leisurely pace. The pro-fluoridationists on the other hand, were discouraged by the vote, felt rejected by fellow townspeople, and had grave doubts about bringing the issue up again in view of the fact that "they don't want to protect their children's teeth."

In the instance of fluoridation the defenders usually have been drawn from the ranks of those who do not hold public office and who do not consider themselves to be members of the Establishment. This is not always the case, however. In civil rights controversies the change agents typically are the disenfranchised; the defenders occupy public office or appear to be close to the sources of existing power. But no matter whether the innovation comes from top down or bottom up, in each situation the defenders are representing value positions which have been important not only to themselves but to larger groups of constituents, and presumably to the maintenance of the culture itself.

In the Boston controversy over de facto school segregation the School Committee Chairman was elected by an overwhelming vote of those who, however bigoted many of them may be, believe they are defending their property values, the integrity of neighborhood schools, and their rights to stand up against those who are trying to push them around. If any of us were faced in our neighborhoods with the prospect of a state toll road sweeping away our homes, we, too, might convince ourselves that we could properly rise up in defense of the same values. The point is not whether the schools should remain segregated; they should not. Rather as change agents we must be concerned with the values held by the opposition and must recognize that, to a great extent, their values are ours as well. Moreover, it would help if we could grant that, in upholding these values, the defenders—however wrong we believe they are in the stands they take and the votes they cast—are raising questions which are important in our society and which we must answer with them. It is far too easy to dismiss neighborhood schools as a reactionary myth or to hold that they are unimportant in face of the larger objective of reducing intergroup barriers. The issues become far more complex, however, when we grant that neighborhood schools were established because in the judgment of many educators and citizens they had merits apart from the current controversy over segregation. Once having granted this, the problem becomes one of seeking solutions which can minimize the losses in respect to such merits and maximize the gains in respect to integration. I would predict that, if it were possible for the change agents to consider seriously the concerns of the defenders in the case of school integration, many of the latter would no longer feel so embattled and would no longer require the kind of leadership which in Boston has just been renominated overwhelmingly for the School Committee.

But what about the motives of those who lead the opposition to good causes? Are they not apt to seize on virtuous issues simply as ways to manipulate opinion and to rally more support? No doubt this is true. Nonetheless, I think the point still holds that the virtues are there to be manipulated. They can be used as a smoke screen by demagogues only so long as those who follow them are convinced that the agents of change are themselves unscrupulous, un-principled, and unfeeling. Therefore, we add to the anxieties and opposition of those who are being rallied by the demagogues if we dismiss the latter and fail to come to grips with the concerns of those who uphold them.

Of course, demagogues and rabble rousers do more than articulate the values of their followers. They also dare to give voice to the frustrations and sense of helpless rage which these followers feel but usually cannot express. Those who are the targets of change usually do not feel it is safe to give vent to their true feelings. The man who is a demagogue in the eyes of his opponent is usually a courageous spokesman to the follower whom he is serving as a defender.

How the Change Agent Views the Defender

Thus an important implication for the change agent is that the defender, whoever he may be and however unscrupulously or irrationaly he may appear to present himself and his concerns, usually has something of great value to communicate about the nature of the system which the change agent is seeking to influence. Thus if the change agent can view the situation with a sympathetic understanding of what the defenders are seeking to protect, it may prove desirable either to modify the change itself or the strategy being used to achieve it. In certain situations the participation of defenders in the change process may even lead to the development of more adequate plans and to the avoidance of some hitherto unforeseen consequences of the projected change.

It is important, therefore, for those seeking change to consider the costs of ignoring, overriding, or dismissing as irrational those who emerge as their opponents. To ignore that which is being defended may mean that the planned change itself is flawed; it may also mean that the process of change becomes transformed into a conflict situation in which forces struggle in opposition and in which energies become increasingly devoted to winning rather than to solving the original problem.

Outcome of the Defender Role

What happens to the defender role during a period of change is no doubt a function of many factors, such as the nature of the issue, previous relationships between opposing sides, and the various constraints of time, urgency of the problem, and the like. We are all familiar with situations in which defenders and protagonists of change have become locked in fierce conflict until finally the defenders have either won out or been shattered and forced to succumb. Frequent examples can be found in the early history of urban renewal when entire urban neighborhoods, such as the West End of Boston, were destroyed and their defenders swept away as a consequence. It is also possible for conflict to continue indefinitely with neither side able to gain the advantage, to the extent that both sides contribute to the ultimate loss of whatever values each was seeking to uphold. Labor-management disputes which shatter entire communities are instances where the interplay between innovative and defensive forces ceases to be constructive.

Often in communities the defenders of values no longer widely held become boxed in and remain in positions of repeated but usually futile opposition to a series of new influences. The consensus of the community has shifted in such a way as to exclude those who may once have been influential. In their encapsulation these individuals and groups are no longer defenders in the sense the term is being used here; for they no longer participate meaningfully in the changes going on around them.

Finally, as has already been suggested, the defenders may in a sense be co-opted by the change agents, in such a way as to contribute to an orderly change process.

Within school systems the balance between innovation and defense must always be delicate, often precarious. The history of education in this country is full of examples of major innovations accomplished by an outstanding superintendent which, no matter what their success, were immediately eliminated by his successor. Sometimes disgruntled citizens who have been unsuccessful in opposing innovations are better able to mobilize their opposition when no longer faced with powerful professional leadership. Sometimes teachers and staff members who have conformed to but not accepted the changes feel more secure to express their opposition to the new superintendent.

It has been pointed out by Neal Gross and others that the superintendent of a public school system faces the almost impossible task of mediating between the conflicting demands of staff, community, and other groups. He is almost continuously confronted with the opposing influences of innovators and defenders, not to mention the many bystanders within the system who simply wish to be left alone when differences arise. Under the circumstances it may well be that one of the most important skills a superintendent can develop is his ability to create the conditions wherein the interplay between the change agents and defenders can occur with a minimum of rancor and a maximum of mutual respect. As we have seen in New York City and elsewhere, however, controversies do arise—such as civil rights—wherein the superintendent seems unable to play a facilitating role.

In situations that are less dramatic and conflict laden, the superintendent and other school administrators are usually in a position where they can and indeed must be both change agents and defenders. In the face of rapid social change they face the challenge of learning how to foster innovation, while at the same time finding the most constructive ways in which to act in defense of the integrity of their systems. It is also important that they learn how to differentiate between change which may pose real threat and change which is resisted simply because it is new and feels alien. Perhaps most important of all, they have the opportunity of educating the change agents with whom they work, either those inside their systems or those who come from the outside to the point where the change agents perceive, understand, and value the basic functions and purposes of the schools.

The Force Field of the Defender

In human relations training we have frequently used Lewin's force field model as a way to introduce learners to the objective analysis of the forces driving towards and restraining against a desired change. Here, too, we have tended to view the change field through the eyes of the protagonists. I think it would be illuminating in any study of educational innovation to attempt to secure analysis of the force field from defenders as well as change agents at several stages of the innovative process. Comparative analysis of the views of protagonists and defenders might help illuminate the biases of the former and clarify more adequately the underlying origins within the target system of the opposition. It also should provide us with a better understanding of the dynamics of the defender role and how it can be more adequately taken into account in programs of social innovation.

8539